Translation and Localization Project Management

American Translators Association Scholarly Monograph Series (ATA)

As of 1993 John Benjamins has been the official publisher of the ATA Scholarly Monograph Series. Edited by Françoise Massardier-Kenney, under the auspices of the American Translators Association, this series has an international scope and addresses research and professional issues in the translation community worldwide. These accessible collections of scholarly articles range from issues of training, business environments, to case studies or aspects of specialized translation relevant to translators, translator trainers, and translation researchers.

For an overview of all books published in this series, please see
http://benjamins.com/catalog/ata

Managing Editor

Françoise Massardier-Kenney
Institute for Applied Linguistics,
Kent State University (Kent, Ohio)

Editorial Board

Marilyn Gaddis Rose
Binghamton University NY

Peter W. Krawutschke
Western Michigan University (Kalamazoo)

Marshall Morris
University of Puerto Rico (Rio Piedras, P.R.)

Sue Ellen Wright
Institute for Applied Linguistics,
Kent State University (Kent, Ohio)

Volume XVI

Translation and Localization Project Management. The art of the possible
Edited by Keiran J. Dunne and Elena S. Dunne

Translation and Localization Project Management

The art of the possible

Edited by

Keiran J. Dunne
Elena S. Dunne
Kent State University

John Benjamins Publishing Company
Amsterdam / Philadelphia

♾™ The paper used in this publication meets the minimum requirements of
American National Standard for Information Sciences – Permanence of
Paper for Printed Library Materials, ANSI z39.48-1984.

Library of Congress Cataloging-in-Publication Data

Translation and localization project management : the art of the possible /
    edited by Keiran J. Dunne and Elena S. Dunne.
    p.   cm. (American Translators Association Scholarly Monograph Series, ISSN 0890-4111 ;
       v. XVI)
Includes bibliographical references and index.
1. Translating and interpreting--Study and teaching. 2. Business--Translating. I. Dunne,
    Keiran J. II. Dunne, Elena S.
P306.5.T7274   2011
418'.02068--dc23   2011032360
ISBN 978 90 272 3192 5   (Hb ; alk. paper)
ISBN 978 90 272 8324 5   (Eb)

© 2011 – John Benjamins B.V.
No part of this book may be reproduced in any form, by print, photoprint, microfilm, or any other means, without written permission from the publisher.

John Benjamins Publishing Co. · P.O. Box 36224 · 1020 ME Amsterdam · The Netherlands
John Benjamins North America · P.O. Box 27519 · Philadelphia PA 19118-0519 · USA

Table of contents

Mapping terra incognita: Project management in the discipline of translation studies   1
   Keiran J. Dunne and Elena S. Dunne

Part I. Project management in the context of translation and localization business

Strategic views on localization project management: The importance of global product management and portfolio management   17
   Salvatore Giammarresi

Selecting enterprise project management software: More than just a build-or-buy decision?   51
   Alain Chamsi

Part II. Project management knowledge areas

Applying PMI methodology to translation and localization projects: Project Integration Management   71
   Alexandra Zouncourides-Lull

Requirements collection: The foundation of scope definition and scope management in localization projects   95
   Natalia Levitina, PMP

Managing the fourth dimension: Time and schedule in translation and localization projects   119
   Keiran J. Dunne

From vicious to virtuous cycle: Customer-focused translation quality management using ISO 9001 principles and Agile methodologies   153
   Keiran J. Dunne

Effective communication in translation and localization
project management   **189**
    Natalia Tsvetkov, PMP and Veronica Tsvetkov

Risk management in localization   **211**
    Mark Lammers

Part III. Managing human and organizational factors

Rethinking the role of the localization project manager   **235**
    Richard Sikes

Project as a learning environment: Scaffolding team learning
in translation projects   **265**
    Elena S. Dunne

Global virtual teams   **289**
    Willem Stoeller

Relationship management: A strategy for fostering localization success   **319**
    Karen R. Combe

Part IV. Translation and localization project management in action

Managing the challenges of game localization   **349**
    Ping Zhou

Project management for crowdsourced translation:
How user-translated content projects work in real life   **379**
    Donald A. DePalma and Nataly Kelly

Additional resources   **409**
Contributors   **413**
Author index   **417**
Subject index   **421**

Mapping terra incognita
Project management in the discipline of translation studies

Keiran J. Dunne and Elena S. Dunne

> Theory without practice is sterile.
> Practice without theory is blind.
> Unknown

Translation studies: Then and now

In 1972, translation scholar James Holmes delivered a lecture entitled "The name and nature of translation studies" (later published as an article) in which he named and mapped the emerging discipline of translation studies. Borrowing the traditional taxonomy of empirical research, Holmes divided the discipline into two main branches, so-called "pure" translation studies and applied translation studies (see Figure 1).

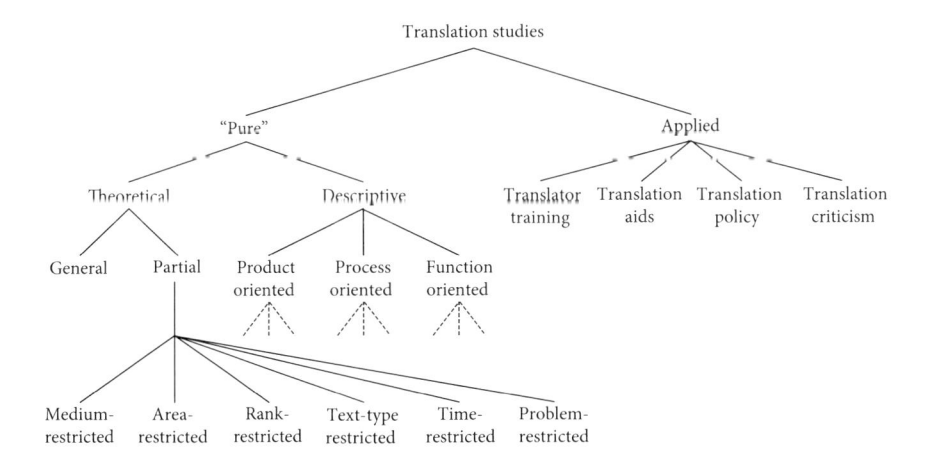

Figure 1. A graphical representation of Holmes "map" of translation studies (adapted from Toury 1995: 10).

He further divided pure translation studies into two sub-branches, theoretical and descriptive translation studies, and identified various sub-areas in each. As Figure 1 illustrates, Holmes mapped the disciplinary territory of theoretical and descriptive translation studies in much greater detail than that of applied translation studies, but such were the lines along which he envisioned the development of the discipline.

Much has changed in the ensuing decades. The digital revolution has moved translation beyond the realm of printed documents into software, websites, multimedia content and databases, giving rise to the concept and practice of localization. At the same time, the shift to an information- and knowledge-based economy (Drucker 1988) and the increased volume and velocity of global trade have fueled a remarkable increase in demand for translation and translation-related services:

> The impetus of economic forces has changed the very structure of the profession, shifting it from a paradigm based on the individual professional, to one based on a cottage industry model, e.g., groups of professionals and small agencies and in-house operations united in professional associations, and finally to a full-fledged service sector.   (Shreve 1998: 6)[1]

The rapid growth and evolution of the language industry has been driven to a great extent by outsourcing of professional translation, which was adopted as a business strategy by most large software publishers in the late 1980s, and became a generalized practice in the early 1990s (Esselink 2003a: 83), thanks in large part to the advent of the Internet. Indeed, in the new millennium, nearly 90% of translation buyers outsource most or all of the work (Beninatto 2006: 4). Finally, the advent of the Web as a commercial publishing platform has greatly increased the complexity of large-scale commercial translation projects to the point that most freelance translators cannot manage such projects on their own. As Esselink observes, "content translation projects are now often considered as localization projects simply because of the complex environments in which the content is authored, managed, stored and published" (2003b: 6–7). As the industry has grown and evolved, so has the range of services offered by language industry companies. Today, translation agencies offer not only translation, but also editing, terminology management, localization, internationalization, proofreading, testing, cross-cultural design, cultural assessment and project management, among other services.

Although professional translation has undergone profound changes in the past several decades, developments in the discipline of translation studies have continued largely in the "pure" areas described by Holmes. Indeed, Holmes did not envisage the

---

1. The United States, Canada and Mexico recognized translation as a distinct industrial sector in 1997 (US OMB 1997), followed by the European Union in 2008 (Eurostat 2008: 81). Today, the market for outsourced language services is estimated to be US$31.5 billion (Kelly and Stewart 2011: 6).

considerable expansion of the applied branch caused by the evolution of the profession and the advent of the language industry, exemplified by the following:

- The diversification and rapid evolution of the skills required in the industry, which pose significant challenges for translator training
- The shift from translation aids, which Holmes identified as lexicological and terminological aids and grammars, to translation technologies such as computer-assisted translation tools, and the subsequent evolution of those technologies from the desktop to corporate servers to the cloud
- The expansion of translation criticism to encompass pragmatic translation quality evaluation and assessment, which are major pain points in the industry today
- The advent of standards development as a significant area of pragmatic focus in the industry[2]
- The need for dedicated project management due to the geographic distribution of outsourced translation teams and to the increasing complexity of the technologies and processes of translation projects

Although the academy has begun to address the needs of the language industry by offering courses on computer-assisted translation, localization, translation as a profession, and project management in curricula and certificate programs, theoretical and descriptive works dealing with these topics are largely absent from the literature. Four decades after the creation of Holmes' model, the time has come to expand the borders of translation studies in recognition of the increasing complexity of the applied branch, and to account for the development of translation as a profession, a business, and an industry. This volume proposes a modest foray in this direction by focusing on the management of translation and localization projects as a necessary – and overdue – addition to the discipline of translation studies.

Why project management?

A number of reasons justify the focus on project management; primary among them is the fact that translation work is typically carried out in the form of *projects*. The Project Management Institute defines a project as a "temporary endeavor undertaken to create a unique product, service, or result" (PMI 2008: 434). Project management expert Robert Wysocki offers a narrower definition of a project as "a sequence of unique, complex and connected activities having one goal or purpose that must be completed by a specific date, within budget and according to specification" (2007: 4). The essential characteristics of projects are *temporariness* and *uniqueness*. The fact that projects are temporary does not necessarily mean that they are of short duration.

---

2. For a comprehensive discussion of language industry standards, see Wright 2006.

For instance, the construction of the Taj Mahal was a twenty-year project. "Temporary" merely signifies means that projects have defined start and end dates; in other words, they are not open-ended. The fact that projects are unique means that a given project may be similar to previous ones, but some aspect of the new project will distinguish it from all others. Finally, projects are shaped by constraints, including scope (how much work is involved), quality (how well the deliverables will meet the project requirements), time (how long it will take to complete the project), resources (how much the project will cost, how many people will be required to perform the work, etc.), as well as risks (threats and opportunities) (adapted from Marasco 2004). Given that professional translation is a project-driven undertaking *par excellence*, it is necessary that scholars, educators, trainers and practitioners study and understand the impact of the project environment on the practice of translation, as well as the operative variables and factors at the intersection of translation and project management, in order to improve translation performance and the training of future translators.

Professional translation is highly outsourced, as noted above. It is widely held in the business world that competitive advantage in a given industry – and even long-term survival – is predicated on the development of one or more core competencies (Prahalad and Hamel 1990). Clients outsource translation work precisely because translation is not one of their core competencies. In the language industry outsourcing model, an organization requiring translation into one or more target languages subcontracts the project to a language service provider (LSP), which in turn subcontracts translation and other language-related services to freelancers (see Figure 2).[3] The LSP may also subcontract language-related services to single-language vendors, i.e., companies that work into a specific target language and employ in-house translators, or to in-country contractors. Finally, the LSP may also outsource certain services, such as desktop publishing, to specialized providers. One major consequence of outsourcing is that translation expertise is necessary but not sufficient to thrive in today's language industry. Translators and other industry professionals must also be able to work successfully as part of culturally diverse and often geographically distributed teams.

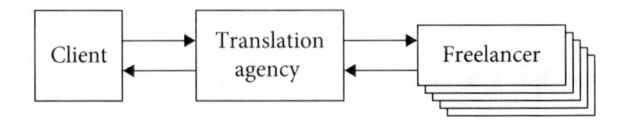

Figure 2. Language industry outsourcing model. Clients subcontract projects to translation agencies, which in turn subcontract work to freelancers and/or to single-language vendors and specialized providers (not shown here).

---

3. The model shown in Figure 2 is deliberately simplified for purposes of illustration; additional entities are often involved.

The outsourcing model shown in Figure 2 illustrates a paradox of the language industry: *most translation agencies do not actually perform translation work,* but outsource that work to others. This observation begs the question: if translation agencies do not perform translation work, then what exactly do they do? The answer: they ensure that the outsourced translation and localization projects awarded to them by clients are completed on time, within budget and according to the client's specification. In other words, they *manage projects*. Thus, the designations "translation agency" and "language service provider" are misnomers: neither accurately reflects the true core competencies of a language industry company, which include sales management, vendor management, and above all, project management (see Figure 3). Sales and marketing involve the acquisition, development and retention of a client base. Vendor management involves the identification and qualification of service providers, such as translators, proofreaders, and so forth (typically referred to as "vendors" in industry); the criteria on which vendors are evaluated may include language pair, subject matter or domain knowledge, tool use and the quality of the specific service, among other things. Finally, project management involves "the application of knowledge, skills, tools and techniques to project activities to meet the project requirements" (PMI 2008:6), namely the delivery of projects on time, within budget and according to the customer's specifications. Project management is *the* core competency of a translation agency, the "hub of the wheel" around which translation and localization activities revolve (Stoeller 2004).

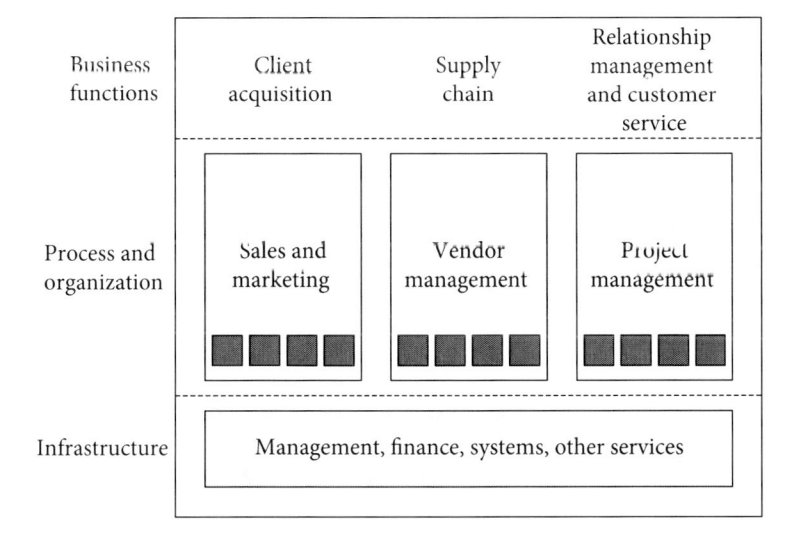

Business functions	Client acquisition	Supply chain	Relationship management and customer service
Process and organization	Sales and marketing	Vendor management	Project management
Infrastructure	Management, finance, systems, other services		

Figure 3. Model illustrating the three core competencies of a prototypical language service provider (adapted from Beninatto 2005:9). The small dark squares represent sub-processes within each of the three main process areas.

Although project management is arguably the foundation of the language industry, it has been largely overlooked as an object of scholarly inquiry and critical pedagogical reflection in the field of translation studies. While several translation scholars have acknowledged the importance of developing project management competencies[4] and others have noted the central role of project management in translation and localization (e.g., Esselink 2000, 2003b; Bowker 2002:131; O'Hagan and Ashworth 2002:18; Mackiewicz 2009:10; Pym 2010:51–52), few works devote more than a cursory treatment to the topic.[5] Likewise, although thousands of books have been written on project management in general, no book-length scholarly work has yet been published on project management in the language industry. This volume proposes to fill this gap.

Bridging the gap between "pure" and applied translation studies

The argument that the disciplinary map of translation studies should be expanded to encompass the management of translation and localization projects should not be taken as a suggestion that previous work in translation studies can or should be ignored. Nor should this argument be taken as a suggestion that translation and localization project management is confined solely to the applied branch of translation studies. On the contrary, given the process-based approach of project management, one could argue that translation and localization project management are ideal objects of study for process-oriented descriptive translation studies, for example. In addition, exploring translation through the lens of project management can help bridge the gap between "pure" and applied translation studies. Focusing on translation and localization project management is one way to build bridges between existing translation scholarship and current professional practice, and offers fertile ground for future research.

Thus, examining the project management areas of communication management and stakeholder management offers a new window through which to study issues of power and politics of translation, as well as ideology and patronage, which have been discussed by scholars such as Lefevere (1992), Spivak (1992), Niranjana (1992) and Venuti (1986, 1995), among others. Works by functionalists such as Reiss (1980), Reiss and Vermeer (1984) and Nord (1997), particularly their notions of text types and of

---

4. See, for example, Shreve (1998, 2000); Anderman and Rogers (2000:66); Fraser (2000:117); Kiraly (2000:121); Baer and Koby (2003:ix); Pym (2003:494–495 nn2); Robinson (2003); Gerzymisch-Arbogast (2005:2); Malmkjær (2006:4); Samuelsson-Brown (2006:33–35, 51–52 and 57–58); Gouadec (2007:117–119); Olohan (2007:58); Sandrini (2008:188); and Maia (2010:450).

5. Notable exceptions include Esselink (2000:427–466), Rico Pérez (2002), Stoeller (2004), Elena Dunne (2011) and Keiran Dunne (2011). In addition, Kiraly (2000) and Washbourne (2009) advocate a project- and team-based approach to translation pedagogy.

the *skopos* of translation, are useful for understanding and describing the processes whereby translation and localization project managers identify project objectives and determine project scope. Studying translation and localization quality management requires the identification of the desired qualities, or characteristics, that the translation should exhibit, and can benefit from work on translation and localization quality assessment and quality control (Dunne 2009), as well as scholarship on translation quality by House (1997), Williams (2004) and others.

In project human resource management, team selection (assessment of qualifications and expertise) and team development (managing team learning and training on the job) are especially critical. Works on translation pedagogy by researchers such as Kiraly (2000), Colina (2003), Kelly (2005) and Angelelli (2009) are an important starting point for the development of on-the-job training for translators or editors, or assessment of the qualifications of team candidates in a specific project. Ignoring existing scholarship and well-established principles of pedagogy and translation training can and often does lead to reinventing the wheel. Work on the cognitive underpinnings of the translation process and the development of translation expertise by Shreve (2002) and Shreve and Angelone (2010), for example, underscores the importance of factors such as deliberate practice, acquisition history, the knowledge accumulation process, cognitive changes occurring in the learning process and differences between novices and experts, among others. Understanding such factors is not only crucial for the development of effective approaches to translation pedagogy and translator training, but also suggests strategies that project managers can adopt to foster successful project outcomes. For example, providing feedback loops and establishing connections between team members enables each project participant to receive continuous, useful feedback about his or her performance and to improve over the course of the project. This philosophy of continual improvement is the cornerstone of quality management principles advocated by the Project Management Institute (PMI) and the International Organization for Standardization (ISO). Managing the process of learning and knowledge in a project provides project manager with a better control of the project and reduces uncertainty that is inherent in all projects, thus improving risk management as well.

Current project management standards, such as the Project Management Institute's *A Guide to the Project Management Body of Knowledge (PMBOK® Guide)*, offer generic project management frameworks that can be applied in any industry. For example, the framework provided by the *PMBOK® Guide* maps project management processes into five process groups (initiating, planning, executing, monitoring and controlling, and closing) and nine knowledge areas (PMI 2008: 43):

1. Project integration management
2. Project scope management
3. Project time management
4. Project cost management

5. Project quality management
6. Project human resource management
7. Project communications management
8. Project risk management
9. Project procurement management

Managing projects in a given domain requires that the generic project management knowledge, skills, tools and techniques described in the *PMBOK® Guide* (or other standard) be adapted for use in that domain. Much information is available in industries that have historically made extensive use of project management, such as construction and software engineering. However, no such body of literature currently exists with respect to translation and localization. Consequently, language industry professionals who seek to apply some elements or the full framework of the *PMBOK Guide* or other project management standards in their day-to-day work are left largely to their own devices.

For example, the estimation and management of the time and cost required to complete the intellectual and creative work of a translation project raises numerous questions. How can one estimate how long a specific translation task will take and how much it will cost? What units should one use when developing pricing structures in translation: words, characters, sentences, hours, pages, lines, or perhaps something else? In order to answer such questions, it is necessary to identify the variables that can impact the duration of a given translation project or task, and also to develop a method for estimating the complexity level of that translation project or task. Theoretical and empirical research on such questions could have a direct, profound impact on translation and localization project management, simultaneously informing and professionalizing the industry.

In sum, there is an acute need for research and scholarship that assesses the impact of the project environment on the practice of translation. This volume represents a first step in that direction. The contributors are seasoned practitioners and scholars who offer insights into the central role of project management in the language industry today and discuss best-practice approaches to the adaptation of generic project management knowledge, skills, tools and techniques for translation and localization projects. Indeed, it must be emphasized that just as there is no single correct translation of a given text or single correct localization of a given product, there is no single correct way to manage translation and localization projects. Given the uniqueness and uncertainty inherent in any project undertaking, it is impossible to prescribe all of the possible decisions via checklists, decision trees, flowcharts and so forth. The project manager must use his or her considered judgment and expertise to balance the competing constraints of scope, cost, time, quality and resources in order to achieve the best possible result. It is for these reasons that translation and localization project management is indeed *the art of the possible*.

This volume is divided into four sections. The first section focuses on project management in the context of translation and localization business. In the first chapter, Salvatore Giammarresi argues that successful localization efforts require a strategic approach in which localization is an integral part of product development. He discusses in detail the global product development process and participants, emphasizing the importance of identifying, documenting and managing stakeholders as well as business, market and product requirements. He also situates product development and localization in the larger context of portfolio management, and examines the implications of a strategic approach to translation and localization (or lack thereof) for businesses, practitioners, students and educators. In the second chapter, Alain Chamsi considers project management from the perspective of language service providers. He argues that the evolution from start-up to mature organization requires a shift from unmanaged, ad hoc processes to formally defined and managed processes. As the LSP's processes evolve, so too must the tools and technologies that support them. Eventually, each LSP must evaluate its project management tools and technologies to determine whether they meet the needs of the organization or must be upgraded or replaced. Chamsi proposes a methodology for identifying the requirements of a project management system, deciding whether to build or buy a project management system, or deciding which off-the-shelf system to choose.

The second section explores the application of project management knowledge areas, i.e., the analytical and interpersonal skills and knowledge required to manage projects described by PMI in the international standard, *A Guide to the Project Management Body of Knowledge (PMBOK® Guide)*. Alexandra Zouncourides-Lull discusses the application of PMI processes to translation and localizations projects, focusing on the knowledge area of project integration management, and provides best-practice guidelines accompanied by examples and illustrations. Acknowledging the basic fact that one cannot determine the project budget, schedule, resources or risks until the project objectives and required work have been defined, Natalia Levitina addresses project scope management and its constituent processes in the context of localization. Underscoring the fundamental role that requirements play in shaping project scope, she pays particular attention to requirements collection. Keiran Dunne discusses the management of time and schedule in translation and localization projects. After examining the concept of the schedule as a descriptive and prospective model of project execution, he discusses PMI's time management framework, illustrating its application to a hypothetical translation project. In the following chapter, Keiran Dunne examines quality management in translation and localization projects. Noting that current best-practice approaches frame quality in terms of customer satisfaction, he observes that quality cannot be *defined*, but rather must be *modeled* based on customer requirements. After exploring some of the challenges inherent in customer-focused quality management and the ways in which these challenges can be compounded by traditional project management approaches, he argues that agile methodologies offer solutions to these problems and proposes a model for the quantitative management of customer-focused translation quality. Next, Natalia Tsvetkov and Veronica Tsvetkov explore project communication management. Noting that excellent communication skills are of paramount importance for *any* PM, they argue that such skills are even more critical for translation and localization project managers, not only because they may interact with colleagues from other departments that have their own cultures, but also because crossing cultural borders is the very essence of translation and localization. The Tsvetkovs propose strategies for addressing personality and cultural differences drawing on the Myers-Briggs Type Indicator, Hall's notion of contexting and Hofstede's theory of cultural dimensions. Finally, the section concludes with a chapter by Mark Lammers, who explores the challenges of managing risks in outsourced localization projects. After proposing a localization risk breakdown structure (RBS) for the categorization of localization project risks, he discusses the PMI risk management framework and illustrates how it can be applied in localization projects. He concludes by examining responses to common risks.

In recognition of the fact that project managers do not manage projects but rather people who perform project work, the third section addresses the management of human and organizational factors within the context of translation and localization projects. Richard Sikes argues that most corporations struggle to understand the relationships between localization, internationalization, and globalization, and suggests that localization project managers (LPMs) are ideally positioned to reduce the friction between these three business processes, but doing so requires additional knowledge and skills that have not traditionally been addressed by training programs or academic curricula. He proposes strategies that LPMs can employ to bridge this gap and enhance their career prospects by raising awareness, educating colleagues and fostering the adoption of best practices. By leading the corporation closer to global maturity, LPMs enhance their career prospects. In the following chapter, Elena Dunne takes a different tack, focusing not on interactions between the project manager and colleagues in the organization *per se*, but rather on interactions between the members of the project team. Noting the uniqueness and uncertainty of projects and the fact that the project environment itself is in constant flux, she suggests that adaptive learning is critical for project success. She explains how the pedagogical technique of scaffolding enables the project manager to foster and manage adaptive learning in the project environment. Next, Willem Stoeller focuses on global virtual teams, that is, teams whose members are distributed across geographic, national, temporal, cultural and/or linguistic borders. Asserting that global virtual teams are the foundation on which localization has established itself as an industry, he explores the challenges inherent in the management of such teams, including risk of communication failure, loss of trust and lack of shared vision. He suggests strategies to address these challenges and presents a critical overview of communications technologies that are commonly used in the management of global virtual teams in translation and localization projects. Finally, observing that localization success depends largely on people and groups that may be unaware of their role as stakeholders in the localization process, Karen R. Combe examines the importance of relationship management in outsourced localization projects. After comparing the challenges and constraints that localization project managers face in client organizations versus vendor organizations, she offers strategies for addressing these factors and proposes tools and processes that can be used to facilitate relationship management.

The fourth and final section examines the integration of project management strategies, tools, techniques and technologies in translation and localization projects. Ping Zhou explores the fast-moving and dynamic environment of game localization. After discussing the activities that comprise a typical multi-platform project as well as the roles and responsibilities of the various project team members, she analyzes and contrasts the two primary approaches to game localization today, post-release and simultaneous shipment ("simship") projects. She then illustrates how the processes of communications, scope, risk and change management can be integrated to maximize the chances of project success. In the final chapter, Donald A. DePalma and Nataly Kelly discuss the application of the community or "crowdsourced" project model to translation. Drawing on focused research into practices in the industry, they present case studies that document the experience of four companies, Facebook, Microsoft, Plaxo and Sun Microsystems, and identify the issues encountered and solutions adopted by each. DePalma and Kelly conclude by analyzing the importance of effective project management in community translation projects, and propose a three-step plan for organizations that seek to make crowdsourcing a repeatable undertaking.

The time has come to put translation and localization project management on the map of translation studies. Examining translation studies through the lens of project management, or conversely, using existing work in translation studies as a springboard to the study of translation and localization project management not only creates new avenues of inquiry and fertile ground for new research, but also offers a way to build stronger bridges between theory and practice. A productive and symbiotic relationship between scholars, researchers, educators, trainers, students and practitioners of translation and localization is needed to study problems plaguing the industry today, some of which are discussed in this volume, and identify solutions to those problems. The application of the various types of project management knowledge, skills, tools and techniques in the realm of translation and localization projects is too vast to be addressed adequately in a single volume. It is our hope that the present work will serve to initiate a conversation between translation studies researchers and scholars, educators and trainers, students, practitioners and language industry stakeholders for the benefit of all.

References

Anderman, Gunilla and Rogers, Margaret. 2000. "Translator training between academia and profession: A European perspective." In *Developing Translation Competence*, Christina Schäffner and Beverly Adab (eds), 63–73. Amsterdam/Philadelphia: John Benjamins.

Angelelli, Claudia V. 2009. "Using a rubric to assess translation ability: Defining the construct." In *Testing and assessment in translation and interpreting studies*, Claudia Angelelli and Holly Jacobson (eds), 13–47. Amsterdam/Philadelphia: John Benjamins.

Baer, Brian James and Koby, Geoffrey S. 2003. "Introduction." In *Beyond the Ivory Tower: Rethinking Translation Pedagogy*, Brian James Baer and Geoffrey S. Koby (eds), vii–xv. Amsterdam/Philadelphia: John Benjamins.

Beninatto, Renato. 2005. "The general theory of the translation company." 46th Annual Conference of the American Translators Association, Seattle, WA, Nov. 10.

———. 2006. "A review of the global translation marketplace." Association of Translation Companies Conference, London, UK, Sep. 21. http://www.atc.org.uk/RenatoBenitatto2006.ppt

Bowker, Lynne. 2002. *Computer-Aided Translation Technology: A Practical Introduction*. Ottawa: University of Ottawa Press.

Colina, Sonia. 2003. *Translation Teaching, from Research to the Classroom: A Handbook for Teachers*. Boston: McGraw-Hill.

Drucker, Peter F. 1988. "The coming of the new organization." *Harvard Business Review* 66 (1): 45–53.

Dunne, Elena. 2011. "Managing risk in translation and localization projects." In *Translationsforschung. Tagungsberichte der LICTRA 2010 IX. Leipzig International Conference on Translation and Interpretation Studies, 19.–21. 5. 2010*, Peter A. Schmitt, Susann Herold and Annette Weilandt (eds), Vol. 1, 171–182. Frankfurt am Main: Peter Lang.

Dunne, Keiran J. 2009. "Assessing software localization: For a valid approach." In *Testing and Assessment in Translation and Interpreting Studies*, Claudia Angelelli and Holly Jacobson (eds), 185–222. Amsterdam/Philadelphia: John Benjamins.

———. 2011. "Integrating project management into translation curricula: The Kent State University experience." In *Translationsforschung. Tagungsberichte der LICTRA 2010 IX. Leipzig International Conference on Translation and Interpretation Studies, 19.–21. 5. 2010*, Peter A. Schmitt, Susann Herold and Annette Weilandt (eds), Vol. 1, 183–195. Frankfurt am Main: Peter Lang.

Esselink, Bert. 2000. *A Practical Guide to Localization*. Amsterdam/Philadelphia: John Benjamins.

———. 2003a. "Localisation and translation." In *Computers and Translation: A Translator's Guide*, Harold L. Somers (ed.), 67–86. Amsterdam/Philadelphia: John Benjamins.

———. 2003b. "The evolution of localization." *The Guide to Localization*. Supplement to *MultiLingual Computing & Technology* 14 (5): 4–7. http://www.multilingual.com/downloads/screenSupp57.pdf

Eurostat [Statistical Office of the European Communities]. 2008. *NACE Rev. 2. Statistical Classification of Economic Activities in the European Community*. Luxembourg: Office for Official Publications of the European Communities. http://epp.eurostat.ec.europa.eu/cache/ITY_OFFPUB/KS-RA-07-015/EN/KS-RA-07-015-EN.PDF

Fraser, Janet. 2000. "What do real translators do? Developing the use of TAPs from professional translators." In *Tapping and Mapping the Processes of Translation and Interpreting: Outlooks on Empirical Research*, Sonja Tirkkonen-Condit and Riitta Jääskeläinen (eds), 111–120. Amsterdam/Philadelphia: John Benjamins.

Gerzymisch-Arbogast, Heidrun. 2005. "Introducing multidimensional translation." In *MuTra 2005 – Challenges of Multidimensional translation: Conference Proceedings*, Heidrun Gerzymisch-Arbogast and Sandra Nauert (eds), 2–15. N.p.: MuTra.
Gouadec, Daniel. 2007. *Translation as a Profession*. Amsterdam/Philadelphia: John Benjamins.
Holmes, James S. 2004. "The name and nature of translation studies." In *The Translation Studies Reader*, 2nd ed., Lawrence Venuti (ed.), 180–192. New York/London: Routledge. Rpt. of Holmes, James S. "The name and nature of translation studies." In *Translated! Papers on Literary Translation and Translation Studies*, 67–80. Amsterdam: Rodopi, 1988.
House, Juliane. 1997. *Translation Quality Assessment: A Model Revisited*. Tübingen: Gunter Narr Verlag.
Kelly, Dorothy. 2005. *A Handbook for Translator Trainers: a Guide to Reflective Practice*. Manchester: St. Jerome.
Kelly, Nataly and Stewart, Robert. 2011. *The Top 50 Language Service Providers*. Lowell, MA: Common Sense Advisory.
Kiraly, Donald C. 2000. *A Social Constructivist Approach to Translator Education: Empowerment from Theory to Practice*. Manchester: St. Jerome.
Lefevere, André. 1992. *Translation, Rewriting, and the Manipulation of Literary Fame*. New York/ London: Routledge.
Mackiewicz, Wolfgang. 2009. "Eröffnungsreden" [Opening remarks]. In *CIUTI-Forum 2008: Enhancing Translation Quality: Ways, Means, Methods*, Martin Forstner, Hannelore Lee-Jahnke and Peter A. Schmitt (eds), 8–11. Bern: Peter Lang.
Maia, Belinda. 2010. "The role of translation theory in the teaching of general and non-literary translation – revisited." In *Meaning in Translation*, Barbara Lewandowska-Tomaszczyk and Marcel Thelen (eds), 437–456. Frankfurt-am-Main: Peter Lang.
Malmkjær, Kirsten. 2006. "Translation programmes and the market." Paper delivered at workshop on teaching translation, Subject Centre for Languages, Linguistics and Area Studies, University of Wales, Swansea, Jan. 20. hhttp://www.llas.ac.uk/resourcedownloads/2421/malmkjaer.doc
Marasco, Joe. 2004. "The project pyramid." *IBM developerWorks*. http://www.ibm.com/developerworks/rational/library/4291.html
Niranjana, Tejaswini. 1992. *Siting Translation History, Post-Structuralism, and the Colonial Text*. Berkeley, CA: University of California Press.
Nord, Christiane. 1997. *Translating as a Purposeful Activity: Functionalist Approaches Explained*. Manchester: St Jerome.
O'Hagan, Minako and Ashworth, David. 2002. *Translation Mediated Communication in a Digital World: Facing the Challenges of Globalization and Localization*. Clevedon, UK: Multilingual Matters.
Olohan, Maeve. 2007. "Economic trends and developments in the translation industry." *The Interpreter and Translator Trainer* 1 (1): 37–63.
Prahalad, C. K. and Hamel, Gary. 1990. "The core competence of the corporation." *Harvard Business Review* 68 (3): 79–91.
Project Management Institute. 2008. *A Guide to the Project Management Body of Knowledge (PMBOK® Guide)*. 4th ed. Newtown Square, PA: Project Management Institute.
Pym, Anthony. 2003. "Redefining translation competence in an electronic age. In defence of a minimalist approach." *Meta* 48 (4): 481–497.
———. 2010. *Exploring Translation Theories*. New York/London: Routledge.
Reiss, Katharina. 1980. *Translation Criticism, the Potentials and Limitations: Categories and Criteria for Translation Quality Assessment*. Trans. Erroll F. Rhodes. Manchester: St. Jerome.

Reiss, Katharina, and Vermeer, Hans J. 1984. *Grundlegung einer allgemeinen Translationstheorie*. Tübingen: Niemeyer.

Rico Pérez, Celia. 2002. "Translation and project management." *Translation Journal* 6 (4). http://translationjournal.net/journal//22project.htm

Robinson, Douglas. 2003. *Becoming a Translator: An Introduction to the Theory and Practice of Translation*. 2nd ed. New York/London: Routledge.

Samuelsson-Brown, Geoffrey. 2006. *Managing Translation Services*. Clevedon, UK: Multilingual Matters.

Sandrini, Peter. 2008. "Localization and translation." In *LSP Translation Scenarios*, Heidrun Gerzymisch-Arbogast, Gerhard Budin and Gertrud Hofer (eds), 167–191. Norderstedt: ATRC Group.

Shreve, Gregory M. 1998. "The ecology of the language industry: Prospects and problems." Keynote address of the Language in Business / Language as Business Conference. Institute for Applied Linguistics, Kent State University, Kent, Ohio, USA. Oct. 8, 1998. Accessed Sep. 1, 2006. http://appling.kent.edu/ResourcePages/ConferencesandWorkshopsPast/LanguageinBusiness/Thursday/01-Shreve.pdf

———. 2000. "Translation at the millennium: Prospects for the evolution of a profession." In *Paradigmenwechsel in der Translation. Festschrift für Albrecht Neubert zum 70. Geburtstag*, Peter A. Schmitt (ed.), 217 –234. Tübingen: Stauffenburg.

———. 2002. "Knowing translation: Cognitive and experiential aspects of translation expertise from the perspective of expertise studies." In *Translation Studies: Perspectives on an Emerging Discipline*, Alessandra Riccardi (ed.), 150–171. Cambridge: Cambridge University Press.

Shreve, Gregory M. and Angelone, Erik (eds). 2010. *Translation and Cognition*. Amsterdam/Philadelphia: John Benjamins.

Spivak, Gayatri. 1992. "The politics of translation." In *Destabilizing Theory: Contemporary Feminist Debates*, Michèle Barret and Anne Phillips (eds), 177–200. Stanford, CA: Stanford University Press.

Stoeller, Willem. 2004. "The hub of the wheel." *The Guide to Project Management*. Supplement to *MultiLingual Computing & Technology* 15 (4): 3–6.

Toury, Gideon. 1995. *Descriptive Translation Studies and Beyond*. Amsterdam/Philadelphia: John Benjamins.

U.S. Office of Management and Budget (US OMB). 1997. "1997 North American Industry Classification System – 1987 Standard Industrial Classification replacement." Washington, DC: OMB. http://www.census.gov/epcd/naics/naicsfr8.pdf

Venuti, Lawrence. 1986. "The translator's invisibility." *Criticism* 28 (Spring): 179–212.

———. 1995. *The Translator's Invisibility: A History of Translation*. New York/London: Routledge.

Washbourne, Kelly. 2009. *Instructor's Resource Manual for Manual of Spanish-English Translation*. Englewood Cliffs, NJ: Prentice-Hall.

Williams, Malcolm. 2004. *Translation Quality Assessment: An Argumentation-Centered Approach*. Ottawa: University of Ottawa Press.

Wright, Sue Ellen. 2006. "The creation and application of language industry standards." In *Perspectives on Localization*, Keiran J. Dunne (ed.), 241–278. Amsterdam/Philadelphia: John Benjamins.

Wysocki, Robert K. 2007. *Effective Project Management: Traditional, Adaptive, Extreme*. 4th ed. Indianapolis, IN: Wiley.

PART I

Project management in the context of translation and localization business

Strategic views on localization project management
The importance of global product management and portfolio management

Salvatore Giammarresi

This chapter examines the strategic position of localization management in high-tech software and Web companies through the phases of requirements development, requirements management, product development and portfolio management. It begins by examining the three functional units that formulate the strategies and planning required to transform an idea into a successful localized product: Global Product Management, Localization Project Management and Portfolio Management. Next, it discusses the product development process and participants. It then addresses the critical importance of requirements and stakeholder identification, and examines in detail the role of the Business Requirements Document (BRD), Market Requirements Document (MRD) and Product Requirements Document (PRD) in the product development process. Finally, the chapter situates localization management in the context of portfolio management and concludes by discussing implications for practitioners, students and educators.

Introduction

When a company undertakes the localization of one or more of its products, it typically does so for one of two reasons: either an international customer has expressed interest in purchasing a localized version of one of the company's products (the reactive approach), or the company has decided to expand into one or more new international markets (the strategic approach). Regardless of whether the impetus to localize is reactive or strategic, a company's initial attempts at localization tend to be painful endeavors. The difficulty of localization is not self-evident. Localization does not involve the *creation* of new products from scratch, but rather the *adaptation* of existing products for use in one or more other locales. It is well-known that creating a product that responds to an existing need in the marketplace and has the potential to become a viable source of revenue is the hardest part of running a business: "nine out of ten packaged products fail. About two-thirds of the high-tech products are destined to fail. In industrial products, the failure rate is 50 percent" (Hodock 2007:12). Creating a successful new product is expected to be far more difficult than *modifying* a successful existing product for international markets – or so one would think.

Successful localization is easier said than done, however. The success of a localization project depends to a great extent on the relative ease with which the product can be adapted for other locales; however the problem is that companies without prior localization experience spend little (if any) time properly identifying and analyzing global product requirements in the hopes of achieving faster time to market. The assumption underlying this practice is that a product is a collection of quasi-independent features that can be easily added or removed without significant impact on the product as a whole. This may be true, depending on the product, and in some cases removing features or reducing their scope can in fact improve time to market. Unfortunately, companies tend to transfer this practice to GILT projects, treating localization as if it were merely another independent feature that can be easily added to or removed from a product, not realizing that localization entails rethinking *all aspects of product design and development*.[1] Indeed, localization can – and often does – require major reengineering work and possibly even a wholesale redesign if the product does not support the display of non-Latin scripts (such as the Cyrillic alphabet or simplified Chinese characters) or right-to-left reading directionality for languages such as Arabic and Hebrew, to cite but two examples. Localization project pain is proportional to the scope of the reengineering and/or redesign effort necessary to create a functional localized version of the product.

As they gain experience in localization, companies learn the hard way the importance of designing software, websites and electronic documents so that they can be localized without the need for reengineering, a process known as internationalization.[2] "The least painful kind of localization process is one in which the product team considers international issues during the initial feature design and coding design stages," as Kano observes (1995:12). "A good rule of thumb to follow is that it takes twice as long and costs twice as much to localize a product if it [i]s not properly internationalized to begin with," advises the Localization Industry Standards Association (Lommel 2003:14).

---

1. The Localization Industry Standards Association (LISA) refers collectively to the business processes of globalization, internationalization, localization and translation using the acronym GILT (Lommel 2003:6; Lommel 2007:53).

2. For detailed information on internationalization, see Urien, Howard and Perinotti (1993); Kano (1995); Luong, Lok, Taylor and Driscoll (1995); Esselink (2000:25–55); Deitsch and Czarnecki (2001); Savourel (2001); Symmonds (2002); Rätzmann, Manfred and De Young (2003); and Smith-Ferrier (2007).

Companies typically attempt to alleviate the pain of localization by identifying and addressing specific internationalization problems that they encounter with the goal of facilitating future localization efforts. However, the tactical approach whereby companies attack discrete "symptoms" of defective internationalization fails to address the root causes of the pain. As Asnes (2007: 33) observes:

> [M]ost published internationalization materials focus only on the tactical code-based issues of internationalization. Those technical tips and descriptions are important, but it's primarily in the business processes around globalizing software development where I see the most organizational pain, delays and expenses endured when companies are reacting to demands of new customers in new locales or are undertaking strategic efforts globally.

Just as localization project pain is evidence of internationalization issues, internationalization issues are themselves symptoms of deeper, more systemic ills.

In the realm of business, a product or service represents a solution to a customer's problem or a means of meeting a customer's need. The identification of a customer problem or need and an idea for solving that problem or meeting that need in a financially viable way are prerequisites for the development of any product or service. However, even if these prerequisites are met, no product or service can be successfully launched without an appropriate detailed plan for developing the idea and bringing the resulting product or service to market. These "laws" of business also hold true for localized products. Moreover, because localized products must cross geographic, linguistic and cultural boundaries, their development must address such international variables as language, culture and local market requirements. International requirements must be identified and addressed *during* product development, not after. In sum, successful localization requires the formulation and execution of an appropriate *enterprise strategy* for developing and releasing each localized product on time, within budget and in such a way that it meets the linguistic and cultural expectations of target users and conforms to the legal and regulatory requirements of each target market.

This chapter will examine localization from a strategic perspective, and will examine the roles that localization project management, global product management and portfolio management play in successful localization efforts. Some might wonder why a chapter on global product management and portfolio management is included in a book devoted to translation and localization project management. Three reasons justify this inclusion. First, in today's economy, in-house translation and localization are an increasing rarity. According to localization market research firm Common Sense Advisory, 87% percent of companies outsource most or all of their translation and localization work (DePalma and Beninatto 2003: 11). In this highly outsourced environment, project managers in translation and localization service providers are often the first people to discover and confront the problems that arise when a company decides to localize an inadequately internationalized product. Indeed, in practice one of the more critical aspects of translation and localization project management is determining the extent to which the source materials have been authored following internationalization best practices, as the failure to do so can have a major impact on the scope of the effort required to create the localized versions, and thus by extension on the project cost and timeline, as noted above. Second, many companies view outsourcing as a way to solve their localization problems by transferring localization-related risks to external service providers. However, outsourcing can only be as effective as the business strategies on which it is based. Outsourcing cannot overcome a lack of effective global product development and/or portfolio management strategies, nor can it be a substitute for such strategies. This explains why many companies view the localization process and concomitant outsourcing as a source of headaches, instead of viewing it as a highly cost-effective way to expand into new markets by leveraging investments in existing products. Finally, in the "flat world" of the twenty-first century, "[a]s businesses continue to expand globally and more countries become wired to the Internet, it will become increasingly important for those businesses to ensure that the products they manufacture and sell are appropriate for the world's markets," as Deitsch and Czarnecki observe (2001:1). In this respect, software engineering has lagged behind more traditional engineering practices, as Deitsch and Czarnecki also point out (2001:1–2). For example, automobile manufacturers produce cars in both left-hand drive and right-hand drive configurations in response to different traffic directionality conventions (i.e., vehicles are equipped with right-hand drive and travel on the left-hand side of the road in the United Kingdom, whereas the opposite is true in continental Europe). In the same way, manufacturers of software applications need to design their products to account for differences in language, culture and local conventions. Localization and internationalization are not "features" that can be retrofitted into a product design after the fact. It is important that translation and localization project management students, educators, scholars, and practitioners be aware of the ways in which global product management and portfolio management shape the very *possibility* of successful localization projects.

Localization strategy and organizational structure

The strategies and planning required to transform an idea into a successful localized product are – or should be – formulated by three different functional groups within a company, namely Global Product Management, Localization Project Management and Portfolio Management (see Figure 1).[3] Although each of these three groups focuses on a different facet of strategy and planning, their approaches are complementary and enable the formulation of a coherent global product strategy.

---

3. Product Marketing is often involved as well, but a discussion of product marketing is outside of the scope of this chapter.

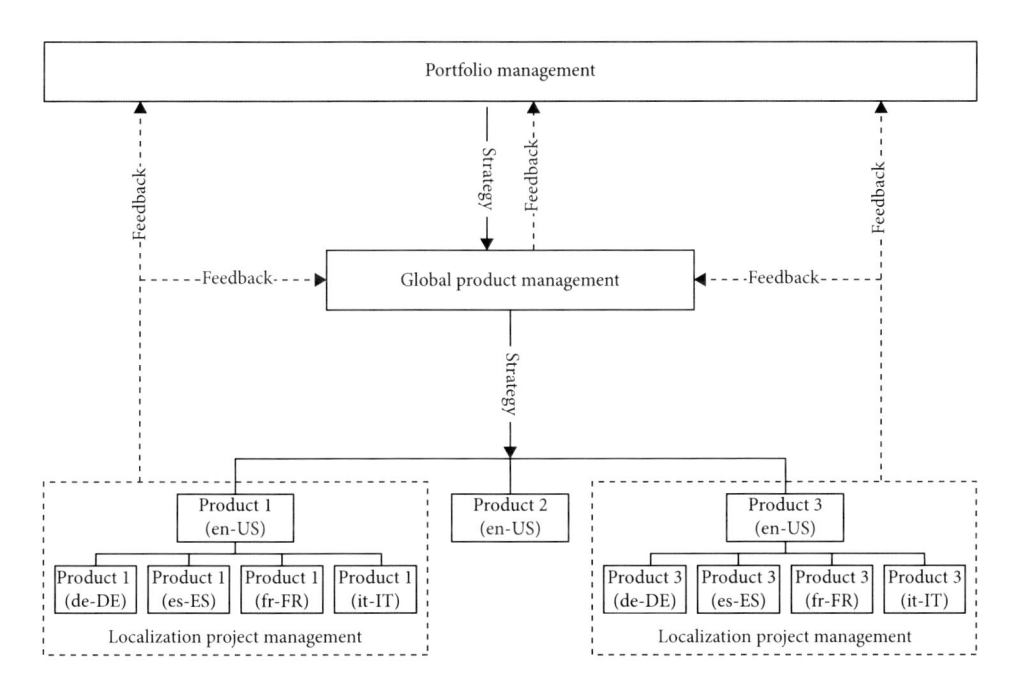

Figure 1. Localization project management, global product management and portfolio management all play a strategic role in successful localization efforts.

Global Product Management defines the overall strategy for each individual product and communicates that strategy to all groups involved in product creation, development, testing, marketing, launch and support. Usually product management takes a broad perspective on development, and focuses on the ways in which the product idea responds to identified customer needs. The product management team must not only conceive a product but also outline the best way to design, develop, test and successfully market and sell it in each locale. Product management is one of the most outward facing functional groups within a company since it relies on direct or indirect customer feedback and must take the competitive landscape into consideration when conceiving and validating the product idea, establishing its financial feasibility and detailing the product requirements. It is important to note that job titles and the way roles and responsibilities are distributed within the organization can vary greatly. The function of product manager may be – and often is – identified using various labels, and may be performed by someone whose job title does not indicate responsibility for product management, such as "chief executive officer" (CEO) or "program manager." Nevertheless, someone must be assigned the responsibility for product management. In recognition of the great variety of titles used in different companies, all references in this chapter to a "project manager," "product manager" or "portfolio manager" are references to the *function* rather than a job title.

Localization Project Management (also often called Localization Management) manages and monitors the implementation of the product localization strategy from a purely engineering and/or operational perspective. Localization project management focuses on determining the most effective way to ensure that the localized product is created on time, with the highest linguistic quality, according to the locale-specific requirements, using the available human and technical resources (both inside and outside the company) and according to the requirements specified by the product management team.

Portfolio Management addresses the overall strategy of all of the products and resources in the company as a whole. It is in portfolio management that the company's overall product strategy and resource allocations, the balance between risk and value, and many other factors are taken into consideration to optimize the company's performance. It is at this level that products and projects are approved, rejected, canceled and modified, and that financial and human resources are allocated on the basis of these project decisions to ensure an optimal mix of products in the company's portfolio based on defined strategic goals.

Because an exhaustive analysis of global product management and portfolio management is well beyond the scope of this chapter, we will focus on start-up, small and medium-sized software and web companies that produce software applications and features.[4] Such companies offer an ideal window through which to examine the importance of global product management and portfolio management to successful localization efforts. On one hand, they typically offer one or at most a handful of products, have a niche expertise and market, and it is costly and time-consuming for them to grow revenues by introducing new products. Localization thus offers them the ability to strengthen their market position and increase revenues while expanding globally (DePalma 2004). On the other hand, although start-up, small and medium-sized software companies are well positioned to benefit from localization, they are usually poorly prepared for it. They often lack a localization manager, a product manager, let alone a Vice President of Products or other senior executive focused primarily on products, and they generally operate without formalized global product development processes. This lack of dedicated global product management and formalized processes reflects the staffing limitations typical in smaller companies, in which each person often covers more than one function, and in which some functions lack an officially designated person. In such companies, the decision to localize one or more products invariably leads to major organizational challenges. What company executives often fail to realize is that localization is not itself the problem; rather, localization merely highlights existing gaps in the organizational structure and competencies,

---

4. Nevertheless, much of what will be discussed, stemming from the author's firsthand experience working in small, medium and large international companies in the software, hardware and web industries for the last 20 years, still applies to other companies and other product types.

i.e., focused global product management and product portfolio management vision, strategy, processes and oversight.

Finally, for the purpose of this chapter, a small company is defined as one that is has up to 100 employees, generates approximately 30 million USD in revenue per year, and has one to three products, whereas a medium company has up to 2000 employees, generates approximately 500 million USD in revenue per year and has up to 10 products. The length of the average product development cycle is estimated to be three to six months.

Localization: A mix of art and science

It has been said that localization is both an art and a science (DePalma 2004; Giammarresi 2005; Dunne 2006a).[5] On one hand, the body of personal and shared experience and the literature on similar localized products that have previously been developed and launched supply the "science," that is, the known facts and the localization procedures that enable repeatable results. On the other hand, every project is unique. The development of any given localized product is shaped by a unique set of parameters, including company culture and practices, the human and financial resources available, market conditions, the type of product being developed, and so forth. Managing these variables constitutes the "art" of localized product development.

The "science" of localized product development includes the following best practices:

- using CAT (computer-assisted translation) tools and TMS (Translation Management Systems) to reduce time and costs of translation while improving consistency;[6]
- using resource files to separate displayable text from source code;
- creating, localizing, reviewing and approving a product glossary, including all text displayed in the user interface (UI), before undertaking any translation of help files or manuals;
- ensuring correct locale-specific display of dates, times, numbers, currencies, addresses, titles and phone numbers;
- ensuring that graphic files do not contain embedded text, and if they must, then ensuring that layered source files are kept and tracked so the graphics can be more easily localized.

---

5. The same can also be said of product management (Mironov 2008), project management (Heerkens 2002), product portfolio management (Brentani 2004), and, more broadly, of running a company.

6. When properly used, CAT tools improve consistency, but consistency is not necessarily synonymous with quality. If the translation is defective, it will be consistently defective.

This list is not exhaustive. Nevertheless, these practices all share a fundamental trait: they can be taught by localization professionals and can be implemented by aspiring localization specialists.

The "art" of localized product development includes the following best practices:

- determining the appropriate scope of localization for a given product based on the company's culture and the products it offers, market conditions, competitors and their products, etc.;
- identifying, gathering and documenting the specific requirements of a given project, taking into account cost, quality, time, scope, and many other factors such as the type of presence the company has in each locale and the perception of the product and brand;
- decomposing the many large and small project tasks into finite deliverables that can be tracked, monitored and analyzed; setting up and executing the proper product strategy; and
- devising a strategy and implementation plan that will allow the company to gain the most benefit from the localization of the product.

Again, this list is far from exhaustive and depends to a great extent on the specific product being localized. Nevertheless, these practices share one critical trait, namely the fact that they cannot be easily taught because they rely on timely, unique and dynamic data that changes as new information is made available and tasks are completed. Both the pace of change and the high variability of localization scenarios make it impossible to codify and therefore teach the potentially infinite number of cases and inter-dependencies that might occur. These practices also require the analysis of the people and the localization processes in place within an organization. Localization processes may need to be modified from one project to another; if none exist, then they will need to be defined and implemented, which can be a daunting task.[7]

Because the specific configuration of variables varies from project to project, the creation of a formulaic, assembly-line approach to development is impossible. The product manager, project manager and portfolio manager must successfully balance the art and science of the development process to enable the creation of a localized product that meets an identified business need and satisfies corporate objectives.

---

7. The Localization Maturity Model (DePalma, Beninatto and Sargent 2006) provides a framework for assessing the status of a company's current localization practices and outlines the various steps and processes companies should implement to improve the return on their localization investment.

The product development process and participants

Localization is based on a strategy that is progressively operationalized over the course of the product lifecycle (see Figure 2). Once the idea for a new product is conceived, the first task is to elicit, analyze and document users' needs as formal requirements. The types of users and the use case scenarios analyzed during this phase of the product lifecycle, known as requirements development, determine the types of markets and locales for which the product will ultimately be suited. If the product is to

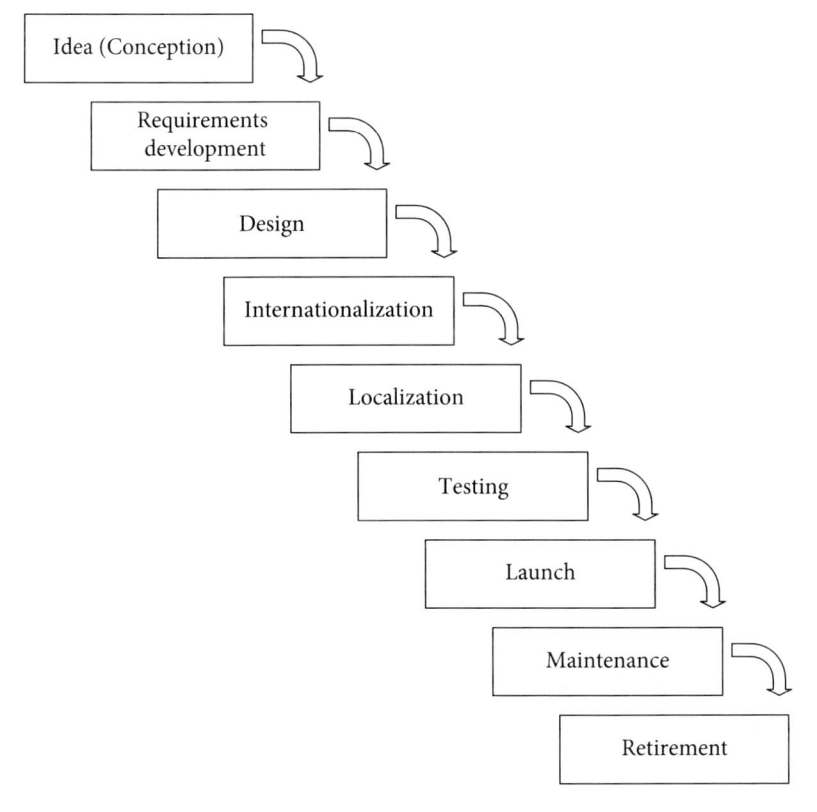

Figure 2. A generic model that illustrates the various phases of a localized Software Development Life Cycle (SDLC) based on a traditional Waterfall methodology.[8]

---

8. As its name implies, the Waterfall method consists of a downward flow from one phase to the next. Each phase needs to be concluded before the following phase can start. This approach offers the benefit of not engaging resources downstream until the upstream resources have completed their tasks. The major disadvantage of the Waterfall development methodology is its relative inflexibility. Over the past decade, new "agile" development methodologies have emerged that are slowly supplanting the Waterfall approach. For a discussion of these methodologies, see Highsmith (2004).

be marketed and sold in locales outside the home market, then users and stakeholders from those locales must be consulted during requirements development. The extent to which the wants, needs, and expectations of all target users are clearly and comprehensively documented during requirements development plays a preponderant role in shaping the very possibility of successful localization efforts later on. The next phase of the product lifecycle, design, specifies the ways in which the requirements will be met. Programmers use the design specification to implement the requirements in a functional software application. The application is therefore internationalized, debugged and tested to ensure that all potential internationalization problems have been successfully addressed and that the product meets the specified requirements. At this point of the product lifecycle, the application is ready to be localized. Following localization, the target versions of the product are tested to ensure that they present all of the functionalities specified in the requirements. The product is then launched, i.e., released to the market, and enters a maintenance phase during which it may be modified as new user needs are identified. Finally, when the product reaches the end of its useful life, support is discontinued and the product is officially retired.

Figure 3 presents a comprehensive view of the functional groups involved in the creation of a localized product, namely Global Product Management, Product Stakeholders, Engineering, Localization Management, Quality Assurance (internal and outsourced), as well as localization vendor(s) and in-country language specialists or reviewers. Figure 3 also illustrates the interactions between these main functions which enable the creation of a localized product. A localized product begins life as an idea that is subsequently conceptualized in business, market and product requirements. While localization is typically understood to encompass the development of internationalized software, the translation of glossaries, user interface strings and documents, as well as localization testing, none of these activities can begin in earnest without clear and complete requirements. The failure to address international market requirements during product development leads to localized products that are "inadequate, over budget, and late" (Asnes 2007: 34).

The critical importance of requirements

Scholars and practitioners (Bacon et al. 1994; Iansiti 1995; Bhattacharya, Krishnan and Mahajan 1998; Cooper, Edgett and Kleinschmidt 2001; Giammarresi 2005; DePalma, Beninatto and Sargent 2006; Dunne 2006b) emphasize the fact that early definition of product requirements and specifications makes product planning, development, implementation, testing and roll-out more efficient and has a direct impact on the product's quality, reducing overall costs and improving total return on investment (ROI) while optimizing time to market.

Localization managers are usually not responsible for authoring or maintaining product requirement documents, yet without such documents they do not have a

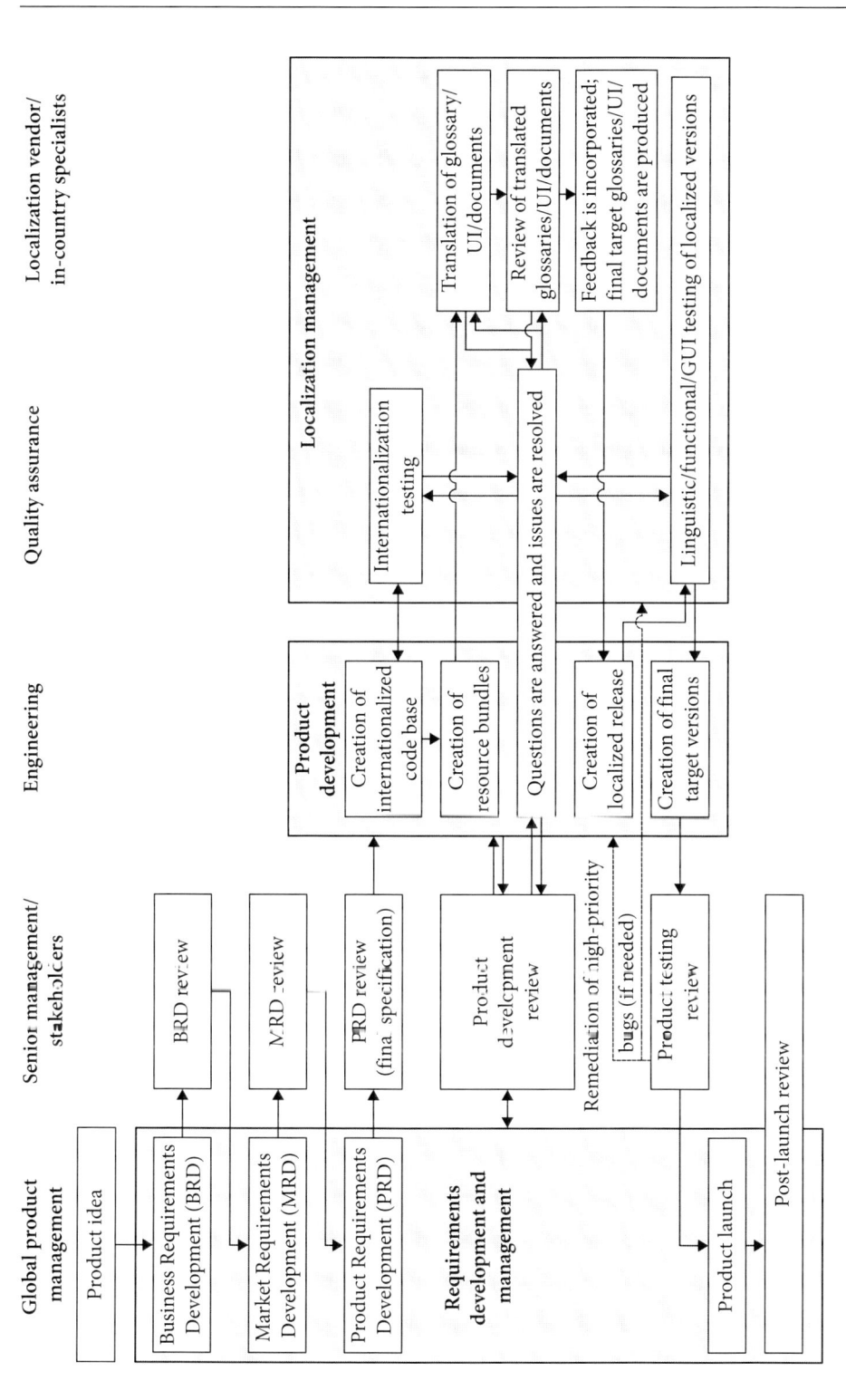

Strategic views on localization project management 27

Figure 3. Localized product development flowchart.

clear understanding of what needs to be localized, and ultimately they cannot successfully perform their job function. While writing requirements documents is often viewed as a waste of time, it is estimated that 40 to 60 percent of bugs found in software products can be traced back to the lack of or incomplete requirements documents (Davis 1993; Leffingwell and Widrig 2003). Likewise, Boehm (1981: 383) notes that up to 65% of software errors originate in the requirements and design phases of the SDLC (see Figure 2). The lack of proper requirements documents has a noticeable impact on engineering and QA (Dunne 2006b). Boehm (1981: 40), citing prior studies in Boehm (1976, 1980), Daly (1977), Fagan (1976) and Stephenson (1976), notes that it is "typically 100 times more expensive to correct [an error] in the maintenance phase on large projects than in the requirements phase." Empirical research by Westland (2002) on software localization projects undertaken by a software publisher that offered products in 31 global markets notes that "the largest single contributor to localization cost was the detection and correction of errors" (3) and supports Boehm's conclusion that "uncorrected errors become exponentially more costly with each phase in which they are unresolved" (8).

Product requirements documents are the output of a process during which the product manager will have to:

- take into account each stakeholder's goals;
- identify and resolve the conflicts among different goals;
- document as many potential use-case scenarios as possible;[9]
- list all the functionality the product will support, which will help engineering clarify the requirements that might not be captured by use-case scenarios;
- list all the components of the product, assigning relative priorities to each and outlining, when possible, the business case for each, taking into consideration the many business, internal and external assumptions, pre-existing business rules, quality requirements, and various internal and external factors and constraints.

Depending on the type of product being developed, the type and size of the company and the number of stakeholders involved, managing requirements can be a highly complex and time-consuming task, requiring dedicated expertise and resources. Over the past two decades or so, requirements engineering has emerged as a discipline unto itself (Kotonya and Sommerville 1998) and an increasingly critical aspect of product development.

---

9. A use-case scenario in software engineering is a description of how a user will interact with a specific functionality of the software, what the user will be able to do and the steps that the user will have to take to accomplish that goal. In simple terms, a use case describes 'who' can do 'what' and 'how' with the system in question. Software products typically encompass hundreds of use-case scenarios. For example, a typical use-case scenario in a word processing software describes the steps the user will need to take to perform a spell-check.

Requirements engineering

Requirements engineering encompasses two distinct processes: requirements development and requirements management (Wiegers 2003). These two processes are often performed by the same person or group, usually in the product management team. During requirements development, product managers conceive, elicit, analyze, specify and validate the product requirements, while in the requirements management phase, product managers direct and oversee the evolution of the requirements as the product goes through the various phases of design, product engineering, quality assurance and various reviews until it is released to the market (see Figure 4). Elicitation is an especially crucial step in the requirements development process that involves gathering feedback from both internal stakeholders and external customers. Product managers should gather information directly (through meetings and surveys) and indirectly (through market research and by analyzing the competitive landscape) to ensure that the requirements are as comprehensive as possible.

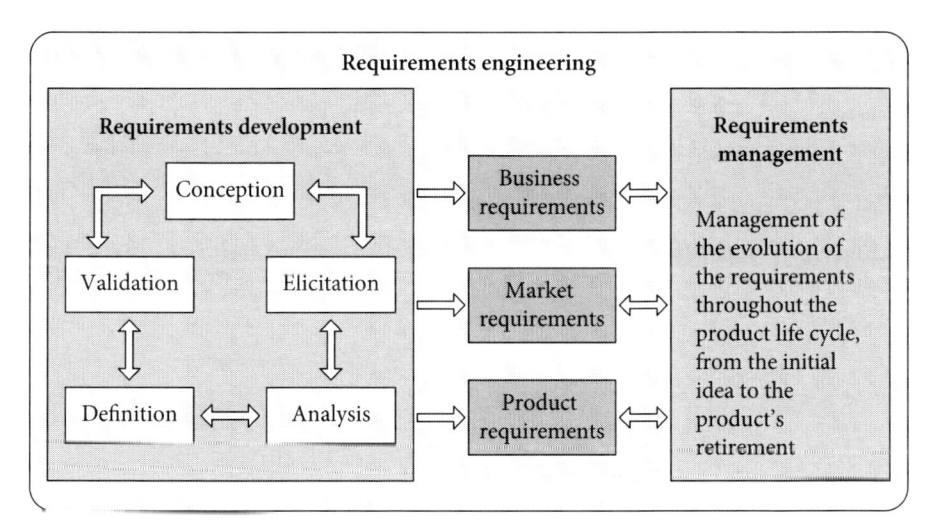

Figure 4. The relationship between requirements engineering, requirements management and the sub-processes within requirements development.

Reviews should be performed at the end of each phase of requirements development, i.e., after the development of business requirements, market requirements and product requirements (Cooper, Edgett and Kleinschmidt 2001, see Figures 3 and 4) to ensure that the project fits within the overall product strategy of the company and that it is appropriately staffed and prioritized. Phase-end reviews involve a twofold decision by product portfolio managers and sometimes by senior management and key stakeholders as well. The first decision is whether to approve, cancel, or place a project on hold. This evaluation is performed in isolation, against a set of parameters, acceptable outcomes and known facts. If the project is approved, then the second decision entails prioritizing the project against all other active and on-hold projects taking into account, among other things, the internal and external resources required and the financial impact. Phase-end reviews are designed to determine whether or not the project objectives can be met. If they can, the project continues; if not, it is terminated. Phase-end reviews are also undertaken to detect and correct errors before proceeding to the next phase of the project.

During requirements development, it is important for the product manager and all stakeholders to remember that "successful product management means delivering the right products at the right time for the right markets" (Ebert 2009: 15). Therefore, while an open exchange of point of views, perspectives and input is necessary, the process of requirements development should never turn into paralysis by analysis. A fine line separates experienced product managers who are able to capture "just enough requirements" (Davis 2005) to release a successful product from those who are unable to do so.

Requirements management is crucial in this respect because requirements evolve continuously and therefore are never truly finalized. During every phase and every phase-end review new information will be available that will enable refinement of the previous requirements. The product manager will continue to modify the requirements with the advice from the stakeholders until at some point (hopefully before the start of the product development phase) a final decision is made as to the product's feature set. In reality, requirements can and most often do change up until the product is officially launched. Requirements management continues even after the product launch as product managers field requests, feedback and input from actual users in various scenarios. This feedback is usually then taken into consideration when the product manager starts outlining the requirements for the following version of the product.

Both requirements development and requirements management present unique challenges. Very often product managers do not have all of the information needed to make final decisions, and as requirements grow in number and complexity they may conflict with one another or may lead to the introduction of new requirements which enlarge the scope of the product and thus require more time and/or resources. It is the product manager's duty to address these challenges; to find, provide and negotiate solutions with the help of the stakeholders; and to keep senior management informed.

Requirements development and stakeholder identification

Arguably the most important aspect of requirements development is identifying and securing the participation of all the relevant stakeholders to ensure that requirements elicitation and analysis are as comprehensive as possible. Identifying stakeholders and determining the appropriate extent of their involvement in the requirements development process is an important but challenging task. If too many stakeholders and/or inappropriate stakeholders are involved, finalizing the requirements will be more difficult. Conversely, if not all appropriate stakeholders are involved there is a serious risk that the product development will be based on incomplete or defective requirements. For example, in-country managers and sales managers should be involved in the requirements development process (although often they are not) to make sure that the major stakeholders who will be promoting and selling the products are aligned in terms of feature set, expectations and ROI. Depending on the types of interactions that in-country offices have with the company's headquarters, the input from in-country managers may be sought later in the product development process, when fundamental business and engineering decisions have already been made, at which point major changes to the product will be prohibitively expensive and/or time-consuming, or even impossible. The following is a list of stakeholders that generally should be involved in product requirements development.

- Global product managers are responsible for product requirements development and requirements management. As such, they are by default the main coordinators of all stakeholder meetings and decisions. The lack of a designated product manager makes it almost impossible to manage the stakeholder consultations.
- The main engineering manager directs all engineering work. Depending on the organization, this responsibility may fall on the lead engineering manager for the product or on the manager of the whole engineering team. More than one engineering manager may be involved in the development of complex products that contain both front-end components (that are visible to the user or that impact the display of information) and back-end components (behind-the-scenes processes and computations), or both hardware and software. Engineering managers are key stakeholders since they manage the development phase of the SDLC (see Figure 2) and provide input on time and resource estimates. Such estimates are particularly important if internationalization is required.
- The localization manager (or localization project manager) determines localization feasibility and manages the localization process, the localization vendors and the internal and external resources, and belongs to the core group of stakeholders.
- Global user interface designers are responsible for the look and feel of the product. Most aspects of localization deal with visualization of data and information; therefore it is paramount that the designers be in tune with the rest of the team and that they help define the requirements. Excluding designers from the requirements development process will effectively delay product development.
- The documentation manager or main document specialist for the product writes all copy contained in the product, including help files and user guides, or manages a team that writes such copy. It is advisable that the documentation manager be involved as early as possible, especially if the company has no prior

localization experience or is developing source and localized versions concurrently for simultaneous shipment, in order to create the master product glossary and plan the documentation authoring and revision timelines so that they fit into the overall localization timeline. Documentation managers and writers also need to be familiar with the concepts of authoring for a global audience, which can help improve the linguistic quality of the localized documentation and reduce translation time.

- The localization quality assurance manager oversees the quality assurance engineers and is responsible for the functional and linguistic quality of the product. He/she must be involved in the early phases of product development in order to provide time and resource estimates and to give input on the overall localization testing phase. This stakeholder is particularly important during the product testing phase-end review (see Figures 2 and 3).
- As their name suggests, in-country general managers are usually responsible for the company's business in a specific country. They should be consulted for their perspective on the features that must be included; not involving them can result in the development of a product that does not respond to the needs of the customers in that market. In-country managers also need to be in the loop on the overall product strategy and scheduled launch timeline in order to prepare all in-country pre-launch activities and to support post-launch promotion and sales activities.
- Global product marketing managers are responsible for marketing the product in specific locales. They should be consulted to help determine the initial product positioning with regard to competing products in each market; a unique marketing and communication plan may be required for each market or group or markets.
- In-country sales managers are tasked with selling the product in a specific country. They need to provide their perspective on the feature set that will make the product most attractive to target customers. In small and medium companies, the in-country general manager generally covers this role.
- Legal counsel is responsible for defining and documenting the initial set of locale-specific legal requirements; a product's Terms of Use and supporting legal documents may be subject to different legal requirements in each country. The failure to prepare appropriate versions that will pass legal muster in each locale can delay or prevent the product launch. In some cases, companies also rely on in-country legal counsel.
- Senior executives also need to participate. Since the functional groups they head will be affected by the product, these executives should have an opportunity to provide their feedback early in the requirements development process. Senior managers also need to be involved to make sure that the product reflects the company's priorities and to be better prepared to review financial and human resource allocations during subsequent portfolio reviews. Company executives

often decline to participate in requirements development stakeholder meetings, not understanding their value, only to provide feedback later in the product development cycle when making changes entails re-work and waste of resources.
- Finally customers are also key product stakeholders and as such their feedback should be valued, although too often companies claim to "know" what customers want without actually trying to find out. It is the product manager's job to present customers' feedback, input and requests within the company; this is what Mironov (2008) calls the "outsider thinking" aspect of product management.

The product manager should be able to identify and engage the appropriate stakeholders throughout the entire product life cycle and determine who must be involved in each phase (core stakeholders) and who merely needs to be kept informed of the progress made (regular stakeholders). For localized products, the core stakeholders generally include the product manager, the main engineering manager and the localization manager. Depending on the extent to which localization work is outsourced, the localization vendor's participation may be required sooner rather than later in the product development process. When localization is heavily outsourced, the localization vendor may even become a core stakeholder. Although treating an external vendor as a core stakeholder is a common practice in many industries, it is relatively rare in translation and localization projects because development companies tend to consider vendors as outsiders rather than as business partners who need to be involved in the process. This flawed perception often leads to project delays, since the vendor becomes involved too late in the localization process to be able to effectively address aspects of the design and/or implementation that hinder localization.

The requirements development process:
Business, market and product requirements

Requirements development comprises three phases that focus sequentially on business requirements, market requirements and product requirements (see Figure 5). The outputs of requirements development are a series of three documents: the Business Requirements Document (BRD), the Market Requirements Document (MRD) and the Product Requirements Document (PRD). Some companies opt to create just one requirements document in order to save time. This approach may be acceptable in smaller projects; however, it is recommended that a three-document approach be used in the majority of projects. It is also recommended that the review of each document be used as an opportunity to finalize the requirements to the extent possible, to check on the status of the project and monitor its feasibility, and also to determine whether the company should further pursue the project by subjecting the product idea or requirement documentation to a thorough review by senior management and the key stakeholders.

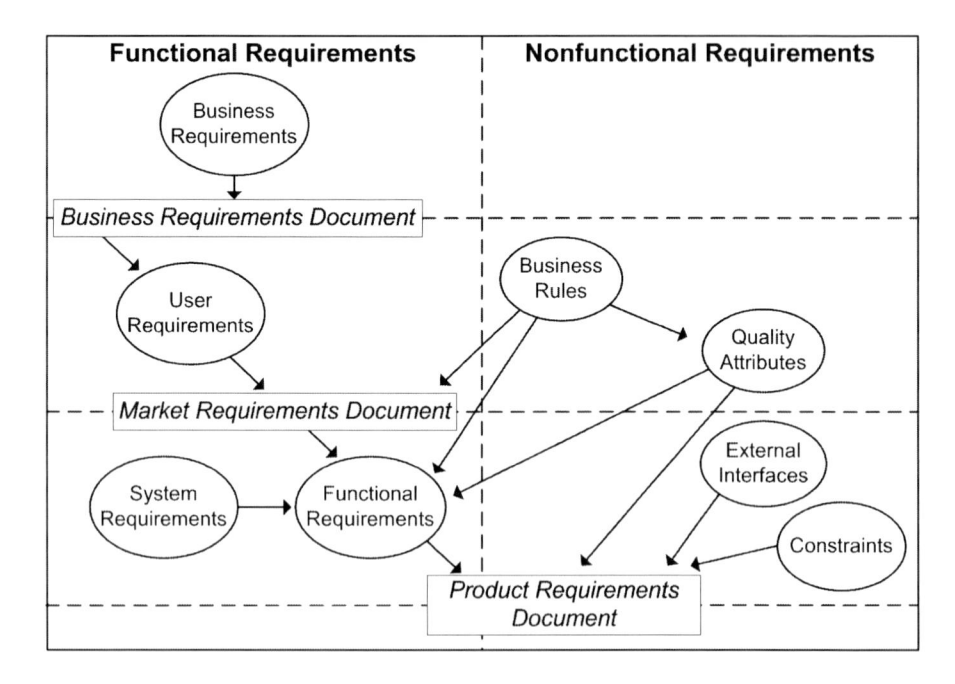

Figure 5. Inputs and outputs of the requirements development process. Inputs are represented as ovals and outputs as shaded rectangles. The horizontal dotted lines represent phase-end reviews. See also Figure 3.

The business requirements document (BRD)

The initial idea for a product should be described in a document that product managers and senior management can share and use as a basis for further discussion. In most companies this first document is called a Business Requirements Document (BRD) (see Figure 5). Wiegers (2003) calls it a Vision and Scope Document and different companies and authors may use other names. Regardless of what it is called, product management professionals and scholars agree that the role of this first document is to identify a business need and to outline the product that can fulfill that need as part of a viable business operation. Because the BRD will lack many pieces of information, it should be considered a discussion-starter, in other words, a document that can be analyzed by different people and groups in the company (primarily senior management and core stakeholders at this stage) in order to obtain feedback and perhaps establish whether it is worthwhile to pursue the product discovery process, modify some of the initial assumptions or just cancel the project. Depending on the product type, a BRD may be more or less complete and detailed, and may range from one to ten pages.

The goal of a BRD is to draft an initial outline of the product and the ways in which it helps customers and fits into both the company's product lineup and the competitive landscape. The solution that a BRD proposes may be either a new product or a feature to be added to an existing product. A BRD should also provide a preliminary outline of supporting business data such as revenue forecasts, market analysis and product strategy. A BRD is usually written by someone in the product development team. Some companies prefer to not use a formal BRD, although the type of information that a typical BRD would contain is collected and discussed in some fashion by someone in the company. Writing a document, reviewing it and maybe holding a preliminary brainstorming session can take some time, but it is time well spent. Companies that fail to invest this time in the early stages of product development often end up embarking on projects that upon closer inspection should never have been started because they diverge from the product suite or the core competencies of the company, or because they offer an insufficient return on investment (ROI). Such projects ultimately waste time and resources. This is particularly true for localized products, given their company-wide implications (see Figure 3).

A BRD should also outline a preliminary product strategy. For example, if a company wants to localize an application into Brazilian Portuguese, and already has a Portuguese version of the product for the European Portuguese market, the BRD should include an outline of how the company and the application will support target-language speaking customers by offering fully translated user documentation, a localized help section on the company's website, as well as access to target-language customer service. In this example, while the Brazilian customers can easily access the Portuguese manuals and help files, it might be a business mistake, given the type of product and the intended audience, to have native European Portuguese speakers in Portugal perform phone support, due to the major differences in pronunciation between the variants of Portuguese spoken in Portugal and Brazil. Not taking such differences into consideration as early as the BRD stage may ultimately delay the product launch, hide the true cost or opportunity of the entire project, or mask the need to hire or subcontract expertise in critical areas. In this hypothetical scenario, the BRD might include a cost/benefit analysis of either setting up a customer service office in Brazil or hiring native Brazilian Portuguese speakers to work in the company's central European customer service office. It is better to identify such issues and projects sooner rather than later and decide early on if company resources should be allocated to these projects.

The BRD and the importance of GILT requirements

In the case of global products, the BRD should contain some high-level indication of the scope of GILT required to release the product successfully. The BRD should answer some of the following questions: should all documentation and online help files be localized for each locale? How will customer support be handled in each locale? What forms of payment will be accepted in each locale? What type of legal requirements should the company fulfill in order to market and sell the product in each locale? The answers to these and many other similar questions allow those gathering the requirements to gain an understanding of the scope of the localization required for each locale as early as possible. Many companies wishing to localize their products fail to properly create a BRD during this first step, particularly when the assigned product manager has no international product experience, and thus undermine their subsequent localization efforts. In this scenario, it is possible that the BRD will contain very little or no information as to the type and extent of the GILT required, and once this information is elicited, later in the product development cycle, it will be harder to address localization-specific issues.

Experienced global product managers should be able to specify the high-level GILT requirements in the BRD working in consultation with the localization manager. At a minimum, a BRD for a global product should indicate the target locales in which the product will be made available and the scope of GILT required for each locale. For example a BRD might specify that the new product should be made available for Spanish-speaking users in both the US and Spain. In this scenario, the BRD might further specify that the US-based users will receive PDF manuals in both English and Spanish; will access a website that has the same top-level domain (.com) and look and feel as the US English website; and will have access to a US-based customer service center, whereas the Spain-based users will only receive PDF manuals in Spanish; will access a website with a Spanish top-level domain (.es) with a different look and feel from the US site; and will have access to the company's main European customer service center in Amsterdam, which will be properly staffed.

If the product has never been properly internationalized, the BRD should outline the required scope of internationalization, and these preliminary internationalization requirements will need to be further refined in consultation with the engineering group. For example, if the product is a Customer Relationship Management system that is intended only for Western European markets, then there will be no need to enable double-byte character support and the application will only need to support the Gregorian calendar. On the other hand, if the product is intended for the Chinese, Japanese and Korean markets, then the product should be able to properly support and display double-byte characters and be able to convert times and dates between the Japanese Emperor Year, the Year of the Republic of China and the Tangun Era calendars. In this case, the BRD review is the perfect opportunity to determine if it is realistic to internationalize and localize the product in the same release.

Companies that have little experience with internationalization are advised to dedicate a product release cycle to internationalizing the core code, and then undertaking phase localization for selected locales in subsequent releases, based on business and marketing opportunities. Phase localization, also known as the staggered approach or pilot localization, entails the localization of a product for one or two locales, usually the most financially viable and/or those that enable the discovery of internationalization issues (for example, Arabic in order to test bidirectionality support). The goal of phase localization is twofold. First, it enables the company to verify that internationalization has been performed correctly. Second, it provides an opportunity to test localization processes within the various in-house groups and in collaboration with the localization vendor(s). Undertaking localization for one or two locales enables the company to identify and fix problems before launching full-scale production, during which the impact of errors and problems will expand proportionally to the number of additional locales. It would be risky to attempt to internationalize and localize a product simultaneously in one release cycle, if this has not been done before. Doing so would increase the chances of missing deadlines and result in a product with an excessive number of software bugs. Once the BRD document is complete, it should be subjected to a phase-end review by senior executives and core stakeholders. Unfortunately many companies, especially start-ups, do not perform proper phase-end reviews and/or prioritization reviews, especially in the initial stages of product development. While it is true that this early in the product's life the incompleteness of the information may preclude a fully informed decision, it is also true that this is the ideal time to halt the development of products that do not fit into the overall strategy of the company.

After the first version of the BRD is provided to the stakeholders, product requirements management starts in earnest (see Figure 4), and from that moment forward until the final version of the PRD is approved, product managers will continuously juggle requirements development and requirements management based on all of the feedback, limitations, constraints and many unforeseen issues that will arise throughout the product cycle, and even after the product is released to the marketplace.

The market requirements document (MRD)

If senior management approves the BRD, the product management team prepares a market requirements document (MRD), also called a Use-Case Document (Wiegers 2003) (see Figure 5). A MRD usually further refines the details of the business problem that the product is meant to solve. It may contain details on the feature set of the product, an analysis of the market segment and the competition, functional and non-functional requirements, a first outline of the priorities of all the desired features of the product, and use case scenarios. In GILT projects, the MRD should also contain additional information such as supported platforms (e.g., the operating system and/or browser versions) and the scope of localization required (e.g., which product features need to be made available and localized for each locale).

Like the BRD, the MRD should be subjected to a phase-end review once completed. At this point, the additional information contained within the MRD will allow senior management and the other stakeholders to make a better informed decision about whether or not to pursue the development of the product with a deeper understanding of the impact and consequences of the required features. Usually the group of stakeholders providing input on the MRD is the same as was involved in shaping the BRD. Depending on the product this may be the right time to involve the head of Customer Support as well. In many companies, the customer support manager is not considered a stakeholder during the requirements phase and becomes involved only after all the requirements have been approved. However, when a company is developing products whose customers rely heavily on customer support (such as mobile devices) or when it is developing products for very large companies that manage multilingual customer support centers, the manager of Customer Support may be involved in the market requirements phase.

During the MRD phase, each stakeholder is required to further define and refine his or her feedback, deliverables, time estimates and dependencies based on the new information available. The product manager also needs to complete the review of user requirements and determine which ones can realistically be implemented in the product, taking into consideration pre-existing business rules and feedback from the other stakeholders. The biggest mistake companies make in this phase is failing to fully investigate and spell out all relevant use-case scenarios and therefore approving or rejecting an MRD based on insufficient data. Use-case scenarios allow product managers to discover non-obvious product requirements that need to be met in order to deliver a fully functioning localized product by simulating the locale-specific environment and the tasks a typical user will perform on the localized version of the product. For example if a product feature requires the user to install a browser plug-in, a use-case scenario analysis can reveal whether such a plug-in is available in all the locales in which the localized product will be made available.

In many web and software companies, the BRD and MRD are combined into one document that carries one name or the other. This usually happens if the same person in the product management team writes both the BRD and the MRD and wishes to further reduce the amount of time spent planning and attending meetings. As noted above, while it may make sense to combine the BRD and MRD documents in small projects, this practice should be avoided in larger and more complex projects in order to allow at least two phase-end reviews during the early product development phases. It is important to note that while the product manager may be the author of both the BRD and MRD, he or she does not and cannot work in isolation. Instead the BRD, MRD and, as we will see, the product requirements document (PRD) are the outcome of many formal and informal discussions about the business needs of the customers, about the business solutions that the company can offer, and about what is feasible and what is not. Although the ostensible author may be the product manager, the final document should reflect the input of all relevant stakeholders.

The product requirements document (PRD)

The output of the third phase of the requirements development process is usually and aptly called the product requirements document (PRD) or Software Requirements Specification (SRS) (Wiegers 2003) (see Figure 5). In small, simple localization projects this may be the only product requirements document created. The PRD focuses on the full feature set of the product and adds further details to the business, user and functional requirements outlined in the MRD and BRD. A PRD should contain mock designs of the various screens or parts of the product that contain a graphical user interface (GUI) in order to disambiguate requirements and more precisely illustrate the user interface workflow, options and features. Many software companies have the engineering team build a working prototype during the PRD phase. A prototype helps the team visually investigate the product requirements that need to be refined or modified by simulating the user-facing aspects of the product. Other companies pair up product managers and designers in order to come up with a full set of mock-ups that visually represent all aspects of the GUI and illustrate the ways in which users will interact with the various components of the software or webpage. The correct visualization of information is a key component of software products in general and of localized products in particular. While the user interface will typically be designed to be the same across locales and accommodate the display of text in each of the supported languages, there will be scenarios in which the use of a single, locale-independent interface will not be possible. In these cases, words, graphics and images may need to be abbreviated, re-positioned and/or changed. In some instances, it might make more sense to change the user interface for a specific language. Developers and casual internal testers will not be able to spot inaccuracies, misspellings, truncated words and the like unless they are proficient in the target languages and know what to look for. Both the prototypes and the mock designs are key tools during the localization process and will eventually be added to the localization kit provided to external vendors. By seeing where the text will be used (its context), how it is used, and how the consumer experience flows from one menu, page, window or dialog box to another in the product, localizers and localization quality assurance engineers will have more information to make better localization choices. This information is especially critical when localization and localization quality assurance are outsourced to external subcontractors.

In companies that combine the BRD and MRD in one document, the PRD should contain all the elements found in the BRD and MRD, such as business background and use-case scenarios plus detailed functional product requirements. PRDs for global products contain more details on GILT requirements, including the following detailed specifications:

- How the product's locale will be determined, e.g. during installation, at each OS startup, when the application is launched or when the user changes language settings
- Which characters and character sets will be supported
- Which UI elements will need to be localized
- What modifications should be performed to non-text elements of the user interface (icons, colors, images) to make the product culturally appropriate for each locale

- The extent of localized help and documentation required
- What other product-related documents or materials need to be translated or localized (for training, marketing, sales, customer service, etc.)
- What input method editors will be supported and how will they behave
- What date, time, calendar, number, currency, address, title, and phone number formats will be supported
- How text searching, sorting, line wrapping, and word breaking will be handled in each locale
- What paper sizes will be supported for display and printing
- What fonts, font sizes, and styles will be supported
- Which keyboard shortcuts will be localized (if any) and how for each locale
- How error messages will be handled in each locale
- Which operating systems and browsers will be supported
- What software and hardware will be supported in each locale
- Which filenames, if any, need to be displayed in the target language
- Which files, if any, will be made available across different localized versions of the product
- What upgrade path, if any, will be supported across languages
- Which websites will be linked to the product, and vice versa
- What locale-specific technical support and sales contact information will be made available
- Which sections, if any, of the company's website will be localized to support the locales of the localized products
- Which release notes and Read Me files will be translated
- Which locale-specific end user license agreements will be translated and/or adapted to comply with locale-specific laws
- What file encoding will be supported for imported files in each locale
- Which locale-specific databases and which versions thereof will be supported in each locale
- How international copyright notices and issues will be treated and regulated
- Which locale-specific examples, demos and audio and videos will be used in each locale
- What are the locale-specific requirements for copying and pasting text
- What are the locale-specific requirements regarding audio, video and animation
- What are the locale-specific requirements based on local business rules, laws, culture, conventions, tax and financial practices
- What are the locale-specific import and export requirements for files
- What are the locale-specific screen layout requirements

The above list is not exhaustive, and can vary greatly depending on the scope, feature set and type of localized product.

Once the PRD is complete, the product should go through a third and final phase-end review to account for any new issues that the stakeholders may have uncovered during the PRD phase and which might prevent the company from further developing the product. Since the PRD is the last formal document that product management will write before the requirements documentation is sent to the Project Management team or to someone in the Engineering team, who will then transform it into an action plan for creating the project deliverables, it is paramount that the product manager clearly state all the key parts of the product that will solve the customer's business problem. Any changes made to the product requirements after the approval of the PRD will translate into exponential increases in product re-work, which in turn will lead to delays, higher localization cost and higher probability of introducing software bugs since there will be less time to properly test the product before launch.

Once the PRD (the "spec" in software jargon) is approved, it is officially handed over to Project Management and Engineering. The date on which this handoff occurs should be the official date on which engineering work starts. In reality, this is hardly ever the case and Engineering may start preliminary work on some portions of the product before the MRD and/or PRD are officially approved by senior executives and the other stakeholders either to save time or to answer requirements feasibility questions that arise during the BRD, MRD and PRD phases. However this practice is also the source of bugs and the cause of major re-work in localization projects if the Engineering team goes too far in its development efforts. In some engineering-driven companies, requirements are dictated by what the engineering team has started developing without proper input from all stakeholders. In such scenarios, companies run the risk of developing solutions to business problems that do not exist.

Planning for and developing localized software products is a delicate balancing act between goals that can conflict at times. Product managers are tasked with resolving these conflicts within the confines of the individual products that they manage. However such conflicts exist at a higher level when taking into account all the products of a company, i.e., when managing the company's overall product portfolio from a holistic perspective. A natural tension exists between the various functional teams within a company. When this tension is healthy, when it is properly managed (by product management, portfolio management and company executives) and when it is oriented toward agreed-upon goals, then companies are in the right position to build great products and prosper. However, this situation tends to be the exception rather than the rule. Only very mature companies achieve a healthy and balanced tension among the various stakeholders and functional groups. In the typical scenario, one or more functional groups take over and do not listen to or value the input of the other stakeholders.

Product portfolio management and localization

Portfolio management has been defined as the process of "resource allocation to achieve corporate new product objectives" (Cooper, Edgett and Kleinschmidt 2001: 1). The term "portfolio management" is a borrowing from the financial world where the ROI of an investment bank is directly related to the mix and quality of the portfolio of investments. Similarly, the overall ROI of a software company is a function of the resources allocated to each product, the mix of products that the company offers and the overall product strategy. Effective portfolio management involves finding the right balance between and diversification of human and financial resources, risk, time to market and technologies. While portfolio management is a well-defined job description and function in financial institutions, such is rarely the case in software and web development companies.

One of the biggest challenges for a software product portfolio manager is to plan a balanced and optimized product portfolio that meets market needs and opportunities while being in line with corporate strategies. Making the right product investments presupposes an accurate picture and understanding of product requirements, strategic importance, value and risk. In this sense, product portfolio management and product management are two sides of the same coin. While product management focuses on the details of each component in each individual product, portfolio management takes a broader perspective, focusing on the contribution that each product makes to the fulfillment of the company's goals and priorities.

Because proper portfolio management requires deep knowledge of each product, the portfolio management function should reside within the product team, especially in software or web development companies, given the inherent complexity of their products. It is during product development that requirements, timing, costs and risks information are gathered, analyzed, and ideally, combined with skill to create a product. Since product portfolio management requires the ability to view all products from many different angles, this task, whether explicit or not, usually falls within the responsibilities of the Vice President of Products or a senior member of the product development group.

Localization amplifies the importance of portfolio management

The need for portfolio management is a natural evolution within a company. As a company expands its product line and the number of locales in which it offers its products, one of the biggest challenges it faces is managing the details of each individual product while keeping an eye on the overall line of products being offered by the company and its competitors. This challenge is the primary reason why companies add layers of management as they grow and why junior managers tend to work at the level of project details, whereas senior managers do not involve themselves with project-level details but rather take a wider, holistic perspective. As a company grows and expands, it needs not only individual product managers and line product managers who manage specific products or product lines, but also a product portfolio manager who looks at all the products and manages globally. In small and medium software and web companies, people are so immersed in the details of individual projects and running the business that portfolio management is usually dealt with indirectly. This state of affairs is another reason why many products do not make it to market or, if they do, why they are late, unsustainable from a business perspective or improperly aligned with the goals of the company.

Portfolio management becomes paramount when developing global products. The decision to localize, market and sell a product for a certain locale has to be made at the highest levels of the company because it often entails a company-wide commitment in terms of investment, strategy and long-term plans. Many localization-specific decisions, such as the deployment and use of translation memory software across departments or the selection of a Language Service Provider (LSP), are not product-specific issues. However, to the extent that they impact multiple products in different stages of development, localization-specific issues require a more holistic perspective.

The six drivers of portfolio management

Portfolio management, like product management and localization, is both an art and science. On one hand, portfolio management involves known factors and processes that can be studied and duplicated; on the other hand, it also involves subjective expert judgment. Portfolio management relies on six drivers: strategy, risk, resource allocation, value, phase-end reviews and portfolio reviews. In the remainder of this section, we will examine each of these drivers in turn.

According to Cooper, Edgett and Kleinschmidt, portfolio management is "about strategy: It is one method by which you operationalize your business strategy" (2001:7). The product must fit within the overall strategy of the company; the decision about how much to invest in a project is determined by the extent to which it advances organizational objectives. Some projects are optional (e.g., those that involve "nice-to-have" attributes), whereas other projects are mandatory (those that involve "must-have" attributes). Internationalization projects fall into this latter category, given the fact that internationalization is a necessary precursor to localization. However, the decision about whether or not to proceed with an internationalization project must weigh the benefits of internationalization and subsequent localization of the new product versus the impact of the diversion of required resources from other competing projects. This type of strategic decision is only possible when one looks at the projects from a very high level. In this sense "[p]ortfolio management provides the link between product strategy and product development. This link is sometimes referred to as strategic balancing" (McGrath 2004:299).

Product portfolio management also "revolves around a portfolio manager's ability to assess and effectively manage risk" (Brentani 2004: xii). As discussed earlier, the main source of localization project risk is lack of or incomplete requirements. Therefore effective risk management necessitates the active participation of executives and stakeholders in the requirements development process and the associated phase-end reviews. When managing localized products, several additional strategies can help mitigate and manage risk. One, for example, is to never rely on just one language service provider, but instead to use at least one primary and one back-up vendor for all localization needs and to ensure that both adopt compatible CAT tools, file handling processes and workflow as those used by the development company itself. Another effective way to mitigate risk during the development of localized software is to conduct pseudo-localization and pilot localization projects that allow early identification of issues and missing information before undertaking systematic localization for all locales. This approach is particularly useful if the company has not previously attempted localization. Pilot programs help fine-tune localization processes within the company and refine roles and responsibilities both internally and with localization vendors.

As Cooper, Edgett and Kleinschmidt observe, portfolio management is also "about resource allocation – how [a] business spends its capital and human resources, and which development projects it invests in" (2001: 7). In a study of sixty companies operating internationally, Chryssochoidis found that the "principal causes of delays in international product rollout were associated with the firm's own internal environment" including "insufficient availability of adequate quality company resources for the development and rollout of the specific new product" (2004: 152). Every company must continuously allocate resources, and as projects progress through different phases, ensure that those resources are allocated properly, meaning that they are aligned with the short- and long-term strategic goals of the company. This is never an automatic process and requires continuous refining. For example, a portfolio review may determine that the company needs to hire an in-house Japanese language specialist and/or tester if it is planning to develop and launch Japanese versions of its software products and intends to become the best in its class in Japan. The conclusion that the company needs to hire a Japanese language specialist and/or tester might not be obvious by looking only at one of the many products the company produces.[10]

Cooper, Edgett and Kleinschmidt also note that portfolio management is about value, i.e., "project selection – ensuring that you have a steady stream of big new product winners!" (2001: 7). In the case of localized software this is exemplified by the concept of language or locale tiering. Portfolio managers and senior executives must

---

10. Human resources are finite within a company; when a company decides to outsource some components of its development, testing and some or all of its localization work, it still has to reconcile the spending and management associated with outsourcing. Too often companies make the mistake of taking a hands-off approach to outsourcing and expect to get back high-quality work.

clearly understand the relative value of localized products in different locales. Tier 1 locales are the first locales in which the localized products will made available either because they offer the best ROI, or because they offer the best match with the company's competitive and market positioning objectives. Locale tiers vary per company and product. Portfolio managers need the input of all other product stakeholders to identify the appropriate tier for a given locale, and thus to determine when and how many resources should be allocated to the creation of the various locale-specific versions of each product.

Lastly and very importantly, "portfolio management is a process" (Grinold and Kahn 1995: 364), which is implemented via regular phase-end reviews and two to four in-depth portfolio reviews per year. Process and strategy go hand in hand, so much so that "the portfolio management process is driven by strategy" (Cooper, Edgett and Kleinschmidt 2001: 270). Phase-end reviews are one of the drivers of effective portfolio management and usually occur at the end of a product stage or phase.

There are two approaches to managing phase-end and portfolio reviews. The first approach is to evaluate projects individually at the end of each phase and determine at that moment the appropriateness of the resource allocation and the strategic fit. This is more of a bottom-up approach, in which the projects, their status and the data at hand heavily determine the outcome of the phase-end review. In this approach, the primary purpose of portfolio reviews is to determine whether the individual decisions made at each phase-end review were accurate, and by extension, whether the resulting portfolio is still aligned with the company objectives.

The second approach is more top-down in nature and is implemented during portfolio review meetings, which are typically held 2–4 times a year. During a portfolio review, senior management examines all projects currently underway, projects on hold, as well as new project ideas. Next, management identifies the "must-do" projects, in other words, projects that must be completed due to their strategic importance. In many companies, senior managers are unaware of the importance of formally identifying must-do projects and of communicating that information throughout the company. The failure to do so typically leads to confusion and double guessing among rank-and-file employees. While portfolio managers are not able to share all the details of their conclusions with the rest of the company, it is extremely helpful to communicate a simple explanation of why, for example, human and financial resources are being diverted to a small and seemingly unprofitable project. Similarly, during portfolio reviews, senior management needs to proactively identify "bad" projects, i.e., projects that on the surface might seem to have potential but that in reality are counter to company strategy or that would negatively impact other projects and products.

The hardest part of this aspect of portfolio management is canceling "bad" projects that are already well into the implementation phase and that for some reason were not identified as such earlier in the development process, or projects that are found to be "bad" once additional information becomes available. It takes courage to cancel a "bad" project that is almost complete. For this reason it is important that early-stage portfolio reviews be particularly detailed and accurate. The further a project proceeds through the development process, the more human and financial resources are invested in that project; it is preferable to cancel bad projects sooner than later. It is important that senior management explain not only project approval decisions, but also cancellation decisions. The failure to do so can damage morale, foster conjectures and rumors, and may lead employees to suspect that senior management makes irrational decisions.

Once all projects have been examined individually, the portfolio review must take a broader perspective and balance the projects to make sure that the final portfolio is aligned with the overall strategy. Balancing a product portfolio entails moving projects from the fast track to the normal track or placing them on the slow track; it can also mean putting projects on hold until the next product portfolio review. In extreme cases, projects are cancelled when they no longer fulfill the business needs of the company. For example, an internationalization project might be terminated if the time and cost prove prohibitive compared to localized product revenue forecasts, if changing market conditions (such as the merger of two competitors) make it unlikely that the localized product will be profitable, or if the diversion of resources required to successfully complete the project is jeopardizing other more strategically important initiatives. Finally, senior managers refine the portfolio and make informed and global decisions about which projects to pursue, which to prioritize as well as the human and financial resources that should be allocated to each.

Conclusions

In most companies, localization managers are in-house experts on the various operational aspects of localization such as managing the translation process, linguistic assets (e.g., glossaries and translation memories), linguistic reviews and language service providers. While current and future translation and localization professionals need to be experts in the specifics of what they do and how to do it, they must also understand *why* they are asked to perform the art and science of localization. In other words, localization managers must understand localization from both tactical and strategic perspectives. They need to be aware of how (and perhaps even if) localization fits into the company's overall strategy, and how their work is shaped by the efforts of other functional teams upstream in the development process.

As we have seen in this chapter, localization can only be as effective as the product development processes, and by extension, as the international business strategies on which it is based. In the absence of effective business and product strategies, the localization manager and team risk being held accountable for problems created earlier in the development cycle that are beyond their control (Dunne 2006b: 113). In addition, localization operations and processes are only as valued as the business needs they fulfill – or are perceived to fill – within a company. In this respect, painful localization projects present opportunities in disguise to proactive project managers, who can play an important strategic role in companies that are making initial forays into international markets (see Sikes in this volume). However, one of the primary challenges facing localization managers today is that they are seldom invited to truly important strategy meetings in which they could proactively address upstream issues, an absence probably caused by the fact that they usually do not have a business mindset (DePalma 2006: 24–25, 34–35).

One solution to this state of affairs is for localization managers to become more aware of the overall business drivers of each product within a company. Academia can play an important role by extending translation and localization curricula to include and emphasize the strategic business aspects of these processes, both within organizations that need to localize their products (which has been the topic of this chapter) and within organizations that provide translation and localization services. As DePalma observes, "Localization must transfer from liberal arts to business school" (2006: 25).

Conversely, businesses also need to rethink their approach to localization. In mature companies, localization is not just an afterthought but is a source of strategic competitive advantage, and an integral part of international product development and portfolio management. In mature companies the localization manager is arguably the product manager's most vital resource; likewise, the localization manager can be invaluable to the company's portfolio manager. It is time for companies to take full advantage of the localization manager's expertise throughout the entire product life cycle.

In conclusion, a successful localization manager thinks and works like a portfolio manager: smart allocation of human and financial resources, proper project selection and strategy ultimately will determine the success of his or her localization projects, and by extension, the company's very own success. Over time, these skills position experienced localization project managers to broaden their careers and possibly become international product managers and product portfolio managers themselves one day.

References

Asnes, Adam. 2007. "Getting projects approved." *MultiLingual* 18 (7): 33–34.
Bacon, Glenn C., Beckman, Sara, Mowery, David, and Wilson, Edith. 1994. "Managing product definition in high-technology industries: A pilot study." *California Management Review* 36 (3): 32–56.
Bhattacharya, Shantanu, Krishnan, V., and Mahajan, Vijay. 1998. "Managing new product definition in highly dynamic environments." *Management Science* 44 (11): S50–S64.
Boehm, Barry W. 1976. "Software engineering." *IEEE Transactions on Computers* C-25 (12): 1226–1241.
———. 1981. *Software Engineering Economics*. Englewood Cliffs, NJ: Prentice-Hall.

Brentani, Christine. 2004. *Portfolio Management in Practice*. Oxford: Elsevier Butterworth-Heinemann.

Cooper, Robert G., Edgett, Scott J., and Kleinschmidt, Elko J. 2001. *Portfolio Management for New Products*. 2nd ed. Cambridge, MA: Perseus.

Chryssochoidis, George M. 2004. *Rolling Out New Products across International Markets: Causes of Delay*. New York/Basingstoke, UK: Palgrave Macmillan.

Daly, E. B. 1977. "Management of software engineering." *IEEE Transactions on Software Engineering* SE-3 (3): 229–242.

Davis, Alan M. 1993. *Software Requirements: Objects, Functions and States*. 2nd ed. Englewood Cliffs, NJ: Prentice Hall.

———. 2005. *Just Enough Requirements Management: Where Software Development Meets Marketing*. New York: Dorset House.

Deitsch, Andrew and Czarnecki, David. 2001. *Java Internationalization*. Sebastopol, CA: O'Reilly.

DePalma, Donald A. 2004. *Business without Borders: A Strategic Guide to Global Marketing*. Chelmsford, MA: Globa Vista Press.

———. 2006. "Quantifying the return on localization investment." In *Perspectives on Localization,* Keiran J. Dunne (ed.), 15–36. Amsterdam/Philadelphia: John Benjamins.

DePalma, Donald A. and Beninatto, Renato. 2003. *How to Avoid Getting Lost in Translation: Buying and Managing Language Services for Global and Multicultural Business*. Chelmsford, MA: Common Sense Advisory.

DePalma, Donald A., Beninatto, Renato S., and Sargent, Benjamin B. 2006. *Localization Maturity Model*. Lowell, MA: Common Sense Advisory, Inc.

Dunne, Keiran J. 2006a. "A Copernican revolution." In *Perspectives on Localization*, Keiran J. Dunne (ed.), 1–11. Amsterdam/Philadelphia: John Benjamins.

———. 2006b. "Putting the cart behind the horse: Rethinking localization quality management." In *Perspectives on Localization*, Keiran J. Dunne (ed.), 1–11. Amsterdam/Philadelphia: John Benjamins.

Ebert, Christof. 2009. "Software product management." *CrossTalk: The Journal of Defense Software Engineering* 22 (1): 15–19.

Esselink, Bert. 2000. *A Practical Guide to Localization*. Amsterdam/Philadelphia: John Benjamins.

Fagan, M. E. 1976. "Design and code inspections to reduce errors in program development." *IBM Systems Journal* 15 (3): 182–211.

Giammarresi, Salvatore. 2005. *La traduzione assistita da computer. Vantaggi e limiti*. Palermo: Compostampa Editrice.

Grinold, Richard C. and Kahn, Ronald N. 1995. *Active Portfolio Management: Quantitative Theory and Applications*. Chicago, Cambridge: Probus.

Heerkens, Gary. 2002. *Project Management*. New York: McGraw-Hill.

Highsmith, Jim. 2004. *Agile Project Management: Creating Innovative Products*. Boston: Addison-Wesley.

Hodock, Calvin L. 2007. *Why (Smart Companies) Do Dumb Things: Lessons Learned From Innovation Blunders: Avoiding Eight Common Mistakes in New Product Development:*. Amherst, NY: Prometheus.

Iansiti, Marco. 1995. "Shooting the rapids: Managing product development in turbulent environments." *California Management Review* 38 (1): 37–58.

Kano, Nadine. 1995. *Developing International Software for Windows 95 and Windows NT*. Redmond, WA: Microsoft Press.

Kotonya, Gerald and Sommerville, Ian. 1998. *Requirements Engineering: Processes and Techniques*. Chichister, West Sussex: John Wiley & Sons.

Leffingwell, Dean, and Widrig, Don. 2003. *Managing Software Requirements: A Use Case Approach*. 2nd ed. Boston, MA: Addison-Wesley.

Lommel, Arle. 2003. *The Localization Industry Primer*. 2nd ed. Fechy, Switzerland: SMP Marketing and The Localization Industry Standards Association.

———. 2007. *The Globalization Industry Primer*. Romainmôtier, Switzerland: The Localization Industry Standards Association.

Luong, Tuok V., Lok, James S. H., Taylor, David J. and Driscoll, Kevin. 1995. *Internationalization: Developing Software for Global Markets*. [New York]: John Wiley & Sons.

McGrath, Michael E. 2004. *Next Generation Product Development: How to Increase Productivity, Cut Costs and Reduce Cycle Times*. New York: McGraw-Hill.

Mironov, Rich. 2008. *The Art of Product Management: Lessons from a Silicon Valley Innovator*. Mountain View, CA: Enthiosys.

Rätzmann, Manfred and De Young, Clinton. 2003. *Software Testing and Internationalization*. Salt Lake City, UT: Lemoine International.

Savourel, Yves. 2001. *XML Internationalization and Localization*. Indianapolis, IN: SAMS.

Smith-Ferrier, Guy. 2007. *.NET Internationalization. The Developer's Guide to Building Global Windows and Web Applications*. Upper Saddle River, NJ: Addison-Wesley.

Stephenson, W. E. 1976. "An analysis of the resources used in safeguard system software development." Bell Laboratories, Draft Paper, August.

Symmonds, Nick. 2002. *Internationalization and Localization Using Microsoft .NET*. Berkeley, CA: Apress.

Urien, Emmanuel, Howard, Robert and Perinotti, Tiziana. 1993. *Software Internationalization and Localization: An Introduction*. New York: Van Nostrand Reinhold.

Westland, J. Christopher. 2002. "The cost of errors in software development: Evidence from industry." *Journal of Systems and Software* 62: (1): 1–9.

Wiegers, Karl Eugene. 2003. *Software Requirements: Practical Techniques for Gathering and Managing Requirements Throughout the Product Development Cycle*. 2nd ed. Redmond, WA: Microsoft Press.

Selecting enterprise project management software

More than just a build-or-buy decision?

Alain Chamsi

Most Language Service Providers (LSPs) have implemented some form of project management system. As the LSP grows and diversifies, the system will initially accommodate increased demands, but continued growth will eventually strain the system to its breaking point. At this critical juncture and under tremendous pressure, the LSP must decide whether to modify the existing system, build a new system or consider buying an off-the-shelf solution. A better approach to making such an important decision is to proactively review the project management system periodically, as part of the organization's ongoing evaluation of its processes and procedures. This chapter provides a methodology and specific tools to facilitate this evaluation and improve the LSP's decision-making process.

Introduction

Project management specialist Dr. Harold Kerzner (2004: 2) defines project management as "the planning, scheduling, and controlling of a series of integrated tasks such that the objectives of the project are achieved successfully and in the best interest of the project's stakeholders." We manage many aspects of day-to-day life in such ways, although we typically do so informally (or even unconsciously). For instance, building a garden shed requires the execution of a series of parallel and sequential steps in a desired time span within an estimated budget. Although this list of tasks in time is seldom captured in either hardcopy or electronic form, it will at least be developed in the mind of the handyman, to a lesser or greater extent. A poorly thought-out plan will most certainly lead to cost and time overruns, disappointment and frustration, and may even result in a shed that resembles a dog house.

In the business world, project management is at the center of most business activities. Over the past 50 years or so, project management methodologies have evolved in tandem with organizational models. Traditionally, organizations were divided into departments, or functional units (e.g., marketing, engineering, documentation, translation, etc.). In organizations that still follow this model, functional managers are responsible for the work of their staff and for delivering this work. In this environment, cross-functional projects tend to pose organizational challenges as project managers have no functional authority and depend on the cooperation of functional managers to obtain the necessary resources for project work. At the other extreme, some organizations are highly projectized; in other words, project requirements are paramount and supersede all others, often to the detriment of the development of the various functional units. In these organizations, cross-functional project teams are assembled for the duration of a project under the direction of a project manager. A third model, the matrix organization, offers a compromise between the traditional hierarchical structure of the functional organization and the flatter managerial structure of the projectized organization. In the matrix model, project team members maintain functional responsibilities in addition to project commitments. This ensures a better balance between the immediate needs of a project and the long-term evolution of the functional areas of the organization.

As organizational models have evolved, so has the role of the project manager. In both projectized and matrix organizations, the project manager is responsible for managing a number of varied functions within an overall project. The complexity of such an endeavor is significant. Reflecting its increasingly central role, project management has become a discipline unto itself (Verzuh 2008: 16–17). Many colleges and universities now offer undergraduate and graduate programs, as well as certificates in project management. Certification in project management is also available through a number of bodies (such as the Project Management Institute and the International Association of Project and Program Management), underscoring the critical importance of project management to the well-being of any organization.

Project management in the translation industry

In the translation industry, the viability and growth of Language Service Providers (LSPs), which are highly projectized organizations, depend directly on the successful management of projects. Despite the inherent importance of this function, LSPs typically pay limited attention to the development of project management processes, and spend even less time reviewing and updating these processes to support their growth and the changing nature of their activities. Likewise, keeping the tools that facilitate project management up to date is often an afterthought, rather than an ongoing management activity. Over time, treating project management with benign neglect can impede growth and lead to shrinking profit margins.

To understand why project management often does not receive the attention it deserves, let us examine the early stages in the life cycle of a typical LSP.

Start-up: The birth of an LSP

During the start-up or birth phase, LSPs are small and initially serve a limited number of clients. They tend to develop expertise in targeted verticals – focused industry segments such as banking, insurance or health care – often in specific language pair combinations. They have very low overhead costs and limited cash resources, and they control their margins by containing costs. The processes of LSPs in the start-up phase are developed to meet the requirements of a limited set of clients and their project management systems are shaped by the need to provide these clients with seamless and predictable service.[1] Such LSPs' project management systems can be described as:

- *Simple:* there are few customer processes to juggle and the volume of work is limited.
- *Low-tech:* because workload manageability is generally not an issue during the start-up phase, the project management system is often paper-driven (sticky notes are also a key feature); more technically-minded LSPs will use some sort of computer-based tracking, such as an Excel spreadsheet.
- *Flexible:* because the system is so simple, it can be easily modified to address exceptions, such as a different source file format. For example, modifying the system may merely entail the use of a sticky note of a different color or the addition of an extra column to a spreadsheet.

Adolescence: LSP growth poses challenges to ad hoc project management processes

As LSPs enter adolescence – the growth phase – they acquire new customers, diversify by moving into new vertical markets and add new language pair combinations. This expansion brings all the challenges that come with delivering services to a broader customer base, specifically having to meet an exponentially growing number of customer requirements, needs and expectations. As the LSP grows and expands, so does its overhead, including office space, communications and connectivity requirements, as well as the cost of the human resources needed to manage this growth. Higher overhead and personnel costs translate into increasing pressure on the LSP's profit margins.

As the LSP moves from the start-up phase to the growth phase, its project management system must evolve to meet expanding customer requirements, including quality assurance processes, billing requirements and a host of other customer-specific items. The project management system must also be able to meet the expanding needs of the LSP itself. Indeed, growth and expansion require the LSP to manage a greater number of suppliers and an ever-increasing number of files being sent back and forth through email, via FTP sites or through other electronic or paper media.

---

1. For the purposes of this chapter, a project management system is understood to encompass the various processes, tools and stakeholder requirements on which the software itself is based.

As they enter and progress through the growth phase, some LSPs recognize the need to replace their original project management system – if in fact there is a formal system – with a more sophisticated one. This may result in the move from paper to electronic workload management. In some cases, technically-minded LSPs will invest in IT resources or external consultants to develop a system that meets their immediate and foreseeable requirements. But this approach is the exception rather than the rule. In most cases, the original project management system simply continues to grow in an unplanned, ad hoc fashion to meet the evolving needs of the LSP. Such a system tends to exhibit the following characteristics:

- It is probably still based in large part on the system used by the LSP during the start-up phase. New pieces of paper and expanded information may have been added, the color-coding may have changed and become formalized or a few more columns and macros may have been included in the Excel spreadsheet, but the original system remains at its core.
- It is no longer simple; on the contrary, the system is now probably quite complex due to its unmanaged growth, and newly hired project managers may require extensive training to be able to use it effectively.
- It is no longer flexible and its adaptability has been compromised. Performing project work on behalf of a new customer who requires a vastly different process (and thus, by extension, major changes to one or more of the system's key components) would be very difficult.

Regardless of whether this ad hoc project management system is based on the LSP's original system or on a more recently developed version thereof, continued growth will lead to a number of issues. Experts in the use of the system will be worth their weight in gold and training new project managers will be a very expensive and time-consuming endeavor. LSP viability will be compromised if there are too few such experts in the organization. (The degree of reliance on such experts is measured by the so-called "Mack truck test" – can the organization survive if one of its project management experts gets hit by a Mack truck?) Most importantly, the efficiency of work processes will be compromised as the limitations of the project management system constrain these processes.

Feeling the pain of immaturity[2]

At some point or another, every LSP will need to re-evaluate the adequacy of its project management system to determine whether the system needs to be upgraded or replaced. Ideally, this evaluation should take place as part of a regular management review of the company's tools and processes. At the very least, an organization should

---

2. For a critical in-depth discussion of the company life cycle and the overall health of the enterprise, see de Geus (2002).

undertake a comprehensive review of its project management system whenever a major change takes place in the scope of its operations, whether the change is driven by significant growth, the provision of new services or the expansion of the organization's client base outside its niche markets, to name a few. More likely, this activity is driven by pain, which can take a number of forms:

- *Perceived excessive workload:* available resources are not used efficiently and their output is thus less than optimal.
- *Customer issues:* complaints about quality, missed deadlines or misplaced work orders all fuel customer dissatisfaction and can affect customer retention.
- *Invoicing woes:* late invoicing can compromise the company's cash flow and its financial health.
- *Reduced margins:* over time, if increased overhead resources (i.e., resources that do not generate revenue directly) are required to manage a given workload, profitability will suffer.

When an LSP applies band-aids to its project management system until the pain becomes unbearable, it ultimately faces the unenviable task of making an expensive decision under duress: the worse the pain, the more acute the need for immediate action.

The problem inherent in this pain-driven reaction is that it tends to limit the range of options that are considered. Time and cost, as the two key drivers of decision-making, will be determining factors: there is limited time to investigate possible solutions and the cost of this investigation in terms of time spent not directly generating revenue, more often than not, leads to a hasty decision that almost guarantees another cycle of pain down the road, as well as more lost time and higher costs in the long run (see Figure 1).

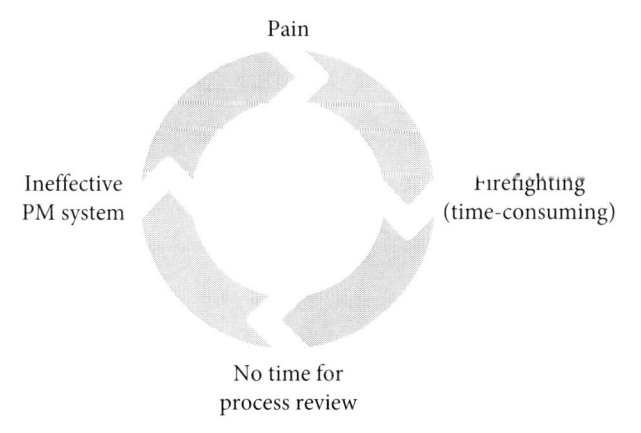

Pain

Ineffective PM system

Firefighting (time-consuming)

No time for process review

Figure 1. The cycle of pain: the greater the duress under which decisions about project management processes and systems are made, the more likely it is that the chosen solution will fail to meet the organization's needs.

As mentioned above, a better approach to decision-making is to develop an ongoing management review cycle of key organizational tools and processes. This ensures that problems in current practices are flagged sooner rather than later, and that adequate needs analysis can be performed and solutions developed without the pressure of time constraints.

Laying the groundwork for a decision

When the project management system no longer meets the needs of the organization, decision-makers typically have three options: modify the existing system, build a new system or buy an off-the-shelf system. In an ideal world, there would be plenty of time to examine all of the options in depth, create a list of all the requirements and attributes of the desired system, prepare detailed cost analysis and return on investment (ROI) studies, and possibly even test some available solutions before deciding which system best meets the organization's needs. And, regardless of the various issues that may hinder this process, *that is exactly what should be done*. But even if this best-practice approach is taken, there are still a number of pitfalls that the organization must strive to avoid.

Human factors

However the organization ultimately decides to proceed, it will have to overcome the most challenging of human traits: resistance to change. Indeed, the organization's existing project management system is rooted in processes developed by its users, and those users have become accustomed to and comfortable with the way it works. Despite constant complaints about its limitations and the need for numerous workarounds to meet the needs of customers, users are familiar with the existing system, and the importance of this familiarity cannot be underestimated. The idea of making fundamental changes to the ways in which people do their job is bound to cause serious misgivings and raise stress levels. Whether consciously or subconsciously, those who are most directly impacted by the planned change, namely the organization's project managers, will erect barriers to the change and, in some cases, may even attempt to sabotage the evolution of the system.

It is necessary to recognize and address this aspect of organizational psychology. There are compelling business reasons to do so, beyond the efficiencies and cost reductions promised by a new system. One reason involves the organization's external language subcontractors. Over time, friendly bonds are forged between project managers and the collaborators to whom they award project work. These subcontractors have probably bailed out the project managers and the company on occasion, when they were in tight spots. In addition, because these contractors are known quantities, the project managers are much more comfortable calling upon them than on lesser-known and/or unproven resources from the company's roster. The need for predictability is very important, but this type of familiarity-based resource selection process may limit or even deny access to potentially higher-quality contributors.

Implementation of a new automated project management system alone is not a panacea for human factor-related issues. Employees and contractors will continue to operate the new system and unless the opportunities for improvement offered by the new system are identified by management, openly discussed and embraced by all users, old habits will simply be incorporated in the new methods and processes and the organization will have missed an opportunity to improve processes and/or resolve problems.

The Systems Development Life Cycle

Designing or updating a project management system is a multi-phase process known as the Systems Development Life Cycle (SDLC). A detailed discussion of the various SDLC methodologies is beyond the scope of this chapter, but most commonly used methodologies include the following steps (see Figure 2):

- *Analysis:* during this phase, the system requirements are identified, as are the shortcomings of the system currently in use.
- *Design:* the actual functional requirements of the system are addressed, including the various tools and processes that are part of its implementation.
- *Development:* it is at this stage that the required software components are evaluated and acquired.
- *Implementation:* this is the rollout phase of the project, from the installation of the software components to the training of the user group.
- *Evaluation:* this phase is often overlooked, despite its critical importance. Once a system is operational, it is essential to continuously evaluate it against benchmarks identified during the analysis and design phases. This evaluation process will ensure that any issues which arise are addressed quickly and appropriately.

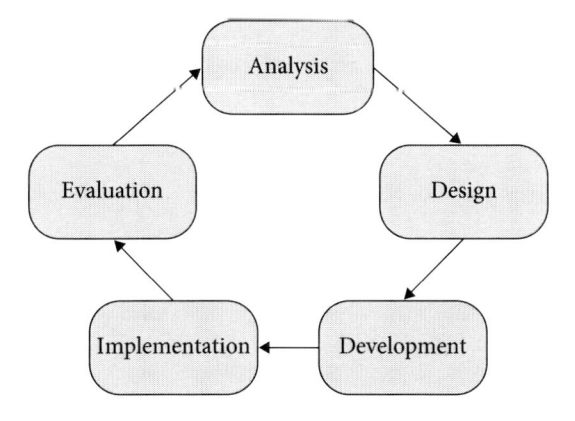

Figure 2. The Systems Development Life Cycle.

As illustrated in Figure 2, collectively these steps comprise an *iterative* process: after deployment of a new or updated system, evaluation begins anew to ensure that the project management system continues to meet the needs of the organization as it evolves.

The first phase of the SDLC, analysis, is arguably the most important. During the analysis phase, the organization empirically defines the requirements of its project management system, without taking into account the features of available systems or, for that matter, those implemented in the current system. It is critical, at this point, that the organization abstract its processes and focus on the actual *needs* that the system must fulfill and not on the system's *functionality*. This is easier said than done, as the line between the two is often blurred. Furthermore, the ability to abstract processes from existing policies and procedures and distill them into their basic elements is not within everyone's ability. Abstraction is especially difficult for practitioners, who are thoroughly immersed in the day-to-day activities of the system. It is also important to remember that the implementation of the current system is based on the evolution of the organization's needs; consequently, the workarounds and quick fixes that have been put into place over time have most likely become an integral part of this system.

A number of methods have been developed to facilitate requirements definition and analysis. For LSPs, a methodology based on the development of use cases is recommended.[3] Each use case describes a specific scenario that corresponds to an activity performed by the LSP. In this way, the various services offered by the LSP and the associated tasks can be broken down into their basic components. The sum total of all the defined use cases represents all of the activities performed within the LSP; the requirements of the project management system can be readily derived from this collection. Throughout the life cycle of the system, new use cases can be created to capture new services being offered or new tasks being performed. This will invariably lead to an evolving requirements list which will in turn drive the continuous improvement of the system and its processes.

In order to analyze the requirements as thoroughly as possible, it is necessary to involve the actual practitioners, i.e., the current project managers. It is these experts who best understand the project management requirements of the organization and the shortcomings of the existing system. Consequently, their input is invaluable. However, as mentioned above, because they have invested themselves the most in the current system, it is possible that they will be the ones who will feel the most threatened by the perception of loss of control and loss of status if the system is changed or discarded: the more peculiarities the existing system has, the more indispensable they will feel. But from a business perspective, concentrating so much mission-critical knowledge in so few people is simply too risky. Because expert users of the system

---

[3]. "A use case in software engineering and systems engineering is a description of a system's behavior as it responds to a request that originates from outside of that system. In other words, a use case describes 'who' can do 'what' with the system in question" (Wikipedia 2010).

may be hesitant to share their knowledge under these circumstances, management will need to reassure them and gain their cooperation in order to move beyond this issue and to the core of the exercise.

The resulting list of requirements should reflect both the current needs of the organization and short- and medium-term needs that are anticipated to arise as a result of planned strategic growth. Such future needs might include diversification into new geographic markets, broadening of the customer base into new vertical segments or into new language combinations, or expansion through acquisition or hiring. This forward-looking exercise greatly reduces the risk of short-sighted decision-making and improves the odds that any system chosen will be adequate for a number of years.

The requirements analysis will not be complete unless the organization spends time defining the reporting tools and techniques that will allow it to accurately measure success and which will provide the performance data necessary to pinpoint the organization's challenges and shortcomings. Such performance metrics allow the organization to engage in continuous improvement of its processes with the goal of enhancing efficiency – and its bottom line.

Cost analysis

Cost analysis is another key component of the analysis phase. The goal of this activity is to calculate the total cost of ownership (TCO) and payback period of each of the options being considered. TCO and payback period data provide benchmarks for comparing different alternatives, such as developing a new system or improving an existing one, and help avoid apples-to-oranges comparisons. The opportunity cost of the various options, namely the cost in terms of lost benefits when one option is chosen over others, also warrants attention, especially when the organization is trying to determine whether to buy an off-the-shelf product or build a proprietary system.

Performance measurement expert Dean Spitzer (2007: 240) defines total cost of ownership (TCO) as follows:

> [TCO] ... is the total cost of a purchase through the entire period of ownership. It takes into account the enormous number of hidden costs in purchasing decisions.... Most post-purchase costs are not anticipated, and therefore they are not *managed*. This often results in huge unanticipated costs – often three to ten times the initial purchase price! For example, a computer can cost $1,000, but the Total Cost of Ownership though its lifetime (including software, upgrades, maintenance, service and replacement) can be as high as $10,000. Obviously, the key trade-off in purchasing decisions is "total price" and "total performance."

In the case of a project management system, the following costs should be taken into account when calculating TCO:

- Software license purchase costs
- Server hardware and software costs
- Hardware and software deployment costs
- Hardware and software warranties and maintenance costs
- Testing costs
- User training costs
- IT personnel costs
- Backup and recovery process costs
- Costs associated with failure or outage
- Cost to upgrade (scalability)
- Other costs, such as infrastructure costs (i.e., floor space, electricity, etc.), may also need to be taken into account if they are relevant to the scenarios being evaluated.

The purpose of the cost analysis exercise is to allow an organization to look beyond the price tag of the solutions being evaluated, and instead, to accurately gauge the *true* cost of deploying each option, thus allowing apples-to-apples and oranges-to-oranges comparisons.

Another useful financial metric is the payback period, defined as "the number of years required to recover a project's cost from operating cash flows" (Brigham and Houston 2007: 373). In the case of a project management system, the payback period is the amount of time required for the TCO of each option being evaluated to be offset by the cost savings – including avoided costs – that it enables. Note that the payback period of a pricier solution may be shorter than that of a less expensive solution if it enables greater cost savings (or cost avoidance). In such cases, the pricier solution may be a better investment, a fact that will not be apparent if TCO is the sole evaluation criterion.

Another useful metric to consider is the opportunity cost of each solution. This measure assigns a value to the opportunities forgone as a consequence of a specific decision. For example, given the reality of finite corporate budgets, the decision to invest in the upgrade of the project management system will preclude a number of other possible expenditures, such as the purchase of new computers, the addition of staff or a number of other opportunities, each of which has a specific value. Therefore, the opportunity cost of upgrading the project management system reflects the value of the investment that would otherwise have been made.

Once the organization has decided to deploy a new or updated project management system, the measure of opportunity cost is only useful for determining whether to buy an off-the-shelf solution or build (or upgrade) a proprietary solution. Choosing to build a proprietary system means assigning internal and/or external IT resources to the task. In this case, calculating the opportunity cost requires that the organization ask the following question: what could these highly-skilled and specialized resources be doing for the organization that they will not be able to do henceforth if they are entirely focused on developing, deploying and maintaining this system? More often than not, the answer to this question leads away from the development of a proprietary solution.

Other considerations

We discussed earlier the need to consider ongoing maintenance costs in the total cost equation when evaluating various alternatives. In the case of most off-the-shelf products, upgrades to the purchased system are covered under an annual maintenance contract whereby the vendor provides ongoing support as well as new releases of the system in exchange for an agreed payment. It is very important to clearly understand what is covered and, especially, what is not covered by the provisions of such maintenance contracts. Some vendors exclude new modules or specific options, but these exclusions may not necessarily be clear from the actual maintenance contract. It is also advisable to inquire about the frequency of past releases and the schedule and content of planned future releases. This information should be assessed as part of the overall evaluation of a vendor's product.

When weighing the option of building a proprietary product, it is also critical to plan ongoing support and development activities. However, such planning is seldom done. One of the advantages of building a custom system is that it will more accurately match the needs of the organization. But if the company is unable to devote adequate support and development staff to solve ongoing problems and implement new functions as required, then the system will quickly become a white elephant.

Identifying the generic requirements of a project management system

Beyond the specific needs of a given organization and the requirements of its customers, there are a number of basic characteristics that any translation project management system should possess. Some of these characteristics should be present in any information system while others are specific to project management and/or translation management systems. In addition, some are non-negotiable, while others are useful functions whose absence may or may not be deal-breakers.

Table stakes

Any translation project management system, whether purchased off the shelf or built specifically to handle the needs of an organization, should have the following characteristics:

- *Simplicity:* it is important that the system not require a lot of training to use and that many (if not most) of its functions be fairly intuitive to end-users.
- *Adaptability/flexibility:* because of the varied nature of customers' needs, it is essential that the system be easily adaptable and flexible enough to handle a variety of work processes in parallel.

- *Scalability:* the system needs to be able to grow with the organization; any system that cannot scale will become obsolete sooner rather than later.
- *Ease and security of access:* because the various contributors in the translation supply chain are scattered across the globe, users must be able to easily access the system from a variety of locations, and must be able to do so securely, as the security of the company's private data and of the customers' files is at stake.
- *Automation of repetitive tasks:* a project management system must free up project managers from repetitive tasks to allow them to focus on the value-added aspects of their work. The system should also reduce the amount of time that project managers spend on each task, thus allowing them to handle a greater volume of work. In this way, automation becomes a productivity multiplier, providing economies of scale and thus better positioning the LSP for growth.
- *Reduction in file management and file transfer overhead*: the system must implement a file management process that eliminates the need for the project manager to manually transfer files from one contributor to the next in the translation supply chain, thus reducing the file handling overhead (through email or via FTP sites, depending on the size of the files) and ensuring that the correct files are available in a timely fashion to those who need them.
- *Reduction of risks of mistakes:* whether in transferring files or in improperly capturing customer requirements, management of a translation project request presents a number of risks of mistakes, and any system that enhances project management by offering pre-defined processes and data and reducing the amount of manual data entry will greatly minimize the risks of error. For instance, a system that provides automatic entry of source file word counts based on the analysis of the files against a translation memory would prevent potential mistakes in the manual entry of this data.
- *Access to relevant data for decision-making:* one of the most critical requirements of a project management system is that it provide its users with easy access to the information needed to successfully manage projects; this includes such essential information as the availability and abilities of suppliers, client-specific information and instructions, and so forth.

Key functions

Along with the characteristics identified above, a translation project management system should implement a number of other key functions. Although these functions are not directly related to the management of projects *per se*, they are nonetheless critical components that round out the project management system into a true enterprise application. These functions include:

- *Report generation:* project management systems are rich with data and this data is a business' most important competitive advantage *if* it is leveraged on

an ongoing basis; to that end, the production of easy-to-tailor reports is a key function of any system.
- *Graphical dashboard*: a dashboard is a customizable reporting screen that displays key business performance indicators in real time in graphical format. Designed to be easy to read (much like the dashboard of a car), this screen provides an overall view of the health of the business at a glance and the ability to drill down to access more specific data as required. In other words, the dashboard automatically pushes high-level data that enables users to gauge the general health of projects and of the organization as a whole. In addition, the dashboard also allows users to manually pull data from the system to gain a more detailed view of specific items.
- *Invoicing module*: an invoicing module allows centralized generation and submission of invoices to customers and from suppliers, which greatly facilitates accounts payable and accounts receivable tracking and administration.
- *Web-based portal:* the provision of a secure web-based portal as a single point of entry for all contributors in the translation supply chain provides a simple solution to the need for easy and secure access described above.
- *Customizable workflows:* the ability to pre-define a variety of workflows (defined as the sequence of tasks required to complete a customer request) for different customers or for different types of projects greatly reduces project preparation time and minimizes the number of repetitive tasks that need to be performed. This increase in efficiency in turn has a direct impact on the company's bottom line.
- *Searchable archives:* the ability to perform full-text searches on archived projects to retrieve data relevant to current projects, using various data filters, enables users to locate specific information more quickly and thus to use their time more efficiently.

Critical interfaces

Whether it is deployed as desktop or web-based software, a translation project management system is designed first and foremost to enable effective translation project management. However, project management systems that provide interfaces to other systems, thereby enabling users to interact indirectly with those systems, offer greater value. These interfaces either provide useful and highly relevant information to the project management system or allow easier downstream data processing. Three interfaces are particularly critical (see Figure 3):

- *Document repository / file management system:* simplified and centralized access to the materials to be translated, without any intervention by the project manager or any other contributor in the translation supply chain, provides a significant reduction in the number of opportunities for error. Indeed, it becomes almost impossible to attach the wrong document to a customer request or to forward an incorrect version of a document as the data of different requests are segregated from each other and version control for each document is handled directly by the system. This automation decreases the amount of time devoted to file administration during the project start-up phase and over the entire course of the project.

– *Computer-assisted translation (CAT) tools:* the interface to CAT tools, when implemented, allows a project manager to incorporate all the relevant CAT tools (such as translation memory and terminology management tools) in the various defined workflows, and can also enable the automation of some of the repetitive aspects of related tasks. For instance, analysis and pre-translation functions can be performed on a set of source files before routing them to a project manager, which facilitates the subsequent project set-up.

– *Accounting software:* even if invoices can be generated and submitted directly from within the project management system, it is still necessary to transfer all of the corresponding financial data to the company's accounting software. If an interface to that software is not available, this data transfer is likely to be a tedious manual process.

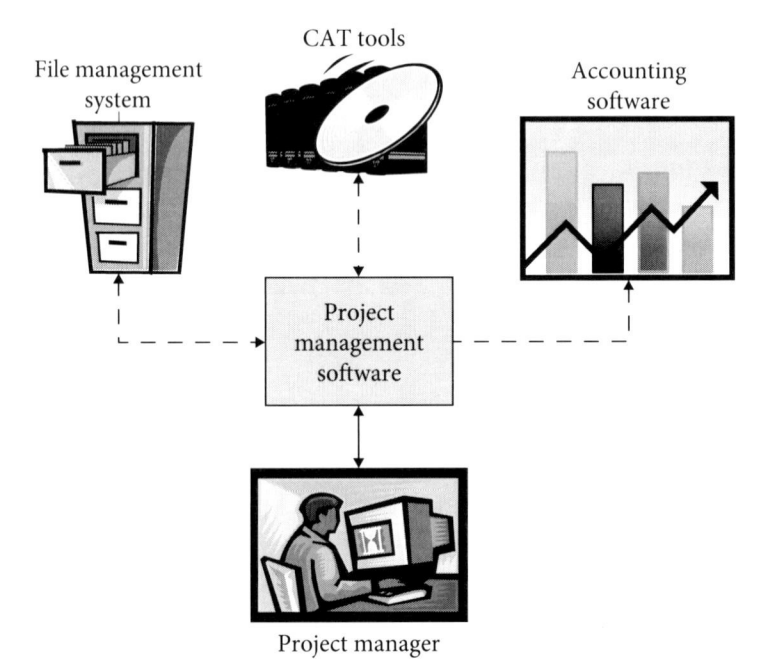

Figure 3. The project manager is the hub of activities in a Language Service Provider.

Making a decision

After requirements analysis and cost analysis have been completed, and key functions and critical interfaces identified, a clear understanding of the requirements of the organization, both financial and functional, will have emerged. This understanding provides a firm foundation on which to make an informed decision as to which project management system is most appropriate.

Starting from the list of requirements

The list of an organization's requirements is, essentially, its shopping list. Once the organization's requirements have been identified, the range of purchase or development options being considered should be narrowed to those that fit within the financial framework identified by the TCO and payback period analyses. The next step is to determine how – or to what extent – the various options meet those requirements. It is critical at this stage not to waver from the chosen baseline, especially when evaluating commercial systems, as vendors may try to deflect attention from their product's shortcomings and/or non-compliance with the list of requirements by touting bells and whistles implemented in their system that, most likely, will add very little value to the LSP's bottom line. Consider, as an example, a trip to the car dealership to purchase a new vehicle armed with your list of must-have features. If your list includes side air bags and you are presented with a vehicle that does not have them, it should not matter that the vehicle has cruise control, heated seated seats and fog lights – all of which are nice features but are only marginally interesting in your eyes – and you should quickly move on to the next vehicle or dealership.

In some cases, promises are made about functionality being available in future releases. (This may also occur during the development of a proprietary system.) To avoid disappointment and protracted battles, commitments to provide functionality at some future date should be included in any signed agreement or contract, and the fulfillment of these commitments should be tied to financial penalties or incentives. More importantly, it is necessary to fully understand the short-term impact that the absence of desired functionality may have on the business. Keeping key stakeholders involved at this stage of the selection process ensures that such issues are clearly addressed and well understood.

Understanding the *true* time to deployment

Various factors influence the amount of time needed for a new project management system to be fully operational in an organization. Note that this milestone is met when the system is being used to *fully manage* the tasks and activities of the LSP, and *not* when the vendor or developer successfully installs the system. Ideally, an appropriate planning cycle will determine the amount of time needed to deploy the new system correctly, and will ensure that the organization can afford to invest this amount of time. Deployment can be staged in phases as a prove-in or test period for the system. For instance, an initial phase may only include a limited number of customers and project management resources. Too often, insufficient attention is paid to post-purchase activities that impact deployment, which inevitably leads to a poor implementation of the system and diminishes the value of the investment.

The following factors determine the *true* time of deployment of a system; it is thus imperative that they be correctly understood and managed:

- *Readiness of the system:* if a system requires customization to be deemed functional or if a later release is required before deployment, such post-installation customization or updates need to be factored into the decision-making process as they will further delay the availability of the system, possibly beyond the preferred or required availability date. The readiness of the system is a larger variable when an organization develops a project management system in house than when it purchases a commercial off-the-shelf system.
- *Configuration of the system:* most systems are fully customizable by the user. It is important to recognize that it will be necessary to invest some time to properly configure the newly-deployed system to meet the needs and requirements of the specific organization and its users. In any event, the system should support standard data transfer methods, enabling users to import existing information from the current system(s) to the new one without the need to resort to workarounds or to create specialized, dedicated utilities. For example, the system might enable users to import customer and supplier data through the use of Comma-Separated Values text files or Microsoft Excel files. Support for standard data transfer methods minimizes the effort required to import critical data and accelerates the availability of the system. Although any project management system under consideration should support standard data transfer methods, such support cannot be taken for granted and must instead be verified. The lack of such functionality may remove the system from further consideration if it requires the manual transfer of enormous quantities of existing data.
- *User training:* as discussed above, simplicity should be one of the key attributes of any project management system. A system that is intuitive and user-friendly will reduce the amount of time required to train its users. However, appropriate training time should be allocated regardless of how intuitive and user-friendly the system may be, and such training should not be assumed to be an insignificant activity as the new system may offer many new functions that the project managers will need to learn how to use.
- *Acceptance testing:* acceptance testing takes place after the system has been installed, and is used by the LSP to confirm that the system does indeed meet the requirements and functions specified during the analysis and design phases of the

SDLC. During those phases, a test plan should be developed for use in evaluating the various purchase or development options being considered. The test plan will comprise use cases that encompass many of the system's basic functions as well as some of the organization's more critical unique needs. The test plan can be further augmented and used upon deployment of the system to accept the system as meeting the agreed-upon functionality within the previously defined parameters. The scope of acceptance testing should be clearly defined in any negotiated contract. Likewise, final payment for the system should be tied to formal acceptance.

Overcoming resistance

The new project management system cannot be said to be successfully deployed until all stakeholders have adopted it as a normal part of the project management process. Although engaging the key users of the system throughout the decision-making process is an effective strategy for fostering buy-in, as discussed above, some users will likely remain resistant to this change. To further accelerate adoption, it is essential to provide adequate and targeted training to all the contributors in the translation supply chain. This training should clearly demonstrate the value of the new system and underlying processes to each stakeholder. It would be a mistake to not pay significant attention to this activity. If users are not convinced that the new system will benefit them, they will only use it grudgingly, undermining much of the good work performed in the planning and decision-making stages.

Conclusion

Regardless of the focus of the decision being made, i.e., whether to build or buy a project management system, or deciding which off-the-shelf system to choose, it is necessary to recognize the three steps involved in the process, namely: (1) the preparation prior to making a decision; (2) the actual decision-making; (3) the implementation of the chosen system in the organization. Too often, much time is spent on the second step but very little time is spent on the other two steps. An excessive focus on decision-making at the expense of preparation and implementation can have negative repercussions on both the ability of the system to meet the business' requirements and its adoption by the various stakeholders.

It is important to note that the methodology discussed throughout this chapter should be followed not merely when selecting enterprise project management software, but when selecting *any* software or information system within an LSP. The fact that LSPs tend to employ ad hoc processes when selecting enterprise project management software has larger implications for the industry as a whole. Unmanaged processes are the hallmark of organizations that are *lowest on the capability maturity scale.*[4] The evolution from start-up to mature organization requires a shift from unmanaged, ad hoc processes to formally defined and managed processes with the ultimate goal of optimizing the ability of those processes to fulfill the LSP's business objectives. It is in an LSP's best interest to attain higher levels of capability maturity, recognizing that this evolution will take time and that the incremental progression from one maturity level to the next is essential to the maturing of the LSP. Likewise, it is in the translation industry's best interest to see as many LSPs as possible attain higher levels of capability maturity. An industry comprised of more mature organizations would be better positioned to meet the evolving needs of customers and partners.

References

Brigham, Eugene F. and Houston, Joel F. 2007. *Fundamentals of Financial Management.* 11th ed. Mason, OH: Thomson South-Western.
Carnegie Mellon University. 2006. *CMMI® for Development, Version 1.2.* Pittsburgh, PA: Carnegie Mellon University. http://www.sei.cmu.edu/downloads/cmmi/CMMI-DEV-v1.2.doc
de Geus, Arie. 2002. *The Living Company: Habits for Survival in a Turbulent Business Environment.* Boston, MA: Harvard Business School Press. (Orig. pub. 1997.)
Kerzner, Harold. 2004. *Advanced Project Management: Best Practices on Implementation.* 2nd ed. Hoboken, NJ: John Wiley & Sons.
Spitzer, Dean R. 2007. *Transforming Performance Measurement: Rethinking the Way We Drive and Measure Organizational Success.* New York: AMACOM.
Verzuh, Eric. 2008. *The Fast Forward MBA in Project Management.* 3rd ed. Hoboken, NJ: John Wiley & Sons.
Wikipedia. 2010. "Use case." http://en.wikipedia.org/wiki/Use_case

---

4. The Software Engineering Institute's Capability Maturity Model describes an evolutionary path for organizational process improvement across five maturity levels: (1) *Initial*: processes are usually ad hoc and chaotic; (2) *Managed*: processes are performed and managed according to documented plans; (3) *Defined*: processes are well characterized and understood, and are described in standards, procedures, tools, and methods; (4) *Quantitatively Managed*: quality and process performance are understood in statistical terms and managed throughout the life of the processes; and (5) *Optimizing*: processes are continually improved based on a quantitative understanding of the common causes of variation inherent in processes (Carnegie Mellon University 2006: 36-38).

PART II

Project management knowledge areas

Applying PMI methodology to translation and localization projects
Project Integration Management

Alexandra Zouncourides-Lull

The Project Management Body of Knowledge (PMBOK® Guide), a comprehensive project management standard published by the Project Management Institute (PMI®), provides a generic project management framework that can be applied to any industry. This chapter focuses on Project Integration Management, one of the nine knowledge areas of the PMBOK® Guide, to provide an overview of the application of PMI project management processes to translation and localization projects. Furthermore, this chapter explains PMI terminology and processes, and provides best-practice guidelines with examples and illustrations. Adhering to project management standards can help translation and localization project managers to build and expand upon their current set of skills and to achieve predictable and repeatable results in their professional practice.

Introduction

In today's society, globalization doesn't just mean outsourcing; it means finding the most appropriate and efficient resources, including human capital, around the world. This state of affairs has created a new type of competition in which individuals who add the most value are scouted and recruited, regardless of their location. Globalization has revolutionized the labor market, and in so doing, has fueled, and continues to fuel, demand for translation and localization, which in turn is driving increased demand for translation and localization project managers. However, the globalization of Human Resource procurement also has serious implications for the practice of project management. As a consequence of the globalization of the labor force, project teams are increasingly multilingual, multicultural and virtual, and project management skills are becoming essential. Thus, as demand for translation and localization project managers continues to expand, so does the set of skills that translation and localization project managers need to survive, and ideally, thrive.

Unfortunately, many people are never properly trained to be good project or program managers but are expected to perform nonetheless. The problem stems from the absence of dedicated degree programs designed to prepare graduates for a career as a translation or localization project manager. Most translation and localization project managers end up in their position by chance rather than design, and have few options when it comes to education and training. Many project managers in the localization industry tend to come into their position for one of the following reasons: (1) they are technically oriented and the company needs someone with technical skills to manage the international versions of their US software releases, (2) they have strong linguistic skills and are considered capable of learning the technical aspects of the business, or (3) they have strong linguistic skills and also display good organizational skills and are promoted to a lead position. This career progression reflects the view that a good project manager must have both technical and linguistic skills to succeed in the localization industry. However, simply possessing these skills does not guarantee that a person will be a good project manager or be able to manage projects successfully. Project managers must also have basic management skills and knowledge of project management fundamentals, and should know how to use different tools and techniques when managing a localization project. Even if they have undergone localization project management training, project managers may still be unprepared to handle some of the challenges they will encounter during their careers.

Project management industry standards, such as *A Guide to the Project Management Body of Knowledge* (*PMBOK® Guide*) from the Project Management Institute (PMI), provide a general, non-industry-specific framework of tools and techniques for managing projects. Current translation and localization project management training tends to focus on domain knowledge strategies and generally does not incorporate PMI standards. Implementing the PMI methodology can be overwhelming for project managers who have not attained the Project Management Professional (PMP®) certification, and even with the certification – which requires a minimum of 3 years of project management experience in addition to a university degree or five years of experience without a university degree just to qualify to sit for the four-hour exam – how to properly apply the generic theoretical concepts to projects within a specific domain is not always evident. For aspiring and current project managers, these standards are a double-edged sword. On the one hand, because the standards are generic, they can be applied to the management of projects in any domain or application area. On the other hand, precisely because they are generic, implementing these project management principles in translation and localization projects can be a daunting task. This chapter seeks to address this problem by looking at one specific knowledge area of the *PMBOK® Guide*, namely Project Integration Management.

The *PMBOK® Guide* is broken down into nine knowledge areas, each of which focuses on a particular management process. These nine knowledge areas are as follows:

1. Project Integration Management
2. Project Scope Management
3. Project Time Management
4. Project Cost Management
5. Project Quality Management
6. Project Human Resource Management
7. Project Communications Management
8. Project Risk Management
9. Project Procurement Management.

This chapter will concentrate on the first knowledge area, Project Integration Management, as it spans all of the process groups by combining and integrating the methods found in all the knowledge areas and covers the project life cycle from initiating, planning, executing, monitoring and controlling, and finally to closing a project. In this way, the Project Integration Management knowledge area gives us a framework in which to discuss best practices for implementing project management principles in translation and localization projects. Furthermore, this chapter provides a roadmap for new project managers, translation and localization educators, and professionals who wish to take a more rigorous approach to localization and translation project management by applying the PMI methodology.

Processes

The Project Integration Management knowledge area can be further broken down into six processes, which are used to manage a project from initiation to conclusion. These six processes are as follows (PMI 2008: 71):

1. *Develop Project Charter:* The process of developing a document that formally authorizes a project or a phase and documenting initial requirements that satisfy the stakeholder's needs and expectations.
2. *Develop Project Management Plan:* The process of documenting the actions necessary to define, prepare, integrate, and coordinate all subsidiary plans.
3. *Direct and Manage Project Execution:* The process of performing the work defined in the project management plan to achieve the project's objectives.
4. *Monitor and Control Project Work:* The process of tracking, reviewing, and regulating the progress to meet the performance objectives defined in the project management plan.
5. *Perform Integrated Change Control:* The process of reviewing all change requests, approving changes, and managing changes to the deliverables, organizational process assets, project documents, and the project management plan.

6. *Close Project or Phase:* The process of finalizing all activities across all of the Project Management Process Groups to formally complete the project phase, or the project itself.

The remaining sections of this chapter will illustrate how each of the six process groups is put into practice in translation and localization projects.

Process group: Develop Project Charter

All localization projects begin from the client side as a requirement to fill a business need. No project can begin without the explicit support of the senior management team in the client organization, as the funds for the project will come directly out of some department's budget. A senior executive sponsors the Project Charter, which formally authorizes the project. For example, if the Vice President of Engineering sponsors the Project Charter, then the project will be funded from the Engineering department's budget. The Project Charter also identifies the justification for undertaking the project (i.e., to satisfy a market demand or meet a legal requirement) and aligns the project requirements and expectations with business objectives. Unfortunately, it is not universal practice to initiate a project with a Project Charter. It is in the project manager's interest to insist on a charter because this document not only authorizes the project, but also specifies the level of authority the project manager will have for decision-making during the project. In the absence of a Project Charter, corporate employees and managers may not all work towards achieving the project objectives, as they will not have been formally mandated to do so. This, in turn, presents challenges for the project manager when she or he must assign internal resources that report to another manager to work on the localization project. In some cases, the project manager may resort to begging or bartering for favors in order to get work done (i.e., the PM needs someone from the foreign field offices to verify translation quality and will send corporate promotional materials in return, such as t-shirts, hats, mugs, or any non-product item with the company logo on it), instead of being able to freely assign a resource. Once the localization project is ready to be outsourced to a vendor, a contract and Project Scope Statement or Statement of Work can serve as the Project Charter for the Language Service Provider(s).

Process group: Develop Project Management Plan

After the project has been authorized to begin on the client side, the next step is to develop the Project Management Plan so that the project can be outsourced to one of more Language Service Providers. This document describes how the project will be developed, monitored and controlled, delivered and closed. The Project Management Plan contains the following subdocuments, which are described in detail below (PMI 2008: 82):

- Project Scope Statement
- Scope Baseline
- Schedule Baseline
- Cost Baseline
- Quality Management Plan
- Human Resource Plan
- Communications Management Plan
- Risk Management Plan
- Procurement Management Plan

Subdocument: Project Scope Statement
Without comprehensive scope requirements, it is difficult to create an accurate budget, define the proper quality requirements or understand the risks associated with the project. In order to correctly define the scope, the project manager must identify all project stakeholders and ensure that their needs are recorded. For example, if the project manager forgets to consult the Legal department while defining the scope of the localization project, she or he may overlook the translation and/or market-specific adaptation of the end user license agreement (EULA), which could delay the launch of the localized product.

PMI defines a stakeholder as a "person or organization (e.g., customer, sponsor, performing organization, or the public) that is actively involved in the project, or whose interests may be positively or negatively affected by execution or completion of the project. A stakeholder may also exert influence over the project and its deliverables" (PMI 2008: 442). Some individuals may have an interest in the project without necessarily being stakeholders. Such individuals should not be allowed to have any influence on the project. Typical localization project stakeholders include the selected contact persons from Engineering, Documentation, Marketing, Technical Support, Quality Assurance, Sales, Legal, Manufacturing, and of course the client. Reflecting current usage in industry, "client" and "customer" are synonymous for the purpose of our discussion. Moreover, the customer could be internal, such as the corporate field offices, or external, such as the end user or a channel partner. The product manager, who is typically part of either the Engineering or the Marketing Department, is responsible for collecting the requirements from the end users. After collecting all of the requirements from the stakeholders, the project manager documents this information in the form of a Project Scope Statement, which then becomes part of the Project Management Plan.

Subdocuments: Scope and schedule baselines
After documenting the scope requirements, project managers usually begin planning their projects by creating a Microsoft Project file that lists all of the tasks which need to be completed. However, this approach is not only faulty but can also increase the risks to the project by overlooking some of the scope requirements, as Microsoft Project is a tool for scheduling rather than planning. Before filling in rows of tasks, the project manager must first verify that all the project requirements have been recorded.

Once the Project Scope Statement is complete, the project manager organizes the requirements into a Work Breakdown Structure (WBS). The WBS can be represented either as a hierarchical organizational chart of the project tasks (see Figure 1), or as a hierarchical outline with sublevels of details (see Figure 2). Any item not listed in the WBS is excluded from the project scope. The WBS provides the project manager with a high-level overview of the total project. These high-level tasks can be further decomposed to display work packages underneath each item (see Figure 3). This decomposition can be performed by the project manager or can be left to the localization vendor if the project manager has no way of determining that level of detail. Incomplete scope requirements increase the risk of scope creep (i.e., unanticipated and/or uncontrolled changes to the scope), as in the example above in which the project manager forgets to consult the Legal Department and overlooks the translations of the EULA. Scope creep, in turn, increases project risks, such as risks of delays and added costs. For this reason, it is crucial that the project manager create the WBS before scheduling each task, thus verifying the project scope. The WBS provides a scope baseline, which then becomes part of the Project Management Plan.

Once the scope is locked down and approved, the next step would be to arrange the WBS components into an Activity List (see Figure 4), which PMI defines as "a documented tabulation of schedule activities that shows the activity description, activity identifier, and a sufficiently detailed scope of work description so project team members understand what work is to be performed" (2008: 418). The project manager then sequences the activities in the order in which they must be performed to execute the project, and specifies the duration of each activity (in other words, of each task). Activity definition, activity sequencing, and activity duration estimation enable the creation of the project schedule baseline, which then becomes part of the Project Management Plan.

Managing projects using PMI methodology 77

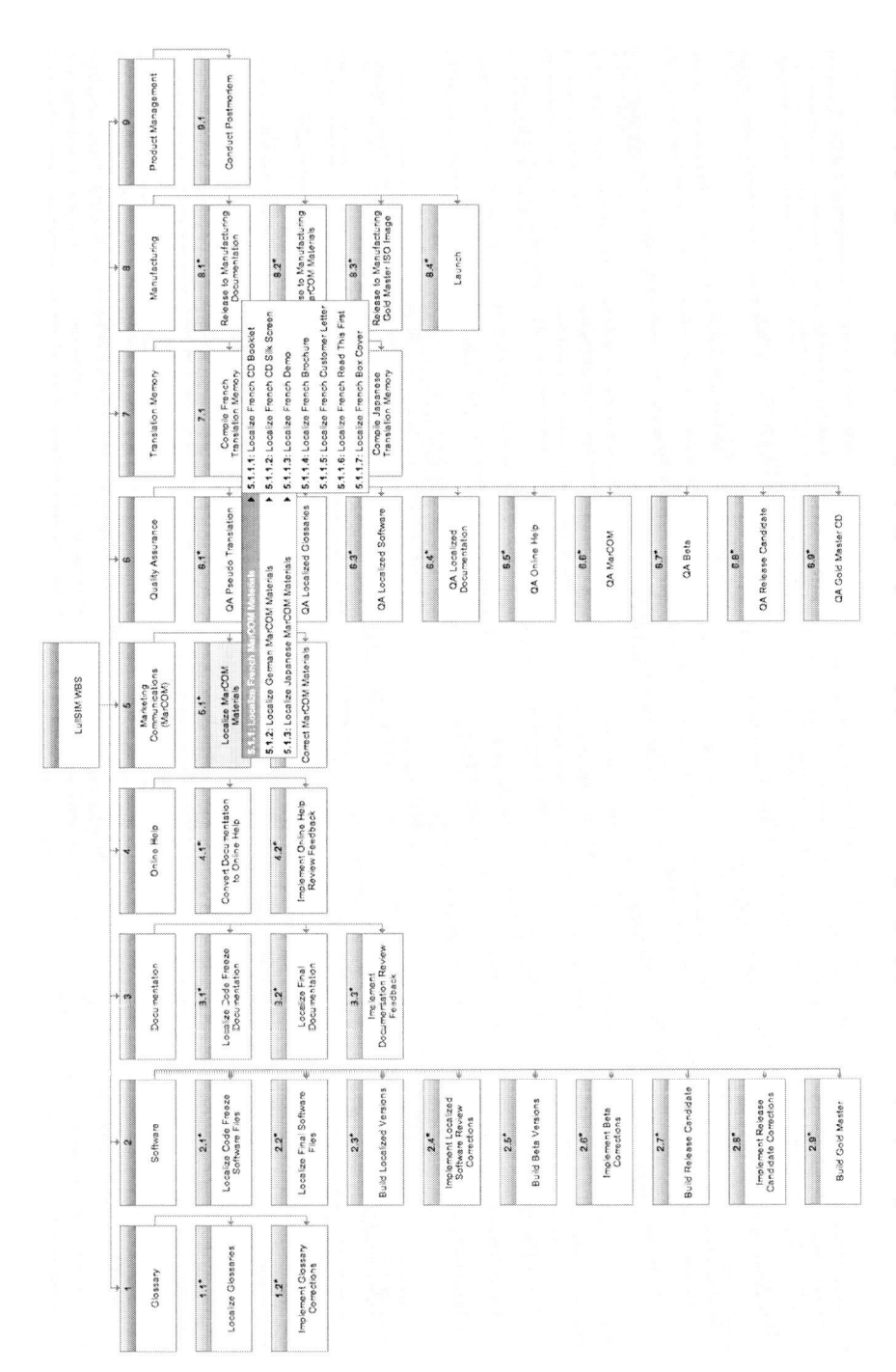

Figure 1. A software localization WBS displayed in organizational chart view from *Project Integration Management Simulation 2010*, www.doublemasters.com. © 2010 Double Masters.

1 **Glossary**
   1.1 Localize Glossaries
      1.1.1 Localize French Glossary
      1.1.2 Localize German Glossary
      1.1.3 Localize Japanese Glossary
   1.2 Implement Glossary Corrections
      1.2.1 Correct French Glossary
      1.2.2 Correct German Glossary
      1.2.3 Correct Japanese Glossary

2 **Software**
   2.1 Localize Code Freeze Software Files
      2.1.1 Localize French Code Freeze Software Files
         2.1.1.1 Localize French Code Freeze Database Files
         2.1.1.2 Localize French Code Freeze UI Files
         2.1.1.3 Localize French Code Freeze Error Messages
      2.1.2 Localize German Code Freeze Software Files
         2.1.2.1 Localize German Code Freeze Database Files
         2.1.2.2 Localize German Code Freeze UI Files
         2.1.2.3 Localize German Code Freeze Error Messages
      2.1.3 Localize Japanese Code Freeze Software Files
         2.1.3.1 Localize Japanese Code Freeze Database Files
         2.1.3.2 Localize Japanese Code Freeze UI Files
         2.1.3.3 Localize Japanese Code Freeze Error Messages
   2.2 Localize Final Software Files
      2.2.1 Localize French Final Software Files
         2.2.1.1 Localize French Final Database Files
         2.2.1.2 Localize French Final UI Files
         2.2.1.3 Localize French Final Error Messages
      2.2.2 Localize German Final Software Files
         2.2.2.1 Localize German Final Database Files
         2.2.2.2 Localize German Final UI Files
         2.2.2.3 Localize German Final Error Messages
      2.2.3 Localize Japanese Final Software Files
         2.2.3.1 Localize Japanese Final Database Files
         2.2.3.2 Localize Japanese Final UI Files
         2.2.3.3 Localize Japanese Final Error Messages
   2.3 Build Localized Versions
      2.3.1 Build French Running Software
      2.3.2 Build German Running Software
      2.3.3 Build Japanese Running Software
   2.4 Implement Localized Software Review Corrections

Figure 2. A portion of the same software localization WBS shown in Figure 1 displayed in hierarchical outline view from *Project Integration Management Simulation 2010*, www.doublemasters.com. © 2010 Double Masters.

Control Account ID: 2.2.1	Control Account: Localize French Final Software Files
WBS ID: 2.2.1.1	Work Package: Localize French Final Database Files

Responsible Organization:
Project Manager, Engineering will hire contractors or outsource this work.

Description:
Localize the English SQL files into French.

File Name:
25 files named Software/Database/EN/ *.sql

File Format:
SQL

Words:
10,000

Schedule Milestone:
Translated files must be reviewed and approved before Engineering will create localized builds.

Deliverable:
French Database files

Output:
Software/Database/FR/*.sql

Technical Requirements:
1. All files must be saved in UTF-8 format.
2. These files must be localized using a computer aided translation tool, which generates a translation memory file. The database translations will then become part of the overall French LullSIM project translation memory database.
3. All final files must be archived in Perforce.

Limits and Exclusions:
1. All translations and translation memory files belong to Lullnet.
2. File names cannot be changed and must be returned in the directory structure shown in Output.

Figure 3. An example of a work package with its associated WBS dictionary from *Project Integration Management Simulation 2010*, www.doublemasters.com. © 2010 Double Masters.

Activity Identifier	WBS ID
Localize French Glossary	1.1.1
Localize German Glossary	1.1.2
Localize Japanese Glossary	1.1.3
Review French Glossary	6.2.1
Review German Glossary	6.2.2
Review Japanese Glossary	6.2.3
Correct French Glossary	1.2.1
Correct German Glossary	1.2.2
Correct Japanese Glossary	1.2.3
Conduct Pseudo Translation	6.1.1
Fix Pseudo Translation Errors	6.1.2
Localize French Code Freeze Software Files	2.1.1
Localize German Code Freeze Software Files	2.1.2
Localize Japanese Code Freeze Software Files	2.1.3
Localize French Final Software Files	2.2.1
Localize German Final Software Files	2.2.2
Localize Japanese Final Software Files	2.2.3
Build French Running Software	2.3.1
Build German Running Software	2.3.2
Build Japanese Running Software	2.3.3
Review French Localized Software	6.3.1.1
Review German Localized Software	6.3.1.2
Review Japanese Localized Software	6.3.1.3
QA French Localized Software	6.3.2.1
QA German Localized Software	6.3.2.2
QA Japanese Localized Software	6.3.2.3
Implement French Software Corrections	2.4.1
Implement German Software Corrections	2.4.2
Implement Japanese Software Corrections	2.4.3
Build French Beta Version	2.5.1
Build German Beta Version	2.5.2
Build Japanese Beta Version	2.5.3
Conduct Functional QA of French Beta	6.7.1
Conduct Functional QA of German Beta	6.7.2
Conduct Functional QA of Japanese Beta	6.7.3
Implement French Beta Corrections	2.6.1
Implement German Beta Corrections	2.6.2
Implement Japanese Beta Corrections	2.6.3
Build French Release Candidate	2.7.1
Build German Release Candidate	2.7.2
Build Japanese Release Candidate	2.7.3

Figure 4. An example of an Activity List from *Project Integration Management Simulation 2010*, www.doublemasters.com. © 2010 Double Masters.

Subdocument: Cost Baseline

Many project managers pad costs when creating their budgets to cushion against possible overruns in the event that one or more tasks costs more than expected. Although this is an accepted practice in the industry, it is an inaccurate way of estimating since it does not truly reflect the cost per task, nor does it make provisions for any risk that could impact the project budget. Risks impact the cost of the project and need to be individually quantified in monetary terms. However, current translation and localization project management practices typically overlook the significance of risk factors and their potential impact on the budget (see Lammers in this volume). This deviation from standard project management practices and failure to account for risk properly represents a significant flaw in current industry approaches to translation and localization project management.

Current approaches to translation and localization project budgeting present similar problems. For most localization project managers, the project budget is equivalent to the cost of performing the tasks and producing the deliverables laid out in the Statement of Work. However, the budget as defined by standard project management practices contains not only the aggregated localization costs but also includes the contingency and management reserves (see Figure 5). Contingency reserves should be included in the project budget as a matter of course. Indeed PMI's *A Guide to the Project Management Body of Knowledge* unequivocally states that "[c]ontingency reserves are part of the funding requirements" (2008: 173). On the other hand, management reserves may not necessarily be part of the funding requirements. Their inclusion (or exclusion) depends on the policies of the company for which the project manager works.

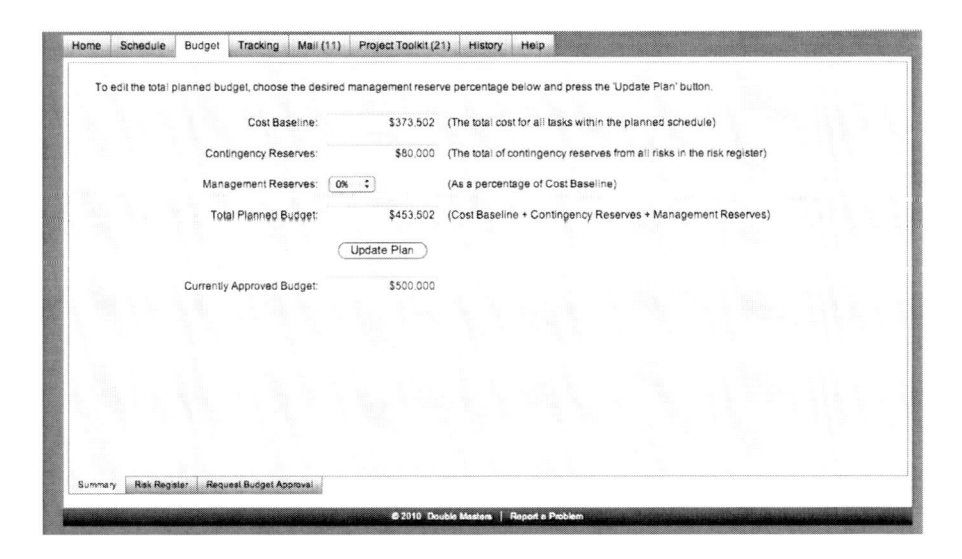

Figure 5. Budget from *Project Integration Management Simulation 2010*, www.doublemasters.com. © 2010 Double Masters.

In order to create the project budget, the project manager should begin by obtaining an accurate estimate of the cost of each work package, preferably from the translator or localizer who will do the task. Another way to calculate the cost of each work package is to employ parametric estimating, which uses a standard rate for each task. Parametric estimating is a standard process used in translation and localization projects. Referring to the sample work package shown in Figure 3, "Localize French Final Database Files," let us suppose that one English word translated into French costs $0.08 per word. If the English source file, meaning the work package "Localize French Final Database Files," has 10,000 words, then the cost to translate that work package into French would be calculated using the following parametric estimation: 10,000 * $0.08 = $800. The aggregated estimate of costs of all the work packages in the WBS defines the cost baseline, which is included in the Project Management Plan. The cost baseline is fundamentally the cost to localize the items listed in the Statement of Work.

Next the project manager should determine the amount of contingency reserves needed for the project. Contingency reserves can be expressed in terms of either time or money, although in translation and localization projects they typically consist of additional funds set aside to be used if and when needed. Contingency reserve funds are calculated during cost and risk management planning by assessing the risks associated with the project and assigning a dollar amount to those risks. The project manager should compile a list of risks associated with the project and enter them into a risk register. The risk register contains information about "identified risks, root causes of risks, lists of potential responses, risk owners, symptoms and warning signs, the relative rating or priority list of project risks, a list of risks requiring response in the near term, a list of risks for additional analysis and response, trends in qualitative analysis results, and a watchlist of low-priority risks" (PMI 2008: 302). After compiling the list of project risks, the project manager assigns a monetary value to each. This value is calculated using quantitative risk analysis, such as sensitivity analysis, expected monetary value analysis, some form of simulation or modeling, or can be based on expert advice. For localization projects, expected monetary value analysis is probably the easiest way to assign a monetary value to a risk. The project manager can estimate the monetary impact of a risk event either by creating a decision tree that plots the probability of occurrence and determines the outcome value, or just by simply multiplying the probability of a risk event by the impact of the event on the project cost.

To illustrate the latter approach, let us suppose that a stakeholder in Engineering tells the project manager that there is a 20% chance that the software source file word count may be higher than estimated but that this cannot be confirmed. Given that information, the project manager would enter the risk event and its corresponding probability into the risk register. The project manager would then determine the impact on the cost of the project if the software source file word count were in fact higher, most likely using parametric estimating. Let us suppose for the purpose of our discussion that the cost would increase by $100,000. In this case, the probability of occurrence (20% or .20) multiplied by the impact of the event ($100,000) is $20,000, so this risk identification and quantification technique requires that $20,000 be budgeted for contingency reserves for this specific risk event. The sum of all monetary risk values within the risk register determines the total amount of money that needs to be budgeted for contingency reserves.

The last step in creating the project budget is to allocate management reserves. Management reserves are funds to be used at the discretion of the manager or sponsor of the project for unforeseen risks. Management reserves usually comprise a percentage of the overall project or a preset amount based on historical data. Depending on company policies, project managers may not be able to include management reserves in the project budget without corporate approval. However, as noted above, contingency reserves should always be included in the project budget. When contingency reserves are used, the project manager should continuously update the budget as the project progresses. Contingency and management reserve funds are not part of the cost baseline, which is used to measure project performance, but are included in the total budget.

Subdocument: Quality Management Plan
The Quality Management Plan for a typical localization project should detail the project-specific standards concerning software (internationalization requirements), documentation and marketing collateral (localization and formatting requirements), quality metrics, and quality checklists. In addition, the Quality Management Plan should define how Quality Assurance (QA) should be executed during the project and how Quality Control (QC) should be used for inspection of those deliverables that did not pass QA and need to be reworked. The Quality Management Plan does not contain the test plans for QC, such as an automated script used to ensure that the localized software strings do not corrupt the software build, but rather the QA requirements that would go into the test plans, like requiring the use of the target-language glossary as the translation baseline for the localized strings. Furthermore, the Quality Management Plan must include the acceptance criteria, in addition to the quality control metrics (i.e. no bugs in the localized software product) to be used during the project and for QC.

Subdocument: Human Resource Plan
According to PMI, "[t]he Human Resource Plan documents project roles and responsibilities, project organization charts, and the staffing management plan, including the timetable for staff acquisition and release" (2008: 216). This document also specifies how the team members will be acquired, developed and managed, as well as the criteria for releasing them from their assigned tasks. Most localization plans do not list criteria whereby a determination can be made that a resource is no longer needed and/or can be made available for another project; it is generally assumed that all the members who worked on the project will be available until the last deliverable has been formally accepted. The absence of release criteria can be problematic for the project manager if

an issue occurs later in the project and the personnel are no longer available (for example, the lead translator is working on another project). By documenting the criteria for releasing the resources, the project manager mitigates some risk and efficiently uses the resources, avoiding future fire drills in the event that it becomes necessary to replace or recover a resource, especially at the end of the project.

Subdocument: Communications Management Plan
Effective communications result from the project manager's commitment to spend a large percentage of his or her time interacting with team members, disseminating project status and performance information to all concerned parties, ensuring that project requirements are met, and keeping everyone up to date on project activities. Identifying the project stakeholders as well as the type(s) of information each of them needs is essential. Communication with various project stakeholders requires the use of many different methods of communication, such as email, teleconferences, face-to-face meetings, written documents, and verbal instructions. In addition to the methods of communication, the project manager must know how many channels of communication exist. "The total number of potential communication channels is [n * (n − 1) / 2], where n represents the number of stakeholders" (PMI 2008: 253). For example, if the project manager identifies stakeholders as one person from each of the six departments within the organization (Engineering, Documentation, Marketing, Sales, Technical Support, Quality Assurance) plus their respective managers or VP, plus three members on the project team, plus one client, there are a total of 16 project stakeholders. In this scenario, the total number of potential channels of communication equals 120: [16 (16 − 1) / 2 = 120 channels]. When a project contains this many channels of communication, sending the same information to each stakeholder as a one-size-fits-all strategy will not work and will only cause confusion. Therefore, the project manager must carefully plan who will receive what kind of communication, how and when. The project manager will provide different levels of detail to different stakeholders depending on their relative position in the organizational hierarchy. As a general rule, the higher the stakeholder is in the organizational chart, the less detail is required. For example, let us suppose that the project manager is providing a status report on the localization project to the Vice President of Engineering. In all likelihood, the VP does not need to see the complete Microsoft Project file and only wants to be informed about the localization milestones and end dates, critical earned value management metrics, trend reports, and any high-level risks posing threats to the project. If the project manager is required to give more details to the project sponsor, visual aids such as the network diagram of the project schedule, one of the views in the Microsoft Project file depicting the flow of scheduled tasks, or the WBS are also useful tools. Team members, on the other hand, will all need to have access to the WBS and know which parts they are responsible for, and they will also need to have access to the project schedule and Project Management Plan. Furthermore, stakeholder interaction must be clarified. For example, will the in-country reviewer interact directly

with the localizer or will the linguistic review feedback be documented so that it can be archived as part of the project? The direction of interaction, frequency, and methods of communication are documented in the Communications Management Plan, which in turn becomes a subdocument in the Project Management Plan.

Subdocument: Risk Management Plan
Most localization project management plans do not contain a Risk Management Plan, as the impact of risks on the budget, schedule, and total project are as a general rule not thoroughly analyzed. Managing risks involves more than just labeling a risk as high, medium or low; it means having the ability to determine the probability that an event will occur in the future and devising a strategy to address that event and the challenges or opportunities it presents. Risks, by their very nature, can make or break a project. Understanding what qualifies as a risk and how to quantify risks takes time and experience.

Unlike the risk register discussed above in the cost baseline, which quantifies the rating or relative priority of each risk, the Risk Management Plan defines how risks will be addressed, the stakeholder risk tolerances, as well as the roles and responsibilities for each risk category. Project managers tend to take a negative view of risks and see them as a threat. However, in practice, some risks are positive and should be exploited to help make the project a success. PMI describes strategies for responding to both negative risks (threats) and positive risks (opportunities). The strategies for responding to negative risks are as follows (PMI 2008: 303–304):

- Avoid (eliminate the risk by reducing scope)
- Transfer (divert management of the risk by getting a guarantee, warranty or buying insurance)
- Mitigate (reduce the probability or impact of the risk by being proactive)
- Accept (accept residual risk that cannot be managed proactively or effectively and assign contingency reserves)

The strategies for positive risks are as follows (PMI 2008: 304–305):

- Exploit (assign a resource to ensure that the opportunity occurs)
- Share (form teams or joint ventures to better take advantage of the opportunity)
- Enhance (add more resources to increase the probability of and/or the positive consequences of the opportunity)
- Accept (a passive strategy: take advantage if the opportunity occurs)

If resources become available earlier than anticipated, the project manager can choose to begin certain tasks earlier than originally scheduled. For example, if only two resources are needed to localize the software and one finishes earlier, the resource that finished early could then begin to work on the documentation. However, future task dependencies in the schedule may be negatively impacted in case of rework, and therefore, the positive aspects of the risk have to be weighed against any potential negative impact. A good tool to use for estimating activity duration is the *program evaluation and review technique* (PERT), which calculates the weighted average or estimates an approximate range of an activity's duration. When evaluating the impact on the schedule for the above example, the project manager estimates the optimistic outcome (O) of accelerating the task, the most likely outcome (L) and also a pessimistic outcome (P) in case accelerating the task would require rework. The PERT formula for determining the expected outcome is (O + 4L + P) / 6. For example, if the project manager has determined that the optimistic duration of the accelerated task would be 20 days, the most likely duration would be 30 days, and the most pessimistic duration, assuming subsequent rework, would be 45 days, the result would be (20 + 4 (30) + 45) / 6 = 31 days duration. Since PERT uses a weighted average formula to determine the expected outcome of the duration, and since there is a wide variation between the optimistic and pessimistic values, the project manager will also need to determine the standard deviation (or sigma, σ) to establish the relative confidence associated with the estimated duration. To determine the standard deviation, the project manager subtracts the optimistic number from the pessimistic number and then divides it by 6. This translates into (45 − 20) / 6 = 4.2 days, or 4 days (σ) if we round to the nearest whole integer, meaning that the task would take 31 days, plus or minus 4 days. The project manager would then update the schedule to reflect a duration of 35 days for the accelerated task. Statistically speaking, one standard deviation (1 σ) represents a 68.3% probability of completion or confidence level in the estimated duration. If the project manager wants a higher degree of confidence in his or her estimates, he or she can calculate the completion times that correspond to two standard deviations (2σ) and three standard deviations (3σ). To calculate 2σ, the project manager would take the mean, in this case 31 days, and add to or subtract from it two times the standard deviation. This translates to 31 days plus or minus 8. For 3σ, the calculation would be 31 days plus or minus 12. The confidence levels in the estimated durations corresponding to 2σ and 3σ are 95.4% and 99.7%, respectively (see Table 1).

Table 1. Confidence levels of estimated durations. For the purpose of this illustration, standard deviations are rounded to the nearest whole integer.

σ	Probability	Standard deviation	Shortest estimated duration	Longest estimated duration
1	68.3%	4 days	27 days	35 days
2	95.4%	8 days	23 days	39 days
3	99.7%	12 days	19 days	43 days

After changing the duration of the task, the project manager would then view the schedule's network diagram and determine what effect this change has on the subsequent activities and the impact on the schedule as a whole before deciding if accelerating the task is feasible. If the desired result is to shorten the project schedule, the project manager could then repeat this exercise and update the schedule to reflect a duration of 27 days, covering the other end of the range of confidence, to see what impact the duration change has on the schedule and project before choosing a course of action. This is an example of the *Exploit* strategy. PERT analysis can be used to estimate not only activity durations, but costs as well.

Subdocument: Procurement Management Plan
The Procurement Management Plan describes how the project resources and materials will be procured and how the contract will be administered, for example, if dealing with multiple sellers (in the language industry, typically, Language Service Providers). Given that most project managers on the client side adhere to their company's general legal policies, a Project Management Plan may or may not include this subdocument, especially if the buyer has been using the same seller for multiple projects. Localization contracts are mostly, if not all, *Time and Material* contracts. This means that the buyer pays for any localization costs incurred during the project in much the same way as a company would temporarily hire a localizer, instead of outsourcing the work to a localization service provider. Other contract types are also viable, such as *Firm Fixed Price* contract, which "involves setting a fixed total price for a defined product or service to be provided" (PMI 2008: 322). Many localization contracts do resemble the *Firm Fixed Price* contract in that the units of labor, material rates, and even penalties for substandard deliveries are included in the terms. However, such contracts are usually not used in the localization industry as localization projects begin before the source files (e.g. US software product) are completed. In localization projects, the scope is almost never frozen before the project begins and can change after the final software source files have been provided for localization. If on the other hand the scope of the project is not subject to change, such as the translation of a published literary article, then a *Firm Fixed Price* should be the preferred type of contract. It is important that the project manager understand the different types of contracts available, as certain business scenarios may warrant the use of other types of contracts besides the *Time and Material* contracts typically used in the industry.

Process group: Direct and Manage Project Execution

Once the Project Management Plan has been developed, a kickoff meeting is held with all stakeholders to discuss roles, schedules, milestones, risks and all project related activities. This meeting marks the official project start. Thereafter, the project manager will spend approximately 50% of the time managing the execution of the project (PMI 2008: 16). To effectively manage all aspects of the project, the project manager will have to focus on the schedule's critical path as the main instrument in controlling the project and its high-level risks. The critical path is the path of activities in the schedule that has the longest duration and zero float (slack). The critical path is so named because it determines the project completion date: even if all of the non-critical path tasks are delivered on time and on budget, if any task on the critical path is delayed, the project duration will be extended, and the project budget will most likely be affected as well. Therefore, instead of micromanaging each line item in the project schedule, the project manager primarily needs to monitor the critical path to ensure success, as the critical path can change depending on the actual completion of a task. Of course, the project manager will keep an eye on the other tasks as well, but there is no need to micromanage each line item in the schedule, or pay extra to expedite tasks with positive float (i.e., tasks that have some slack between them), as they have no impact on the critical path or the project schedule. By managing the critical path, the project manager can control the schedule and budget with confidence. A project manager can even manage the team more effectively by allowing members to take time off during crunch time if their tasks are not on the critical path.

When using Microsoft Project, the critical path can be found in the network diagram, which is one of the view options in the project schedule. The network diagram boxes highlighted in red indicate the critical path. Also, when viewing the project Gantt Chart, the Gantt bars and links in red identify the critical path. As the project progresses, some tasks may be completed earlier than expected while others may take longer than expected. As a result, the critical path may also change. This in turn may cause the priority of a risk to change as well. Consequently the project manager must continually update the schedule, risk register and Project Management Plan to reflect changes. In general, if the project is already late, adding resources will make it run even later due to the risk of rework. In this case, the project manager should use the technique of fast tracking to manage the project. Fast tracking involves starting tasks in parallel instead of waiting for one task to finish before another begins. The default relationship in the project schedule is finish-to-start (FS) which means that a task cannot start until its predecessor has been completed. To fast track one or more tasks, the project manager has to change the relationship from finish-to-start (FS) to start-to-start (SS) in Microsoft Project.

Another technique the project manager can use to bring the schedule back on track is "crashing," whereby the project manager compresses the schedule without exceeding the current budget if the project budget is constrained, or with the least incremental cost if the project budget is not constrained. The project manager can do this by applying more resources to a task or re-allocating them to other tasks. When crashing the schedule in a project whose budget is not constrained, the project manager should focus on accelerating the critical path tasks that add the least amount of cost, which in turn adds the least amount of risk. When crashing the schedule in a project whose budget is constrained, the project manager should first focus on accelerating non-critical tasks so that resources can be shifted responsibly to the critical path. Another way to crash the schedule in a budget-constrained scenario would be to move resources around. For example, if there is an expensive resource on the critical path and a good resource on the non-critical path, the project manager could consider switching them in order to stay within budget. The biggest concern with schedule compression is the risk of rework.

Process Group: Monitor and Control Project Work

Reporting progress
Project management standards require that status reporting be precise so that each task is accounted for with regards to cost and schedule. Current project management practices report status as a percentage of the overall project, for example, 50% complete. But what exactly does completion mean? Should completion be measured at the level of a task or at the level of the entire project? If at the level of the task, how does one measure completion? Activity duration or work effort? And how can one ascertain that a project is 50% complete overall when translation and localization projects typically comprise numerous interdependent tasks? The project manager cannot determine if the project is ahead or behind schedule with regards to the budget with such vague progress reporting.

Earned value management (EVM) offers a solution to this problem. Like many other interesting tools and techniques that were initially conceived for government use, earned value management was adopted by the United States Government in the 1960s as a form of performance reporting for the Department of Defense. By the 1990s, EVM had become the standard progress reporting method for all government programs. PMI subsequently adopted this method of reporting, and it is now considered standard practice in the project management community. It is worth noting, however, that earned value management only measures cost and schedule performance, not quality.

Reporting is based on the duration and cost of each task. Each task reported in the schedule is listed in the performance report along with corresponding start and end dates, as well as cost. The cost and schedule baselines are then compared to the actual performance, which enables the project manager to identify any variances and trends.

For example, let us suppose that we want to measure the performance of the work package called "Localize French Final Database Files" shown in Figure 3. For the purpose of this illustration, we'll say that this task is scheduled to take 20 days at a cost of $8,000. Proportionately, the cost of the task is $400 per day or $2,000 per business week, assuming a five-day work week. This anticipated per-day or per-week cost is known as the planned value (PV). If the task is scheduled to take 20 days and cost $8,000, one would expect that after 5 days, $2,000 of the budgeted cost would have been consumed and that the task would be 25% complete, assuming a constant, or non-variable, daily throughput. If after one week the localization vendor reports that the actual cost (AC) of the first five days of work is only $1,800 and that the task of localizing those files is 20% complete, then the earned value (EV) is then calculated as

20% of the budgeted costs, i.e., (20% * $8,000) or $1,600. Just because the actual cost is less than the planned value does not necessarily mean that this is a positive result. The cost variance (CV), which measures the difference between the earned value and the actual cost (EV – AC), is negative (-$200) in the case of this hypothetical localization task. A negative cost variance indicates that the task is running over budget, i.e., the task will incur a higher cost than planned for the amount of work scheduled. However, cost variance does not provide a total overview of the task. The schedule variance (SV), which measures the difference between the planned progress and the actual progress (EV – PV), is negative (-$400) as well in the case of the sample localization task, indicating that the task is also behind schedule. The aggregated costs of each task can be used to calculate the project's PV, EV, AC, as well as CV and SV, which are then used to render a snapshot of the total project performance. To understand the significance of positive and negative cost and schedule variances, the project manager would use the guide shown in Table 2.

Table 2. Cost and schedule variances and their impact on a task or project.

Numeric value	CV	SV	Explanation
Positive	+		Task or project is under budget
Positive		+	Task or project is ahead of schedule
Negative	–		Task or project is over budget
Negative		–	Task or project is behind schedule
Mixed	–	+	More money than planned was spent to bring the schedule back on track
Mixed	+	–	Enough resources may not have been assigned

To better understand the overall effect of this task on the project budget and schedule, the project manager needs to look at other metrics as well. She or he can use the cost and schedule variances to determine the cost performance index and the schedule performance index, which provide a more granular indication of how well a task or project is doing. The cost performance index (CPI) provides an indication of cost efficiency by comparing the earned value to actual cost using the formula CPI = EV / AC. In the case of our sample task, the CPI shows that only $1,600 / $1,800 = 0.89. In other words, $.89 worth of work planned has been completed for each $1 spent. This means that at this point in time, unless a change is made, the task will have cost overruns. Along similar lines, the schedule performance index (SPI) provides an indication of schedule efficiency by comparing earned value to planned value using the formula SPI = EV / PV. With regard to the sample task, the SPI shows that only $1,600 / $2,000 = 0.80. In other words, $.80 worth of work has been completed for each $1 scheduled. This figure indicates that less work has been completed at this juncture than was planned in the schedule, and unless a change is made, the task will be incomplete on the scheduled completion date. Schedule and cost performance indexes are standard reporting tools and are used most commonly in a project. To understand the significance of the CPI or SPI, the project manager would use the guide shown in Table 3.

Table 3. Schedule and cost performance indexes and their impact on a task or project.

Index	= 1	> 1	< 1
CPI	On target	Under budget	Over budget
SPI	On target	Ahead of schedule	Behind schedule

Just because a task does not cost as much as planned does not indicate that the project is on track for a successful outcome. Using variance analysis, the project manager can determine exactly where problems exist and take corrective action to get the project back on track. With each progress report, the project manager will use the variance analysis to determine if the status of any risk in the risk register has changed, either from low to high or from high to low priority. Based on the progress report and the occurrence of risks, the project manager will adjust the contingency and management reserves accordingly.

Process group: Perform Integrated Change Control

The Perform Integrated Change Control process entails "reviewing all change requests, approving changes, and managing changes to the deliverables, organizational process assets, project documents, and project management plan" (PMI 2008: 432). The project manager should expect that at some point during the project, someone will request that a change be made to the scope. This change request may come in the form of a direct request (e.g. the Sales team would like a Czech version of the product after the project has already started), or may stem from other change requests identified from defects by Quality Assurance or Quality Control, such as pseudo-translation corrective action.[1] For example, if during pseudo-translation an engineer discovers that large sections of the source code contain hard-coded strings, then those particular software files will need to be internationalized before localization can begin. This would constitute a change to the scope of the project, and as such would have to be reviewed for approval. Depending on the size of the company, changes to the scope of a project are reviewed and evaluated either at the business unit level or at the enterprise level. Some companies have a Change Control Board, which is a formal group that evaluates requests and determines which changes to the scope are accepted or rejected. If a Change Control Board or similar group does not exist within

---

1. Pseudo-translation involves the automatic replacement of source-language content by random target-language characters (hence the term "pseudo-translation") to test the localizability of a software application.

the company, then the project manager will need to consider each change request in terms of its potential impact on the project, schedule and cost. If a change request is approved, the schedule baseline will need to be updated. Otherwise, baselines should not be changed but should merely be controlled by managing the variances identified in the performance report.

Managing access to documents, file updates and file versions is another form of integrated change control. Most companies use configuration management systems, meaning source control software, to manage and control access to project files, code and documents. If the company does not have such software for controlling access to documents, the project manager should record access rights in the Project Communications Plan.

Process Group: Close Project or Phase

At the end of the project or phase, the project manager must accept or reject the corresponding deliverable(s). If a deliverable has a defect, the deliverable is then reworked until it is deemed acceptable according to the project quality control criteria. Once the project manager has formally accepted the deliverable, then the seller can invoice for the accepted deliverable and the project manager closes that phase of the project. All files should be archived either upon formal acceptance or completion of the project. As part of the project closure, the project manager should prepare a lessons learned document listing all of the issues encountered and recommendations for future projects. It is also advisable that she or he reward team members for working on the project, even if they are not direct reports. Managing people is an important skill that all project managers must learn. Without human resources, the most precious component of any project, the project manager will never be successful.

Conclusion

Just as there are standards for internationalization (i.e. World Wide Web Consortium (W3C), Unicode) and localization (i.e., TMX, TBX, GMX, XLIFF) that span many industries, there are also standards for project management. The *PMBOK® Guide* from the Project Management Institute provides a framework and guidelines for managing projects, using various tools and techniques. Project managers in the localization industry should embrace and employ these standards as a matter of course, as should the organizations that employ them. Technical and linguistic skills should not be the only criteria considered for promoting someone to the role of project manager; basic management skills and an understanding of project management processes and of the project life cycle are also important. Using project management tools such as the WBS and critical path can help the project manager to better control projects. By locking down the project scope, the WBS makes it easier for the project manager to control scope creep. In similar fashion, the critical path helps the project manager prioritize and focus on the activities that directly impact the overall project timeline and costs. The project network diagram and critical path are also useful tools for managing team members and controlling scope. When asked if a task can be squeezed into the schedule, the project manager will be armed with precise information and thus will be able to make an informed decision instead of working the dates to try to accommodate a request or crashing the project unnecessarily. Also, the project manager will be able to share resources when needed if those resources are working on tasks that are not on the critical path. Using these basic tools can help the project manager create good team relationships and show a solid understanding of all the project's components.

By adhering to standard methodologies, the project manager will no longer depend on padding to create the budget and will know each task's exact cost, along with the associated contingency and management reserves. The project manager will manage risks according to their impact on the budget and schedule, and will monitor project performance more precisely using earned value management. Ideally, the localization vendors or localization contractors will report their weekly status using earned value metrics, ensuring consistency and accuracy in progress reporting. And finally, just as the project has a formal beginning, so must it have a formal ending. All projects must be officially closed when the deliverables are accepted and the sellers must be paid. Documenting lessons learned is standard procedure and should be delivered after the project has been completed. Using the PMI methodology may not only help the project manager ensure success on a project by drawing on different tools and techniques, it may also help protect and promote the project manager's career by expanding and adding value to his or her current skill set.

References

Double Masters LLC. *Project Integration Management Simulation 2010*, www.doublemasters.com
Project Management Institute (PMI®). 2008. *A Guide to the Project Management Body of Knowledge (PMBOK® Guide)*. 4th ed. Newton Square, PA: Project Management Institute, Inc.

Requirements collection
The foundation of scope definition and scope management in localization projects

Natalia Levitina, PMP

Managing project scope is essential to ensure that the project includes all the work required, and only the work required, in order to meet the project objectives. Requirements collection and scope definition are the foundations of scope management. Requirements specify the project's product or service and shape the project scope, which in turn defines what must be done to fulfill the requirements and complete the project according to the specification. This chapter discusses scope management in localization projects. Drawing on the Project Management Institute's *A Guide to the Project Management Body of Knowledge (PMBOK® Guide)*, the chapter examines the five processes that comprise scope management: requirements collection, scope definition, work breakdown structure creation, scope verification and scope control. It then discusses the application of these processes in localization projects, focusing primarily on requirements collection.

Introduction

In an old tale a man comes to a hat tailor with a piece of fur and asks the tailor to make him a custom hat. Before he leaves, the man wonders whether the fur is big enough to make two hats and so he asks the tailor, "Can you make two hats out of this piece?" "Sure," the tailor answers. The man hesitates: "How about three?" "No problem," the tailor answers. "Five?" exclaims the man in disbelief. "Absolutely," replies the tailor. And on it goes until finally the man settles on eight hats and returns home quite content with the deal. One week later, the man returns to the tailor's shop to pick up his order and is surprised to receive eight tiny hats, each one big enough for a mouse. One might say that the moral of the story is "don't be greedy." However, this tale also illustrates an important lesson in project management: one must define the project requirements, and by extension, the project scope as clearly and completely as possible to obtain the desired results.

In the realm of project management, requirements are defined first and foremost as "quantified and documented needs and expectations of the [project] sponsor, customer, and other stakeholders" (PMI 2008: 105). Requirements specify what the project's product or service should be; what it should do (i.e., what problems it should solve); approximately how long the project should take and approximately how much it should cost; and how its relative success will be evaluated. Requirements shape the project scope, which defines what must be done to fulfill the project requirements and complete the project according to the specification.

Requirements collection and scope definition are cornerstones of project management. As the tale above illustrates, a clear understanding of precisely what needs to be produced is essential to avoid project failure. In addition, the project manager needs to quantify the amount of work that must be done to be able to determine how long the project will take and how much it will cost. Ensuring that the project includes all the work required for successful project completion and only the work required is the goal of project scope management.

According to the Project Management Institute's *A Guide to the Project Management Body of Knowledge (PMBOK® Guide)*, scope management comprises five processes (2008: 103):

1. *Collect Requirements* – The process of defining and documenting stakeholders' needs to meet the project objectives.
2. *Define Scope* – The process of developing a detailed description of the project and product.
3. *Create WBS* [Work Breakdown Structure] – The process of subdividing project deliverables and project work into smaller, more manageable components.
4. *Verify Scope* – The process of formalizing acceptance of the completed project deliverables.
5. *Control Scope* – The process of monitoring the status of the project and product scope and managing changes to the scope baseline.

This chapter discusses the application of scope management as described in the *PMBOK® Guide* to localization projects in order to demonstrate how the processes of requirements collection and scope definition can be standardized. Depending on the organizational structure and capabilities of the company requiring localization service (the client), scope management may be performed by a project manager in the product management or localization department of the development organization, or by a project manager in the language service provider (LSP) to which the project work is being subcontracted. This chapter examines scope management primarily from the perspective of the client, rather than that of the service provider and focuses on a generic software localization project that includes localization of the software user interface, as well as translation of the accompanying documentation, training materials and marketing materials. Finally, in recognition of the fundamental role that requirements play in shaping the project scope, the focus will be primarily on requirements collection within the larger context of scope management.

Scope management process: Collect requirements

Requirements collection is the first step of the scope management process. As its name suggests, the goal of this step is to define and document the project requirements. In a localization project, the requirements collection process focuses on gathering an initial set of high-level requirements, such as the target languages and locales and the identification of final deliverables (such as software, documentation and marketing materials). These high-level requirements are progressively elaborated and further refined in subsequent steps of the scope management process, i.e., scope definition and WBS creation. High-level requirements are collected from the business case and the project stakeholders.

A business case describes the justification for undertaking the project and identifies the needs that the project will meet. A business case may take the form of a structured written document or a verbal agreement or request. The goal of localizing a product or content for other markets is typically to increase revenue in particular countries; the business case for doing so is generally based on favorable return on investment (ROI) analysis. For example, a business case may include sales forecasts and ROI projections showing that revenues generated by localized product sales will exceed the cost of localizing that product and supporting the localized version(s). Alternatively, a company may decide to localize a product at a loss if representation in a given country is a strategic objective.

Stakeholders are defined as people, groups, and organizations that can affect or be affected by the project's objectives and/or outcome, such as the project sponsor, the development team, the customer and the project manager, among others. Stakeholders are not confined to the person or team sponsoring the project. In other words, the person who signs the check is an important stakeholder, but not the only one. Identifying the main stakeholders and ensuring that they review and approve all of the requirements and deliverables are essential steps in project scope management. If some stakeholders do not have an opportunity to review and approve the requirements, deliverables and/or the project plan, there is a great risk that the project deliverables will not be accepted and the project as a whole will fail. Stakeholder requirements typically include only high-level information and represent identified needs and, ideally, expectations (i.e., unidentified needs) for a given project.

In industries that focus on product development, such as software and manufacturing, it is important to understand the difference between project requirements and product requirements. Project requirements focus on conditions that a project must satisfy to be deemed successful, such as business, timeline and delivery objectives. Product requirements, on the other hand, describe capabilities that the product must possess or conditions that it must meet, such as technical, performance or security criteria, for the project to be deemed successful. Because localization does not involve development but rather the adaptation of products, many localized product requirements are identical to those of the source materials on which the localized versions are based.

Many organizations streamline project management by formalizing common project requirements, such as the use of a Content Management System (CMS), as organizational requirements and by developing checklists to capture them during requirements collection. Creating a set of organizational requirements that never or nearly never changes helps a company focus on the unique requirements of each project and improves the effectiveness of planning. It is interesting to note that the same requirements may be classified as project requirements by some organizations and as organizational requirements by others. (This classification may even vary across departments in the same organization). For example, some organizations determine the target languages and locales during requirements collection on a project-by-project basis. Other organizations, especially those that perform localization into multiple languages as a matter of course, define target languages and locales as organizational requirements: the company translates all materials into a given set of languages or uses a matrix to specify which components are translated into which languages.

The output of the requirements collection process is requirements documentation, which can range from a simple checklist to one or more descriptive documents. All subsequent cost, schedule and quality planning is based upon the requirements documentation. High-level localization project requirements can be divided into five main categories: (a) target start and/or completion date; (b) project components; (c) file formats; (d) target languages and locales; and (e) volume per component per language/locale combination.[1] Localization requirements documentation typically also specifies internationalization requirements, delivery requirements, quality requirements, terminological requirements, as well as business and organizational requirements. In the sections that follow, we will examine each of these categories of requirements in turn.

Target start and completion dates

During the project planning phase, the project manager must collect information that will help him or her determine when the project can be ready to start and when it must be completed. Localization projects typically start when the source content is released to manufacturing, unless simultaneous shipment of the source version and one or more target versions is required.

Many software companies have a simship (simultaneous shipment) policy, which means that localized versions of software products are released to the market at the same time as the source version (typically, English). A simship policy may apply only

---

1. Certain high-level requirements such as file formats and volume typically undergo further refinement during scope definition and WBS creation. However, we will examine them in detail in this section since they are core localization requirements.

to software or to both software and accompanying documentation. In localization projects, a finish-to-start dependency typically exists between the English software Release to Manufacturing (RTM) schedule and the localization project schedule. This means that localization cannot begin until the development of the source materials is complete. Even when the source deliverables are completed later than scheduled, the localization project may still have to be completed by the RTM date for all the target languages. In such cases, additional resources and/or funds may be required to complete the project in the shorter time frame, depending on the severity of the delay.

In simship scenarios, project managers may have to work backwards from the required end date, e.g., the planned shipment date, to calculate a project start date. Simship projects often require schedule compression, which can be achieved by fast-tracking project tasks (i.e., by scheduling tasks that were originally supposed to be performed sequentially to be performed in parallel instead), by assigning additional human resources to shorten the duration of one or more project tasks, a technique known as "crashing" (PMI 2008: 156) (e.g., assigning three translators to the translation of a 30,000-word Help system enables the project manager to reduce the duration of translation by up to two-thirds), or by adopting a streaming model of file delivery, whereby a constant flow of localizable content is provided to vendors. This latter approach is discussed in greater detail in the Delivery requirements section below.

Identification of project components[2]

A typical localization project undertaken by a software development company may include all of the following components or any combination thereof:

- Software
- Documentation and/or online Help
- Training materials (training guides, presentations, multimedia)
- Marketing materials (website, collateral materials, multimedia)
- Technical Support Knowledge Base

Each component presents different requirements, due to the various file formats involved, activities that must be performed, tools that must be used, processes that must be followed and volumes of translation and other work that must be accomplished to create the localized versions of each. For example, training materials and help systems

---

[2]. "Project components" are understood here as a high-level description of the project deliverables. Generally speaking, scope definition in "projects that have a product as a deliverable" involves "translating high-level product descriptions [requirements] into tangible deliverables" (PMI 2008: 114). However, scope definition in localization is determined first and foremost by the *tangible characteristics of the existing products that need to be localized* (i.e., components, file formats, word counts, internationalization, etc.).

typically contain far more translatable content than software components. Likewise, the tasks required to create localized versions may vary from component to component: the creation of a localized software component may require building and testing in addition to translation, whereas the creation of a documentation component may require desktop publishing (DTP).[3] Because different components present different requirements, the scope of each is usually defined independently.

File formats

As part of the scope definition process, the project manager must determine in which file format(s) the content has been authored and/or will be submitted for localization, as well as the format(s) in which the final deliverables must be provided. The specific workflow steps of a given localization project strongly depend on the file formats in which the project receivables have been authored. For example, HTML files are documents; as such, they can be considered to be finalized once translation, editing, proofreading and client review (if applicable) have been completed. In contrast, files authored in DITA (an XML-based format) are not documents; the generation of documents from DITA files requires the use of a publishing engine to produce an output whose structure and content are defined by a map and whose format is defined by a style sheet.[4] In other words, DITA localization involves translation and editing of DITA content, as well as publishing, testing and proofreading of the output of the publishing engine for each identified target output (PDF, Web Help, etc.). The translation of files authored in page layout and design programs such as Adobe FrameMaker, InDesign and Illustrator requires DTP and DTP quality assurance stages.

Aside from specific workflow steps, each file format may require its own file preparation process, which in turn impacts the project cost and timeline. For example, translation memory tools do not directly support FrameMaker or InDesign files, so one must save or export such files in a format supported by the tool, e.g., *.MIF (Maker Interchange Format) in the case of FrameMaker files and *.IDML (InDesign Markup Language) in the case of InDesign files.

---

3. Desktop publishing (DTP) is the process of laying out text and graphics to create a page, graphic, publication, book, or magazine. Localization DTP differs from the standard authoring-related DTP process in that it does not involve the creation of a new layout design, but rather the replication of the look and feel of the source layouts using target content (with a few exceptions; for example, Asian files must use Asian fonts).

4. The Darwin Information Typing Architecture (DITA) was originally developed as an internal documentation architecture by IBM, which donated it to the standards consortium OASIS (Organization for the Advancement of Structured Information Standards) in March 2004. Version 1.0 of the DITA specification was approved as an OASIS standard in April 2005. For an overview of DITA, see Day, Priestly and Schell (2005).

Target languages and locales

Once the project components have been identified, both the target languages and the locales of the various localized versions must be specified (e.g., French-France vs. French-Canada). It is important to specify the locale in addition to the language for both linguistic and technical reasons. For example, Portuguese spoken in Brazil (Brazilian Portuguese) differs from Portuguese spoken in Portugal (Iberian Portuguese), as does Spanish spoken in Mexico compared to Spanish spoken in Spain. Users in each country are typically sensitive to such differences and the product acceptability may be compromised if the same linguistic version is launched in multiple countries. With respect to technical issues, the failure to account for locale during software development can result in broken functionality when moving from one locale to another.

The specification of components that require localization may vary depending on language/locale. As mentioned earlier, some companies choose to translate all the materials for all software products into a standard set of languages, whereas others identify target languages and locales on a project-by-project basis. In some cases, depending on the results of market research and/or ROI analysis, the company may decide not to deploy a certain product to a specific region or it may decide to only translate marketing materials and to leave the product software interface in English. The translation of some components, such as Technical Support Knowledge Bases (KB), may prove prohibitively time consuming and costly due to the sheer volume of content. Rather than leave KB content untranslated, some companies offer machine translation of KB content.[5] The use of machine translation is discussed in greater detail below. In any event, the project manager needs to know which components require localization for each language/locale combination.

Volume per component per language/locale combination

The project manager needs to estimate the volume of work required to localize each component in order to be able to estimate the total work effort – and thus the duration and cost – of the project. On one hand, the project manager may need this information for budget projections. For example, she or he may want to plan the following year's budget prior to the start of the fiscal year and may estimate the amount by multiplying

---

5. For example, as of late 2007, between 3% and 30% of Microsoft's support Knowledge Base (KB) was professionally translated, depending on the language pair. Since it is economically unfeasible to translate the entire Knowledge Base, Microsoft offers users the option of reading raw (unedited) machine translation of articles where no human translated version is available. In late 2007, the rates at which users reported that machine translated articles answered their questions (15.77%–25.03%) compared favorably with those of human-translated articles (18.97%–30.84%) (Kaplan 2007).

the preliminary volume of each product by number of localized versions thereof. On the other hand, the project manager also needs to gather scope information, and by extension duration and cost information, simply to determine whether a given project is feasible given budget and scheduling constraints. Finally, it is important to itemize the volume of translation work per component because not all components will necessarily be localized for a given target market, as noted above, and because language service providers and freelancers often charge different translation rates for different types of components (e.g., software user interface content, document content, etc.).

Initial word count calculations performed during requirements collection are often preliminary or tentative, since in many cases project planning is performed while the development of the source-language product is still underway. Different techniques and metrics are used to measure the volume of the linguistic and non-linguistic tasks that comprise a localization project.

Measuring the volume of linguistic tasks

The word is the most commonly used unit for calculating the volume of translation, editing and proofreading work in the localization industry.[6] Hourly metrics are typically used to calculate the volume of other linguistic work such as terminology extraction or linguistic review.

Once the list of components and corresponding target languages/locales has been created, each component must be analyzed to determine the number of translatable words it contains. The word counts of the various components are then mapped to the list of target languages/locales per component to determine the total number of words per component per language/locale combination. Determining the precise number of translatable words in a given component is typically a process unto itself in localization projects and is carried out using translation memory (TM) technology, which enables the reuse of previously translated materials in new or updated versions of software or documents. For example, let us suppose that version 1.0 of a product was translated using TM technology, and in the new version, 1.1, only 20% of the text content has changed. When the content of the new files is analyzed using a translation memory produced during the translation of version 1.0 of the product, it is determined that 80% of the new material can be translated by re-using, or leveraging, material from the TM, whereas the remaining 20% of the content is identified as new text for translation. Translation memory tools parse texts and segment them into smaller chunks called translation units (TUs). In practice, texts are most commonly

---

6. The word is the most common unit of scope estimation for translation from English into other languages. Units other than words are used to estimate the scope of translation from certain languages into English. For example, the scope of translation from agglutinative languages such as German and Turkish into English is typically calculated based on the number of lines in a file (e.g., approximately 50 characters per line), whereas the volume of translation from Asian languages into English is typically calculated based on the number of characters.

segmented at the sentence level, although segmentation at the paragraph level is also possible. When new text is analyzed using a TM tool, the text is parsed, segmented, and compared to the contents of one or more existing translation memories. The results of the analysis are categorized as follows:

- *100% matches*: new segments that are identical to TUs which have already been translated. Such segments require no translation and little or no editing. Some translation memory tools also offer a so-called exact or in-context match category. Exact matches indicate text that was previously translated within the same file or document and that is both preceded and followed by the same segments as before. Such segments rarely need to be reviewed and thus typically incur no cost.
- *Fuzzy matches*: TUs that are similar but not identical to previously translated TUs (e.g., "The house is red" vs. "The house is blue"). Fuzzy matches are often broken down into more granular subcategories.
- *New words*: segments for which no similar TU is found in the TM or whose variable match percentage is less than the minimum match value specified in the TM tool settings.

Because the work effort required of the translator is inversely proportional to the matching percentage, LSPs have developed a sliding-scale pricing model for each category of matching, where rates increase as the matching percentage decreases.

Translation memory technology provides no up-front benefit in a particular project if there is no existing translation memory against which to leverage the new content. Nevertheless, the use of translation memory may still enable time and cost reductions if there is a substantial amount of repetition within and/or across project components. Any relevant legacy translation memories should be analyzed to determine which TM (or combination of TMs) will enable the maximum amount of content reuse in the new project. If the existing translation memories were created using a tool other than the one that will be used in the current project, a TM conversion effort may be required. In any event, the project manager must evaluate the availability, content and format of translation memories to account for the impact of translation leveraging on work duration estimates (and by extension, on the project budget and schedule). In the absence of existing translation memories, the project manager should decide whether to use a translation memory tool in order to capture content for re-use in subsequent releases, thus enabling future savings.

It is critical to determine both the total word count as well as the correct word match breakdown in a project in order to correctly define the project scope and plan properly. For example, one might think that the work effort and thus the schedule and budget of a project containing 300,000 words would be completely different from those of a 50,000 word project. But if the first project contains 250,000 words of exact matches (no cost) and 50,000 new words, and the second project contains 50,000 new words, the net translation work effort required in the two projects would be very similar. However, this "leverage effect" may only hold true for translation tasks. For example, if the project requires software testing, such testing may have to be performed on a complete set of files, in which case the work effort, and by extension the schedule and budget, will vary significantly.

Measuring the volume of non-linguistic tasks
Localization project tasks are not confined to translation and linguistic work, but also include engineering, dialog box resizing, testing, screen capturing, desktop publishing and more. Dialog box resizing, for example, is required because translation from English into Western European languages can cause text to expand in length by 30% or more. Translation-related expansion during software localization requires that dialog boxes be resized to accommodate the expansion. In such projects, one must know the number of dialogs to properly estimate the scope of the resizing effort. When translating documentation, one must calculate the number of localizable screenshots and graphics plus the number of pages in the documentation in order to estimate the scope of the screenshot capturing and desktop publishing effort. Multimedia project scoping requires careful examination of all Flash, audio and video components and requirements. For instance, one might choose to localize a complete package of on-screen text, an actual product demo and the corresponding audio track, or just the audio track (and leave the rest in the source language).

Likewise, the project manager must know what types of testing will be carried out and how the tests will be performed to estimate the scope of the corresponding work effort. In many software localization projects, portions of software testing can be automated, especially if the corresponding source product testing has already been automated. In such cases, a computer program performs tests that would otherwise have to be conducted manually. Localization testing includes user interface (UI) testing, during which keystrokes and mouse clicks are recorded and played back to compare obtained and expected results, and functional testing, which assesses the product's compliance with functional requirements. Manual testing is a very time-consuming process, and test automation is an effective way to reduce testing costs and duration. Automated tests for a source-language product should be created with localization in mind so that the tests performed on the source version of the product can be successfully replicated on localized versions and when performed on native operating systems using locale-specific input (such as text written in the Cyrillic alphabet or in Kanji characters, for example).

Testing of Help systems and websites focuses on issues different from those involved in software testing. Testing of Help and website components can be partially automated (for example, checking for broken or missing links). However, many tasks still must be performed manually, such as checking for corrupted characters and verifying proper formatting.

Internationalization requirements

Internationalization, which is often abbreviated as "i18n," is the process of designing software so that it can be localized or adapted to take into account the linguistic, cultural, technical and regulatory requirements of other locales. A software product is said to be "internationalized" if it can correctly display languages written in other scripts (e.g., Cyrillic, Kanji, etc.) and if it correctly supports locale-dependent representation of data (e.g., dates, times, calendars, imperial and metric measurements, etc.) without the need for redesign. Although the theory and practice of internationalization were originally developed by and for software engineers, the concept of internationalization as "localization enablement" is also applicable to developers and authors of other forms of digital content, including web designers and technical communicators. Internationalization of content refers to the process of ensuring that materials to be translated or localized contain no cultural references, images or colors that would be considered inappropriate or offensive to users in other countries.

Knowing whether a product is correctly internationalized is an important part of the scope management process as it can significantly impact the volume of work needed to localize the product and ancillary materials. Software created without localization in mind must be internationalized before it can be localized. The Localization Industry Standards Association states that "[a]s a general rule, it is best to assume that it takes twice as long and costs twice as much to localize a product if it is not properly internationalized to start with. In the case of computer code, the difference can be much greater" (Lommel 2007: 17).

Delivery requirements

Another important requirement that the project manager must define early in the project planning process is the manner in which the source files will be submitted from authors to the project manager, from the project manager to the LSP, and from the LSP back to the project manager. File submission can be performed in three ways: via a one-time handoff, in batches, or on a streaming basis. The approach adopted generally depends on whether localization is being performed after the source development project or in parallel with it.

For example, let us suppose that an English software product development project is underway at a software company, with the English documentation scheduled to be finalized on April 1 and RTM scheduled for May 1. Let us further suppose that as part of the localization of the software product, the documentation needs to be translated into 5 languages and contains 60,000 words. For the sake of simplicity we will assume that the outsourced portion of this project only involves translation, editing and proofreading.

In this scenario, the project manager can wait until April 1 to receive all of the final source files from the authors and then send them all at once to an LSP for translation, i.e., submit the files via a one-time handoff. The disadvantage to this approach is that the LSP would need to hire a large team of translators, editors and proofreaders for each language to produce the target versions of the documentation by May 1. The use of a large number of translators increases the risk of inconsistency and other translation quality problems.

Alternatively, the project manager can adopt a batching process. In other words, she or he can make arrangements with the writers to provide finalized portions of the documentation in batches prior to April 1, and then send the batches to an LSP for translation as they become available. In this way, for example, the project manager might arrange to send the LSP a first batch of files containing 20,000 words on March 1, a second batch containing an additional 20,000 words on March 15 and a final batch of 20,000 words on April 1. This strategy offers two major advantages. First, because it enables localization to start before development of the source product and/or authoring of the source files are complete, this approach narrows the time gap between the finalization of the source files and the completion of the corresponding localized materials, thus enabling the localized versions of the product to be released to market sooner. Second, this approach allows the LSP to use a smaller team of translators, editors and proofreaders, which typically enables greater terminological and stylistic consistency in the translations. On the other hand, because this approach involves multiple batches of files, it also increases the managerial and administrative overhead for authors and project managers in the client organization as well for project managers in the LSP if the file handoffs and submissions are not fully automated.

Finally, the project manager can arrange for individual files to be submitted to the LSP for localization on a streaming basis, as soon as they are created by writers. In the hypothetical scenario discussed above, this approach might result in files being sent to an LSP as early as January or February. The streaming approach is particularly well suited to projects that involve relatively simple workflow (such as translation, editing and proofreading) and whose file handoffs and submissions are automated. One disadvantage of this approach is that the volume and sequence of file handoffs to the LSP are more unpredictable, as they are tied directly to the relative productivity of the documentation team. Another disadvantage is that it multiplies waste in the event that materials authored during the development cycle are ultimately omitted from the final deliverables, since those materials will already have been localized during the development cycle.

Quality requirements

Localization projects may be well planned, cost-effective and delivered on time, but if the quality of the final product does not meet the customer's requirements, the entire project may be considered a failure. Thus, it is essential to capture the customer's quality requirements during the project planning phase. In the localization industry, customer quality requirements are commonly formulated in terms of adherence to style guides and compliance with approved terminology.

Adherence to source language style guide
Although adherence to a source style guide during the authoring process is by definition beyond the scope of localization, it can have a significant positive impact on localization projects. A style guide leads to syntactic and terminological consistency in source materials. Syntactic consistency, in turn, offers two major benefits when it comes to translation or localization. First, standardizing the syntax of specific types of sentences (such as instructions and error messages) can decrease costs by reducing the number of words to be translated (for example, "Click OK" vs. "Select the OK button") and by increasing the amount of repetition in the source materials. Translation memory tools treat identical source sentences as repetitions. Once the first occurrence of a given segment has been translated, subsequent repetitions can be translated automatically by applying this translation across the project. Greater consistency in the source materials translates into a greater number of exact and fuzzy matches during translation, reducing overall translation costs. Although the total savings in a one-language localization project may not be significant, the impact can be considerable when a company supports dozens of languages. Second, adherence to a style guide minimizes stylistic variation in the source materials, and as a result, helps disambiguate those materials. This in turn reduces the number of queries translators might otherwise submit to clarify the meaning of source sentences. Addressing queries is a challenging task. Any delay in responding to translators' queries can negatively impact the project schedule and cost. In addition, translators working in different languages will typically pose different questions. Managing large numbers of queries submitted by multiple translators in multiple languages becomes a significant overhead and a cost in itself. It is more cost effective to prevent inconsistencies that can lead translators to submit queries than to address queries as they arise. Again, since content is typically translated into multiple languages, the net impact of this strategy rises in proportion to the number of supported languages.

Adherence to target language style guide
Ensuring that translators follow the same common set of style guidelines in a given target language is as important as having writers follow a source language style guide. Some software companies develop their own translation style guides for every language, whereas others rely on language service providers for this service. A style guide may provide rules on tone, register, and typographic conventions such as usage of quotation marks, numbers and hyphenation, among many other things.[7]

---

7. For downloadable style guides in 91 languages, see Microsoft (2011).

Terminological requirements

The creation of a reliable glossary is a cornerstone of the localization process. This step should be completed before undertaking any other translation-related steps in a project.[8] Ideally, a source language glossary is created during the design phase of the product development cycle, and each term is documented along with its definition and examples of usage. A glossary helps content creators choose appropriate terms and employ them consistently so that users (and translators) are not confused by the use of different terms to refer to the same concept.

The glossary should be provided to the localization team, translated in its entirety and approved by the client organization prior to translation of any product content. If target glossaries are approved while the content is still being developed, then translation of the content can begin as soon as the source files are finalized, thus shortening the translation turnaround time, and by extension, the time to market.[9] Additionally, an approved glossary will answer many of the translators' terminological questions that would otherwise require the submission of queries, and enable editors, proofreaders and reviewers to avoid making unnecessary and/or purely preferential changes. In sum, the use of approved glossaries during authoring and translation helps to ensure terminological consistency in all languages.

Terminology-related requirements in localization projects include the following:

– Identifying source terms, documenting definitions and examples of usage, and submitting the terms, definitions and examples to subject matter experts for review. Some companies have developed detailed organizational requirements and dedicate linguists to these tasks. Such companies typically undertake glossary development work as part of the process of authoring the source documents. Other companies perform this work on a more ad hoc basis as part of the localization process.
– Measuring the volume of terminology translation.
– Determining whether the translated terms will be reviewed, and if so, identifying subject matter experts in the appropriate domains. Terminology review is typically treated as an important or even mandatory step. Time, financial or human resource constraints may preclude a full review of the localized software or documentation, but it is advisable at a minimum to review the glossary since the terminology it contains is used across all of the product components.
– Determining how to make the glossary accessible to all users (including translators, reviewers, and ideally, content creators).

---

8. In theory, glossary creation is a core localization requirement. In practice, however, whether or not glossary creation is treated as a core requirement by authoring teams depends to a great extent on the maturity of localization processes within the organization (DePalma, Beninatto and Sargent 2006: 28, 53, 59).

9. Vesey defines time to market as "the elapsed time between product definition and product availability" (1991: 23).

Business and organizational requirements

As noted above, many organizations streamline project management by formalizing common project requirements as business or organizational requirements. In the realm of translation and localization, examples of typical business or organizational requirements include translation memory tool and translation management system usage, machine translation usage and content management system usage.

Translation memory tools and translation management system usage
Translation memory tools have been used in the localization industry for over 15 years. Today, it is difficult to find a translation or localization service provider that does not take advantage of translation memory technologies, which are available in both client (desktop) and server-based configurations. As noted above, desktop translation memory tools enable cost savings thanks to leveraging of previous translation. Server-based technology, also called Translation Management Systems (TMS), offers additional benefits including automated workflows, TM and glossary centralization, and connections to Content Management Systems. Most large companies require service providers to use a specific technology and adhere to a specific process and/or automated workflow during their translation and localization projects.

Machine translation usage
Machine translation is a technology that performs translation of text or speech from one human language into another. Unlike translation memory, which is designed to *assist* human translators, machine translation actually *replaces* human translators. At the present time MT technology is mainly used in combination with translation memories and post-editing by professional translators or editors. First, content is leveraged using one or more existing translation memories. Any translation units that have not been not pre-translated (leveraged) using the TM then undergo machine translation. The machine translated units are then edited by professional translators and/or target language post-editors. One common exception to this practice is machine translation of Knowledge Base content that is generally not post-edited, but rather published as is.

Over the past two decades, the advent of large collections of machine-readable documents (i.e., corpora) in both structured and unstructured formats, coupled with the decreasing cost and increasing computational power of computer hardware, has enabled major strides in the field of machine translation. Today, machine translation is increasingly seen as a commercially viable option for certain vertical markets and applications (e.g., the translation of Knowledge Base content mentioned above). Three types of MT technologies are currently used in industry: rule-based, statistical and hybrid MT.

The first type, rule-based MT relies on a set of grammatical and linguistic rules, as well as on a dictionary, to translate data. Because grammatical and syntactic rules vary from language to language, a distinct set of rules must be created for each language pair (such as English to German, German to Russian or Arabic to French). Creating rule-based MT software is a very time-consuming process. Rule-based machine translation output may be grammatically quite accurate but typically requires a great deal of editing because rule-based MT lexicons generally do not contain customer- or industry- specific data. The second type of MT, statistical MT technology, makes use of bilingual corpora to translate text of similar kinds. Bilingual text corpora are analyzed to create a statistical translation model, which is then used to translate new documents. Statistical MT systems can be continuously improved by providing corrective feedback to help them "learn" what errors they are making. This process, which is referred to as "training" the statistical MT engine, requires large amounts of domain-specific data and is a time-consuming process. Each language pair must be prepared for and processed individually. However, because the training process enables the system to learn, statistical MT can sometimes produce higher quality output that requires minimal editing. Finally, the third type, Hybrid MT combines statistical and rule-based translation methodologies, either by applying rules to a statistical engine or by using statistics to correct an output from a rule-based MT.

Determining whether a project can (or should) be executed using MT has traditionally been a long-term, organization-wide decision as it requires a substantial investment and preparation; this explains why MT usage is typically specified as an organizational requirement by the client. However, this may change: some language service providers have begun to offer machine translation service as a part of their translation workflow, enabling clients to test the viability of machine translation for their applications without actually having to develop or acquire MT systems themselves. The decision to use such a service may impact the project budget; it may also impact translation quality if editing steps are not built into the process. These factors must be addressed when considering the possible use of machine translation.

Content Management System usage
Many large organizations use Content Management Systems (CMS) to manage the creation, version control and lifecycle of their documents. If content to be translated is authored or stored in a CMS, certain procedures must be followed to extract the data from the CMS. Because most Translation Management Systems (TMS) can connect to CMS systems, the process of extracting translatable files and submitting translated versions back to the CMS can be automated, which is typically referred to as a CMS/TMS integration. In order to develop a smooth CMS/TMS integration, the CMS system must have a good metadata scheme and labeling system that allows content owners to indicate within the CMS which files/versions should be translated into which language(s). The CMS must also be able to properly mark and classify the language and version of translated files when they are returned to the system. For example, suppose that version 1.1 of a given source file is extracted from a CMS for translation into French and German, and that during the translation process, the source file is updated and is now identified by the CMS as version 1.2. When the finalized French

and German translations are returned to the CMS, it is important to correctly associate them with version 1.1 of the source file, not version 1.2, as well as with the previous French and/or German versions (if any), and to store the translations as part of the correct object or folder.

Depending on whether (a) a CMS/TMS integration is available; (b) an integration is possible but will need to be implemented; or (c) the files will be extracted from and submitted to the CMS manually, both the project scope and timeline may change.

Scope management process: Define scope

The scope definition process involves the development of a detailed description of the project and product. Requirements documentation serves as one of the main inputs into the scope definition process. Other documents that play an important role during this phase are organizational process assets such as project scope templates and post-mortem notes from similar previous projects. Project scope templates provide a list of all the potential requirements that must be defined and/or researched when managing a given type of project. Post-mortem notes contain information on what went well and what did not go well in previous projects. This information helps the project manager take previous mistakes into account when planning new projects to ensure that those mistakes are not repeated.

During scope definition, the localization project manager (either in house or at an LSP) progressively elaborates the set of requirements captured during requirements collection to specify them at a more granular level; organizational requirements are used if applicable. The output of the scope definition process is a detailed project scope statement, which includes but is not limited to the following:

- *Product scope description:* a document that details the characteristics of the product or service per the project requirements.
- *Project deliverables:* a list of the outputs that constitute the project product or service.
  Project acceptance criteria: the process and criteria by which the product or service will be deemed acceptable by the customer, for example compliance with a standard or specification, or completion prior to a given deadline.
- *Project assumptions:* a list of assumptions and a description of the impact on the project should those assumptions prove false. Assumptions may be listed within the project scope statement or as a separate document.

A project scope statement may also specify what is excluded from the project scope, as well as constraints (for example, a set budget or a trade show deadline).

In the paragraphs that follow, we will discuss the list of deliverables, acceptance criteria and assumptions.

List of deliverables

The list of deliverables is defined during the scope definition processes, and is one of the main inputs to the subsequent scope management process, WBS creation. As noted above, the components identified during requirements collection comprise a high-level list of the project deliverables. This high-level list is subsequently expanded and formalized during scope definition. The list of localization deliverables includes both final deliverables and intermediate deliverables. Final deliverables include the localized versions of all components (for example, built and tested localized product, documentation, help, collateral), as well as the project translation memory and glossary. The final deliverables are usually specified by stakeholders during the requirements collection process. However, additional deliverables may subsequently be added during the scope definition process. For example, a stakeholder in a client organization may be unfamiliar with translation memory tools and therefore may not request a TM as a deliverable. The localization project manager would later add the TM to the final deliverable during the scope definition process. The TM deliverable might be further broken down per component (software, documentation and marketing) during the WBS creation process, depending on the needs and requirements of the client organization. Intermediate deliverables include status reports and query reports, and are usually spelled out during WBS creation as well.

Acceptance criteria

As their name suggests, acceptance criteria are a set of requirements that a product or project must meet to be deemed acceptable by the customer. Preliminary acceptance criteria are established by project stakeholders during requirements collection. Passing functional and/or other forms of acceptance tests, meeting delivery deadlines and not exceeding the budget are common examples of high-level acceptance criteria in software development projects.

In the localization industry, acceptance testing often takes the form of client review. There are many possible justifications for subjecting project deliverables to client review. One of the most common is the fact that although translation is typically performed by professional translators, in many cases those translators are unfamiliar with the corporate culture of the client on whose behalf they are translating. It is the company's own personnel who are best positioned to determine whether the target materials are consistent with the company's brand, messaging and international communications strategies. Some companies use in-house or in-country reviewers; others rely on the help of internal or external subject matter experts (e.g. distributors).

Some projects are subjected to a higher degree of scrutiny than others. Depending on the level of visibility and scrutiny, the complexity of the content and other factors, the project stakeholders may decide to conduct multiple levels of review and quality assurance. Most projects require human resources that have specific knowledge or expertise. For example, only translators specializing in medical, chemistry and marketing translations may be allowed to work on a new drug pamphlet. During the planning phase it is critical to decide whether or not project deliverables will undergo review, and if so, by whom, when, and according to what criteria. If the content varies significantly per component, it may be necessary to submit different components of a project to different reviewers (for example, to send documentation to an application engineer and to send marketing materials to a marketing specialist). Such decisions are usually made during the WBS creation process.

Assumptions

Assumptions must be outlined during scope definition since the project scope, cost and timeline all depend to some extent on these assumptions. For example, suppose an assumption is made during a multimedia localization project that Flash source files will be provided for localization. The project costs and schedule calculations will be based on this assumption. If source files are subsequently not provided, the localization team will have to recreate editable source files, in which case both the cost and duration of the project will increase.

In a product development environment where it is critical to minimize time to market, the localization cycle very often starts while the product is still being developed. If the requirements documentation does not specify whether the localized products should be shipped simultaneously with the English version and/or whether files will be delivered in batches or on a streaming basis, the localization project manager makes these assumptions during the scope definition process. Other assumptions might include the scope of client review as well as the identification of who will be responsible for performing the review in each language.

Scope management process: Create Work Breakdown Structure (WBS)

A Work Breakdown Structure (WBS) is a "deliverable oriented hierarchical decomposition of the work to be executed by the project team to accomplish the project objectives and create the required deliverables, with each descending level of the WBS representing an increasingly detailed definition of the work" (PMI 2008: 116). The work breakdown structure must account for all of the work specified in the project scope statement, including project management. Anything not included in the WBS is technically outside of the project scope. The WBS creation process involves the decomposition, or subdivision, of project deliverables and project work into progressively smaller components in order to make the project more manageable. The lowest level of the WBS consists of individual work packages, i.e., chunks of work that can be scheduled, budgeted and monitored, and organized by phase (see Figure 1).

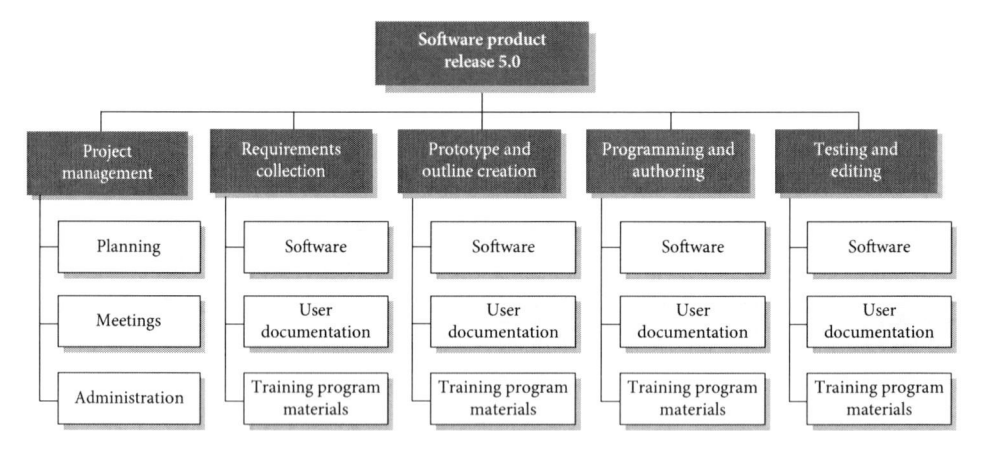

Figure 1. A sample work breakdown structure for a generic software development project, organized by phase (adapted from PMI 2008: 119).

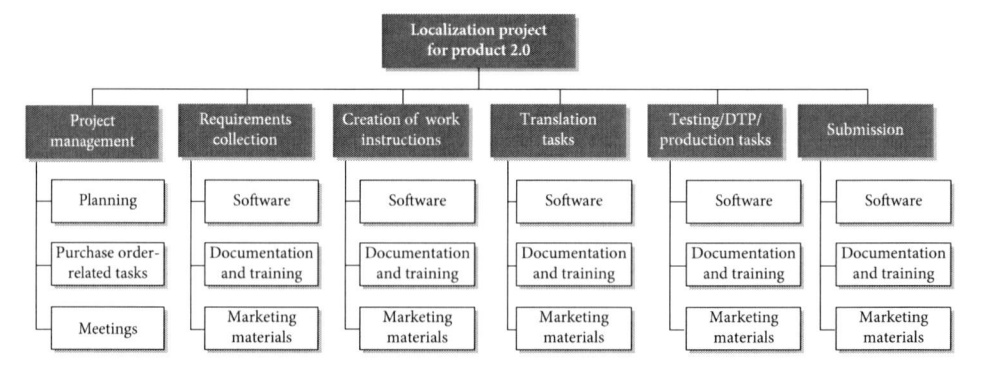

Figure 2. A sample work breakdown structure for a generic software localization project, organized by phase.

LSPs and companies that require their services may designate a localization project WBS using different names, such as a RFQ (request for quotation), a scope statement, a project plan, or work instructions, depending on a given company's policies. During the creation of a localization project WBS, the work is decomposed based on the project deliverables that need to be created and subdivided into individual phases reflecting either the various components that must be produced or the activities that must be performed to create those components. Figure 2 presents an illustration of a generic software localization project whose components include software, documentation and training materials, as well as marketing materials.

High-level requirements documented during requirements collection may be specified in greater detail during the WBS creation process. For example, the final determination of word counts and concomitant translation memory statistics can only be performed after receiving finalized source files, as noted above, and thus these calculations are typically carried out as part of WBS creation process by either the software company itself, by an LSP, or both (e.g., when a counter-analysis is performed by an LSP to confirm numbers provided by a client).

The outputs of the WBS creation process include a work breakdown structure that defines all deliverables at a work package level, as well as a WBS Dictionary, which provides more detailed information about components in the WBS, including but not necessarily limited to the following:

- Description of work
- Milestones
- Schedule
- Cost estimates
- Quality requirements
- Acceptance criteria
- Technical information
- Required resources

In addition to quality requirements, acceptance criteria and technical information, it is important to discuss required resources.

Required resources

Identification and assignment of appropriate human resources at the task level occurs during WBS creation. It is for this reason that the list of required resources is defined as an output of the WBS creation process. A localization project in a client organization can be outsourced to a number of freelancers, a few single language vendors (SLVs), one or a few multiple language vendors (MLVs) or any combination thereof. An LSP, in turn typically manages the project and outsources most of the project work to freelancers (e.g., translation, editing, proofreading, testing, etc.).

When selecting vendors from which to solicit a Request For Quotation (RFQ), one must consider resource-related requirements, such as the expertise of the different vendors in the appropriate subject area(s) and language(s); the quality of their work; the depth of their experience as well as their ability to support the required tools and processes (i.e., TM, MT, CMS and/or TMS, as discussed above); and price (especially if the decision to undertake the project is contingent on not exceeding a limited budget). Some vendors specialize in certain industries or certain localization activities. A typical localization project comprises a wide range of activities, which may include translation, testing, engineering quality assurance, desktop publishing and audio recording, among others. Small or medium-sized LSPs may not possess the requisite expertise or have access to adequate resources to perform all of these activities.

The decision to outsource a localization project to multiple vendors will impact the project budget. Outsourcing typically increases in-house overhead management costs by multiplying the number of financial records, invoices and queries that must be addressed and generally speaking expands the amount of communication work required of the project manager. Therefore project scope and budget factors must be considered when deciding whether (or to what extent) to outsource project work, defining vendor strategy, as well as selecting and hiring vendors during a new project.

The imperative of scalability dictates that a company pre-qualify vendors to be able to handle large projects and/or to execute multiple projects simultaneously without encountering resource bottlenecks. Many companies create detailed vendor selection and qualification processes. Depending on the complexity of the processes, vendor selection and/or approval may take several months. In such cases, if a new vendor needs to be approved by the client organization to perform a new service or to work on an additional language during a given project, the project manager will have to begin the vendor selection far enough in advance to ensure that the vendor has been qualified when needed.

Scope management process: Verify scope

Scope verification is one step in the formal acceptance of the project deliverables, and consists of an inspection of the project output to ensure that the project requirements have been met: the customer (or a customer representative) compares the original project scope and acceptance criteria with the delivered materials and signs off on all the deliverables – or not, as the case may be. If any deliverables are not accepted, the reason for non-acceptance is documented and a change request may be issued to repair the defect, resulting in additional work and/or rework.

Localization organizations typically verify the project scope throughout the project life cycle as part of their monitoring and controlling processes. Since work is often performed in batches, clients generally do not wait until the conclusion of all batches to verify the scope of the project deliverables. Instead, the scope is verified incrementally upon the submission of each completed batch. For example, suppose that the work of a software localization project is divided into three batches. After the submission of the first batch, the project manager can verify that all of the files in the batch have been translated in their entirety. He or she can also confirm that the list of submitted target files matches that of the source files provided for translation. If any files are missing, the project manager can request re-delivery of all files or of the missing files only. At the end of the project, all final deliverables are checked against the project scope and acceptance criteria either by project manager or by other team members.

Scope management process: Control scope

Even when projects are planned very carefully, changes are inevitable. The main purpose of the scope control process is to monitor the project and make sure that changes to the scope baseline are documented and managed. Three components of the project plan are used to control scope: the scope management plan, the scope baseline, and the change management plan. The scope management plan specifies how the scope shall be managed and controlled. The scope baseline provides a snapshot of the most current version of the project scope, and is used as point of reference enabling the comparison of expected results to actual results in order to determine whether any action is required. If so, the change management plan defines the processes for managing project changes. Requirements documentation and work performance information are also useful for comparing the actual scope to the baseline. Changes in scope typically require formal change requests. Approved change requests in turn require changes to the project plan, WBS and WBS dictionary documents (i.e., description of work, schedule, costs, etc.).

Change requests are common in localization projects. For example, one or more additional languages/locales may be added during the course of a project. Another common scenario is a change in word count: for example, a Help system translation project originally estimated to contain 50,000 words is expanded to include 80,000 words of Help plus a separate 5,000 word Release Notes document. Change requests are necessary not only when the volume of translatable content increases, but may also be required when technical specifications for a deliverable file are modified. For example, a change in the resolution of a video file (i.e., from 320 × 240 to 720 × 480 pixels) would require re-work and the creation of a new output file.

Conclusion

Collecting requirements, defining the scope, creating the work breakdown structure, verifying the scope and controlling the scope are key scope management processes. Effective scope management begins with the clear and comprehensive definition of project requirements, and an understanding of the ways in which those requirements are interconnected and may affect the project: scope changes may affect cost, time and/or resources; quality requirement changes may affect resources, risk, and/or cost; and so on. If we reconsider the story discussed in the introduction of the man who wanted eight hats made out of a single piece of fur, we are in a better position to understand the errors that the man made in managing his project: he should have defined the parameters and sizes of the hats that he desired as project requirements, and when he changed the scope of the project from one hat to eight, he should have added resources in the form of another seven pieces of fur. Localization projects are no different in this respect. Before undertaking a new localization project it is important to document all of the project requirements and to define and manage the project scope to maximize the likelihood of project success. The scope management process described by PMI and discussed in this chapter offers a repeatable methodology for doing precisely that.

References

Day, Don, Priestly, Michael and Schell, David. 2005. "Introduction to the Darwin Information Typing Architecture: Toward portable technical information." IBM developerWorks (Sep. 28). http://www.ibm.com/developerworks/xml/library/x-dita1/

DePalma, Donald A., Beninatto, Renato S. and Sargent, Benjamin B. 2006. *Localization Maturity Model: Applying a Capability Maturity Model to Technology, Product and Website Globalization*. Lowell, MA: Common Sense Advisory.

Kaplan, Richard. 2007. "Using translation automation to improve access and content quality." Keynote presentation. Localization World conference, Seattle, WA, Oct. 18.

Lommel, Arle. 2007. *The Globalization Industry Primer*. Romainmôtier, Switzerland: LISA.

Microsoft. 2011. "Download international style guides." Microsoft Language Portal. http://www.microsoft.com/Language/en-US/StyleGuides.aspx

Project Management Institute (PMI). 2008. *A Guide to the Project Management Body of Knowledge (PMBOK® Guide)*. 4th ed. Newtown Square, PA: Project Management Institute, Inc.

Vesey, Joseph T. 1991. "The new competitors: They think in terms of 'speed-to-market.' " *The Executive* 5 (2): 23–33.

Managing the fourth dimension
Time and schedule in translation and localization projects

Keiran J. Dunne*

> The whirligig of time brings in his revenges.
> Shakespeare
>
> How does a project get to be a year behind schedule? One day at a time.
> Frederick P. Brooks
>
> La stratégie est la science de l'emploi du temps et de l'espace.
> Je suis, pour mon compte, moins avare de l'espace que du temps.
> Pour l'espace, nous pouvons toujours le regagner. Le temps perdu, jamais.
> Napoléon Bonaparte

In recognition of the importance of time as a project constraint, this chapter discusses time and schedule management in translation and localization projects. It begins by considering the schedule as an explanatory and forecasting model of project execution. The chapter then discusses the standard time management framework provided by the Project Management Institute's *A Guide to The Project Management Body of Knowledge (PMBOK® Guide)*, examining each of the constituent processes in turn and illustrating their application in a hypothetical translation project.[1]

Introduction

In 1969, while conducting doctoral research in financial control of civil engineering projects at the University of Manchester, Martin Barnes designed a course called "Time and money in contract control," which adopted an integrated approach to cost

---

*   The author wishes to thank Matthew Conheady for the helpful feedback he provided during the preparation of this chapter.

1.   Although a hypothetical translation project is presented for purposes of simplicity, the concepts discussed in this chapter are relevant to localization projects as well.

and time.[2] During one of the seminars, Barnes noted that managing a "contract" entails not only controlling cost and time, but also the delivery of what is specified in the contract. To illustrate this point, Barnes sketched a triangle on an overhead projector slide and labeled the three corner points as cost, quality and time.[3] Barnes then placed a coin on the slide, which appeared as a black circle on the screen, and moved it around the triangle to illustrate the emphasis of one factor at the expense of the other two in a given contract. This impromptu exercise led Barnes to the conclusion that an effective way to conceptualize the management of a contract is to decide where on the triangle the black circle should be located to best meet the client's objectives, representing the ideal balance of the competing constraints in that particular contract, and to maintain that position until delivery of whatever is specified in the contract. Thus was born one of the most enduring concept models in project management, the project management triangle (see Figure 1). This model illustrates the interdependence of the variables of cost, quality and time: if constant performance (i.e., scope) is a given, then a change to any side will affect one or both of the other sides, which is sometimes expressed in the form of the adage, "fast, good, cheap: pick any two." This interdependence is considered so axiomatic that it has become known as the law of triple constraints (Beath 1986; Kezsbom, Schilling and Edward 1989; Miller 1989). In recognition of this axiomatic relationship between these three project variables, the project management triangle is often referred to as the "iron triangle" (Kliem 1994). Project constraints are not confined to cost, quality and time, but may also include scope and resources, among others. The operative constraints and the relationships between them vary from one project to the next.

In the current market for translation and localization services, time is arguably the most critical constraint. Indeed, at the 2011 Localization World conference in Barcelona, Derick Fajardo from Nuance observed that "cost rules, quality is assumed, but in the end, schedule wins" (quoted in Beninatto 2011). Likewise, Tim Young from Cisco, when asked during the keynote panel at this same conference which metric is the most important for internal clients, replied without hesitation, "on-time delivery" (quoted in Beninatto 2011). Nevertheless, translation and localization project managers, and the organizations that employ them, must not allow urgency to override other constraints. *A Guide to The Project Management Body of Knowledge (PMBOK® Guide)*, a project management standard published by the Project Management Institute (PMI), provides a framework and repeatable methodology for identifying, evaluating and balancing constraints.

---

2. The information in this paragraph is drawn from Barnes (2006) and APM (2010: 21–23).

3. Barnes later decided that the third corner point should be changed from quality to performance, "because what you want from a completed project is that it does what it was supposed to do. I've been trying to tell people this for years but I can't get them to change it!" (qtd. in APM 2010: 22).

```
            Cost
             /\
            /  \
           /    \
          / Scope\
         /        \
        /_____\
     Time          Quality
```

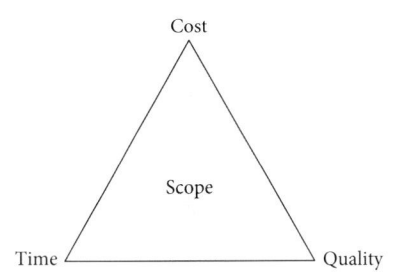

Figure 1. The project management triangle.

A fundamental difference exists between time and the other constraints identified above. It is possible to adjust the project budget to account for cost variances, and to modify the staffing plan to add human resources to the project if necessary. Likewise, quality can be enhanced or sacrificed, and the project scope can be increased or decreased if need be. Time, however, is finite: once consumed, it cannot be reclaimed. "Time is the scarcest resource, and unless it is managed, nothing else can be managed," as Peter Drucker has observed (1967:51). In recognition of the critical importance of this constraint, this chapter uses the time management framework provided by the Project Management Institute (PMI) to illustrate how and to what extent time and schedule management can be standardized in translation and localization projects.

Schedule as a model of project execution

The creation of a schedule is the process of estimating how, when and by whom each element of work in the project scope will be carried out. In other words, much as the project management triangle discussed above is a model of project constraints, a project schedule is a model of project execution that represents and approximates the work, time and resources required to complete the project, and the sequence in which the various project tasks shall be undertaken. Thus, a schedule is at once an explanatory model and a forecasting model. it simultaneously represents and enables the management of the reality of the project. In this respect, a schedule is similar to an itinerary whereby a traveler projects how (and when) he or she will get from point A to point B. The schedule, like the itinerary, is an approximation: the true duration of the project or trip cannot be known with certainty until it has been completed. Along similar lines, a schedule, like an itinerary, represents merely one of multiple possible models of the journey from point A to point B.

Although the notion that a schedule is a project model may seem self-evident, the Project Management Institute (PMI) distinguishes between a "schedule" and a "schedule model." The latter term was introduced in the initial edition of the *Practice Standard for Scheduling* (PMI 2007). PMI defines "schedule model" as a *tool*, i.e., "a dynamic representation of the project's plan for executing the project's activities developed by the project team's applying the scheduling method to a scheduling tool using project specific data such as activity lists and activity attributes" (2007:100). By contrast, PMI defines the term "project schedule" as the *input or output* of the schedule model tool, i.e., "the planned dates for performing schedule activities and the planned dates for meeting schedule milestones" (2007:97). In introducing the term "schedule model" and drawing a distinction between the tool in which a schedule is created and the output of that tool (2008:129), PMI has arguably created an unnecessary terminological and conceptual confusion. A schedule models project execution; it does not (and cannot) model itself (Uyttewaal and Woolf 2011). Thus, the term "schedule" as used in this chapter is understood to be a model of project execution; no distinction is drawn between the medium in which the schedule is created and the medium in which it is represented or displayed.

Project time management

A Guide to The Project Management Body of Knowledge (PMBOK® Guide), a project management standard published by PMI, provides a generic time management framework that can be applied to schedule modeling and management in any industry. According to PMI, time management comprises six processes (2008:103):

- Activity definition
- Activity sequencing
- Activity resource estimation
- Activity duration estimation
- Schedule development
- Schedule control

These processes are presented by PMI and discussed in this chapter as discrete undertakings, reflecting the fact that each entails the use of distinct tools and techniques. In practice, however, these processes can and often do overlap, and some or all of them may need to be performed more than once over the course of a project. The sections that follow discuss each of these processes in turn and illustrate their application to a hypothetical translation project.

Defining activities

Before any work can be performed or scheduled, the project manager must identify precisely what work needs to be done. Thus, the first process of project time management, defining activities, focuses on "identifying the specific actions to be performed to produce the project deliverables" (PMI 2008:129). The process of defining activities is roughly akin to reverse engineering. During the scope definition process, the project manager begins by identifying the deliverables that need to be produced. He or she then subdivides, or decomposes, those deliverables into their constituent components to create a work breakdown structure (WBS). At some point thereafter, during the activity definition process, the project manager identifies the activities that must be carried out to produce each component. The main difference between WBS creation and activity definition is that in WBS creation the outputs of decomposition are defined as deliverables and sub-deliverables, whereas in activity definition the outputs are defined as activities.

The project manager performs decomposition until the project activities are defined at a sufficient level of granularity to enable adequate duration estimates (to create the project schedule), cost estimates (to create the project budget) and independent work assignments (to create the project staffing plan). Activity definitions may be shaped not only by the scope and parameters of the given project, but also by enterprise environmental factors such as organizational culture and infrastructure (including the specific software used to carry out various activities), as well as by organizational process assets such as policies, procedures, templates or post-mortem documentation from similar past projects.

An example will help to illustrate the processes of decomposition and activity definition. The Dynatorch Company of Paducah, Kentucky, USA is a specialized manufacturer of CNC motion control equipment and software designed for plasma and oxyfuel cutting. The company's products include Dynatorch CNC Plasma Cutter software. For the purposes of this discussion, we will imagine that the company is entering the Canadian market and that as part of this expansion, it has worked with its in-country distributors to localize the CNC Plasma Cutter software for that market. We will further imagine that Dynatorch has decided to work with a language service provider (LSP) to translate the CNC Plasma Cutter user guide into French for Canada rather than further burdening its in-country distributors.[4] This user manual consists of a 120-page Microsoft Word document (*.doc) that includes 57 screenshots from the Dynatorch CNC Plasma Cutter software (some of which are used multiple times) as well as 5 drawings that presumably have been produced using CAD (computer-assisted design) software. For the purposes of this discussion, it is assumed that the language service provider will outsource the language-related project work (e.g., translation and proofreading) and that the translators will not work directly in the source Word document but rather in a dedicated translation environment using computer-assisted translation (CAT) tools.

In this hypothetical project, the ostensible deliverables comprise the French version of the user manual in Microsoft Word *.doc format and the corresponding

---

4. The author wishes to express his gratitude to Dynatorch for permission to use the company's CNC Plasma Cutter user manual (Dynatorch 2006) as the basis for this hypothetical scenario.

translation memory in *.tmx (Translation Memory eXchange) format. Performing a high-level decomposition of the deliverables, we might identify the constituent components of those deliverables as target (translated) text, target versions of the screenshots created using the localized versions of the software, target drawings in which translated text has been substituted for the original English text, and a translation memory database.[5] However, this level of decomposition is not sufficiently granular to enable estimates of the time and human resources required to create the components, and by extension the deliverables. Thus, further decomposition would be necessary to identify the individual activities required to create these components.

For instance the creation of target versions of the five drawings requires further decomposition. Even if source CAD files are available, extraction of text from the drawings into a format that is compatible with CAT tools tends to be a labor-intensive manual process. Although utilities designed to enable extraction of text from CAD files do exist, they generally do not identify and extract all instances of translatable text (such as scripts that contain variables and comments). Given the modest number of drawings and limited amount of text that they contain, the most time-efficient approach would be to mask the text embedded in the drawings and replace it with editable callouts in the Word document. This would entail drawing a text box at the location of each occurrence of text embedded in a drawing and typing the corresponding text. This approach would enable the text associated with the five drawings to be processed by a CAT tool along with the rest of the text in the Word document. In this way, it would not be necessary to import (or copy and paste) the text into the CAD files, save target versions of the drawings, and then insert the target drawings into the target Word document. Finally, this modified source document could be provided to Dynatorch as part of the deliverables for re-use if or when the company decides to enter other international markets, thus saving time in future projects. Assuming that this is how the translation of the text embedded in the drawings will be handled, a list of the activities needed to complete the Dynatorch project is presented in Table 1.

The activity list presented in Table 1 is not exhaustive and represents but one possible way to complete the project. Depending on the project requirements and/or project processes, other activities might also be necessary, such as style guide creation, termbase creation, editing, pre-translation using existing translation memories, machine translation, and client review, among others. In addition, some of the activities listed in Table 1 could be further decomposed. For example, project closure might involve several steps, including but not necessarily limited to archiving project files, conducting a project post-mortem, updating project documentation and conducting a customer satisfaction survey.

---

5. This chapter draws a distinction between a *document*, defined as "an exchange artifact that provides information to someone" (Gollner 2009: 3) and *text*, defined as the written information contained in a document.

Table 1. A list of the activities needed to complete the Dynatorch project. Note that items are not presented in strict chronological order.

Receive project approval
Develop schedule
Acquire resources
Prepare for kick-off meeting
Kick-off meeting
Insert editable callouts to mask text embedded in drawings
Import modified Word document into CAT tool
Save project file
Translate project file
Capture target screens from localized software
Output target Word document from translated project file
Integrate target screen captures into target Word document
Format target Word document
Proofread target Word document
Retake target screen captures as needed
Update TM to reflect linguistic changes
Output contents of TM in *.tmx format
Finalize graphics and formatting in target Word document
Deliver finalized target document, revised source document and *.tmx file
Invoice project
Close project

Sequencing activities

Once the project manager has defined the activities that must be performed to create the deliverables, he or she must determine the sequence in which they will be carried out in the project. This in turn requires that the PM identify the dependencies between the various activities. Broadly speaking, dependencies can be divided into three categories: mandatory, discretionary and external (PMI 2008: 139–140). Mandatory dependencies may reflect contractual obligations, such as a stipulation that the language service provider use a specific translation or localization tool, or may be inherent in the work being undertaken. For example, a target-language document cannot be proofread until the source-language document has been translated. Discretionary dependencies, by contrast, are optional and may be defined based either on best practices in the domain or on the judgment of the project manager that a specific sequence of activities is preferable to other possible and acceptable sequences. For example, the project manager may define a discretionary dependency between terminology development and client review prior to translation to minimize the risk of subsequent re-work (see Dunne 172–173 and 178–180 in this volume). Finally, as their name suggests, external dependencies reflect a relationship between some aspect of the project and an external activity. For instance, in-country regulatory approval of a pharmaceutical product may be required before the product can be authorized for sale in that market (and by extension, before the translation of the product's packaging, documentation and marketing materials can begin).

The sequence of activities is shaped not only by dependencies but also by the nature of the logical relationships between the activities. The Project Management Institute identifies four types of logical relationships (PMI 2008:138):

1. *Finish-to-start (FS)*. The initiation of the successor activity depends upon the completion of the predecessor activity. For example, the publication of a document cannot start until creation of the document has finished. This is the most common type of logical relationship.
2. *Finish-to-finish (FF)*. The completion of the successor activity depends upon the completion of the predecessor activity. For example, the authoring of a book cannot finish until the authoring of the last chapter has finished.
3. *Start-to-start (SS)*. The initiation of the successor activity depends upon the initiation of the predecessor activity. For example, editing or revision of a document cannot begin until authoring of the document has begun. (Note that in this example, it would also be necessary to delay the start of the editing by introducing a lag to allow time for the authoring of some content.)
4. *Start-to-finish (SF)*. The completion of the successor activity depends upon the initiation of the predecessor activity. For example, suppose a company has purchased a new accounting system, and does not want to remove the old system from service until the new one enters operation. When employees start to use the new system (predecessor activity), the old system can be retired (successor activity). This type of logical relationship is rarely used.

The project manager evaluates the types of dependencies and logical relationships between the various project activities in order to determine the sequence in which the activities should be performed to complete the project according to the customer's specification. Referring to the activities that comprise our hypothetical project scenario (see Table 1), finish-to-start logical dependencies exist between text extraction and translation; translation and desktop publishing; screen capturing and desktop publishing; as well as desktop publishing and proofreading, to cite a few examples.

The definition of the dependencies and logical relationships between the various project activities enables the creation of a project network diagram, which provides a visual representation of the various activities and the causal linkages between them, much like a flowchart (see Figure 2). The project network diagram constitutes the skeleton of the project schedule. It presents the various activities that comprise the project as well as the sequence in which they must be performed, but not the specific dates and times when each activity will be scheduled to begin and finish. To be able to schedule the various activities and determine how long the project will take, the project manager must identify the human resources required to carry out the project activities as well as the duration of those activities. The processes of estimating the required human resources and the durations of the activities are the focus of the following section.

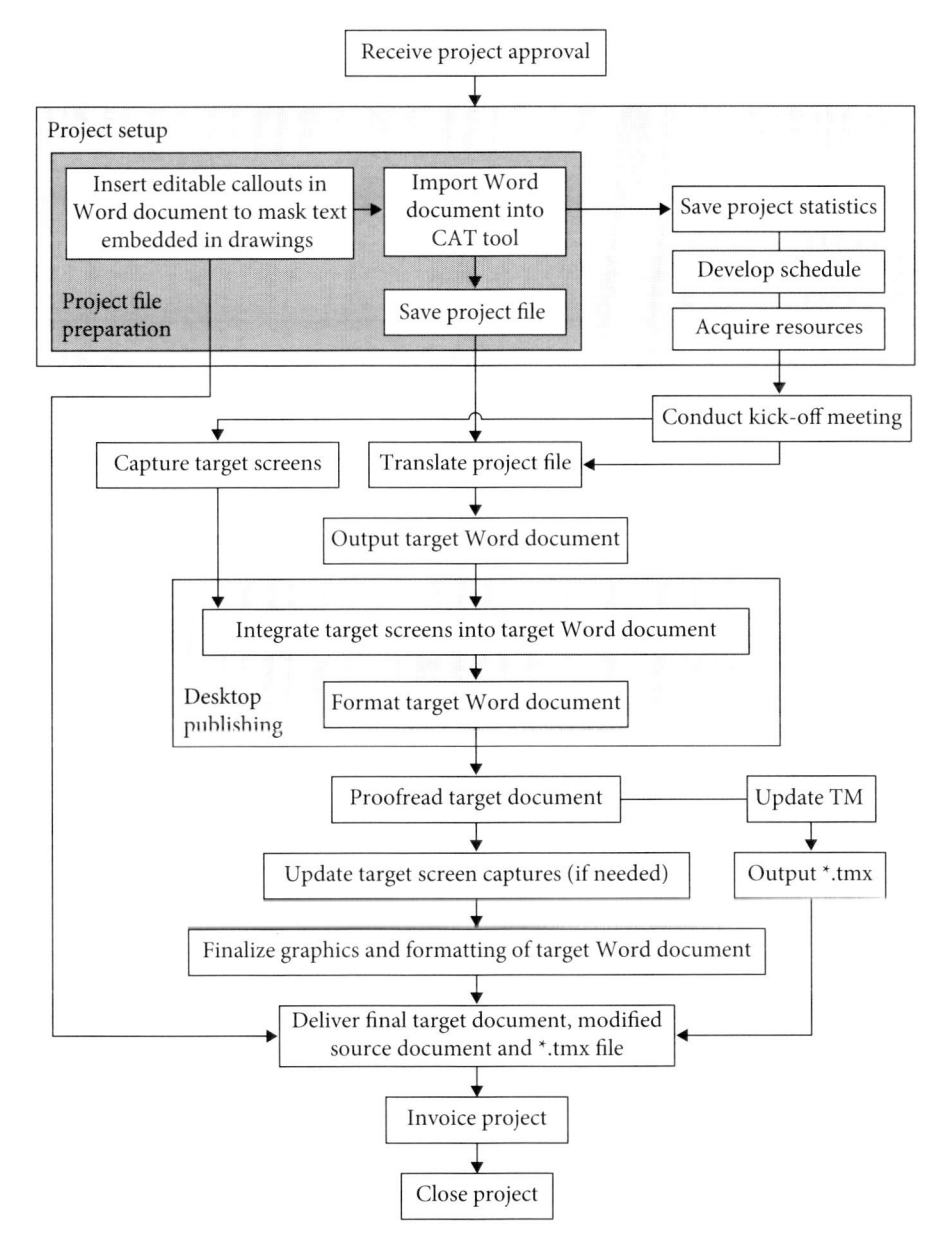

Figure 2. A project network diagram that illustrates the sequence and dependencies between the activities that comprise the Dynatorch project scenario. Solid arrows represent finish-to-start logical relationships.

Estimating activity resources

Once the project manager has defined the project activities and the sequence in which they must be performed, it is necessary that he or she undertake a high-level estimate of the human, material and financial resources required to complete the project. In outsourced translation and localization projects, the primary goal of this preliminary estimate is to identify the number and types of human resources (i.e., freelancers and other service providers) needed to perform the various project activities, such as translation, proofreading, testing, terminology development, and so forth. This initial estimate of human resources takes into account not only the project activities that must be performed but also preliminary project requirements, which may include but are not necessarily limited to language pair, locale and directionality; subject matter expertise; professional experience; and technological skills. Comparing the required resources to the available resources enables the project manager to identify and address any gaps (or recommend that the organization not pursue the project in the event that the required resources are unavailable and cannot be acquired).

Table 2. The activities that comprise the hypothetical Dynatorch project and a preliminary estimate of the human resources required to complete them.

Activity	Required human resource
Receive project approval	Project manager
Develop schedule	Project manager
Acquire resources	Project manager
Prepare for kick-off meeting	Project manager
Kick-off meeting	Entire project team
Insert editable callouts to mask text embedded in drawings	DTP specialist
Import modified Word document into CAT tool	Project manager
Save project file	Project manager
Translate project file	FR-CA translator
Capture target screens from localized software	Localization specialist
Output target Word document from translated project file	Project manager
Integrate target screen captures into target Word document	DTP specialist
Format target Word document	DTP specialist
Proofread target Word document	FR-CA proofreader
Retake target screen captures as needed	Localization specialist
Update TM to reflect linguistic changes	FR-CA proofreader
Output contents of TM in *.tmx format	Project manager
Finalize graphics and formatting of target Word document	DTP specialist
Deliver finalized target document, modified source document and *.tmx file	Project manager
Invoice project	Project manager
Close project	Project manager

For the purposes of this discussion, it is assumed that the language service provider selected by Dynatorch to carry out the project has in-house project management, desktop publishing (DTP) and localization staff and outsources the language-specific work of translation and proofreading to external subcontractors. Given those assumptions, and given the activities defined in Table 1, the human resources required to complete the Dynatorch project would include a translator of English into French for Canada; a proofreader of English into French for Canada; a project manager; a DTP specialist; and a localization specialist (see Table 2).

Estimating activity durations

After performing this initial estimate of the required resources, the project manager must estimate "the number of work periods needed to complete individual activities [using the] estimated resources" (PMI 2008: 146). In this respect, it is important to note that work effort and duration are not synonymous. Work effort represents the total amount of labor required to perform an activity, that is, the total amount of focused, uninterrupted work, whether consecutive or non-consecutive, expressed in hours or days. Duration represents the total elapsed time between the start of an activity and its completion, expressed in business or working days; weekends, holidays, vacations and other non-work periods are not included in duration calculations. The work effort and duration of a given activity may differ considerably. For example, if a translation project requires eight hours of work to complete, but the translator assigned to the activity can only devote two hours per day to it, then duration of the activity will be four days even though the total work effort is only eight hours. Activity duration is shaped not only by human resource availability, but also by the efficiency of the work time:

> If a person could be focused 100 percent of the time on a task, he or she could accomplish 10 hours of work in 10 hours. Such a person would indeed be unique, for it is more likely that his or her work will be interrupted by e-mail, beepers, meetings, coffee breaks, and socializing. Several estimates have been made regarding the percentage of a person's day that he or she can devote to project work. Past data that I have collected from information technology professionals indicates a range of 66 to 75 percent. More recently, among the same client base, I have seen a downward trend in this percentage to 50 to 65 percent. Using the 75 percent estimate means that a 10-hour task will require about 13 hours and 20 minutes to complete. That is without interruptions, which, of course, always happen. (Wysocki 2007: 165)

It is because of such interruptions that the amount of time spent at work is not equal to the actual time spent working (Robinson, Chenu and Alvarez 2002: 44).[6] Interruptions

---

6. A decrease in the number of interruptions is often cited as one reason why teleworkers are more productive than employees who work in the office (Illegems and Verbeke 2003; Verbeke 2006).

impact duration not only because they prevent the project team member from working on the activity at hand, but also because they entail task-switching. "Every time a worker is interrupted, it takes additional time to get to the level of productivity attained prior to the interruption," notes Wysocki (2007: 167). In other words, an interruption extends the duration by an amount of time greater than the interruption. Empirical studies demonstrate that performance degradation tends to increase with the complexity of the task (Speier, Valacich and Vessey 1999; Bailey and Konstan 2006) and that interruptions can have a residual effect well beyond the point in time at which the interruption occurs (Bailey and Konstan 2006). In any event, the project manager must estimate both the work effort and the duration of each project activity: work effort information is needed for quoting and billing, whereas duration information is needed for estimating completion dates and scheduling.

Various techniques can be used to estimate the work effort and duration of project activities, including expert judgment, analogous estimating, parametric estimating, and three-point estimating (PMI 2008: 149–151). As its name suggests, expert judgment involves the estimation of duration based on the knowledge of those who have much experience with the matter at hand. Analogous estimating is a technique whereby actual data from similar past projects is used to extrapolate, or project, the durations of activities in the current project. The reliability of the results obtained using analogous estimating depends on the degree of similarity between the previous projects and the current one. Parametric estimating is similar to analogous estimating in that it too relies on historical data, but extrapolates estimates by performing statistical analysis on historical duration data. The reliability of the results obtained using parametric estimating depends on the robustness of the statistical model and of the historical data. Finally, the three-point estimating technique involves a probabilistic calculation of the expected duration of an activity. Three-point estimating acknowledges that duration is itself a random variable and that the duration of a given activity will vary if repeated several times under identical conditions, and takes account of risk and variation in the estimation process. Thus, using the three point technique requires the preparation of three duration estimates: an optimistic estimate (the duration expected if everything goes perfectly); a pessimistic duration (the duration expected if everything that can go wrong does go wrong but the activity is completed nevertheless); and a most likely duration (the duration expected under normal or typical conditions). The estimated duration (E) is then calculated using the formula $E = (O + 4M + P) / 6$, where O is the optimistic estimate, M is the most likely estimate and P is the pessimistic estimate.

In the language industry, as in many other industries, work effort is typically estimated by dividing the volume of work by baseline productivity rates (or metrics) for each activity. This would be relatively straightforward if human translation was a mechanical process, rather than an intelligent, knowledge-based activity (Wilss 1994, 1996a, 1996b). The process by which translation input (source text) is transformed into output (target text) is inherently subjective: a target text represents the sum of all of the inferences and choices made by the translator, and the inferences and decisions made by one translator may be different from those that another translator would make. The subjective nature of human translation and the fact that the rate of translation output is affected by a host of factors, not the least of which is the individual translator himself or herself, raise fundamental questions about the very possibility of defining generic productivity rates.[7] The challenges of estimating translation and localization work effort and activity durations are compounded by the relative dearth of empirical translation and localization productivity data. In the absence of large-scale studies or industry initiatives to develop and validate productivity metrics, estimates are generally based on individual expert judgment or analogous estimates from previous projects completed by a given company or organization.

Various factors affect the calculation of output. For translation of English to/from Romance languages, output is typically estimated at approximately 2,500 words of source text per day (Bass 2006: 77; Chriss 2006: 35; McKay 2006: 88). As Bass points out, estimates of productivity in translation of English to/from Asian languages that require the use of an IME (Input Method Editor) are somewhat lower, ranging from 1,500–2,000 words per day (2006: 77).[8] These high-level baseline productivity rates notwithstanding, translation output can fluctuate significantly, from several hundred words a day to over 10,000 words a day, depending on many factors, not the least of which is the individual translator.[9] For example, the following factors will generally increase daily output:

- Clear scope and requirements
- The availability of a reliable (and, ideally, client-approved) translation memory
- The availability of a reliable (and, ideally, client-approved) terminological database
- The availability of style guides and of a corpus of pre-screened/pre-approved reference materials

---

7. In 2003, the Localization Institute announced the Localization Metrics Initiative (LMI), whose stated goal was "to define units of measurement primarily in the areas of time, cost, and quality to allow participating companies not only to track changes internally, but also to compare their numbers with industry averages" (Localization Institute 2003). The initiative was quietly shelved in 2005. Along similar lines, in 2004 the Localization Industry Standards Association announced that it would undertake work on GMX-C, a standard designed to "provide a notational mechanism for establishing the complexity level of a given task" in order to enable the relative quantification of work effort (Zydron 2004). GMX-C had not evolved beyond the level of an initial specification when LISA declared insolvency in late February, 2011.

8. The source-text word is generally used as the base unit when estimating productivity of translation of English to/from Romance languages. Other base units are also used, including characters per hour or day in the case of Asian languages, and lines of text per hour or day in the case of agglutinative languages such as German and Turkish.

9. For additional discussion of generic factors that should be considered when performing estimates, see Kliem and Ludin (1998: 69–70).

- Extensive experience, knowledge and expertise of the translator within the domain
- A history of performing similar work for this particular client
- Large project size (mental and administrative setup time represents a smaller proportion of the work effort in larger projects than in smaller projects, all other things being equal; for example, a single 10,000 word translation project requires less work effort than five unrelated 2,000 word projects of similar complexity in a given domain)
- Small number of files: administrative overhead is proportional to the number of project files
- Linear text (e.g., lengthy prose as in user documentation as opposed to isolated user interface strings)
- Translation in a WYSIWYG ("what you see is what you get") tool that enables display of the text in context
- Absence or limited number of cultural issues in source files
- Factual accuracy and limited number of flaws in source files
- Availability of subject-matter experts who can respond promptly to questions as they arise during the project
- The use of proven technology (e.g., CAT tools)
- Repetition in and across project files (assuming a CAT tool is used)
- Terminological and stylistic consistency in the source content

The absence of the items listed above will generally decrease daily translation output, as will the following factors:

- The newness or uniqueness of the domain
- The complexity of the source files and/or of the project domain
- Poor quality of the source files (which may manifest itself as unedited text, inconsistent formatting or markup, factual errors, and so forth)
- Syntactic, stylistic and/or terminological inconsistency in the source files
- The inability of the translator to display in context the text to be translated
- The need to manually confirm consistency of usage within or across files (e.g., between a user interface on one hand and Help or documentation on the other hand)
- The use of new or unproven technology (e.g., CAT tools)
- Source materials that require extensive cultural adaptation
- Translation into a language that requires the use of an IME
- The use of a translator who is working outside of her/his area of specialization

In addition, a translator's productivity may vary significantly over the course of a given project, particularly during software localization projects. Translation of user interface strings is inherently more time-consuming than translation of documentation. "In understanding text, a reader must not only be able to integrate information within sentences but also make connections across sentences to form a coherent discourse representation," as Rayner and Sereno observe (1994: 73). Making such connections is a relatively straightforward process when translating linear text such as user documentation. Such is not the case when translating software strings. Due to their non-linear structure and lack of narrative thread, software programs cannot be "read" in the same way as prose" (Dunne 2009: 197). Consequently, it can take up to ten times longer to translate a given number of words of user interface strings compared to the equivalent number of words of user documentation. Significant productivity variations such as these must also be taken into account when estimating work effort and activity durations in localization projects.

No validated, standardized metrics currently exist for other translation- and localization-related activities, such as proofreading, editing, desktop publishing or screen capturing. For example, some desktop publishing specialists or departments/companies quote the work by page. However, the scope of required work may differ from page to page within a given document. Moreover, work effort may differ by an order of magnitude (or more) depending on the tool and format in which the work is being performed (e.g., an Adobe InDesign document or Adobe FrameMaker book compared to a Microsoft Word document). Although most language service providers have presumably developed their own approach to estimating the work effort required to complete various project activities, guidelines, recommendations or research on possible factors that might impact the estimation of work effort or duration of translation- and localization-related activities are conspicuously absent from the literature. Given the custom nature of translation and localization work, and the number of factors that influence the work effort and duration of the various types of activities, it seems likely that the process of work effort and activity duration estimation will always depend largely on the expertise of the individual estimator (Forsyth 2006). In any event, an estimate by a definition nothing more than an educated guess (or a "guess in a clean shirt," to borrow a phrase from Ron Jeffries). "Apart from all of [the] factors that can influence activity duration, the reality is that durations will vary for no reason other than the statistical variation that arises because the duration is in fact a random variable" (Wysocki 2007: 168). Thus, paradoxically, the precise work effort and duration required to complete a given activity cannot be known until that activity has actually been completed.[10]

---

10. The problem with this approach is that most translation projects are billed using fixed-price contracts, according to industry expert Don DePalma (personal communication). Work effort estimates have a direct bearing on project cost estimates: costs are approximated by multiplying the estimated work effort (i.e., volume) by the appropriate cost metric, such as words of translation by the corresponding per-word cost of translation, or hours of proofreading by the corresponding hourly cost. These issues are exacerbated when translation or localization is carried out in parallel with Agile development projects, in which the scope is not fully defined upon project launch.

Having discussed the concepts of work effort and activity duration, and examined certain challenges associated with the estimation of work effort in translation and localization projects, let us now turn our attention back to the hypothetical Dynatorch project to illustrate the process of work effort estimation using the activities that comprise this scenario. In the sections that follow, we shall discuss in turn the estimation of work effort of the activities listed in Table 1. For the purposes of this discussion, it is assumed that the estimated work effort of the activities performed by the project manager, desktop publishing specialist and localization specialist reflects a work efficiency rate of 75%.

Receipt of project approval
For the purposes of this discussion, it is assumed that the project approval is received from the client in the form of a signed fax. Since this activity involves no work effort on the part of the project team, it has zero duration.

Schedule development
Given the relatively low technological complexity of this project and the limited number of constituent activities, it is estimated that schedule development would take at most one hour. Note that the project manager could create the project network diagram and preliminary schedule upon receipt of project approval, but finalization of the schedule would be contingent on the completion of file preparation and resource acquisition.

Resource acquisition
In this hypothetical scenario, the project manager would need to ensure that the DTP and localization specialists have no other commitments that might interfere with the schedule. He or she would also need to secure commitments from two external subcontractors, namely one translator and one proofreader. The major potential obstacle to doing so would be the domain of the project (i.e., CNC plasma torch cutting). For the purposes of this discussion, it is assumed that the project manager works on a regular basis with four French Canadian translators who have either formal training or work experience in mechanical engineering, and who also offer translation, editing, proofreading and testing services. Thus, the project manager would not need to locate and assess any new human resources in this scenario. If neither the DTP nor the localization specialist has any schedule conflict, and if both the translator and proofreader promptly commit to the project, it is estimated that this activity would take at most one hour. However, if the project manager does not know whether the preferred translator and preferred proofreader are available, the PM will need to send inquiries to each and allow several hours for them to respond. He or she would also need to allow for the possibility that the recipients will not respond or be unavailable, in which case it would be necessary to contact the next most qualified candidate. In

this latter scenario, the project manager might still estimate the work effort at 1 hour but estimate the duration as a full business day or more.

Project kick-off meeting
For the purposes of this discussion, it is assumed that the meeting will be held online using a Web conferencing tool. The work effort associated with the logistical preparations, creation and distribution of the agenda and other documentation is estimated at one hour, and the duration of the meeting itself is estimated at 30 minutes.

Insertion of editable callouts in source Word document to mask text embedded in drawings
Given the limited scope of the required work (five drawings containing 291 words, of which 112 are repeated), it is estimated that at most one hour would be required to complete this activity.

Preparation of project file
Importing the modified Word document into the CAT tool and saving the project file are two discrete activities in the project activity list (see Table 1). However, since they require the use of the same material resource (a CAT tool) and would presumably be performed sequentially by the same human resource (the project manager), these activities would typically be considered as one file preparation activity for scheduling purposes.

The amount of time required to import a Word document into a CAT tool and save the corresponding project file depends on a number of factors, including the size of the document, the extent of complex formatting (such as bulleted lists, tables, text boxes and callouts), the number of graphics, the number of styles, and the CAT tool being used, among other things. Many tools convert Word documents to and from Rich Text Format (*.rtf) in the process of text extraction. When such tools are used, the time required for text extraction (and the likelihood of problems) increases in proportion to the number of pages and the number of graphics in the file. In this case, based on the length of the document (120 pages), number of graphics (69 total, not all of which require adaptation), and drawing on prior experience extracting text from Word documents of a similar length, the project manager might estimate the duration of this activity at 15 minutes.

Many CAT tools enable text analysis in addition to extraction. This analysis compiles project-level statistics about the total number of translatable words in all source files, the number of words that can be fully or partially pre-translated using an existing translation memory, as well as the number of words in segments that are fully or partially repeated within and across project files.[11] It is assumed in this scenario that

---

11. Repetition and partial TM matches are evaluated on a sliding scale that can be defined by the user, but which typically ranges from 50% or 75% to 99%.

no translation memory is available for use in the project and that the translation of the user manual is thus being undertaken from scratch. The analysis of the modified Word document reveals that the source materials contain 31,300 words of translatable text, of which approximately 2,100 words are repeated. This information would serve as an input to estimations performed using word-based metrics, such as estimates of translation and proofreading work effort.

Translation of project file
As noted above, translation work effort is typically estimated using productivity metrics expressed in terms of words of source text per hour or day, with a rate of 2,500 words of source text per day being considered average. However, the domain of this hypothetical project (CNC-controlled plasma torch cutting) is relatively complex. In addition, it would be necessary during translation to ensure that the target-language terminology used in the manual is identical to that used in the user interface of the localized software (to avoid confusing the target users). In light of these considerations, the project manager might want to estimate the translation work effort in this project using a slightly more conservative metric of, say, 2,000 words of source text per day, or 250 source words per hour (assuming an eight-hour work day). Dividing the total volume of the translation (~31,000 words of source text) by the productivity rate (2,000 words of source text per day), yields an estimate that 15.5 work days would be required to complete the translation. However, the project manager might take into account the fact that the source materials contain 2,100 repeated words. Although this amount of volume appears roughly equivalent to one day's worth of productivity, the translator would still need to view and confirm these leveraged segments in context. Consequently, the project manager might decrease the estimated effort by less than a full work day to, say, 15 work days.

Capture of localized screens
The amount of time required to take screenshots depends on many factors, including the availability of installed and properly configured versions of the localized software from which to capture the screens (or, alternatively, the time required to install and configure the target software); the complexity of the software; the familiarity of the person capturing the screens with that software; the complexity of the procedures that the user would have to follow to display the screens to be captured; and the availability of a script or other documentation of those procedures, among other things. For the purposes of this illustration, it is assumed that the client has provided a VMware virtual machine image on which the localized software has been installed and properly configured, in addition to the script and sample files used in the creation of the source screen captures. Thus, relatively little setup time would be required. In addition, three dialog boxes account for more than 20 of the 57 screens in the manual. For example, the dialog box that displays the machine parameter settings contains 14 different tabs. Thus, the person capturing the localized screens would merely move from tab to tab,

updating the settings on each tab to reflect those of the source image, and capture an image of each tab as a separate screen. Given these considerations, the project manager might estimate that it would take three minutes to create each localized screen capture. Since the manual contains 57 unique screens (some images are used more than once), the total work effort associated with this activity would be estimated at three hours.

Output target Word document from translated project file
Drawing on prior experience generating target files from similar translated project files, the project manager might estimate the duration of this activity at 10 minutes.

Desktop publishing
"Desktop publishing" is an umbrella term for adaptation of non-text or presentational aspects beyond mere text, such as tables, bulleted lists, graphics, pie charts, scanned images, photos, advanced diagrams, and so forth. In this project, desktop publishing would entail replacement of the English screen captures with the corresponding target versions and formatting of the target Word document (which includes updating the table of contents). Since these activities would presumably be performed sequentially by the same person – the desktop publishing specialist – they would typically be considered as one desktop publishing activity for scheduling purposes.

Assuming that the target screens are properly labeled and organized, replacing the 63 source screen captures with the corresponding target versions would take at most one hour. Likewise, since this is a very simple document, updating the formatting and table of contents after integration of the target screen captures would take at most one hour. Thus, the aggregate total work effort of the desktop publishing activities is estimated to be two hours.

Proofreading of target Word document
Proofreading is a monolingual activity performed after translation that "focuses on checking for typographical errors, incorrect hyphenation and spelling, and improper formatting" (ASTM International 2006: 10). For the purposes of this discussion, it is assumed that the proofreader will work on the electronic version of the document and correct typos and other linguistic errors directly in the Microsoft Word file. As with translation, proofreading work effort is estimated using a productivity rate expressed in words per hour. Benchmark productivity rates published by professional organizations such as the Society for Editors and Proofreaders (2011), the Association of Freelance Editors, Proofreaders & Indexers (2011), and by translation and localization practitioners (Esselink 2000: 445; Müller 2007: 42) generally range from 2,000–3,000 words per hour depending on the complexity of the material, the formatting, the relative frequency of errors, and other factors. Given the technological complexity of the source material as well as the number of screenshots and graphics, the project manager would probably opt to estimate the work

effort using a more conservative productivity metric of 2,000 words per hour. The volume of the text amounts to 31,000 words. At 2,000 words per hour, proofreading this amount of text would require 15.5 hours.

Note that the project manager does not take account of repetition in the text when estimating the proofreading work effort. CAT tools automatically leverage and reuse translations of repeated segments, once those segments have been translated. However, proofreading is an entirely manual process and is subject to the inherent limitations of human memory. A proofreader does not necessarily notice or remember which segments are repetitions and which are not. The proofreader simply verifies the entire text, as well as the graphics and the formatting of the document. Consequently, repetition within or across project materials does not decrease the scope of the proofreading work effort.

Retaking of target screen captures
Assuming that the localization specialist has extensive experience in screen capturing and a good eye for detail, there will be few (if any) problems with the initial set of target screen captures. In this case, the project manager might budget one hour for possible retaking of screenshots.

Updating of translation memory to reflect linguistic changes
Assuming that the translator and proofreader have formal training and/or professional experience in the domain, the project manager might estimate the work effort of this activity at one hour.

Outputting contents of translation memory in *.tmx format
The duration of this activity is estimated at ten minutes.

Finalization of graphics and formatting of target Word document
Assuming minimal changes to the graphics and formatting, we will estimate that 30 minutes would suffice to finalize the document for delivery.

Delivery of modified source document, finalized target Word document and *.tmx file
For the purposes of this discussion, the modified source document, finalized Word document and translation memory will be delivered via upload to the client's secure FTP site. Performing the upload and confirming receipt of the files will take 15 minutes.

Creation and submission of project invoice
Assuming the use of templates or financial accounting software, fifteen minutes would suffice to complete this activity.

Project closure
For the purposes of this discussion, it is assumed that closure would entail an internal post-project review and archival of the project files and documentation. It is estimated that one hour would be necessary to complete this work.

Contingency reserve
Finally, project activity duration estimates may also include a schedule contingency reserve, which is also called a buffer or management reserve (PMI 2008: 151). Schedule contingency reserve is typically calculated as a percentage of the total duration of the project schedule (e.g., 5–10%). For example, the total duration of all activities in the hypothetical Dynatorch project is 19.2 business days. If the project manager wanted to include a 10% reserve in the schedule as a contingency against risks, then he or she would simply define an activity called "project buffer" or "management reserve" with a duration of 2 business days and schedule it immediately prior to delivery.

Used in conjunction with project scope data, productivity metrics enable the project manager to estimate the work effort associated with the various project activities, which in turn permits him or her to complete resource planning and finalize the project schedule.[12] It is important to note, however, that duration estimates are in fact *estimates*, rather than measurements. Indeed, work effort estimates may subsequently need to be adjusted to account for the assignment of human resources whose productivity rates are significantly higher or lower than those used to calculate the initial estimates. Likewise, work effort may prove to be greater or less than initially estimated due to any number of variables, such as those described above. Thus, it is critical that the project manager actively monitor the performance of the team to be able to identify potential problems and take corrective action on a timely basis.

Developing the schedule

Schedule development is the process whereby the project manager plans the precise dates on which each activity, and by extension the project as a whole, will start and end. Inputs to the schedule development process include (a) the list of project activities; (b) the project network diagram (i.e., the sequence of project activities); (c) the estimated work effort of each activity; and (d) the resources required to complete each activity. Inputs to the schedule development process may also include the project scope statement, if it contains constraints or assumptions that impact the schedule, enterprise environmental factors, such as scheduling or project management

---

[12]. In an analogous fashion, cost metrics are used in conjunction with project scope data to estimate how much the various project activities will cost, which in turn permits the project manager to complete cost budgeting and finalize the project budget.

software, as well as organizational process assets such as policies, procedures, templates or post-mortem documentation from similar past projects.

Schedule development is typically performed with the assistance of specialized software, such as Microsoft Project, AIT Projetex, JiveFusion Collaborate, MultiTrans Prism and Plunet Business Manager. The project manager first enters the date on which the project will begin. For the purposes of this discussion, it is assumed that the hypothetical Dynatorch project will begin at the start of business on Monday, March 21 with receipt of the client's approval to proceed. After entering the project start date, the project manager defines the working days and times during which work can be scheduled. For example, the full-time work week in most Western countries extends from Monday to Friday and comprises seven or eight hours per day. Weekends and holidays are not considered working days. Default working days and times of various locales are typically defined in scheduling software, but the PM can adjust the information as circumstances warrant (as in the case of "rush" projects, for instance). We will assume for the purposes of our hypothetical project that the work week extends from Monday through Friday and that working days comprise eight hours, 8:00 am to noon and from 1:00 pm to 5:00 pm.

After defining and/or modifying the working days and/or times, if necessary, the project manager enters the list of activities in the scheduling software and defines the sequence in which they must be performed (see Figure 3). (Note that this may already have been done as part of activity definition, activity sequencing and creation of the project network diagram.) More specifically, the project manager defines the sequence by specifying the predecessor(s) of each activity (except for the first, which has no predecessor). Scheduling software typically defines finish-to-start logical relationships between predecessor and successor activities. For example, referring to Figure 3 the predecessor of project file preparation (Task 3) is insertion of editable callouts in the source Word document (Task 2).[13] In other words, project file preparation cannot begin until editable callouts have been inserted in the source Word document to mask the text embedded in the drawings. In some cases, multiple activities may share a common predecessor. For example, referring again to Figure 3, Tasks 13 and 14 share proofreading of the target Word document (Task 11) as a predecessor. The linkage of multiple successor activities to a single predecessor in the project network diagram implies that the successor activities will be performed in parallel. However, undertaking activities in parallel may or may not be advisable or even possible, depending on the specific activities and the required human resources. Thus, decisions about parallel scheduling are typically made later in the schedule development process.

---

13. *Activity* and *task* are synonyms that denote "a component of work performed during the course of a project" (PMI 2008: 426).

	Task Name	Predecessors
1	Receive project approval	
2	Insert editable callouts in source Word doc	1
3	Prepare project file	2
4	Develop schedule	3
5	Acquire resources	4
6	Prepare for kick-off meeting	4
7	Kick-off meeting	5,6
8	Translate project file	7
9	Capture target screens	7
10	Output target Word document	8
11	Desktop publishing	9,10
12	Proofread target Word document	11
13	Retake target screen captures as needed	12
14	Update TM to reflect linguistic changes	12
15	Output contents of TM in *.tmx format	14
16	Finalize graphics/formatting of target doc	12,13
17	Contingency reserve	16
18	Deliver modifed source doc, target doc & TM	2,14,16,17
19	Invoice project	18
20	Close project	19

Figure 3. Preliminary project schedule draft in which activities and activity predecessors have been defined.

Next, the project manager enters the estimated work effort of each activity (see Figure 4). The scheduling software uses this information to calculate the corresponding finish date. For example, as noted above, the hypothetical Dynatorch project assumed to start on March 21 at 8:00 am. Referring to Figure 4, the first activity, receipt of project approval, is a project milestone and as such has zero duration. Since the first activity has zero duration, the system assumes that the second, extraction of text from the CAD drawings, will begin at 8:00 am on March 21. The estimated duration of this activity is 15 minutes. Consequently, the scheduling software automatically calculates that the extraction of text from the CAD drawings will finish at 8:15 am on March 21, at which point the successor activity, file preparation, can begin. Moreover, scheduling software distributes the work effort over working hours and days, thus automatically converting work effort to duration. For example, the work effort of translation in the Dynatorch project is estimated to be 15 working days, as noted above. Referring again to Figure 4, translation is scheduled to begin on March 21 and finish on April 11. Thus, although the estimated work effort is 15 working days, the duration of the activity is actually 22 calendar days (reflecting the fact that weekends are not working days).

	Task Name	Predecessors	Duration	Start	Finish	Resource Names
1	Receive project approval		0 days	Mar 21	Mar 21	PM
2	Insert editable callouts in source Word doc	1	1 hr	Mar 21	Mar 21	DTP specialist
3	Prepare project file	2	15 mins	Mar 21	Mar 21	PM
4	Develop schedule	3	1 hr	Mar 21	Mar 21	PM
5	Acquire resources	4	1 hr	Mar 21	Mar 21	PM
6	Prepare for kick-off meeting	4	1 hr	Mar 21	Mar 21	PM
7	Attend kick-off meeting	5,6	30 mins	Mar 21	Mar 21	PM,Translator,Proofrea
8	Translate project file	7	15 days	Mar 21	Apr 11	Translator
9	Capture target screens	7	3 hrs	Mar 21	Mar 21	Proofreader
10	Output target Word document	8	10 mins	Apr 11	Apr 11	PM
11	Perform desktop publishing	9,10	2 hrs	Apr 11	Apr 11	DTP specialist
12	Proofread target Word document	11	15.5 hrs	Apr 11	Apr 13	Proofreader
13	Retake target screen captures as needed	12	1 hr	Apr 13	Apr 13	Localization specialist
14	Update TM to reflect linguistic changes	12	1 hr	Apr 13	Apr 13	Proofreader
15	Output contents of TM in *.tmx format	14	10 mins	Apr 13	Apr 13	PM
16	Finalize graphics/formatting of target doc	12,13	30 mins	Apr 13	Apr 13	DTP specialist
17	Contingency reserve	16	2 days	Apr 13	Apr 15	
18	Deliver modifed source doc, target doc & TM	2,14,16,17	15 mins	Apr 15	Apr 15	PM
19	Invoice project	18	15 mins	Apr 15	Apr 15	PM
20	Close project	19	1 hr	Apr 15	Apr 18	PM

Figure 4. Preliminary project schedule in which activities, durations, start and finish dates, and resource assignments have all been specified.

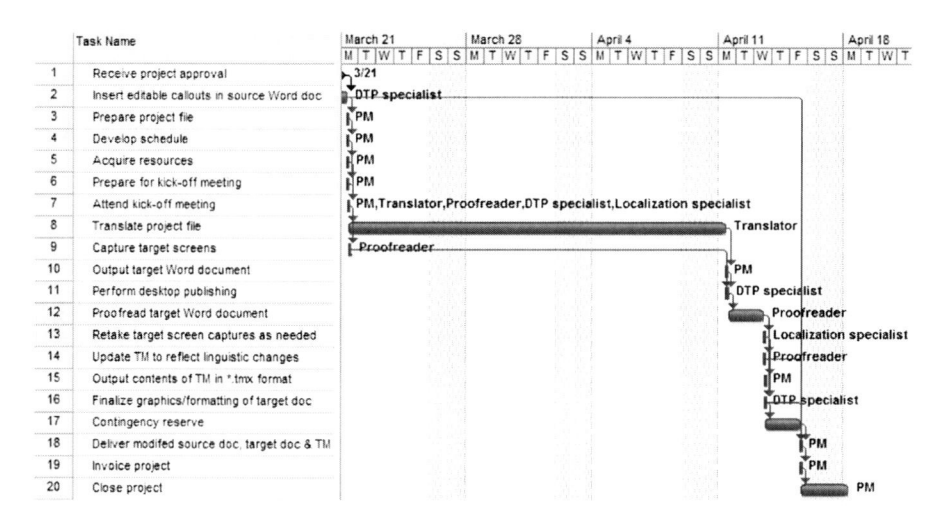

Figure 5. Gantt chart illustrating the sequence and duration of the various activities that comprise the hypothetical Dynatorch project. Each horizontal bar represents an activity and each arrow represents a predecessor-successor relationship.

	Task Name	Predecessors	Duration	Start	Finish
7	Kick-off meeting	5,6	30 mins	Mar 21	Mar 21
8	Translate project file	7FS+3 days	15 days	Mar 24	Apr 14
9	Capture target screens	7FS+3 days	3 hrs	Mar 24	Mar 24

Figure 6. Preliminary Dynatorch schedule in which a three-day lag has been specified between the project kick-off meeting and both translation and target screen capturing.

Finally, the project manager assigns a human resource to each activity (see Figure 4). If any project team member is only available for a limited number of hours per day, the project manager specifies the percentage of time that the team member can devote to his or her activities. Likewise, the project manager may also need to specify the percentage of work efficiency of project team members who are working in house, as discussed above. The project manager will also need to define FS dependencies for so-called "bottleneck" activities that are subject to resource constraints, such as those for which a single human resource is available (e.g., those that will be performed by the DTP specialist and by the localization specialist in the hypothetical Dynatorch project). Once all of the information about the activities, dependencies, work effort and human resource assignments has been entered, and necessary adjustments made to account for resource limitations or work efficiency, the preliminary schedule is complete.

Once the project manager has completed the preliminary schedule, he or she must determine whether it is viable as is or whether further refinements or modifications are required. If the client has specified a deadline, the primary consideration is whether the preliminary schedule will enable completion of the project on or before that deadline. If so, then the project schedule may not require modifications. Such is not usually the case in real-world projects, however. In addition, changing circumstances may impose new scheduling constraints in addition to those inherent in the dependencies and logical relationships between project activities, and the availability of the requisite human resources. For example, let us suppose that Dynatorch has promised to localized version to the software available to the translation team via the company's testing server, but discovers on the morning of Monday, March 21 that the server has suffered a catastrophic hardware failure over the weekend of March 19 and 20. In this scenario, Dynatorch contacts the language service provider at the start of business on March 21, advises the project manager of the problem. Furthermore, Dynatorch promises to create a virtual image of a desktop installation of the localized software, copy the virtual image to an external hard drive, and ship the hard drive to the language service provider by the end of business on March 23. In this case, because a localized copy of the software will not be available for target screen capturing or for consultation by the translator, the project manager might want to insert a lag, or delay, of 3 business days between the project kick-off meeting (Task 7) on one hand, and translation of the project file (Task 8) and capture of target screens (Task 9) on the other hand (see Figure 6).

If the preliminary schedule does not enable the completion of the project by the client's stated deadline, the project manager must decide whether to (a) decrease the project scope to the point where the project can be completed in the specified time frame; (b) decline to undertake the project; or (c) decrease the length of the schedule to meet the specified deadline. The first two alternatives are generally not viable options when managing outsourced translation and localization projects, so they will not be discussed here further. The following section will examine some of the ways in which the project manager can decrease the total duration of the schedule.

Schedule compression

In order to determine where and how the schedule can best be shortened, the project manager must first determine the project's critical path. When a schedule calls for activities to be performed in parallel, multiple paths can be traced through the project network diagram from initiation to conclusion. The critical path corresponds to the sequence of activities whose duration is the longest and that has no slack or float. Slack and float are synonymous terms that designate the amount of delay that can be tolerated in the starting time or completion time of an activity. Free slack or float corresponds to the amount of delay that can be tolerated without delaying the start of an immediate successor activity, whereas total slack or float corresponds to the amount of delay can be tolerated without delaying the completion of the project or violating a schedule constraint (PMI 2008: 435, 451; Wysocki 2007: 201). Thus, the critical path is the sequence of activities that determines the total project duration.[14] A delay in the completion of any activity located on the critical path will in turn delay the completion of the project. Once the project manager has identified the critical path, he or she can begin to examine the ways in which it can be shortened to enable project completion by the client's deadline. The process of shortening the schedule without changing the project scope in order to meet an imposed deadline or other schedule constraints is called *schedule compression* (PMI 2008: 156). Schedule compression techniques include crashing and fast-tracking.

Crashing involves the analysis of cost and time tradeoffs to ascertain what actions will enable the greatest reduction in schedule duration for the least amount of cost increase and with the least risk to project objectives. Examples of crashing in translation and localization projects could include paying rush fees to external subcontractors to expedite the completion of their activities, and assigning additional human resources to activities of relatively longer duration, an approach known as resource loading. In mathematical terms it would appear that assigning a second human resource to a given activity would decrease the estimated duration of the activity by half, that assigning a third human resource would decrease the estimated duration by two thirds, and so forth. However, duration is merely *influenced* by the number of human resources assigned to an activity; duration does not necessarily decrease in direct proportion to the number of people working on the activity. For example, different human resources may exhibit significantly different levels of productivity. In addition, the amount of administrative overhead rises in proportion to the number of people involved in a project, as does project risk. For instance, the more people assigned to a translation activity, the greater the risk of communication problems, stylistic and/or terminological inconsistencies, and errors that may require rework and thus delay completion of the activity. In any event, crashing is only an option for activities that

---

14. For more information and an illustration of critical path, see Lammers 230–232 in this volume.

can be expedited and/or partitioned among multiple resources. As Brooks observes, "When a task cannot be partitioned ... the application of more effort has no effect on the schedule. The bearing of a child takes nine months, no matter how many women are assigned" (1995: 17).

Fast-tracking is a schedule compression technique whereby activities that are normally performed in sequence are performed in parallel instead. An example will serve to illustrate this concept. Let us suppose that a project involves 10 business days of translation and five days of editing. Let us further suppose that the project manager normally defines a finish-to-start logical relationship between translation and editing.[15] In this scenario, the total duration of the activities is 15 business days (see Figure 7).

Figure 7. When a finish-to-start logical relationship is defined between two activities (here, translation and editing), those activities are performed in sequence.

Now let us suppose that the client requires that translation and editing be completed in 11 business days. In this scenario, the project manager could fast-track the editing activity by scheduling it to overlap with translation. For example, the project manager could change the logical relationship between translation and editing from finish-to-start to finish-to-finish and introduce a lag of four hours to enable editing of the final day's worth of translation. The net effect of this change would be to compress the schedule for the two activities from 15 business days to 10.5 business days (see Figure 8). In this scenario, the translator would be responsible for providing material to the editor on a rolling basis.[16]

Figure 8. Defining a finish-to-finish logical relationship between two activities causes them to be performed in parallel. The use of a lag may be necessary if the two tasks cannot finish simultaneously.

---

15. This example uses translation and editing for purposes of illustration only. Generally, it is not advisable to define finish-to-start logical relationship between translation and editing as doing so prevents timely feedback from the editing process to the translation process and increases the risk of rework. (For more information, see Dunne 170–171 in this volume.)

16. Server-based translation management systems that enable real-time collaboration can facilitate fast-tracking by eliminating the need for manual handoffs.

Alternatively, instead of changing the logical relationship between translation and editing in this scenario, the project manager could also compress the schedule by dividing the translation and editing work into, for example, five batches. As the translator completed each batch, the project manager would make it available to the editor. Partitioning translation and editing in this way would enable the project manager to decrease the duration of the two activities from 15 business days to 11 business days. This approach would increase the amount of coordination and communication associated with the two activities because the project manager would need to manage five sets of file handoffs from the translator to the editor, rather than a single handoff upon completion of translation as in the sequential schedule illustrated in Figure 7.

Once the project manager has made sufficient changes to enable the project to be completed by the required deadline, he or she must examine the human resource assignments to identify any conflicts or availability problems that may have resulted from the schedule compression. Once the schedule has been finalized, the project manager saves a baseline that he or she will subsequently use to compare planned progress and actual progress as part of the project monitoring process. Finally, the schedule development process may also require updates to other project documents. For example, the cost baseline may need to be modified if schedule compression will require payment of rush fees to subcontractors. Likewise, the risk register may need to be updated to account for any new threats or opportunities identified (or created) during schedule development. (For more information on the project risk register, see Lammers 219–222 in this volume.)

Controlling the schedule

By definition projects are unique, so work effort and duration estimates necessarily involve an element of uncertainty. Indeed, translation- and localization-related work effort is influenced by a wide range of variables, as noted above, and duration is a variable in and of itself. Ultimately, the schedule is a model that represents the project manager's educated and considered best guess as to the amount of time needed to complete the project. That being the case, the project manager cannot simply assume that all of the estimates will be accurate, but rather must monitor actual durations and compare them to planned durations to determine whether the project is on schedule, ahead of schedule or behind schedule.

Monitoring should be performed frequently enough and at a level of detail sufficient to allow early identification of variances and prompt corrective action. Variances can be both negative and positive. A negative schedule variance indicates that an activity (or project) is behind schedule, whereas a positive variance is an activity (or project) that is ahead of schedule. Negative variances typically result from activities that take longer than planned to complete. Some negative variances are cause for more concern than others. Negative variances associated with an activity not located on the critical path will generally not affect the completion date unless the slippage exceeds the activity's total float. Negative variances associated with critical path activities, on the other hand, are more serious because a delay in any critical path activity will in turn cause a delay in the completion of the project as a whole. Thus, the project manager should closely monitor all activities on the critical path for evidence of slippage. Positive variances would appear to be good news to the project manager. After all, it is far easier to fill time when it becomes available than to reclaim time once it is lost. However, positive variances can also cause problems if the project manager wants, needs, or is directed to remain ahead of schedule. Any schedule change, whether it is driven by a positive or negative variance, requires that the resource schedule for subsequent activities be adjusted accordingly. Such adjustments may cause problems if any human resources are not available during the new time frame in which their activity is scheduled.[17] Finally, the project manager can also compare the percentage of use of schedule contingency reserve to the percentage of completion of work at a given point in time to take the project's pulse. The use of contingency reserve at a rate lower than that of project progress (e.g., 50% of the project work has been completed and 20% contingency has been used) suggests that the project will completed on schedule. Conversely, the use of reserve at a rate that exceeds project progress suggests that the project will be completed late.

Schedule control involves not only monitoring project progress, but also revising the schedule as needed. Revisions may be warranted due to variances, as discussed above, or by changes to the project scope. Scope is treated as fixed for the purposes of scheduling, but can and often does change due to the uncertainty inherent in projects and the dynamic nature of the business environment. For example, referring to the hypothetical Dynatorch project scenario, the project manager might be contacted by the client in the latter stages in the project requesting the translation and insertion of a disclaimer that Dynatorch's legal counsel has just drafted to meet new legal requirements in Canada.

Since changes to project scope are not an uncommon occurrence, translation and localization project managers should plan for them. This can be done by defining a project change management process that addresses questions such as the following:

– Who can request changes?
– What are acceptable reasons for requesting changes?

---

17. Traditional project time management treats the critical path as primarily activity-driven and resource-independent. Critics argue that time management should focus on the longest sequence of activities as determined not only by activity dependencies, but also by resource constraints. This approach is known as the critical chain method. For more information, see Goldratt (1997) and Newbold (1998).

- How will change requests be submitted (i.e., via a form, template, etc.)?
- How will the project manager determine the impact of proposed changes on the schedule?
- Who will review change requests?
- Who will approve or reject change requests?
- If a change is approved, how will the schedule be updated?

Finally, as part of the project planning process, the project manager should also determine the format in which and the frequency with which the client will receive status updates. The progress reporting system should provide timely and accurate status information without adding significant overhead, and the reports should be easily understood by those who use them (Wysocki 2007: 321). Reports typically provide high-level information about the percentage of completion, based on duration, human resource effort or cost, and display the information in graphical format that enables the viewer to understand the project status at a glance. An example of a graphic status report is presented in Figure 9.

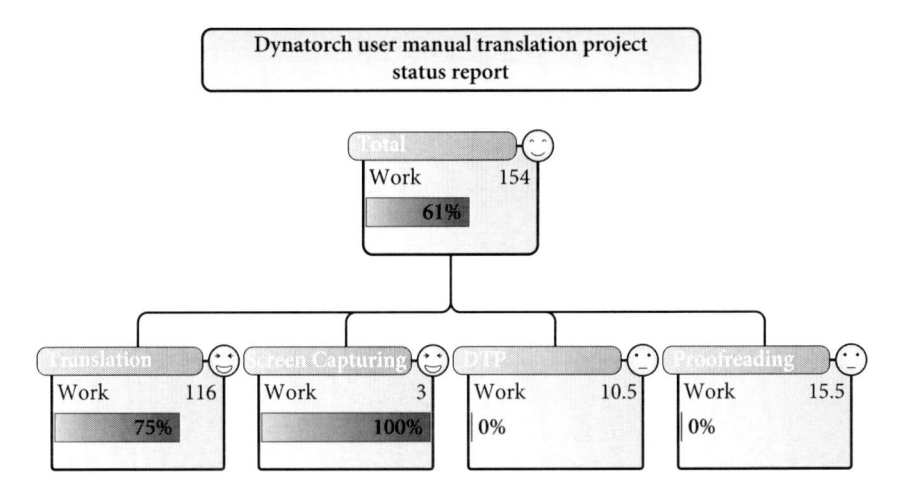

Figure 9. Sample status report illustrating the percentage of project work completed. Happy face = ahead of schedule; smiley faces = on schedule and indifferent face = not started. (Due to space limitations, not all activities are shown.)

Conclusion

Time and schedule are critical project constraints, but they are not the only constraints, nor are they necessarily the most important ones in a given translation or localization project. A schedule (and by extension delivery by a specified date) is not a goal or objective in itself. "The purpose of the schedule [is] planning, not goal-setting," notes DeMarco (2001:57). In other words, one must distinguish between doing the project right and doing the right project. Although each pays an important role in project success, it is crucial to recognize that doing the project right is a logistical consideration, whereas doing the right project is a business consideration, and the latter should take precedence over the former (Heerkens 2006:5). Consider the example of the procurement of the B-1B bomber by the U.S. Air Force in the 1980s. "Although the program ran close to budget and on schedule, the performance of the aircraft [was] a problem to which even proponents admitt[ed]," observes a case study of risk management in the program, which concludes that the program "[met] budget and scheduling constraints by not meeting performance goals" (Bodilly 1993:vi). The key point is that on time-delivery, and by extension adherence to the schedule, is necessary but not sufficient to achieve a successful project outcome. A project completed on time and within budget may still be deemed a failure if it does not generate value or effectively address the problem(s) it was undertaken to solve.

Competing constraints must be carefully balanced to optimize the value realized by the project. In the current market, although clients hold certain expectations about translation and localization project schedules, those expectations often do not reflect a clear understanding of project scope and of the time required to complete the work. Consequently, when requesting translation or localization services, clients may request (or stipulate) a deadline that is risky or unreasonable not out of malice, but simply because they do not know what the project will entail. Conversely, in the current market, suppliers often cannot say "no" or do not know when or how to do so; as Sikes (2007) observes, the response to a request for translation or localization services tends to be "yes" by default, even when the ratio of work volume to available time poses significant risk. The problem with this heroic approach to project management is that urgency can govern the *scheduled* completion of a project, but it cannot govern the *actual* completion date (Brooks 1995). Translation and localization project managers, and the organizations that employ them, must resist the temptation – or pressure, as the case may be – to allow urgency to trump other constraints when developing and managing project schedules and to move into the realm of post-heroic project management. The time management processes described by PMI and discussed in this chapter offer a standardized framework and repeatable methodology for doing just that.

Instead of responding "yes" by default to requests for specific deadlines or for decreases in the length of project schedules, translation and localization project managers should instead use such requests as an opportunity to discuss the risks and constraints with the project requestor, present one or more alternatives, and weigh the various options with respect to the requestor's objectives. This approach offers several advantages. By presenting alternatives and discussing the advantages and drawbacks to each, the translation or localization project manager ensures that the project requestor is in a position to make a fully informed decision about how to proceed, and that the requestor shares the responsibility and accountability for whatever decision is ultimately made. This approach also helps the parties to confirm that the requestor's requirements and expectations are aligned with the supplier's capabilities, thus minimizing the risk that one party, or both, will be dissatisfied by the project outcome (i.e., a proverbial win-lose or lose-lose situation).

Finally, research is needed to assess and quantify the impact on translator productivity of the factors discussed in this chapter. Research is also needed to identify other relevant variables that shape translation and localization performance, and to assess the influence thereof. Validated productivity data would provide an empirical basis on which to estimate the amount of time required to perform translation and localization tasks, and by extension, to complete translation and localization projects. The development and sharing of such information would be of great benefit to clients, practitioners, educators, scholars and students of translation and localization – in sum, to all industry stakeholders.

References

Association for Project Management (APM). 2010. *A History of the Association for Project Management*. Buckinghamshire: APM. http://apm.org.uk/sites/default/files/0.10.6_APM_History.pdf

Association of Freelance Editors, Proofreaders & Indexers. 2011. "FAQs [Frequently Asked Questions]." http://www.afepi.ie/faqs.htm

ASTM International. 2006. F 2575 – 06. *Standard Guide for Quality Assurance in Translation*. West Conshohocken, PA: ASTM International.

Bailey, Brian P. and Konstan, Joseph A. "On the need for attention-aware systems: Measuring effects of interruption on task performance, error rate and affective state." *Computers in Human Behavior* 24: 685–708.

Barnes, Martin. 2006. "Some origins of modern project management – A personal history." *PM World Today* VIII: 8 (August). http://www.pmforum.org/viewpoints/2006/08_4.htm

Bass, Scott. 2006. "Quality in the real world." In Perspectives on localization, Keiran J. Dunne (ed.), 69–94. Amsterdam/Philadelphia: John Benjamins.

Beath, Cynthia Mathis. 1986. Managing the User Relationship in Management Information Systems Projects: A Transaction Governance Approach. Ph.D. dissertation, University of California at Los Angeles.

Beninatto, Renato. 2011. "Three takeaways from Localization World Barcelona." *Localization Industry* 411 (Renato Beninatto's blog), June 21. http://www.l10n411.com/2011/06/three-takeaways-from-localization-world.html

Bodilly, Susan J. 1993. *Case Study of Risk Management in the USAF B-1B Bomber Program*. RAND Note N-3616-AF. Santa Monica, CA: RAND.

Brooks, Frederick P. 1995. *The Mythical Man-Month: Essays on Software Engineering*. Reading, MA: Addison-Wesley.

Chriss, Roger. 2006. *Translation as a Profession*. N.p.: Lulu.

DeMarco, Tom. 2001. *Slack: Getting Past Burnout, Busywork, and the Myth of Total Efficiency*. New York: Broadway Books.

Drucker, Peter F. 1967. *The Effective Executive*. New York: Harper & Row.

Dunne, Keiran J. 2009. "Assessing software localization: For a valid approach." In *Testing and Assessment in Translation and Interpreting Studies*, Claudia V. Angelelli and Holly E. Jacobson (eds), 185–222. Amsterdam/Philadelphia: John Benjamins.

Dynatorch. 2006. "Dynatorch CNC plasma cutter software user's manual." Paducah, KY: Dynatorch. http://www.dynatorch.com/downloads/SWManualNew4.doc

Esselink, Bert. 2000. *A Practical Guide to Localization*. Amsterdam/Philadelphia: John Benjamins.

Forsyth, Darryl. 2006. "Determiners of accuracy when making an expected duration estimation: The role of 'past' event/task saliency." Research Working Paper Number 7. Research Working Paper Series, Massey University Department of Management and International Business. http://www.massey.ac.nz/massey/fms//Colleges/College of Business/MIB/Documents/Working Paper Series/working paper 7 - darryl.pdf

Goldratt, Eliyahu M. 1997. *Critical Chain*. Great Barrington, MA: North River Press.

Gollner, Joe. 2009. "The emergence of intelligent content." *Whitepapers Old & New – The Fractal Enterprise*. http://jgollner.typepad.com/files/the-emergence-of-intelligent-content-jgollner-jan-2009.pdf

Heerkens, Gary. 2006. *The Business-Savvy Project Manager: Indispensable Knowledge and Skills for Success*. New York: McGraw-Hill.

Illegems, Viviane and Verbeke, Alain. 2003. *Moving Towards the Virtual Workplace: Managerial and Societal Perspectives*. Cheltenham, UK/Northhampton, MA: Edward Elgar.

Kezsbom, Deborah S., Schilling, Donald L. and Edward, Katherine A. 1989. *Dynamic Project Management: A Practical Guide for Managers and Engineers*. New York: Wiley.

Kliem, Ralph L. 1994. "The invisible cornerstone: The people side of project management." *Systems Practice* 7:6 (December) 699–705.

Kliem, Ralph L. and Ludin, Irwin S. 1998. *Project Management Practitioner's Handbook*. New York: AMACOM.

Localization Institute. 2003. "2003 special edition localization management roundtable." http://www.localizationinstitute.com/switchboard.cfm?category=roundtable&display=title&ID=10&Agenda=yes

McKay, Corinne. 2006. *How to Succeed as a Freelance Translator*. N.p.: Two Rat Press.

Miller, William C. 1989. *The Creative Edge: Fostering Innovation Where You Work*. New York: Basic Books.

Müller, Eva. 2007. "Measures to achieve quality in localization." *MultiLingual* 18:7 (Oct –Nov): 38–45.

Newbold, Robert C. 1998. *Project Management in the Fast Lane: Applying the Theory of Constraints*. Boca Raton, FL: St. Lucie Press.

Project Management Institute (PMI). 2007. *Practice Standard for Scheduling*. Newtown Square, PA: Project Management Institute.

———. 2008. *A Guide to the Project Management Body of Knowledge (PMBOK® Guide)*. 4th ed. Newtown Square, PA: Project Management Institute.

Rayner, Keith and Sereno, Sara C. 1994. "Eye movements in reading: Psycholinguistic studies." In *Handbook of Psycholinguistics*, M. A. Gernsbacher (ed.), 57–81. San Diego, CA: Academic Press.

Robinson, John P., Chenu, Alain and Alvarez, Anthony S. 2002. "Measuring the complexity of hours at work: The weekly work grid." *Monthly Labor Review* (April): 44–54.

Sikes, Richard. 2007. "Creating a framework for saying 'no.'" *MultiLingual* 18:5 (July–August): 37–42.

Society for Editors and Proofreaders. 2011. "FAQs: Using copy-editors and proofreaders." http://www.sfep.org.uk/pub/faqs/fusing.asp

Speier, Cheri, Valacich, Joseph S. and Vessey, Iris. 1999. "The influence of task interruption of individual decision-making: An information overload perspective." *Decision Sciences* 30:2 (Spring): 337–360.

Uyttewaal, Eric and Woolf, Murray. 2011. "A call to action: What is a project 'schedule?'" MPUG (Microsoft Project Users Group), Jan. 13. http://www.mpug.com/News/Pages/A-Call-to-Action-What-is-a-Project-Schedule.aspx

Verbeke, Alain. 2006. *Growing the Virtual Workplace: The Integrative Value Proposition for Telework*. Cheltenham, UK/Northhampton, MA: Edward Elgar.

Wilss, Wolfram. 1994. "Translation as a knowledge-based activity: Context, culture, and cognition". In *Language, Discourse and Translation in the West and Middle East*, Robert de Beaugrande, Abdullah Shunnaq and Mohamed Helmy Heliel (eds), 35–44. Amsterdam/Philadelphia: John Benjamins.

———. 1996a. *Knowledge and Skills in Translator Behavior*. Amsterdam/Philadelphia: John Benjamins.

———. 1996b. "Translation as intelligent behaviour." In *Terminology, LSP and Translation*, Harold Somers (ed.), 161–168. Amsterdam/Philadelphia: John Benjamins.

Wysocki, Robert K. 2007. *Effective Project Management: Traditional, Adaptive, Extreme*. 4th ed. Indianapolis, IN: Wiley.

Zydron, Andrzej. 2004. "GILT metrics – Slaying the word count dragon." *Globalization Insider* 13 (4.1). http://www.lisa.org/globalizationinsider/2004/11/gilt_metrics__s.html

From vicious to virtuous cycle
Customer-focused translation quality management using ISO 9001 principles and Agile methodologies

Keiran J. Dunne

> Quality is value to some person.
> Gerald Weinberg
>
> Agility might be said to be about encountering all of the problems so early and so often that the effort to fix them is less than the pain of enduring them.
> Ron Jeffries

This chapter discusses the challenges of customer-focused quality management in outsourced translation and localization projects. Current quality management theory, which frames quality in terms of customer satisfaction, suggests that quality cannot be *defined*, but rather must be *modeled* based on customer requirements. However, most customers cannot state their quality requirements and no consensus currently exists as to the operational definition of quality as a variable in translation and localization projects. These challenges are exacerbated by traditional project management approaches, in which customer quality assessment is undertaken in the final stages of a project based on preferences (unidentified needs) rather than requirements (identified needs). Agile project management methodologies offer effective strategies for overcoming these problems, but require significant changes in approaches to project management and to client review, as well as a greater degree of client involvement.

Introduction: Quality is in the eye of the beholder

The phrase "beauty is in the eye of the beholder" is a truism in art and literature. Over the past thirty years, this phrase has also firmly established itself in the realm of business, where "quality" substitutes for "beauty." As Peter Drucker observed in 1985:

> "Quality" in a product or service is not what the supplier puts in. It is what the customer gets out and is willing to pay for. A product is not "quality" because it is hard to make and costs a lot of money, as manufacturers typically believe. That

> is incompetence. Customers pay only for what is of use to them and gives them value. Nothing else constitutes "quality." (228)

Indeed, in the current market, quality is not viewed as an absolute but rather is framed in terms of customer satisfaction.[1] This makes perfect sense: after all, any company that wants to remain in business must satisfy its customers. However, the notion that quality is whatever the customer says it is presents significant challenges in language projects.

Translation and localization project management students, scholars, educators and practitioners who seek guidance on quality management can consult project management standards, such as *A Guide to the Project Management Body of Knowledge (PMBOK® Guide)* published by the Project Management Institute (PMI), or dedicated quality management standards, such as those published by the International Organization for Standardization (ISO). Currently, the approach most widely adopted in industry is that of *ISO 9001:2008, Quality Management Systems*, which has been implemented by over one million organizations in more than 175 countries (ISO 2011). ISO quality management principles have also been widely adopted in the realm of project management. In fact, the Project Management Institute explicitly states that its approach to quality management is intended to be compatible with that of ISO (PMI 2008: 190). Thus, using the ISO 9001:2008 standard as a frame of reference, this chapter examines some of the problems inherent in the customer-focused approach to quality management in outsourced translation and localization projects, and discusses some possible solutions to those problems.[2]

The process-based approach to project management

The ISO 9000 family of standards shares a common point of departure with project management standards such as the *PMBOK Guide* in that they all advocate the adoption of a process-based approach. A process is any managed activity or set of activities in which knowledge, skills, tools, techniques and resources are used to transform inputs into outputs (ISO 2008: vi; PMI 2008: 37) (see Figure 1). Examples of processes in translation and localization projects include, but are not limited to, scope definition, requirements development, terminology extraction, translation and proofreading.

---

1. A customer is a person or an organization that receives the project deliverables, and not merely the person who pays for the project; a customer can be internal or external to the organization (ISO 2005: 10).

2. Although a number of translation-specific product and process quality standards exist, they have achieved little visibility beyond the relatively closed circle of language industry practitioners (Kelly, Beninatto and DePalma 2008). For a detailed overview of language industry standards, see Wright (2006).

Customer-focused quality management using ISO and Agile 155

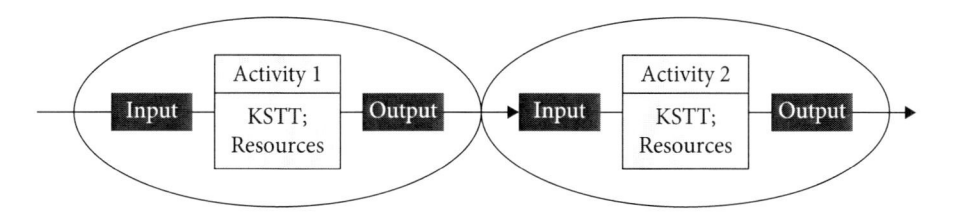

Figure 1. A process is an activity or set of activities whereby knowledge, skills, tools, techniques (KSTT) and resources are used and managed to accomplish the transformation of inputs into outputs.

Often the output from one activity comprises the input to the subsequent activity. For example, in a translation project, the output of termbase creation comprises an input to translation; the output of translation comprises an input to editing; and so forth. According to ISO, "[t]he application of a system of processes within an organization, together with the identification and interactions of these processes, and their management to produce the desired outcome, can be referred to as the 'process approach' " (2008: vi).

The process-based approach to quality management

The process-based approach to quality management emphasizes the importance of four fundamental concepts:

1. understanding and meeting requirements,
2. considering processes in terms of added value,
3. obtaining results of process performance and effectiveness, and
4. improving processes on a continual basis and based on objective measurement (ISO 2008: v–vi).

According to ISO, achieving quality is a matter of *specifying and meeting customer requirements* (see Figure 2). Before beginning a project, the customer and vendor consult in order to ensure that the customer requirements are properly understood and documented. This documentation, in turn, provides the specification against which the product will ultimately be evaluated to assess its conformance to the requirements. The vendor then develops and implements the project and product quality plans needed to meet the specified requirements. The set of project and product quality plans constitutes the vendor's quality assurance (QA) processes. During the creation of the product, measurement and analysis of the output are performed at each step to ensure compliance with the vendor's QA processes and standards. These verifications, which comprise the vendor's quality control (QC) procedures, ensure the proper implementation of QA processes and conformance of output to QA standards.

Upon completion and delivery of the product, measurement and analysis are conducted with respect to the customer's requirements, and feedback is solicited from the customer in order to identify areas for improvement.

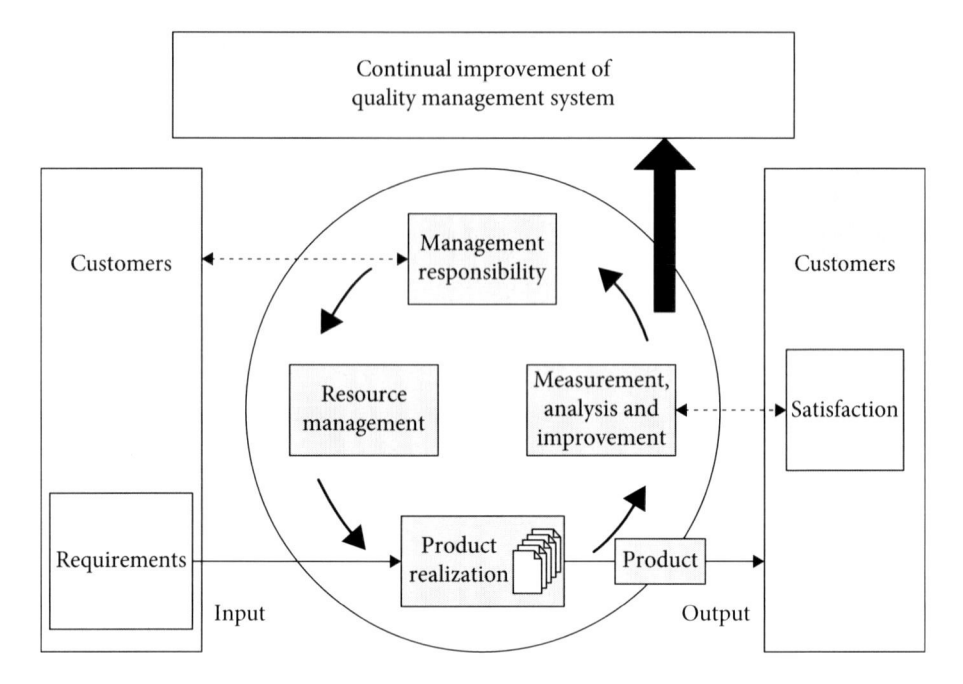

Figure 2. A process-based approach to quality management. The solid arrows represent value-adding activities, whereas the dotted arrows represent the flow of information.

Critical characteristics of process-based, customer-focused quality management

Three aspects of the customer-focused approach to quality management merit special attention for the purposes of our discussion: (a) the specific meaning of the noun "quality," (b) the criticality of requirements, and (c) the distinction between conformance to requirements and customer satisfaction. In the sections that follow, we shall examine each of these three notions in turn.

Quality: A source of fundamental terminological confusion

The noun "quality" can mean both *degree of excellence* and *an intrinsic characteristic, property or attribute*. This polysemy is the source of a fundamental terminological confusion. In common usage, "quality" is typically understood to mean "degree of excellence." However, neither the ISO 9000 family of standards nor *The PMBOK Guide* equates the concept of quality with degree of excellence. In ISO parlance, quality is understood in terms of intrinsic characteristics, properties or attributes. Indeed, the ISO 9000 standard explicitly defines quality as the "degree to which a set of inherent *characteristics* fulfils *requirements*" (ISO 2005:7; emphasis in the original). *The PMBOK Guide* in turn uses the ISO definition of quality as its own (PMI 2008:190, 345, 445). Consequently, the phrase "quality management" as used by ISO and PMI does not mean *management of quality*, understood as excellence, but rather *management of qualities*, understood as intrinsic characteristics that influence the ability of the product to meet the customer's requirements.[3]

An example will serve to illustrate this distinction. Suppose a customer orders a metric ton (1000 kg) of the chemical compound isopropanol, commonly known as isopropyl alcohol or rubbing alcohol (chemical formula: $[CH_3]_2CHOH$) from a chemical supplier. Isopropanol has a number of qualities, such as appearance, boiling point, flammability, flash point, melting point, odor, pH, solubility, stability, toxicity, vapor density, vapor pressure, and volatility, among others. In this scenario, "quality management" describes the management of those qualities or characteristics that influence the ability of the isopropanol to meet the customer's requirements. The relevant qualities would depend on the requirements specified by the customer, and by extension, on the intended use, i.e., as an antiseptic, a fuel source, a solvent for lipophilic compounds such as oils, or something else. Thus, customers who intend to use the isopropanol as a fuel source will be more concerned about thermodynamic qualities than those who intend to use it as an antiseptic, for instance. Similarly, the requirements in a translation project would vary considerably depending on the text type (e.g., user manual vs. marketing brochure) and the wants, needs and expectations of the users in a given target locale, among other things.

Thus, quality is not an *absolute*, but rather a *construct* whose operational variables are the characteristics of the product or service that impact its ability to fulfill the requirements specified by the customer (or that impact the customer's perception that the requirements have or have not been met). The requirements should specify both the product (formal characteristics) and the intended use of the product (fitness for use characteristics). The fact that the customer's requirements are themselves contextually bound and depend on the specific objectives that the project was undertaken to meet (e.g., to respond to market demand, fulfill a customer request, meet a legal requirement, etc.) underscores the inherent constructedness and fundamentally subjective nature of customer-focused quality. In sum, in the customer-focused approach, creating a universally valid definition of quality is a logical impossibility. Instead, quality must be *modeled* on a per-project basis. The importance of this distinction cannot be overstated.

---

3. For a detailed discussion of the ISO quality management philosophy, see Praxiom (2008).

The criticality – and conundrum – of requirements

"Quality" ultimately reflects the extent to which customer requirements are accurately and adequately captured, communicated, and expressed in the final product. However, this concept of quality as the fulfillment of customer requirements poses significant challenges. Capturing, communicating and meeting requirements is inherently difficult because what customers say they want is often not what they really need, and what they say they want may not be correctly heard, understood, communicated or implemented by the project team (see Figure 3). Requirements collection is arguably one of the most challenging and risky aspects of scope definition, and by extension, of project management:

> If the project manager blindly accepts what the clients say they want and proceeds with the project on that basis, then the project manager is in for a rude awakening. Often in the process of building the solution, the client[s] [learn] that what they need is not the same as what they requested. Here you have the basis for rolling deadlines, scope creep, and an endless trail of changes and reworks. It's no wonder that 70-plus percent of projects fail. (Wysocki 2007: xxxiv)

In 2008, IAG Consulting published the results of a study of requirements gathering in software development projects carried out by 110 midsized and Fortune 1000 companies in North America. The study examined projects in excess of $250,000 that delivered "significant new functionality" to their organizations; the size of the average project was $3 million. The study found that in 68% of companies surveyed, project success was deemed improbable due to a failure to adequately or properly gather requirements: "Projects *might* succeed – but not by *design*" (Ellis 2008: 1). In addition, 50% of this group's projects were categorized as "runaways," defined as projects that exhibited any two of the following three characteristics: (a) exceeding the allotted timeline by more than 80%; (b) exceeding the estimated budget more than 60%; (c) delivering less than 70% of the required functionality. Such results confirm and reinforce Berry's conclusion that developers are doing a good job of implementing of what they *think* customers want, but they are doing a poor job of *knowing* what customers want (2000: 44).

In translation and localization projects, the challenges of requirements gathering are exacerbated by the introduction of variables such as foreign languages and cultures:

> [T]he Skopos of the translation must be formalized and clearly set out before the translator can actually start work. The process of defining the Skopos of a translation is included in what is called the translation brief (Vermeer 1989, Kussmaul 1995 and Nord 1997). We can look at the translation brief as a form of project specification which sets out the requirements for the service / product to be provided. Ideally, such a brief would be quite specific about the intended

Customer-focused quality management using ISO and Agile   159

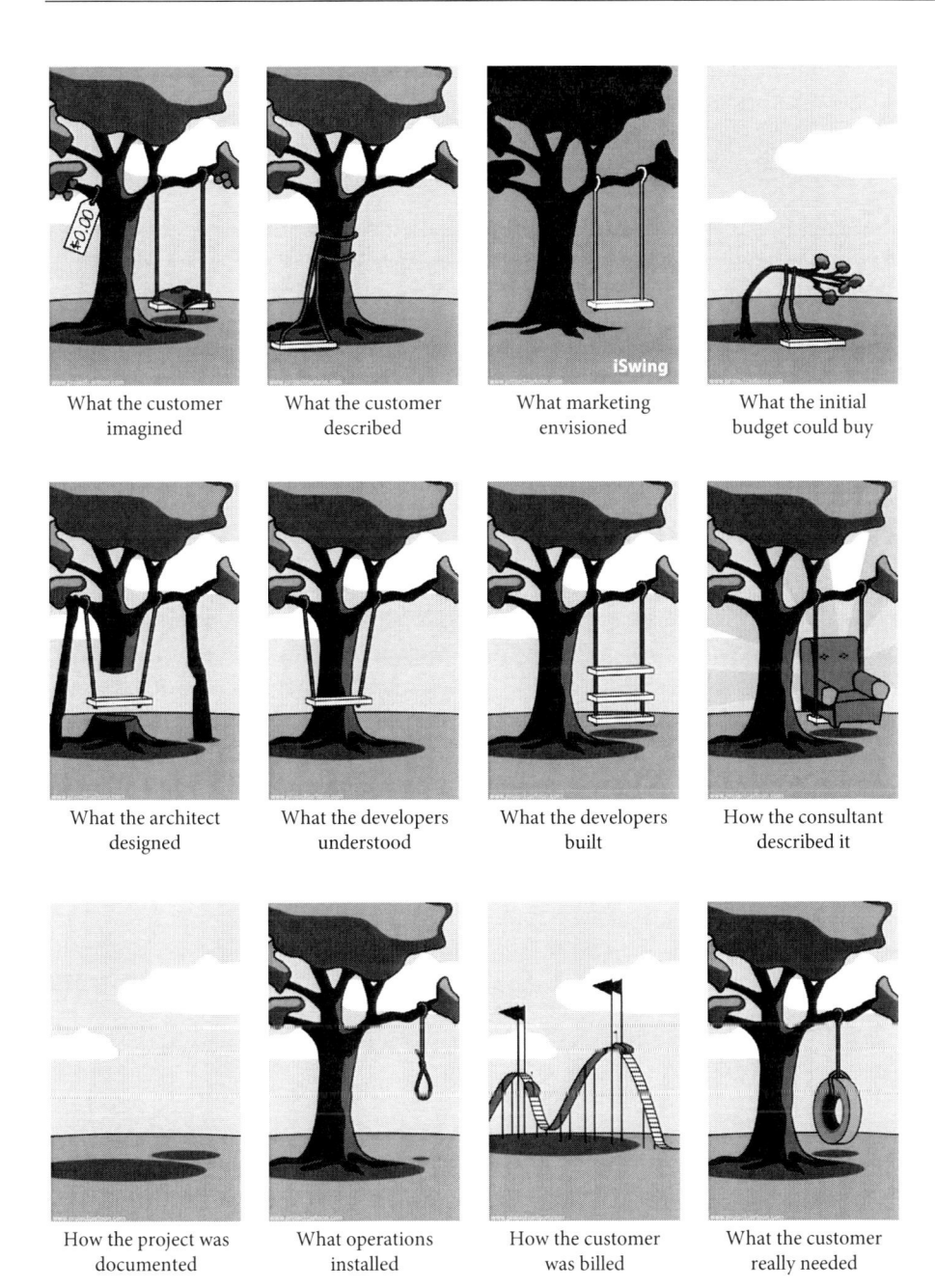

What the customer imagined	What the customer described	What marketing envisioned	What the initial budget could buy
What the architect designed	What the developers understood	What the developers built	How the consultant described it
How the project was documented	What operations installed	How the customer was billed	What the customer really needed

Figure 3. The wants-needs gap: the difficulty of determining, communicating and meeting customer requirements. Adapted from "How projects really work," © 2006 projectcartoon.com.

> function of the translation, the target audience, the time, place and medium as well as purpose. The problem with this concept is that the client who initiates a translation is rarely a language professional and usually has no specialized linguistic knowledge.
> (Byrne 2006: 39–40)

Thus is born a vicious cycle: customer-focused quality management requires that clients specify their requirements; however, translation customers often *cannot* specify their requirements because that they have little or no knowledge of the languages, cultures, conventions, and legal requirements of the target locales (Dunne 2006). In fact, lack of such knowledge plays a major role in many clients' decision to outsource translation in the first place (Shreve 2000). These problems are magnified in localization projects, which present a greater degree of complexity than document translation projects.

For these reasons, the bidirectional flow of information and communication about requirements portrayed in Figure 2 is often lacking in translation and localization projects, with the result that the specification is unclear and/or incomplete. In the absence of a clear, comprehensive set of *identified* customer needs (requirements), "quality" is shaped largely by *unidentified* customer needs (expectations). In such cases, the responsibility for specifying requirements falls upon the service provider by default (Koo and Kinds 2000).[4] However, undertaking project work without having first documented the customer's requirements as clearly and completely as possible represents a significant deviation from the principles of customer-focused quality management and represents a significant source of project risk, as we shall see. After all, the degree to which a product or service conforms to the customer's requirements cannot be evaluated if those requirements have not been clearly and completely specified. Moreover, proceeding on the basis of expectations is ill advised since the customer's expectations may ultimately prove to be very different from those of the service provider.

Conformance to requirements and customer satisfaction are not synonymous

The third aspect of the ISO 9001 approach to quality management that is critical for our discussion is the fact that that ISO clearly distinguishes between conformance to requirements and customer satisfaction: "[m]onitoring of customer satisfaction requires the evaluation of information relating to *customer perception as to whether*

---

4. This problem is compounded by language industry quality standards, which "vary widely and are prone to subjective interpretation by individuals and organizations alike" (Kelly, Beninatto and DePalma 2008:1). For a critical discussion of quality assessment in the realm of software localization, see Dunne (2009).

the organization has met the customer requirements" (ISO 2008: vi; emphasis added). In other words, the customer's *perception* as to whether the requirements have been met trumps formal compliance with those requirements. Conformance to the specification is necessary, but not sufficient in itself, to ensure customer satisfaction. PMI echoes ISO, noting that customer satisfaction "requires a combination of conformance to requirements (to ensure the project produces what it was created to produce) and fitness for use (the product or service must satisfy real needs)" (2008: 190).

The evaluation of conformance to requirements and fitness for use are known as *verification* and *validation*, respectively (see Figure 4.) Verification and validation underscore the criticality of clear, complete requirements. Suppose, for example, that the customer's needs are not specified clearly and completely, that the needs evolve over the course of the project and ultimately diverge from the specification, or that the specification addresses formal characteristics but not the intended use of the product. In any of these scenarios, a significant gap may exist between what the requirements specify and what the customer tacitly wants or expects. In such cases, the product may conform perfectly to the specification, such as it is. However, there is a risk that validation will reveal the fact that what has been produced is ultimately not what the customer wanted or needed (see Figure 2).

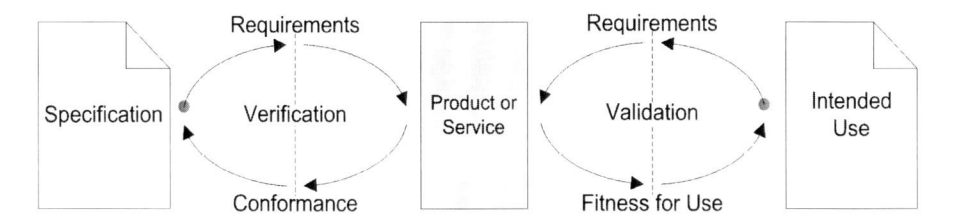

Figure 4. Verification evaluates internal quality by assessing conformance to specified requirements (left-hand loop), whereas validation evaluates external quality by assessing fitness for use (right-hand loop).

To avoid client dissatisfaction and perceptions of poor product and/or service quality, it is critical to document the customer's requirements as clearly and completely as possible *before* commencing the project. The requirements specification should encompass both the formal characteristics of the product as well as the intended use of the product. Project success is subsequently measured by the degree to which the client perceives that (a) the deliverables fulfill the specified requirements, and (b) the deliverables are fit for their intended use(s). The process of identifying, documenting and fulfilling requirements is easier said than done, however, and these challenges can be exacerbated by the project management methodology, as we shall see.

The relationship between requirements and project management methodology

The foregoing discussion suggests that the project management methodology should be chosen based on the relative clarity with which the project requirements, and the ways to fulfill them, are understood and specified. In the past decade, this idea has gained mainstream acceptance in the realms of software engineering and product development, but it does not yet appear to have firmly taken root in the language industry. In the following sections, we will examine the main approaches to project management and the ways in which they influence the ability of the project team to achieve quality results by meeting the customer's requirements.

The linear or "waterfall" model

Traditional project management practices arose and evolved in the first half of the twentieth century in the fields of engineering and construction, in which project teams "expected (and got) a clear statement from clients as to what they wanted, when they wanted it, and how much they were willing to pay for it" (Wysocki 2007: 45). Because the project teams clearly understood what the customer needed and how to provide it, they were able to create clear, comprehensive project plans. Moreover, because those plans did not generally require subsequent modification, the path from plan to goal was linear: adherence to the initial project plan sufficed to fulfill the customer's requirements.

The expectation that project teams would receive a clear and complete set of requirements prior to beginning any project work gave rise to the traditional project management approach known as the linear or "waterfall" model (see Figure 5). As its name suggests, the linear model proceeds in sequential fashion. Each phase must be completed before the subsequent phase can begin.

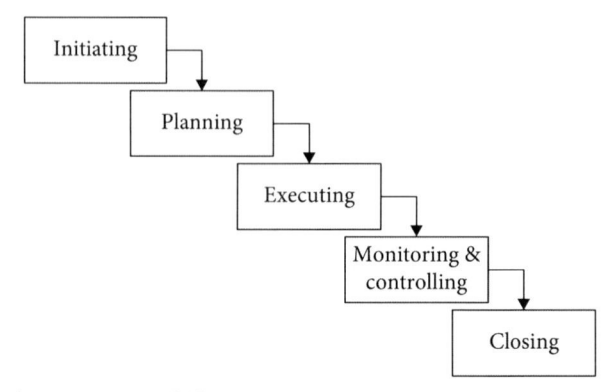

Figure 5. The linear or "waterfall" approach to project management (adapted from PMI 2008: 40 and Wysocki 2007: 49).

Experts point out that the problems with the linear approach are twofold.[5] First, it forces a comprehensive determination of client needs up front, during the scope definition phase. However, as we have seen, this is not always possible, especially in translation projects. In addition, because it calls for phases to be completed in lock-step, the linear approach is change-intolerant: the customer does not see or use the project deliverables until the project is complete. In the absence of upstream feedback loops, lessons learned during the execution and monitoring phases cannot be used to update or improve the project plan. Likewise, changes requested by the customer after the project has been launched will not only disrupt the schedule, but may also require rework in upstream processes, which in turn may delay the project completion. In the worst-case scenario, the project will have to be undertaken in its entirety a second time, incurring schedule and/or budget overruns of up to 100 per cent (Royce 1970/1987). An example will serve to illustrate the problems inherent in the linear project model.

> During a trade fair in the 1990s, a company drafted a Romanian/German bilingual contract, stipulating the delivery of 3,000 cars, half black, half yellow. Obviously, the firm wanted 1,500 yellow cars and 1,500 black. What happened (as a result of mistranslation) was that all products had yellow hoods (half yellow) while the rest was black (the other approximate half). The contractor did not accept them and a new lot with the correct specifications had to be manufactured. The initial products were delivered to the domestic market and became taxis.
> (Cismas 2010: 492)

In this case, the failure to confirm the correctness and completeness of the requirements prior to production combined with any form of customer inspection prior to delivery resulted in the production of 3,000 cars that were refused by the customer, requiring that the project be undertaken a second time in its entirety. Although this may be an extreme example, it nevertheless illustrates the high risk of rework associated with the linear project management model given the lack of customer feedback prior to delivery, if either the project requirements or the work that must be performed to fulfill those requirements are poorly understood.

As noted above, one of the fundamental aspects of the process-based approach to quality management is considering processes in terms of added value. In other words, quality management seeks to minimize the number of non-value-adding processes. The linear model actually hinders the achievement of this goal if the project presents a significant degree of uncertainty.

---

5. See for example Wysocki (2007: xxxii–xl and 44–47); Kerzner and Saladis (2009: 1–59); and Kerzner (2010: 1–11).

The incremental or "staged delivery" model

One way to address the problem of unclear, incomplete or changing project requirements is to adopt an incremental approach, whereby project work is partitioned or divided into chunks, each of which is undertaken according to the initial set of requirements. Intermediate and final deliverables may subsequently undergo multiple iterations based on customer feedback before the customer formally accepts them (see Figure 6). Because it is change-tolerant, the incremental approach can help reduce both the risk and the scope of rework compared to the linear approach. The incremental model encourages the customer to evaluate intermediate deliverables and suggest improvements. The smaller the chunks into which the project is partitioned, the earlier in the execution phase the chunks are evaluated, and the greater the frequency with which the customer provides feedback, the better the project team is positioned to identify any changes to requirements. Incrementally updating the project specification to reflect evolving requirements helps the project team to ensure that the deliverables are aligned with the customer's wants, needs and expectations. The incremental model also allows the customer to confirm much earlier than the linear model that the project is delivering the desired value.

Many project managers end up adopting an incremental approach not by design but rather by necessity in the latter stages of projects because they fail to specify customer requirements clearly and completely during scope definition or they fail to capture evolving requirements after project launch. Indeed, in 2007 project management expert Robert Wysocki noted that most PMs with whom he had discussed the problem of unclear and changing requirements over the previous several years admitted that "they deliver according to the original requirements and then iterate one or more times before they satisfy the client's current requirements" (2007: xxxiv). In other words, these project managers provide the client with a complete set of deliverables and then perform one or more rounds of rework until the customer is satisfied, much like the producer of the "half black, half yellow" cars discussed above.

Viewed from this perspective, the linear model can be thought of as an instance of the incremental approach that includes only one increment. Rework undertaken to satisfy the updated or complete set of customer requirements constitutes a second increment in addition to the one performed in the traditional linear model. Although this *ad hoc* approach comprises two increments, it lacks the partitioning of work, staggered deliveries and feedback loops that characterize the true incremental approach, and thus is more rightly considered a modified version of the waterfall model (see Figure 7).

Although Wysocki argues that "discovering the requirements during execution/construction is so inefficient and detrimental that we will assume that no competent and right-thinking person would do so" (2007: 103), his remarks suggest that this is in

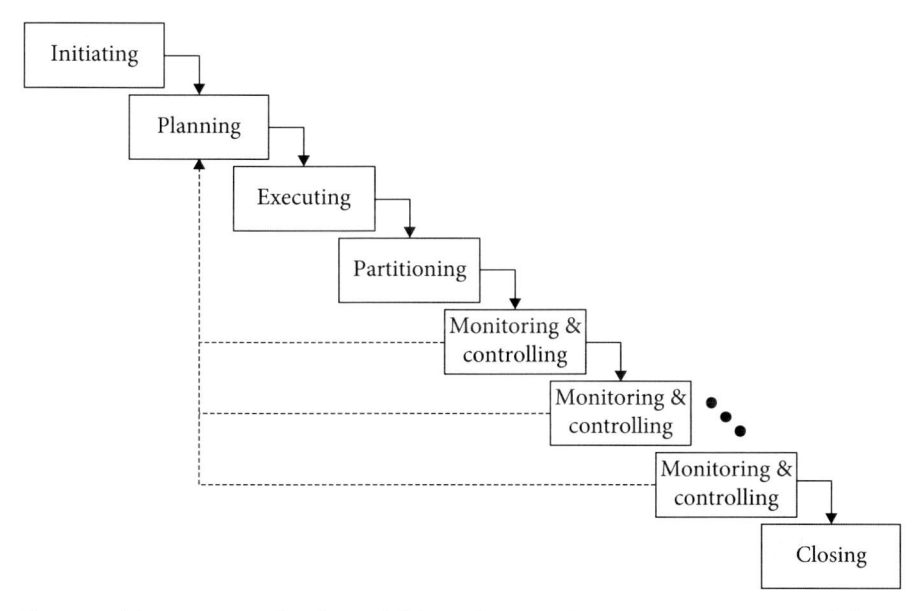

Figure 6. The incremental or "staged delivery" approach to project management (adapted from PMI 2008: 40 and Wysocki 2007: 50, 59). Variants include the Spiral model (Boehm 1986, 1988) and Rapid Application Development (Martin 1991).

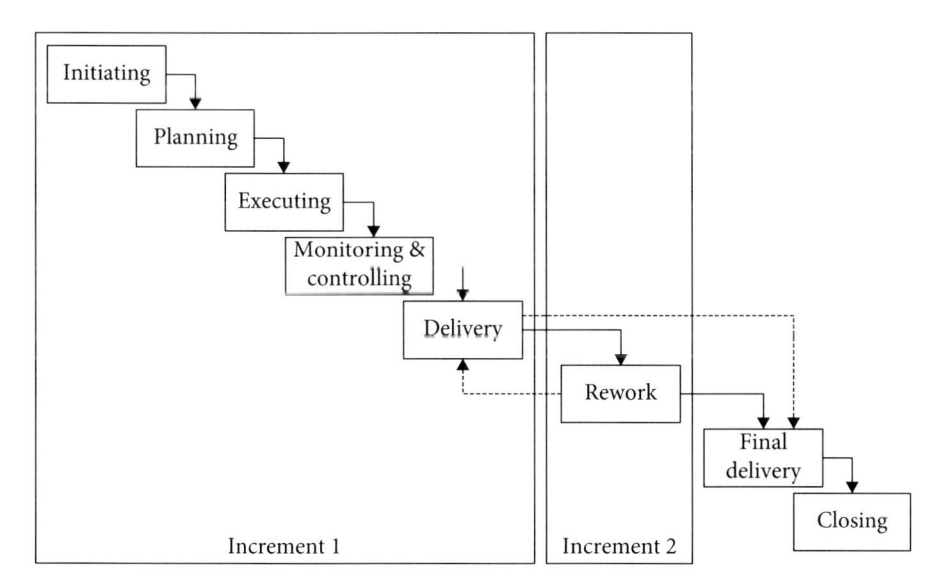

Figure 7. The modified waterfall approach. Although it comprises two increments, this model differs in fundamental ways from the true incremental approach (see Figure 6).

fact precisely what a significant number of project teams are doing.[6] Indeed, Wysocki also notes that he asks the managers of these team why they do not adopt an approach that incorporates iteration if they know they will ultimately iterate. "The silence in response to that question is deafening," he observes (Wysocki 2007: xxxiv).

The iterative model

The advent of the information society and the knowledge economy, and the concomitant shift from tangible to intangible products have exacerbated the difficulty of gathering clear and complete requirements from customers prior to undertaking project work. Today, customers who are asked to describe what they need typically reply, "I can't tell you what I want, but I'll know it when I see it" (Berry 2000: 92; Boehm 2000: 99). This state of affairs suggests that requirements gathering should focus on rapid prototyping in order to facilitate the emergence and discovery of the customer's needs. However, it is also important to recognize that customer needs are not static. Customers may think they recognize what they want in an early prototype, but as they interact with subsequent prototypes, they often gain a clearer understanding of precisely what they need, and thus their requirements evolve.[7]

When requirements cannot be specified in advance but rather emerge over the course of the project, attempting to create a comprehensive specification during the planning phase is an exercise in futility (Brooks 1987). Instead, what is needed is a flexible approach in which change is not merely *tolerated*, but rather *expected* and *embraced*. As Laufer and Hoffman observe, "in a dynamic environment, project management is not about performing to plan, with minimal changes. It is about meeting customer needs, while coping successfully with unavoidable changes" (1998: 2; 2000: xxi). That is precisely the philosophy on which the iterative approach is based.

As its name suggests, the iterative model consists of a series of iterations, or short development cycles, each of which builds on an incomplete solution and brings it one step closer to being a complete solution (see Figure 8). At the completion of each iteration, the customer evaluates what has been accomplished thus far and provides feedback to the project team. In addition, a planning activity is conducted: newly identified requirements are documented and the next iteration is planned. In the iterative approach requirements emerge and are integrated progressively over the course of the project;

---

6. Wysocki's observations are based on more than 40 years of experience in project management, during which he has developed more than 20 project management courses and trained more than 10,000 project managers (2006: v).

7. In some application domains, requirements cannot be completely known until the users have used the product, a phenomenon that Humphrey has described as the "requirements uncertainty principle" (1995: 313–314); along similar lines, Wegner's Lemma holds that it is not possible to completely specify an interactive system (1995).

change is thus an integral part of the life cycle. In this respect, the iterative model is fundamentally different from the incremental approach, in which the requirements are specified during project planning and subsequently refined (if need be) during the monitoring and controlling phase. In addition, the iterative project model requires a higher degree of customer involvement in the project than the incremental approach.

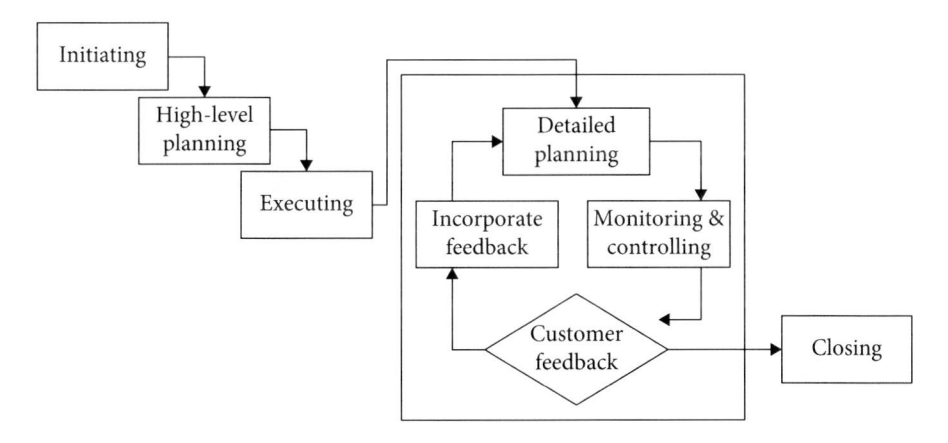

Figure 8. The iterative approach to project management (adapted from PMI 2008: 40 and Wysocki 2007: 52).

Agile methodologies

Today, the incremental and iterative models discussed above are generally referred to as "Agile" methodologies. In fact, "Agile" is an umbrella term for a number of methodologies whose core values differ in fundamental ways from those of traditional approaches. The term derives from the *Manifesto for Agile Software Development* (Beck et al. 2001), which enunciates these core values and groups them under the Agile banner:

> We are uncovering better ways of developing [products] by doing it and helping others do it. Through this work we have come to value:
>
> *Individuals and interactions* over processes and tools
> *Working [products]* over comprehensive documentation
> *Customer collaboration* over contract negotiation
> *Responding to change* over following a plan
>
> That is, while there is value in the items on the right, we value the items on the left more.[8]

---

8. Following Highsmith's example (2004: 10), the generic noun "products" is substituted here for the original "software" to emphasize the broader relevance of the Agile approach.

Although these core value statements ostensibly describe software development, they are directly relevant for, and applicable to, project management (Highsmith 2004). Agile project management approaches are founded on the presumption that changing requirements are a given. Consequently, they embrace change and stress reliability of results instead of stability and predictability of process.

In sum, clear and comprehensive requirements are the foundation of customer satisfaction and project success. However, requirements and the work that must be undertaken to fulfill them cannot always be clearly identified and specified before undertaking project work. The project management methodology should be chosen accordingly. The linear approach is indicated when both the requirements and what must be done to fulfill them are clearly understood and specified. The incremental approach is indicated when the requirements are clearly understood and specified but what must be done to fulfill them is not. Finally, the iterative approach is indicated when neither the requirements nor what must be done to fulfill them is clearly understood and specified (see Figure 9).

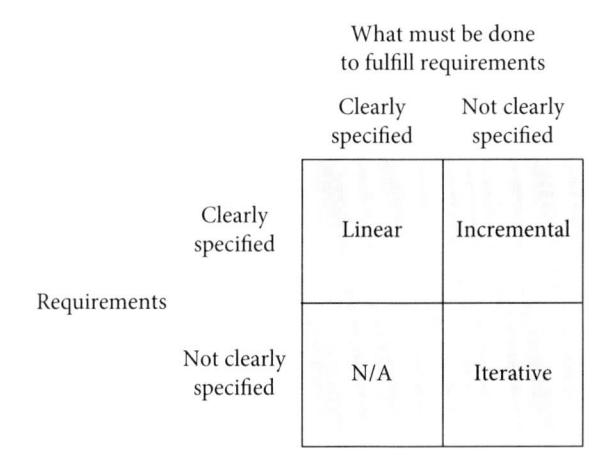

	What must be done to fulfill requirements	
	Clearly specified	Not clearly specified
Requirements: Clearly specified	Linear	Incremental
Requirements: Not clearly specified	N/A	Iterative

Figure 9. A taxonomy of project management approaches based on the relative clarity of requirements and of what must be done to fulfill them (adapted from Wysocki and McGary 2003: xxvii).

The typical translation and localization project model

The fact that customers often cannot provide a clear, correct, comprehensive specification of requirements in translation and localization projects, as discussed above, suggests that incremental and iterative approaches are better suited to these types of projects than the linear model. However, the adoption of incremental and iterative approaches seems to be exception rather than the norm in translation and localization project management.[9]

Translation, editing and proofreading (TEP) form the core of the traditional translation project model. "TEP is based on Gutenberg's printing requirements, where the author submitted the manuscript, someone typeset it, and somebody else reviewed the galley proofs as many times as necessary to make sure that no typos made it to the final print run," as Beninatto and DePalma point out (2007:2).[10] The linear TEP approach made sense when authoring and publishing were separate professions, and texts were published using offset printing. In the early twenty-first century, however, this linear approach is increasingly anachronistic. "Today, virtually all publishing is digital to some extent, whether content is delivered electronically or in print," as Kasdorf observes (2003:1).

Although authoring and publishing have undergone profound transformations over the past quarter-century due to the digital revolution and the advent of desktop publishing, translation project management has been slow to react to these developments. Today, TEP remains at the heart of the typical translation and localization project model, which comprises the following phases (Beninatto and DePalma 2007:2–3, 5; ForeignExchange Translations 2011; Jonckers 2008:7; Leary and Nock 2009:18; Lionbridge 2009:9; Shaefer and Koh 2010:19, 21):[11]

- Project planning, including the following sub-processes:
  - Scope definition
  - Requirements development
  - File preparation (extraction of translatable text from source files and pre-translation, if applicable; sometimes called "pre-processing" or "pre-production")
- Translation
- Editing
- Integration of translated text into files (also called "formatting," "desktop publishing," and "engineering," depending on the types of files involved)

---

9. This situation is not confined to the language industry. A 2009 survey of software developers by Forrester Research found that the largest single category of respondents was the 30.6 per cent who indicated that they do not use a formal process methodology (West and Grant 2010:2).

10. A synopsis of the 2007 Beninatto and DePalma report is available on the Common Sense Advisory blog under the title, "The end of localization Taylorism" (Oct. 27, 2007) (http://globalwatchtower.com/2007/10/16/end-of-tep/).

11. Other activities listed by some sources include glossary preparation, translation memory updates and post-project review.

- Proofreading in final layout (also called "testing," "linguistic testing" and "verification"; implicitly includes correction of any problems identified)
- Client review in final layout (implicitly includes the subsequent implementation of any requested changes)
- Creation of final target files (sometimes called "final production")
- Delivery

These project phases tend to be presented, discussed and diagrammed in an explicitly sequential way (e.g., Leary and Nock 2009: 18; Shaefer and Koh 2010: 19; Beninatto and DePalma 2007: 5; see also DePalma and Kelly Figure 1 in this volume). Moreover, reference is generally not made to either iterations or feedback loops. These observations suggest that the typical project model remains predominantly linear (see Figure 10). Indeed, "[m]ost translation agencies still operate this way," observe Beninatto and DePalma (2007: 2), who liken the sequential process model to "localization Taylorism."

> In today's TEP translation environment, companies adopt a sequential process where – in its simplest form – the work passes hand from the client to the vendor, which in turn hands it to the translator, who returns it to the vendor, who sends it to the editor, who returns it to the vendor, who delivers it to the client.
> (Beninatto and DePalma 2007: 6)

Internationalization expert and industry veteran Tex Texin concurs with Beninatto and DePalma, noting that "[i]t is ironic that the localization industry, an industry specialized in adaptation and customization, has been insistent on its existing process model and is not adapting itself" (2010: 3).

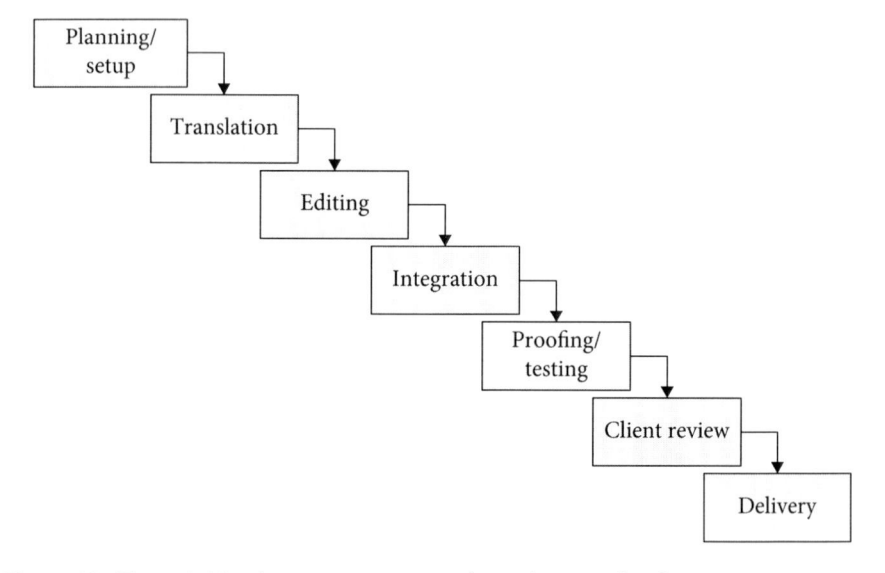

Figure 10. The activities that comprise a typical translation or localization project are undertaken in sequential fashion.

The major problem with the linear translation and localization model is that client review (i.e., validation, see Figure 4) is the final phase before delivery. Consequently, customer feedback is not received until all of the linguistic work has been completed, at which point it is too late to integrate that feedback into the translation and editing processes. Because client review tends to focus on end-item inspection and detection and correction or errors (QC) rather than prevention of errors (QA), this approach fuels rework and increases the risk of schedule and budget overruns. In other words, in the linear translation and localization model the language service provider provides the customer with a complete set of deliverables and then performs one or more rounds of rework until the customer is satisfied, much like the producer of the "half black, half yellow" cars discussed above. The typical language industry product model thus reflects a "modified waterfall" or two-step incremental approach (see Figure 11).

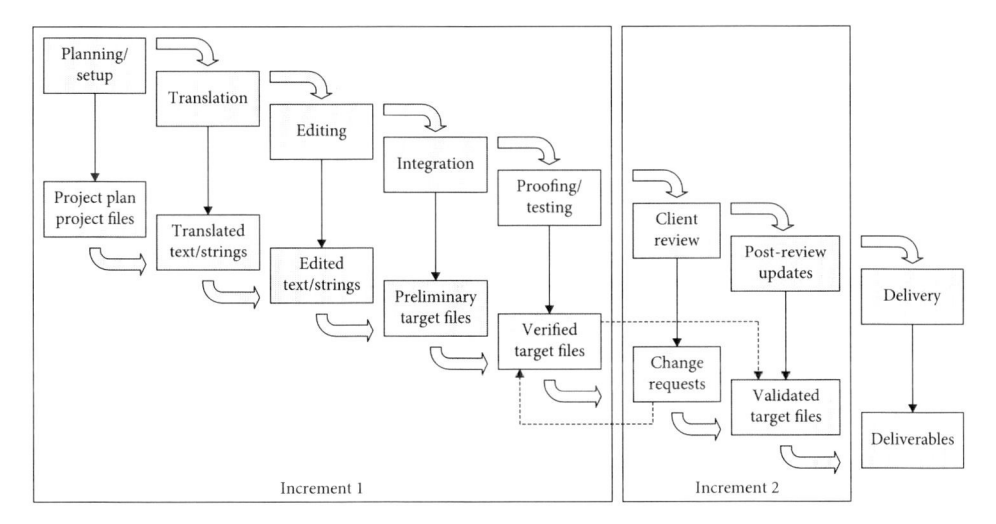

Figure 11. Modified waterfall project model. Production of verified target files constitutes the first increment, and implementation of changes requested following client review (i.e., validation) comprises the second increment.

Client review reveals and magnifies quality management problems

More often than not, clients lack the expertise and/or human resources needed to evaluate the acceptability of translation and localization deliverables. "With a few notable exceptions, the average language services buyer is still in the early phases of localization maturity," notes Txabarriaga (2009: 4). Not wishing to take the quality of the work for granted, or to release the product to the market and leave the responsibility for discovering possible quality problems to end users, clients typically delegate the task of translation assessment to in-country staff or third parties such as in-country distributors or external service providers. In theory, the review process should be a collaborative undertaking designed to ensure that product reflects the client's wants, needs and expectations. In practice, the review process is often ill-defined, confrontational and wasteful. "Unfortunately, in many cases, the process is antagonistic rather than collaborative. The problem revolves around the central issue of quality expectations," as Bass observes (2006: 87).[12]

For example, suppose that the scope of a given project does not include client review. In this scenario, the LSP delivers the files and considers the project to be complete. At some point after the delivery, the client (or a representative thereof) conducts a unilateral review of the materials, identifies "problems" and brings them to the attention of the LSP. In the absence of a formal process for documenting quality expectations as requirements and ensuring compliance of the products to those requirements, the post-delivery review and request for changes will at the very least strain the relationship between the client and LSP, and in a worst-case scenario, could lead to litigation. If the contract merely stipulated that the LSP provide a translation and did not specify requirements beyond the target language and possibly the target locale, then the LSP may claim to have completed the work according to the specification, such as it was, thus absolving the LSP of the responsibility to perform rework free of charge. The client, on the other hand, may deem the translation unacceptable for any number of reasons. For example, the client may feel that the translation is too literal (or not literal enough), or may object to the terminology or style used in the translation even if they are not incorrect *per se*. The list of possible points of discord is nearly endless. The problem in this scenario is that the LSP may have indeed provided precisely what the client requested and done so according to the project specification; yet the client may well be dissatisfied. In such cases, both parties are right, but neither party wins by proving it is correct. This scenario represents a classic lose-lose situation.

Explicitly including client review in the project scope does not necessarily resolve such problems in and of itself. For example, assessment of a translation presupposes that the reviewer possesses *at a minimum* appropriate knowledge of the source and target languages and cultures, relevant subject-matter expertise, as well as knowledge of translation and localization processes, tools and methodologies. If the reviewer does not possess the full array of required skills, there is a good chance that he or she will actually *introduce* errors rather than improve the translation (Wang 2007; Goldsberry 2009). Likewise, if the scope of the task is not clearly defined, the reviewer will typically evaluate the translation based on his or her personal terminological and stylistic preferences. Using preferences as a yardstick against which to

---

12. For further information, see Bass (2006: 84–88), Txabarriaga (2009) and Dunne (2009: 215–220).

assess the translation is perfectly acceptable, provided they are identified and formalized during the project planning phase (Stoeller 2008). Assessing translation based on preferences without having first identified and captured those preferences in the form of a specification amounts to *discovering* quality requirements after the work has been completed, which, as noted above, "is so inefficient and detrimental that we will assume that no competent and right-thinking person would do so" (Wysocki 2007: 103). However, that is precisely what many translation and localization project managers are doing. Instead of proactively eliciting feedback about preferences, language service providers (LSPs) often discover them after the translation has been completed when reviewers request seemingly "preferential" changes. LSPs typically perceive such change requests as unnecessary or even abusive (Wang 2007); however, clients see them as evidence that earlier project phases are not adding as much value as they could or should be.[13]

From vicious to virtuous cycle

How, then, can customer-focused quality be managed and delivered in translation and localization projects? How can the vicious cycle that we have described be transformed into a virtuous cycle? First, the primary focus of project quality management must be the *customer*. The customer's wants needs and expectations (and by extension, those of the target audience who will ultimately make use of the translation or localization) shape the *project quality requirements*. In turn, the specifics of the project, including the business objectives, the characteristics of the target audience and the time, place and medium in which the deliverables will be made available shape the *product quality requirements*. Finally, the specific characteristics of the deliverables to be produced shape the *process quality requirements* governing the production, verification and validation of the project's product(s). In other words, customer-focused project quality management requires the abandonment of the traditional bottom-up approach that works from the linguistic surface structure of the text to target-audience conventions and finally to pragmatics (Nord 1997). What is needed instead is a top-down approach that proceeds from the customer's pragmatic goals to the context and audience of the communication, and finally to the formal linguistic structure or surface attributes of the deliverables. This top-down approach to quality management is presented graphically in Figure 12.

---

13. Much like Henry Ford, who famously said in reference to the Model T that "any customer can have a car painted any colour that he wants so long as it is black" (1922: 72), such LSPs seem to be suggesting that clients can have any translation they want as long as it is the one that the LSP is offering.

```
             ┌─────────────────────────────────────┐
             │     Client (user) quality needs     │
             └─────────────────────────────────────┘
                   │                    ▲
              influence            depend on
                   ▼                    │
             ┌─────────────────────────────────────┐
             │     Project quality requirements    │
             └─────────────────────────────────────┘
                   │                    ▲
              influence            depend on
                   ▼                    │
             ┌─────────────────────────────────────┐
             │    Product quality requirements     │
             └─────────────────────────────────────┘
                   │                    ▲
              influence            depend on
                   ▼                    │
             ┌─────────────────────────────────────┐
             │    Process quality requirements     │
             └─────────────────────────────────────┘
```

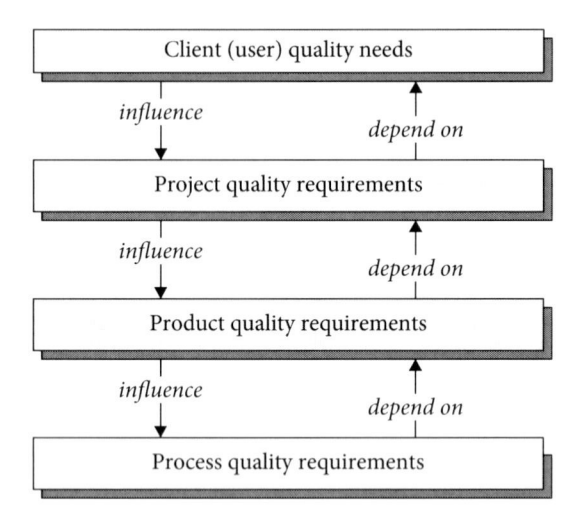

Figure 12. Customer-focused quality breakdown structure.

Because the perception of project quality depends on the customer's requirements, quality cannot be universally *defined*, but rather must be *modeled* for each project. The project quality model must account for the formal characteristics of the translated text or localized product, as well as the characteristics of the text or product that shape its fitness for the intended use. To enable quantitative measurement, the characteristics that comprise the quality model must be defined operationally. As Heiman (2001: 49) observes, "an *operational definition* defines a construct or variable in terms of the operations used to measure it." Finally, quality must be modeled not only in terms of the project's product(s), but also in terms of the project's processes. A project quality management process model should include four components: (a) quality requirements analysis; (b) quality design; (c) quality measurement; and (d) continual quality improvement.[14] In the sections that follow, we will examine the application of this generic quality management process model to translation and localization projects.

---

14. The traditional view is that quality management comprises four components: quality planning, quality control, quality assurance and quality improvement. Bawane and Srikrishna (2010) substitute quality requirements analysis, quality design, quality measurement and continual quality improvement for the four traditional components. This re-mapping not only aligns more closely with product development methodologies (which are often the driving force behind translation and localization projects), but also avoids the conflation of quality assurance and quality control that typically plagues localization projects (Dunne 2006).

A process model for the quantitative management of customer-focused translation quality

Quality requirements analysis

Quality management begins with the identification and classification of the project stakeholders and their quality requirements, i.e., the characteristics that influence the stakeholders' perception that the product meets their requirements and is fit for the intended use. It is essential that the project manager identify the reasons why the project is being undertaken, as well as the intended purpose that the translation or localization is intended to fulfill. Translation and localization requirements are determined at a high level by the context of the communication and the goals that the client or desires to achieve via that communication, which we may characterize as *pre-textual variables*. The requirements of a given translation or localization may vary dramatically depending on the reasons why the project is being undertaken; a translation or localization can only be evaluated as "good" or "poor" to the extent that it fulfills, or fails to fulfill, the intended business and communicative objectives. Achieving those objectives requires that the translators know and understand them.

Next, it is necessary to elucidate the parameters of the specific communicative situation(s), which we may characterize as *contextual variables*, as clearly and completely as possible. In particular, it is of paramount importance to ascertain *to whom* the translation or localization will be directed. The audience plays a preponderant role in shaping translation and localization project requirements. Indeed, translation scholars agree that the receiver is (or should be) the primary factor that determines the characteristics of the target text (Reiss and Vermeer 1984; Nord 1997). What constitutes an "adequate" translation or localization may vary dramatically depending on the target audience. Consequently, it is important that the project manager consult with the stakeholders to specify the degree of loyalty that the translation should exhibit to the source text and to the intentions of the source author (Nord 1997). A text requiring translation or a product requiring localization functions as a set of signs that is read and understood by readers or users. Different readers or users may understand the set of signs in different ways. For this reason,

> it is problematic to speak of '*the* source text' unless we really only mean source-language words or sentence structures. The meaning or function of a text is not something inherent in the linguistic signs; it cannot simply be extracted by anyone who knows the code. A text is made meaningful by its receiver and for its receiver. Different receivers (or even the same receiver at different times) find different meanings in the same linguistic material offered by the text. We might even say that a 'text' is as many texts as there are receivers.
>
> (Nord 1997: 31)

An example will serve to illustrate this point. Different cultures have different expectations about the explicitness with which information should be presented (Hall 1976). In high-context cultures, such as France or Russia, much information is encoded in the context rather than in the message. By way of contrast, in low-context cultures such as the United States, most information is explicitly encoded in the message. For instance, the packaging of frozen pizza sold in the U.S. typically directs consumers to cook the pizza before eating it. Thus, the packaging of DiGiorno frozen pizza advises that the pizza is "not ready to eat" and that it is necessary to "cook thoroughly." The DiGiorno cooking instructions also include the warning "Do not eat pizza without cooking" for good measure. Likewise, the packaging of Red Baron frozen pizza directs consumers to "cook before eating." Such labeling is not found on the packaging of frozen pizzas sold in French grocery stores, such as Jacques Fournil's Pizza Braisia, Buitoni Fraich'Up or Findus frozen pizzas, nor on the packaging of those sold in Russia, such as Дон Густо Пицца Ассорти (Don Gusto Assorted Pizza) made by ОАО «Звездный» or Пицца Ассорти (Assorted Pizza) made by ООО «Прод-Торг». In these countries, it is simply understood that the consumer will cook or heat the pizza before consuming it. Explicit instructions to cook frozen food before eating it are common in low-context cultures, but such messages risk being perceived as unnecessary or even condescending in high-context cultures. In this case, a translation that faithfully reproduces the message of the source text might well be deemed unacceptable by the client or by end-users.

This example underscores the importance of focusing on the goals and objectives of the project and on the wants, needs and expectations of the target audience when specifying translation requirements, rather than on the characteristics of the source text. A given text, expression or utterance is not adequate or inadequate in and of itself, but is only adequate or inadequate to the communicative function that it is intended to fulfill. The adequacy of a translation is not a quality inherent in a target text, but rather is a quality assigned to the target text by an evaluator from his or her particular point of view (Nord 1997; Dunne 2009). It is thus critical that the project manager identify as early as possible in the project planning phase the person or persons who will be responsible for reviewing, approving and accepting project materials.

Aside from the target audience, other contextual variables that the project manager must identify include the time, place and medium by which the target materials will be made available, the degree of internationalization (in localization projects), as well as any target-culture statutory and/or regulatory requirements that apply to the project, as such variables shape the characteristics of the target materials to be created. Pre-textual and contextual variables collectively comprise what is referred to in the literature as the "translation brief" (Fraser 1996). "[T]he translation brief does not tell the translator *how* to go about their [sic] translating job, what translation strategy to use, or what translation type to choose. These decisions depend entirely on the translator's responsibility and competence" (Nord 1997: 30). Thus, the brief answers the questions "who" (and "for whom"), "what," "where," "when" and perhaps most critically, "why" with respect to the project being undertaken, but it does not specify *how* the nuts-and-bolts work of translation should be performed.

The problem with the concept of the translation brief as presented in the literature is that it does not address client (or client reviewer) preferences. Answering the questions "who," "what," "where," "when" and "why" is necessary but not sufficient to ensure the creation of a translation that meets not only the client's *requirements* (identified needs), but also the client's *expectations* (unidentified needs). The *how* of translation must also be specified with respect to the project objectives, communicative context and target audience. In other words, the variables that shape the translation specification must be operationally defined at a more granular level to avoid potential preference-based disagreements during client review, or worse, after the files have been delivered. Translation is not a mechanical undertaking, but rather an intelligent, knowledge-based activity (Wilss 1994, 1996a, 1996b). The process by which translation input (source text) is transformed into output (target text) is inherently subjective: a target text represents the sum of all of the inferences and choices made by the translator, and the inferences and decisions made by one translator may be different from those that another translator would make. It follows that there is no single correct translation of a given text, but rather multiple possible translations that may be more or less suitable for a given target audience and intended use, a fact that is well documented in the literature (Bar-Hillel 1960; Quine 1964; Savory 1968; Macklovitch, Nguyen and Lapalme 2005). Translation scholars argue that "the actual procedures [whereby the translation is created] are entirely up to the translator as a competent expert in translation" (Nord 1997: 117). However, clients often do not defer to the translator as *the* competent expert. In this respect, language projects differ in fundamental ways from other types of projects. Everyone is an expert when it comes to his or her personal experiential knowledge. Thus, it is hardly surprising that people who grow up speaking a language and who use it every day in their personal and professional lives often consider themselves qualified to judge language use, regardless of their actual level of expertise (Kaplan and Baldauf 1997: 3). This may explain the truism attributed to H. G. Wells that "no passion in the world is equal to the passion to alter someone else's draft."

Since translation is essentially a decision-making process (Levý 1967; Darwish 1998, 1999, 2008), translation quality management requires that the range of decision-making choices be limited to those options that the client deems acceptable. To use ISO parlance, translation quality management involves controlling the characteristics of the target materials that influence the customer's perception that the target materials meet the customer's requirements and are fit for the intended use. Those characteristics can be controlled by specifying the range of acceptable choices that the translation team can make. This requires that the project manager and the project team work closely with the client reviewer to specify the potential acceptable choice or choices for the relevant qualities (characteristics) of the target materials.

Quality design

After gathering the preliminary set of requirements from the project stakeholders, the project manager should create a project quality model in which the pre-textual variables represent the top-level or primary requirements and the contextual variables comprise the secondary requirements. The project manager should then further decompose the contextual variables, and specify the quality characteristics of the text itself (see Figure 13):[15]

- Cultural, linguistic and/or social conventions associated with the medium
- Constraints imposed by the time, place and/or medium
- Target audience demographics; educational level; knowledge of domain in general and product in particular; role with respect to text or product; needs and expectations; etc.
- Other requirements not stated by the customer but necessary for the specified or intended use, where known (ISO 2008: 7)
- Text-related requirements shaped by the pre-textual and contextual factors
    - Linguistic style requirements
        - Target-language conventions, including abbreviations; acronyms; active vs. passive voice; capitalization; designation of user interface terms; forms of address (informal vs. formal; singular vs. plural; imperative vs. indicative; etc.); grammar; punctuation; register; relative degree of explicitness; etc.
        - Other client- or project-specific requirements
    - Terminology requirements[16]
        - Conventional or standardized target equivalents; copyrighted terms; non-translatables; etc.
        - Other client- or project-specific requirements
    - Visual style requirements
        - Colors; fonts, graphics; line spacing; margins; page size; white space; etc.
        - Other client- or project-specific requirements.

It is essential that the characteristics that comprise the quality model be specified as clearly and comprehensively as possible, and that they be measurable. Specifying the characteristics of the deliverables before project work is undertaken establishes a shared understanding among the project team and the stakeholders not merely of *what*

---

15. This list is not exhaustive.

16. Wright (2001) and Dunne (2007) argue that terminology is the single most critical characteristic in specialized translation. Lionbridge estimates that 15% of all translation and localization project costs stem from rework, and that inconsistent terminology is the primary cause (2009: 10).

deliverables will be produced but also *how* they will be produced. This shared understanding in turn diminishes the risk of customer dissatisfaction during the project. Once documented, the linguistic style requirements, terminological requirements and visual style requirements can be used as a formal specification against which to verify compliance during verification and validation (see Figure 4). In this regard, it is also important to specify who will have final decision-making authority with respect to questions of style, usage, ambiguity and other items not addressed by the project specification.

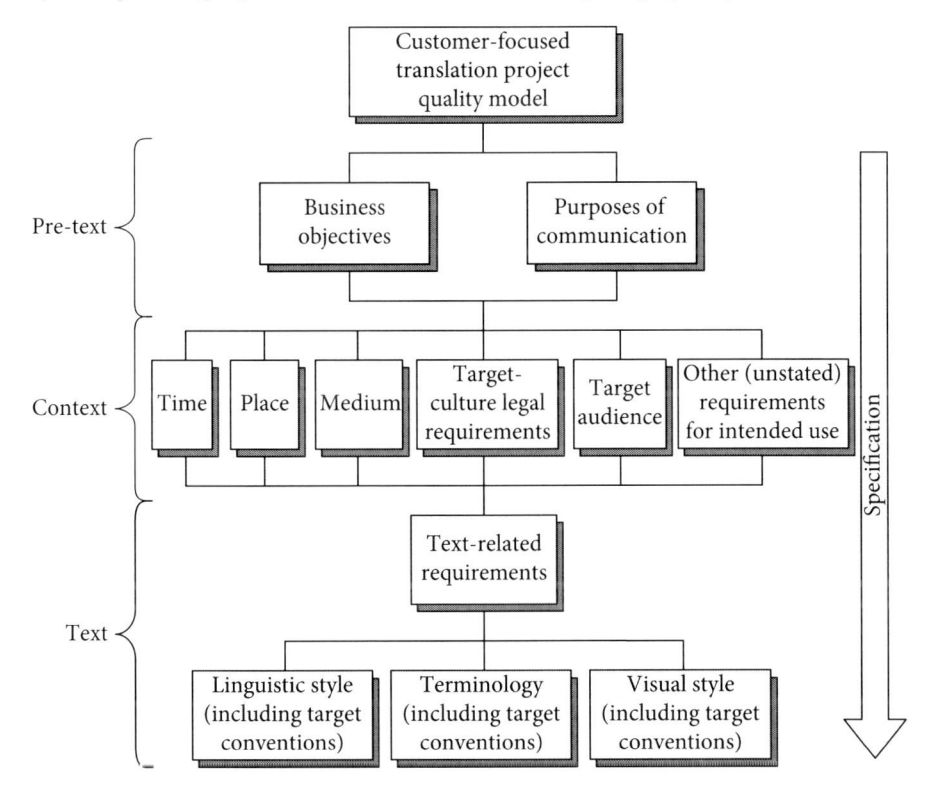

Figure 13. Translation project quality model. The specification of pre-textual, contextual and textual requirements mirrors that of business, market and product requirements in product development (see Giammarresi in this volume for a discussion of the product development process).

Once the quality requirements have been modeled, the project quality assurance and quality control processes must be defined. Quality assurance involves the establishment of the monitoring, measurement, analysis and improvement processes needed to (a) demonstrate conformity to project requirements; (b) monitor customer *perception* as to whether the organization has met the customer's requirements; and (c) continually improve the effectiveness of the quality management system, focusing on prevention rather than on detection and correction of problems. Quality control is a set of procedures designed to confirm that the translation conforms to the requirements, and relies on end-item inspection (systematic or random) to identify defects and quantify the frequency thereof. Quality control is typically performed using project quality metrics. Metrics should be selected (or created) based on the project's business goals and objectives. To create a metric for the evaluation of translation quality, the project manager must (a) determine the relative criticality of each quality characteristic (e.g., via a ranking or weighting); (b) establish the procedure by which each quality characteristic will be measured; and (c) establish measurement scales for the various characteristics. Measurement scales can reflect the degree of satisfaction of the requirements. For example a simple binary scale can be used (e.g., unsatisfactory or satisfactory); if a more nuanced evaluation is required, a multiple-category scale may be preferable (exceeds requirements, target, minimally acceptable and unacceptable) (ISO 2001:4). The linguistic style requirements, terminological requirements and visual style requirements can form the basis of the quality metric.

Quality control should not focus on ensuring accuracy, equivalence or consistency between the source and target materials, unless these characteristics have been explicitly specified as requirements. Indeed, this approach may cause more problems than it solves. As the above example of the pizza cooking instructions illustrates, a translation that communicates precisely the same information in precisely the same way as the original text may lead to customer and/or end-user dissatisfaction. Instead, quality control should focus above all on ensuring the *adequacy* of the translation with respect to the project goals, the intended function of the target materials and the target audience. "If the purpose of a translation is to achieve a particular function for the target addressee, anything that obstructs the achievement of this purpose is a translation error," as Nord observes (1997:74). Conversely, anything that does *not* obstruct the achievement of this purpose is *not* a translation error. Such should be the philosophy governing quality control. Documenting linguistic style requirements, terminological requirements and visual style requirements and using these requirements as a formal specification during verification and validation operationalizes this philosophy. It limits both the range of acceptable decisions that can made by the project team and the risk of uncontrolled preferential changes by the client reviewer(s).

Quality monitoring and measurement

Once the requirements have been captured and documented, the quality model has been created and the QA and QC processes have been defined, the project manager must monitor the quality of the intermediate and final deliverables. Such monitoring entails measurement of the actual values of the selected characteristics using the project quality metric via verification (confirmation that the translated text or localized product fulfills the specified requirements) and validation (confirmation that the translated text or localized product is fit for the intended use or uses) (see Figure 4). Depending on the requirements of the specific project, measurement may be systematic (full review) or random (spot-checking). Spot-checking is the preferred approach: if proper quality management and quality assurance processes have been implemented, subjecting the materials to a comprehensive review generally does not add sufficient value to warrant the extra time and cost. However, in the case of regulated industries or projects in which the cost of failure is prohibitive (i.e., medical devices and pharmaceuticals), systematic review may be warranted regardless of the confidence levels associated with the QA processes.

Continual improvement

Continual improvement involves the remediation of any problems or defects uncovered by quality control. Quality control should be incremental or iterative to enable continual improvement over the course of the project.[17] In other words, the feedback from verification and validation should be used to refine the project requirements as well as the quality assurance and quality control processes throughout the project. This feedback loop facilitates the identification and elimination of the root causes of problems in keeping with ISO 9001 quality management principles (ISO 2008: 12).

Finally, continual improvement also requires that the organization monitor the customer's perception as to whether the project requirements have been met, using customer satisfaction surveys, user opinion surveys, and so forth (ISO 2008: 12). Discrepancies between quality control measurements and customer satisfaction measurements suggest misalignment between the customer's requirements and expectations and/or problems with the delivery of the service. Such issues should be addressed promptly.

Agile approaches are well suited to translation and localization projects

Given the strong likelihood that requirements will progressively emerge and/or evolve over the course of a given translation or localization project, an Agile project management methodology should be adopted. Requirements specification, like planning as a whole, should not be a one-time event but rather an iterative process that can potentially span the entire project lifecycle. PMI refers to this iterative process as *progressive elaboration*. "Progressive elaboration involves continually improving and detailing a

---

17. Note that in the context of quality management "iterative" does not simply mean "repeated." Each iteration builds on the previous one so that problems and errors identified in a given iteration can be avoided in subsequent iterations. The key point is that the iterative approach enables progressive improvement.

plan as more-detailed and specific information and more accurate estimates become available. Progressive elaboration allows a project management team to manage to a greater level of detail as the project evolves" (PMI 2008:7).

To illustrate the application of this principle, let us consider a generic translation project. During the planning phase, the project manager gathers information from client-side stakeholders (e.g., the product manager and/or project manager) about the business objectives and communicative purposes of the translation; the time, place and medium by which the target materials will be made available; high-level characteristics of the target audience; target-culture legal or statutory requirements (if known); and the degree of "loyalty" that the translation should exhibit to the source text and the intentions of the author. Collectively, these characteristics comprise the preliminary requirements (see Figure 14).

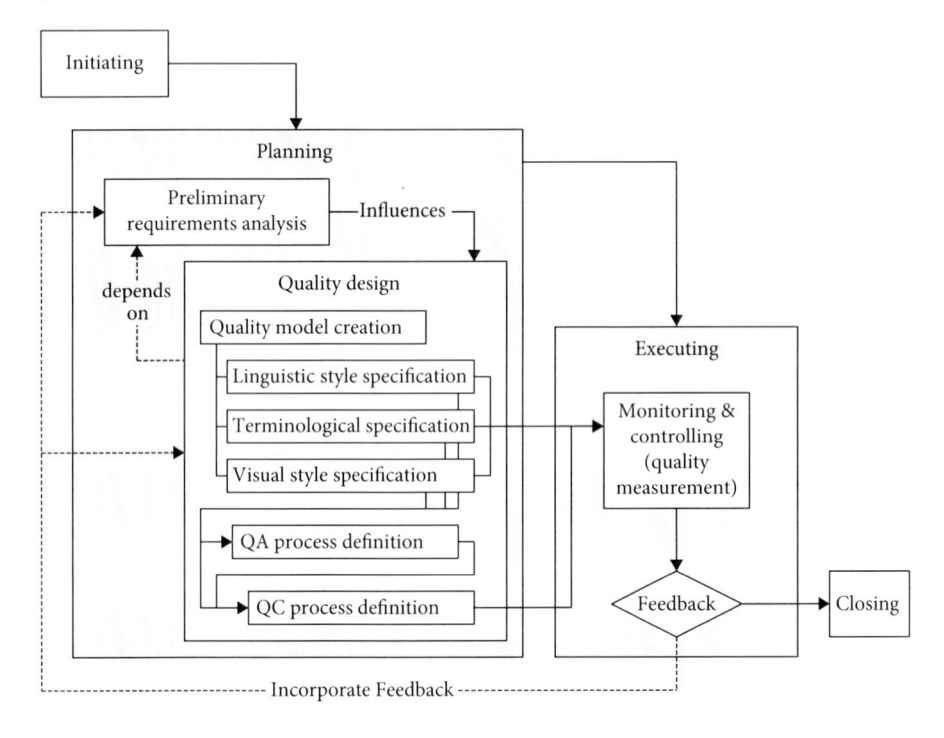

Figure 14. Agile approach to translation and localization quality management.

Next, the project manager engages in quality design. First, he or she consults with the project team to specify the contextual requirements in greater detail, including but not limited to more granular characteristics of the target audience; target-culture legal or statutory requirements not identified by client; cultural, linguistic and social conventions associated with the medium; as well as constraints or restrictions imposed by the medium. The project manager then oversees a collaborative consultation between the project team and the client reviewer, in-country representatives and/or end users to specify the text-related requirements, including linguistic style, terminology, and visual style. The specification of contextual and text-related requirements must be performed in parallel for each language (and possibly for different locales within a given language as well, depending on the specific project). Once the preliminary project quality model is complete, the QA and QC processes can be defined accordingly.

During the project execution phase, tasks should be completed and subjected to review in batches. This approach offers multiple advantages. First, it enables incremental error correction, which not only ensures punctual remediation of defects, but also provides data about types and frequency of errors. This information can be provided to the project team to prevent further propagation of such errors. In this way, iterative feedback loops help the project team continually improve its efficiency. In addition, incremental client review provides feedback to the planning process in general, and to quality requirements analysis and to quality design in particular. For example, client review of initial batches of translation may reveal stylistic, terminological or other requirements that were not captured during the project planning phase. The Agile approach enables the project manager to update text-related specifications and/or QA and QC processes to reflect the emergence or identification of new requirements, thus continually improving the project specification.

Conclusion

Adopting a customer-focused, Agile approach to quality management in translation and localization projects increases the likelihood that the deliverables will conform to the specification, be deemed fit for the intended use, and satisfy the client. Over time, the collection of quantitative data demonstrating consistent conformance to specification, fitness for intended use and customer satisfaction by LSPs can instill in clients the confidence and trust necessary to move beyond systematic review to random quality control or spot-checking (except in highly risky domains where the cost of failure is prohibitive, as noted above).

There is one significant caveat, however. The customer-focused, Agile approach presupposes active participation and continual feedback from the client, client reviewer, and/or end users (ISO 2001: 4). This represents a sea change from the traditional "throw-it-over-the-wall" approach to translation and localization (Aberdeen 2006), in which clients provide all of the source materials to the language service provider and expect to receive target versions at the specified date and price, while involving themselves as little as possible in the nuts and bolts of project processes. Many clients do not wish to participate in incremental or iterative translation or localization cycles, preferring (or requiring) instead that the deliverables be subjected to end-of-cycle review. "Many clients have no interest whatsoever in the 'mechanics' of the translation process and may even regard such information as the responsibility of the translator," as Byrne observes (2006: 40). However, if clients want, need and/ or expect translation and localization deliverables that are adequate for the intended use, they must provide a clear, comprehensive requirements specification to the language service provider during the project planning phase. Absent a clear, comprehensive project specification, clients should adopt an Agile approach to translation and localization in collaboration with their service providers in order to facilitate the progressive emergence, identification and refinement of project requirements. If the client cannot or will not agree to an incremental or iterative approach to quality management, then the service provider takes on the project at its risk and peril because the client is insisting on a "throw-it-over-the-wall" approach, which is a recipe for problems for the reasons discussed above.

Although the approach proposed here represents a significant change in the status quo, it is in the interest of all project stakeholders to embrace this change. Moreover, it is also in the interest of scholars, educators, students and practitioners of translation and localization project management to embrace this change. Quality is value, as Peter Drucker reminds us, and value is in the eye of the beholder. If language service providers are perceived by clients as providing little or no value, then they are in fact providing little or no value. If clients have no basis on which to assess translation or localization quality (or value), then there is a high risk that they will perceive translation and localization as undifferentiated offerings, fueling the common (mis)perception of translation and localization as commodity services.

References

Aberdeen Group. 2006. *The Next-Generation Product Documentation Report: Getting Past the 'Throw It over the Wall' Approach*. Boston, MA: Aberdeen Group.
Bar-Hillel, Yehoshua. 1960. "A demonstration of the nonfeasibility of fully automatic high quality translation." *Advances in Computers* (1): 91–163.
Bass, Scott. 2006. "Quality in the real world." In *Perspectives on Localization*, Keiran J. Dunne (ed.), 69–94. Amsterdam/Philadelphia: John Benjamins.
Bawane, Neelam and Srikrishna, C. V. 2010. "A novel method for quantitative assessment of software quality." *International Journal of Computer Science and Security* 3 (6): 508–517.
Beck, Kent et al. 2001. "Manifesto for Agile software development." http://agilemanifesto.org/
Beninatto, Renato S. and DePalma, Donald A. 2007. *Collaborative Translation: The End of Localization Taylorism and the Beginning of Postmodern Translation*. Lowell, MA: Common Sense Advisory.
Berry, Daniel M. 2000. "The requirements iceberg and various icepicks chipping at it." IEEE Long Island Section. http://www.ieee.li/pdf/viewgraphs/iceberg.pdf
Boehm, Barry. 1986. "A spiral model of software development and enhancement." *ACM SIGSOFT Software Engineering Notes* 11 (4): 22–42.
———. 1988. "A spiral model of software development and enhancement." *[IEEE] Computer* 21 (5): 61–72.

———. 2000. "Requirements that handle IKIWISI, COTS, and rapid change." *[IEEE] Computer* 33 (7): 99–102.
Brooks, Frederick P., Jr. 1987. "No silver bullet: Essence and accidents of software engineering." *[IEEE] Computer* 20 (4): 10–19.
Byrne, Jody. 2006. *Technical Translation: Usability Studies for Translating Technical Documentation*. Dordrecht: Springer.
Cismas, Suzana Carmen. 2010. "Risk assessment and mitigation in drafting translation contracts." In *Proceedings of the International Conference of Risk Management, Assessment and Mitigation (RIMA '10)*, Mircea Grigoriu et al. (eds), 491–495. N.p.: WSEAS Press.
Darwish, Ali. 1998. "Translation as a decision making process under constraints." http://www.translocutions.com/turjuman/abstracts.html
———. 1999. "Towards a theory of constraints in translation." http://www.translocutions.com/translation/constraints_0.1.pdf
———. 2008. "Translation as a decision making process under constraints." In *Optimality in Translation*, 147–243. Patterson Lakes, Australia: Writescope.
Drucker, Peter F. 1985. *Innovation and Entrepreneurship: Practice and Principles*. New York: Harper & Row.
Dunne, Keiran J. 2006. "Putting the cart behind the horse: Rethinking localization quality management." In *Perspectives on Localization*, Keiran J. Dunne (ed.), 95–117. Amsterdam/Philadelphia: John Benjamins.
———. 2007. "Terminology: Ignore it at your peril." *MultiLingual* 18:3 (April/May): 32–38.
———. 2009. "Assessing software localization: For a valid approach." In *Testing and Assessment in Translation and Interpreting Studies*, Claudia V. Angelelli and Holly E. Jacobson (eds), 185–222. Amsterdam/Philadelphia: John Benjamins.
Ellis, Keith. 2008. "Business analysis benchmark. The impact of business requirements on the success of technology projects." IAG Consulting. http://www.iag.biz/images/resources/iag%20business%20analysis%20benchmark%20-%20full%20report.pdf
ForeignExchange Translations. 2011. "Web globalization." http://www.fxtrans.com/services/web.aspx
Ford, Henry with Crowther, Samuel. 1922. *My Life and Work*. Garden City, NY: Doubleday.
Fraser, Janet. 1996. "The translator investigated: Learning from translation process analysis." *The Translator* 2 (1): 65–79.
Goldsberry, Lonie. 2009. "Becoming a successful translation manager (part one)." *GALAxy [Globalization and Localization Association] Newsletter* (Q4). http://www.gala-global.org/articles/becoming-successful-translation-manager
Hall, Edward T. 1976. *Beyond Culture*. Garden City, NY: Anchor Press-Doubleday.
Heiman, Gary W. 2001. *Understanding Research Methods and Statistics*. 2nd ed. Boston and New York: Houghton Mifflin.
Highsmith, Jim. 2004. *Agile Project Management: Creating Innovative Products*. Boston: Addison-Wesley.
Humphrey, Watts. 1995. *A Discipline for Software Engineering*. Reading, MA: Addison-Wesley.
International Organization for Standardization (ISO). 2001. *ISO/IEC 9126-1:2001(E). Software engineering – Product quality – Part 1: Quality model*. Geneva: ISO.
———. 2005. *ISO 9000:2005(E). Quality management systems – Fundamentals and vocabulary*. 3rd ed. Geneva: ISO.
———. 2008. *ISO 9001:2008(E). Quality management systems – Requirements*. 4th ed. Geneva: ISO.

———. 2011. "ISO 9000 – Quality management." International Organization for Standardization. http://www.iso.org/iso/iso_catalogue/management_and_leadership_standards/quality_management.htm

Jonckers. 2008. "Achieving localization excellence." http://www.jonckers.com/wp-content/uploads/brochure_achieving_localization_excellence.pdf

Kaplan, Robert B. and Baldauf, Richard B. 1997. *Language Planning from Practice to Theory*. Clevedon/Philadelphia: Multilingual Matters.

Kasdorf, William E. 2003. *The Columbia Guide to Digital Publishing*. New York: Columbia University Press.

Kelly, Nataly, Beninatto, Renato S. and DePalma, Donald A. 2008. *Buyer-Defined Translation Quality: Illuminating the Customer's Perspective on What Good Language Services Mean*. Lowell, MA: Common Sense Advisory.

Kerzner, Harold. 2010. *Project Management Best Practices: Achieving Global Excellence*. 2nd ed. New York: John Wiley & Sons.

Kerzner, Harold and Saladis, Frank P. 2009. *Value-Driven Project Management*. New York: John Wiley & Sons.

Koo, Siu Ling and Kinds, Harold. 2000. "A quality assurance model for language projects." In *Translating into Success: Cutting-Edge Strategies for Going Multilingual in a Global Age*, Robert C. Sprung and Simone Jaroniec (eds), 147–157. Amsterdam/Philadelphia: John Benjamins.

Laufer, Alexander, and Hoffman, Edward. 1998. "Ninety-nine rules for managing 'faster, better, cheaper' projects." *ASK: Academy Sharing Knowledge, The NASA Source for Project Management* 7 (March). http://askmagazine.nasa.gov/pdf/pdf7/47990main_47442main_ninety_nine_rules.7.pdf

Leary, Liesl and Nock, Heike. 2009. "Web site localization 101 – Why and how to prepare your web site for Global markets." ENLASO Corporation. http://www.translate.com/Language_Tech_Center/webinars/content/Website-Localization-101.pdf

Lionbridge. 2009. "Building stronger brands around the world: A guide to effective global marketing." http://www.slideshare.net/Lionbridge/building-stronger-brands-around-the-world

Levý, Jiří. 1967. "Translation as a decision process." In *To Honor Roman Jakobson: Essays on the Occasion of his Seventieth Birthday, 11 October 1966*, Vol. 2, 1171–1182. The Hague/Paris: Mouton de Gruyter.

Macklovitch, Elliott, Nguyen, Ngoc Tran and Lapalme, Guy. 2005. "Tracing translations in the making." In *MT Summit X, Phuket, Thailand, September 13–15, 2005, Conference Proceedings: The Tenth Machine Translation Summit*, 323–330. N.p.: Asia-Pacific Association for Machine Translation.

Martin, James. 1991. *Rapid Application Development*. New York: Macmillan.

Nord, Christiane. 1997. *Translating as a Purposeful Activity: Functionalist Approaches Explained*. Manchester: St Jerome.

Praxiom Research Group Limited. 2008. "Theoretical overview of ISO 9000." http://www2.connect.ab.ca/~praxiom/concepts.htm

Project Management Institute (PMI). 2008. *A Guide to the Project Management Body of Knowledge (PMBOK® Guide)*. 4th ed. Newtown Square, PA: Project Management Institute.

Quine, Willard Van Orman. 1964. "Meaning and translation." In *The Structure of Language: Readings in the Philosophy of Language*, Jerry A. Fodor and Jerrold J. Katz (eds), 460–478. Englewood Cliffs, N.J., Prentice-Hall.

Reiss, Katharina and Vermeer, Hans J. 1984. *Grundlegung einer allgemeinen Translationstheorie*. Tübingen: Niemeyer.

Royce, Winston W. 1987. "Managing the development of large software systems: Concepts and techniques." In *Proceedings of the 9th International Conference on Software Engineering (ICSE), Monterey, CA, March 30–April 2, 1987*, 328–338. New York, NY: ACM. Rpt. of "Managing the development of large software systems: Concepts and techniques." In *Proceedings, [Technical Papers of] Western Electronic Show and Convention (WesCon), August 25–28, 1970, Los Angeles, USA*, 1–9.

Savory, Theodore Horace. 1968. *The Art of Translation*. Boston: The Writer.

Shaefer, Anja and Koh, Arnold. 2010. "Localization 101: Getting started with localization." Lionbridge.com. http://www.slideshare.net/Lionbridge/localization-101-5091536

Shreve, Gregory M. 2000. "Translation at the millennium: Prospects for the evolution of a profession." In *Paradigmenwechsel in der Translation. Festschrift für Albrecht Neubert zum 70. Geburtstag*, Peter A. Schmitt (ed.), 217–234. Tübingen: Stauffenburg Verlag.

Stoeller, Willem. 2008. "Why do l10n projects fail? Common failure scenarios for localization projects." *ClientSide News* 8 (2): 16–18.

Texin, Tex. 2010. "Agile localization practices." Internationalization (I18n), Localization (L10n), Standards, and Amusements. http://www.i18nguy.com/l10n/Agile-Localization-Practices.pdf

Txabarriaga, Rocío. 2009. *Best Practices for Client Review Processes*. Lowell, MA: Common Sense Advisory.

Wang, Frank. 2007. "Client review of translation in a localization project." *MultiLingual* 18 (7): 49–52.

Wegner, Peter. 1995. "Interactive foundations of object-based programming." *[IEEE] Computer* 28 (10): 70–72.

West, Dave and Grant, Tom. 2010. *Agile Development: Mainstream Adoption has Changed Agility*. Cambridge, MA: Forrester Research.

Wilss, Wolfram. 1994. "Translation as a knowledge-based activity: Context, culture, and cognition." In *Language, Discourse and Translation in the West and Middle East*, Robert de Beaugrande, Abdullah Shunnaq and Mohamed Helmy Heliel (eds), 35–44. Amsterdam/Philadelphia: John Benjamins.

———. 1996a. *Knowledge and Skills in Translator Behavior*. Amsterdam/Philadelphia: John Benjamins.

———. 1996b. "Translation as intelligent behaviour." In *Terminology, LSP and Translation*, Harold Somers (ed.), 161–168. Amsterdam/Philadelphia: John Benjamins.

Wright, Sue Ellen. 2001. "Terminology and total quality management." In *Handbook of Terminology Management*, Sue Ellen Wright and Gerhard Budin (eds), 488–502. Amsterdam/Philadelphia: John Benjamins.

———. 2006. "The creation and application of language industry standards." In *Perspectives on Localization*, Keiran J. Dunne (ed.), 241–278. Amsterdam/Philadelphia: John Benjamins.

Wysocki, Robert K. 2007. *Effective Project Management: Traditional, Adaptive, Extreme*. 4th ed. Indianapolis, IN: Wiley.

Wysocki, Robert K. with McGary, Rudd. 2003. *Effective Project Management: Traditional, Adaptive, Extreme*. 3rd ed. Indianapolis, IN: Wiley.

Effective communication in translation and localization project management

Natalia Tsvetkov, PMP and Veronica Tsvetkov

> We don't see things as they are, we see them as we are.
> Anaïs Nin

Successful communication requires that project managers be aware of and address two major factors: personality (value orientations, mental models, thought patterns, and behaviors of an individual) and culture (attitudes, beliefs and behaviors of a group). Culture is an especially critical factor in translation and localization project management, which by nature involve the collaboration of people from different cultures. We first discuss the identification and classification of personality types using the Myers-Briggs Type Indicator (MBTI), and then examine some of the ways in which personality shapes perceptions of time, conflict resolution and problem solving. Secondly, we explore culture, drawing on Hall's notion of contexting and Hofstede's theory of cultural dimensions, and discuss the impact of culture on perceptions of time, decision-making and business communication. We conclude by proposing practical strategies for addressing personality and cultural differences in a project communication plan.

The role of communication in project management

The ability to communicate effectively is perhaps the most important skill to have at work and in life. Regardless of what we do, whether we are expressing ideas, experiences or feelings, we always want other people to understand what we mean and to then react accordingly. Excellent communication skills are of paramount importance for translation and project managers. Indeed, it is generally held that project managers spend 80% of their time communicating (Treasury Board of Canada Secretariat 1999:2; PM4DEV 2009:94). It is easier to identify problems created by poor communication than to identify ways to solve those problems. However, this chapter proposes strategies to avoid them altogether.

Localization project managers must negotiate two distinct factors that affect communication. The first factor involves inherited and learned individual personality traits. With the help of psychometric instruments, the vast array of different personalities can be identified and classified with an eye to improving communication. The most widespread personality assessment tool in the business world is the Myers-Briggs Type Indicator (MBTI), which is discussed in detail below. The second important factor is the culture of the people with whom one works. By "culture" we mean the set of attitudes, beliefs and behaviors that are shared by members of a group (i.e., a nation). The impact of culture is obvious in day-to-day work with contacts overseas, where people live and work in their native cultures. Cultural dimensions are less obvious when working with colleagues and fellow team members at the office, even if the office environment brings together people from different countries. One might expect foreigners living abroad to be well adjusted and "culturally acclimated," but people generally do not drift completely away from the core values they grew up with. Try as one might, it is nearly impossible to "go native." People's cultural background affects their way of thinking, mostly in unconscious ways, and influences their decision-making process, the value they ascribe to individual goals versus group goals, and their perception of time.

Before exploring the impact of culture and personality on communication, it is important that we first clarify the model of communication on which our discussion is based, as well as the parameters that influence the relative success of communication.

Communication model

How does communication take place between people? The basis of most communication models is the notion that an *Idea* travels from the *Sender* through a *Channel* to the *Receiver*. Communication is shaped not only by these four basic components, but also by (1) encoding and decoding the idea into a message in verbal and nonverbal vocabularies, (2) "noise" that interferes with the transmission, and (3) feedback from the receiver to the sender. Thus, the process of communication has come to be thought of as circular and simultaneous (see Figure 1).

Meaning does not merely flow from sender to receiver, but rather remains in the mental data banks of both sender and receiver. In fact:

> the idea does not travel, only the code (the words or the patterns of sound or print) travels. The meaning a person attaches to the words received will come from his or her own mind. The interpretation is determined by the listener's own frame of reference, culture, ideas, interests, and past experiences – just as the meaning of the original message is fundamentally determined by the sender's mind and frame of reference. (Szalay 1981:135)

Communication is said to be successful if the message that is received is the same as the one that the sender meant to send. When the sender and receiver share similar frames of reference, they are both likely to assign similar meanings to a given message. However, memories, past decisions, values, beliefs, distortions, and generalizations all act as filters during communication. The greater the differences between the filters of the sender and receiver, the more likely it is that, while decoding a message, the receiver will assign meaning(s) that differ from the meaning(s) that the sender intended.

When people have different cultural backgrounds, the potential for failed communication between them rises in proportion to the distance that separates the frames of reference of the sender and the receiver. Because personal and cultural frames of reference differ from one person to another, communicators must make some assumptions regarding the intended meaning; otherwise dialogue is impossible. Communicators ascribe meaning to the messages they exchange based on their personal and cultural frames of reference. However, by understanding the cultural frame of reference of their interlocutor(s), intercultural business communicators can improve their ability to understand, and be understood, correctly. Given the fact that PMs spend as much as 80% of their time communicating, it is critical that they understand the frames of reference of the different types of people with whom they are in regular contact, whether they are colleagues in the office or colleagues in international virtual project teams. Understanding others' frames of reference will enable more effective communication, thus enhancing the likelihood of successful project outcomes.

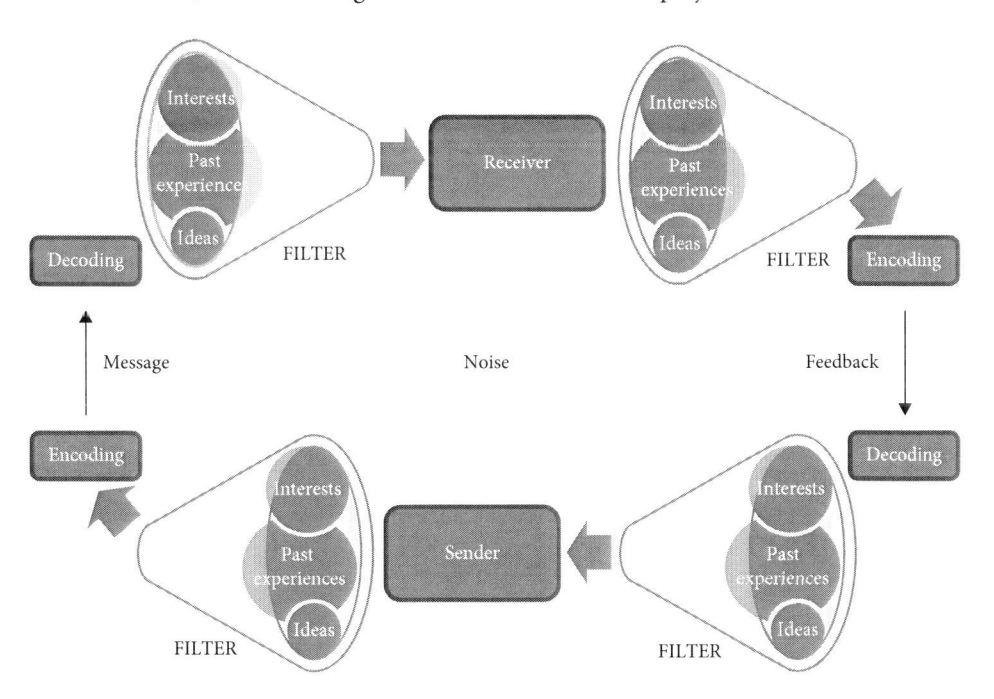

Figure 1. Communication model.

Myers-Briggs Type Indicator (MBTI)

Successful communication involves a variety of factors, including a myriad of personality types. Whether or not we realize it, we give and receive information differently based on our personality preferences. In this regard, the Myers-Briggs Type Indicator (MBTI) is invaluable for project managers and no doubt explains why it is a part of the Project Management Institute's (PMI) project management framework. We recommend engaging a certified MBTI instructor for training on self-assessment and for assistance in understanding the implications of the self-assessment with regard to project management and communicating with others.

The MBTI was developed in the 1940s by Myers and Briggs and was based on Carl Jung's theory of psychological types. The MBTI is the most widely used personality inventory assessment in the world, and has been translated into 20 languages. Because different cultures may interpret the meaning of a given term very differently, alternate versions of the inventory have been customized and validated for use in languages and cultures in which a straight translation of English-language terms would yield inaccurate results. Today, more than 2 million people worldwide take the assessment each year (Briggs Myers et al. 1998: 9). Some companies even add the four-letter MBTI personality type acronyms to employees' business cards, which serves to facilitate communication. The MBTI categorizes personality types via four dichotomies, which indicate one personal preference versus another (see Table 1).

A total of sixteen different combinations of preferences are possible, corresponding to sixteen different personality types. For example, Isabel Briggs Myers describes the INFP type as follows:

> Idealistic, loyal to their values and to people who are important to them. Want an external life that is congruent with their values. Curious, quick to see possibilities, can be catalysts for implementing ideas. Seek to understand people and to help them fulfill their potential. Adaptable, flexible, and accepting unless a value is threatened. (The Myers and Briggs Foundation)

The sixteen types are typically organized using a table layout created by Isabel Briggs Myers (an INFP) (see Table 2).[1] MBTI type tables convey meaningful information about relationships between the sixteen personality types. The order of types in the table is always the same; there is a pattern in the quadrants in the top and bottom halves, and in the left and right halves.

---

1. For more information on the sixteen MBTI types, see The Myers & Briggs Foundation (2011).

Table 1. The four MBTI dichotomies (Briggs Myers et al. 1998:6).

Extraversion-Introversion Dichotomy (attitudes or orientation of energy)	
Extraversion (E)	**Introversion (I)**
Directing energy mainly toward the outer world of people and objects	Directing energy mainly toward the inner world of experiences and ideas
Sensing-Intuition Dichotomy (functions or processes of perception)	
Sensing (S)	**Intuition (N)**
Focusing mainly on what can be perceived by the five senses	Focusing mainly on perceiving patterns and interrelationships
Thinking-Feeling Dichotomy (functions or processes of judging)	
Thinking (T)	**Feeling (F)**
Basing conclusions on logical analysis with a focus on objectivity and detachment	Basing conclusions on personal or social values with a focus on understanding and harmony
Judging-Perceiving Dichotomy (attitudes or orientation towards dealing with the outside world)	
Judging (J)	**Perceiving (P)**
Preferring the decisiveness and closure that result from dealing with the outer world using one of the Judging processes (Thinking or Feeling)	Preferring the flexibility and spontaneity that result from dealing with the outer world using one of the Perceiving processes (Sensing or Intuition)

Table 2. Distribution of the sixteen MBTI types across the U.S. population calculated using inferential statistics (Briggs Meyers et al. 1998: 298, 385–386).

ISTJ	ISFJ	INFJ	INTJ
11.6%	13.8%	1.5%	2.1%
ISTP	ISFP	INFP	INTP
5.4%	8.8%	4.4%	3.3%
ESTP	ESFP	ENFP	ENTP
4.3%	8.5%	8.1%	3.2%
ESTJ	ESFJ	ENFJ	ENTJ
8.7%	12.3%	2.5%	1.8%

Once we become familiar with our own type, and once we understand what each preference represents, it is only a matter of time and practice before we can become proficient in identifying other people's types. For example, ENTPs are already intimately familiar with what being an Extravert, Intuitive, Thinking and Perceiving means, so they can easily recognize those traits in other people. In addition, it is not too difficult to identify a person whose traits are the opposite of our own because such a person's actions would seem diametrically opposed to ours. The more we know about ourselves, the more confident we become about our preferences, abilities and strengths. Table 3 provides a short summary of preferences and strengths as a function of the four MBTI dichotomies.

Table 3. Summary of personal preferences as a function of the four MBTI dichotomies.

Breadth of interests	**Extraversion**	**Introversion**	Depth of concentration
Reliance on facts	**Sensing**	**Intuition**	Grasp of possibilities
Logic and analysis	**Thinking**	**Feeling**	Warmth and sympathy
Organization and stability	**Judging**	**Perceiving**	Adaptability and flexibility

The existence of different personal psychological preferences has practical implications for project managers. Awareness and appreciation of personality differences can be used to improve communication, which in turn results in increased productivity and higher morale. The MBTI assessment is a useful tool for building successful project teams, improving project communication and productivity, managing conflict, and developing effective leadership. A comprehensive discussion of the application of MBTI types in project management is beyond the scope of this chapter, and so we will focus on the application of MBTI knowledge to three main areas that project managers have to deal with every day: perceptions of time, conflict resolution, and problem solving.

Perceptions of time: The role of personality

We all know that there is a finite number of hours in a day. However, although time is immutable, perceptions of time are not and can vary significantly depending on the situation. One of the best descriptions of the relativity of time is the one provided by Albert Einstein: "When a man sits with a pretty girl for an hour, it seems like a minute. But let him sit on a hot stove for a minute and it's longer than any hour. That's relativity" (Einstein 1938, reproduced in Mirsky 2002: 102).

Perceptions of time also vary depending on personality type. Kroeger and Thuesen (1992: 89) summarize the ways in which the different personality types relate to time as follows:

- *Extroverts*: time is to be overpowered and used.
- *Introverts*: time is special, a concept.
- *Sensing*: time is now; there is no time like the present.
- *Intuitive*: time is a set of possibilities; there is always time for one more thing.
- *Thinking*: time is an object, a resource.
- *Feeling*: time is relational and interpersonal.
- *Judging*: time is to be scheduled and controlled.
- *Perceiving*: time can be adapted and added to.

Of the four MBTI preference dichotomies, the Judging vs. Perceiving dichotomy is the one that plays the biggest role in shaping attitudes toward time. Everyone either has a need to control time or to adapt to it. Adapters will never become controllers, and vice versa, so project managers should not try to change the people with whom they work. Instead, project managers should recognize that everyone has his or her natural tendency and try to respect that fact. It is not the job of project team members to fit the mold of the project communication practices as designed and implemented by the project manager; instead, it is the job of the project manager to make accommodations for different personality types.

To better illustrate the difference in the Judging and Perceiving types' perspectives on time, let us look at how each type handles a common situation in which they are stuck in traffic and likely to miss an important meeting. Finding themselves in circumstances beyond their control can cripple Judging types' ability to deal with the situation constructively, as Judging types cannot easily generate alternatives. However, if a person knows that this tendency describes him or her, then he or she can learn to step back and look at the alternatives, e.g., whether to take a different road or to call and cancel the meeting. Perceiving types would react differently in this scenario. Once they realize that they are not going to make it to the meeting, Perceiving types might even be relieved if they are unprepared; they might start thinking about all of the other things that they can do during this unexpected free time, and they might not even think to call to tell their colleagues that they are going to miss the meeting. Having an adaptive nature can help Perceivers address this type of situation more constructively, for example, by cancelling the meeting and rescheduling it for a later time, or perhaps joining it by phone. Whatever one's type may be, it is beneficial to be aware that if Perceiving types could better control time, and if Judging types could better adapt to changing circumstances, both would handle themselves and their time more effectively.

In this respect, knowledge of the MBTI personality types is a double-edged sword: on one hand, such knowledge can enable more effective communication; but on the other hand, project managers who have learned about different types than have a responsibility to "speak the second language" of their team members.

Conflict resolution

People tend to approach conflict resolution in specific predictable ways based on their personality type. During tense situations, people tend to react in the way that feels "natural" to them, which usually leads to results that are not satisfying for anyone. However, once project managers and project team members acknowledge their natural tendencies, they can actually control tense situations if they consciously strive to avoid following their instinct and instead attempt to react in more constructive ways. Suggested constructive approaches to conflict resolution based on personality type are as follows:

- *Extroverts*: listen more; do not try to talk your way out of the situation.
- *Introverts*: talk more and tell your side of the story; people cannot read your mind.
- *Sensing*: look at other circumstances; there might be more to the situation than the facts would indicate.
- *Intuitive*: settle on the details first, and then look at the big picture.
- *Thinking*: express emotions and allow other people to do the same. This is an integral part of conflict, even if you may not see the point of it.
- *Feeling*: say what you really mean; other types will appreciate it. Do not be afraid to come across as too harsh.
- *Judging*: look for the gray areas between black and white and right or wrong to leave more room for others to negotiate with you.
- *Perceiving*: pick a side. While it is always fun to be flexible and/or argue both sides, this does not really help to resolve a conflict.

Problem solving

During conflict resolution, it pays to defer to one's non-dominant side (for example, Introverts should try to talk more). However, in problem solving the reverse tends to be true (except for the Extrovert vs. Introvert dichotomy). The author's experience suggests that approximately half of a typical day of a project manager is spent in problem solving. That being the case, it is important to know what strengths one has and how best to use them. Suggested constructive approaches to conflict resolution based on personality type are as follows:

- *Extrovert*: as you think while you talk, you may start circling at some point, so pay attention when you are repeating yourself, as that does not help to solve a problem. Try to avoid interrupting while others speak, even if they are repeating what you have already said, and especially when others pause, as this is not an invitation to jump in.

- *Introvert*: share your ideas more quickly; do not try to filter them internally. Remember that Extraverts do not have internal filters; so their most recent idea may be very different from the one they had a few minutes earlier. Help them to clarify.
- *Sensing*: try to press project team members to solve the problem at hand. Make sure everyone agrees on the definitions of the terms of the debate and present the facts. While seeing the big picture may be inspirational, it may not help to solve the actual problem.
- *Intuitive*: show everyone why the glass is half-full rather than half-empty and explore as many alternatives as you can without letting "down-to-earth" types hinder your creativity. When it comes to brainstorming solutions to problems, the more ideas are discussed the better (within reason, of course).
- *Thinking*: use your ability to keep everything in perspective to identify when some people over-personalize a situation, even when they have nothing to do with the situation or have no control over it. Keep the group focused on the issues and not the people, but do not go overboard as you will risk being seen as someone who does not care about others.
- *Feeling*: explain the potential impact that a solution may have on people. However, if your personal judgment interferes with a proposed solution, your task is to stay focused on the issue as objectively as you can. Make sure that everyone has a chance to be heard, but keep in mind that it may not be possible for every person who is impacted by a solution to be happy with the result. Trying to forge a consensus about a solution may come at the cost of the fairest solution.
- *Judging*: keep the process goal-oriented. While sidetracks may be fun, they are not necessarily helpful in solving the problem at hand. Make sure that a meeting results in action items, but do not enforce their implementation right away. Instead, wait until it is clear that the action items represent a final decision.
- *Perceiving*: make sure that all of the possibilities are examined. No matter how appealing the first proposal may be, a different and better solution might exist that could save time and money in the long run, so it is important to keep offering solutions in order to avoid overlooking better alternatives. Nevertheless, one must know when to say when: if you play devil's advocate for too long, you may make enemies quickly.

Managing international teams

Translation and localization project management requires that one work with people from a variety of different cultures. These intercultural aspects are both exciting and challenging. To get a better picture of the world in which the translation or localization project manager works, let us imagine that we can shrink the world's population of 6 billion people into a global village of just 100 people, while preserving all existing ratios. As noted by Goodman (2006: X–XI), this village would include:

- 60 Asians
- 14 Africans
- 12 Europeans
- 8 Latin Americans
- 5 people from the USA and Canada
- 1 person from the South Pacific

In this village:

- 22 would speak a Chinese dialect.
- 19 would speak Mandarin.
- 9 would speak English.
- 8 would speak Hindi.
- 51 would be male.
- 49 would be female.
- 82 would be non-Caucasian.
- 18 would be Caucasian.
- 80 would live in substandard housing.
- 67 would be unable to read.
- 50 would be malnourished.
- 24 would not have electricity.
- 7 would have access to the Internet.
- 1 would have a college education.
- 1 would have HIV.

Knowledge of other cultures is fundamental to successful communication. As Goodman notes (2006: XVIII), the workplace is influenced by a number of cultural factors, including language, type of social organization, communication styles – high-context or low-context, face-saving strategies, concepts of authority, non-verbal communication, concepts of time and space, and long- versus short-term orientation. Some of these aspects play a greater role than others in the everyday life of a translation or localization project manager. We will explore these aspects in greater detail in the sections that follow.

Language

English is the recognized language of business. Native English speakers have a distinct advantage in the realm of international business, but being a native speaker could be a handicap as well. It is easy to assume that anyone who understands English has the same cultural references as a native speaker. The motto of the Microsoft Windows International Division is "Global by design, local by experience." However, transforming this motto into reality is easier said than done. Once project managers (or the company for which they work) make the decision to think globally, they must make a conscious effort to learn how the values of others in the world differ from their own. These values are reflected to a great extent in language.

Learning the languages of the countries with which one's organization is conducting projects or in which one's team members live is a major way of overcoming cultural barriers; however, nobody expects a localization manager whose team members come from dozens of countries to be able to speak every one of those countries' languages. The reality is that the project manager might know a few phrases in those languages. In any event, the project manager is advised to follow best-practice approaches when speaking English to non-native speakers in order to increase the chances of successful communication. Simple sentence structures should be used; colloquialisms, abbreviations and idioms should be avoided. Analogies should be used with care, especially those related to sports. For example, people who were not born or raised in North America may not understand the rules of baseball or football even if they have lived in North America for a decade or more. When such people hear others use terms like *home run* or *touchdown*, they may not know what point others are trying to make. In such cases, the message sent is different from the message received, and thus communication is unsuccessful.

It is important to follow up on conversations by providing a written summary. People who have learned a foreign language in school tend to have much stronger reading skills than speaking or listening skills. It is essential that the project manager not confuse a smaller vocabulary pool with a smaller intelligence pool. Putting information in writing gives the members of the group a chance to verify their understanding and provides a historical document that can serve for future reference.

Low-context cultures, high-context cultures and face-saving

In 1976, cultural anthropologist Edward T. Hall published *Beyond Culture*, in which he coined the term *contexting* to describe the relative extent to which contextual information is used to send and decode messages in a given culture. Hall argues that cultures are distributed along a continuum on a scale from low to high context (Hall 1976: 105–116). In a low-context culture such as the United States, or most of Scandinavia, there is more reliance on explicit verbal messages to transmit meaning, and less attention is paid to contextual cues such as nonverbal signals, length and strength of the relationship, and the relative status of the parties involved. In low-context cultures, directness is highly valued and appreciated. Americans often say the phrase "time is money," and they mean it. Getting straight to the point is viewed as a virtue and a consideration of other people's time. In high-context cultures, the opposite is true. Getting to the point quickly is considered uncivilized and rude. In a high-context culture, such as Japan or Arab countries, people communicate their messages in a less direct way; much information remains implicit. The more similar the context, the less the communicator needs to express directly what he or she is trying to say. The delivery of messages is more indirect and more geared towards the consideration of others' feelings than in low-context cultures. Business decisions may be based on information collected through close personal relationships and extensive partnerships, rather than straight factual data, such as return on investment (ROI).

Table 4. Comparing cultures by *context* (Goodman 2006: 28; adapted from Hall 1976).

High context (information is implicit)

Japanese
Indian
Chinese
Arabic
Latin American
Italian
English
French
United States
German

Low context (information is explicit)

When interacting with people from a culture that is **lower on the context scale** than one's own culture, the following approaches are recommended:

– Get to the point quickly and limit the amount of background information that you present.
– Do not imply conclusions; state them specifically so that they are not misinterpreted or misunderstood.
– Use all of the data that you have to support your idea.
– Do not take criticism personally; people from low context cultures may seem rude or blunt. In low context cultures, people separate criticism of the issues from criticism of the people presenting the issues.
– Rules are important, and they are more rigidly followed in this culture than in your own.
– Do not become frustrated if you have to ask additional questions; people from low context cultures do not want to appear condescending by giving you too much information.

- Be careful not to read too much "between the lines." Do not assume that what a person is saying today correlates directly with what was said last week. When in doubt, clarify.
- Personal relationships have less importance in this culture than in your own, and they are kept separate from business relationships.

When interacting with people from a culture that is **higher on the context scale** than one's own culture, the following approaches are recommended:

- Pay close attention to the context in which communication is taking place, i.e., who is speaking, who is not speaking, what is the relative status of the speakers, and what is not being said. In this culture, patience is a virtue, and business cannot proceed until a relationship has been established.
- Preserving harmony is extremely important. Observe carefully how your message is received. Most likely people will never say "no," even if they disagree with you. Learn how disagreement and negative feelings are expressed in that culture.
- Be extremely careful about how you express your disagreement and/or give feedback. Face-saving is extremely important in high context cultures, so do state your disagreement in private, or do it through a third party.
- When you are asked for in-depth information, the expectation is that you will provide a great deal of detail, much more than you would ordinarily provide in your culture. If you give a concise answer, you will be considered unhelpful.
- Personal relationships are essential to successful business partnerships. Be prepared to use a variety of approaches to establish your credibility. Who you know, how willing you are to invest in the relationship, and spending time socializing can matter more than the facts and data you present.

Perceptions of time: The role of culture

Perceptions of time are shaped not only by an individual's personality type, as discussed above, but also by the culture in which the individual lives, and more specifically, by the ways in which that culture views the passage of time.

Edward T. Hall categorizes cultures as either *monochronic* or *polychronic* depending on the ways in which they relate to time (1959: 178; 1976: 17–20; 150–151). People in monochronic cultures tend to conduct activities sequentially, to focus on one thing at a time, to compartmentalize schedules and to separate task-oriented time from personal or social time. In contrast, people from polychronic cultures are comfortable engaging in several tasks or activities simultaneously and tend to place higher emphasis on people and relationships than on schedules or on completion of tasks. Drawing upon Hall's work, David A. Victor argues that business cultures can also be classified as monochronic or polychronic, depending on how they view time (Victor

1992: 234–241). Countries with monochronic business cultures, such as the United States, Great Britain, English-speaking Canada, Australia, Germany, and the majority of Scandinavia tend to have the following characteristics:

- Personal relationships are subordinate to schedules.
- Schedules are used to coordinate activities.
- Appointment times are rigid.
- One task is handled at a time.
- Breaks and personal time are sacred, regardless of personal ties.
- Time is perceived as inflexible and tangible.
- Work time is clearly separated from personal time.
- Each activity is seen as separate from the organization as a whole.
- Tasks are measured by how long they take.

Countries with polychronic business cultures, such as Italy, Greece, most of Latin America, Arabic speaking countries, and most of Asia, tend to have the following characteristics:

- Schedules are subordinate to personal relationships.
- Relationships are used to coordinate activities.
- Appointment times are flexible.
- Many tasks are handled simultaneously.
- Breaks and personal time are subordinate to personal ties.
- Time is perceived as flexible and fluid.
- Work time and personal time are not clearly separated.
- Activities are integrated into the whole organization.
- Tasks are measured as part of the organization's larger goals.

These perceptions influence the majority of the business activities a localization project manager performs every day. Knowing and understanding a vendor's perception of time can help the project manager avoid schedule slippage and organize meetings in the most productive way for all involved. Project managers from monochronic cultures leading teams of which some or all members are from polychronic cultures should try to be more flexible and remember that people from those cultures are already trying their best to accommodate what they likely see as inflexibility on the project manager's part.

An example from our personal experience will help to illustrate this phenomenon. Natalia once sent a request form on a Wednesday to a project manager in Italy, writing that she needed a financial report on the previous month's activities, and that she needed it "A.S.A.P." ("as soon as possible"). On Friday morning Natalia received a PDF that contained a lot of pretty diagrams, which was not what she needed. The document that she received was useless to her. Unfortunately, at that point in time it was already night in Italy; therefore, her report to her manager was going to be late.

Looking back on the situation, we realize that this communication failure was due in part to different perceptions of time and in part to differences in the contexts in which Natalia and the receiver of her message were working. Natalia's frame of reference for "A.S.A.P." was "by tomorrow morning." For Mario, who was in Italy where the philosophy of *dolce far niente* (sweet doing nothing) was invented, 48 hours was very reasonable. Natalia had been working with Excel spreadsheets all week, so she assumed that of course he would send her a report containing his raw data in Excel that she could use as the basis for her report. Mario, on the other hand, had just completed a report for his manager for a road show presentation that required a lot of diagrams, so his decision on how to present the report was heavily influenced by his most recent assignment. How should Natalia have phrased her request? In retrospect, she should have stated what she needed more explicitly: "I need a report as well as supporting data in an Excel spreadsheet on Friday by 10:00 a.m. Pacific Standard Time (PST)."

Dimensions of culture

In 1980, Dutch psychologist Geert Hofstede published his groundbreaking work, *Culture's Consequences: International Differences in Work-Related Values*. This monograph, based on two surveys conducted in 1968 and 1972 that generated some 116,000 questionnaires, "explores the differences in thinking in social actions that exist between members of 40 modern nations" (Hofstede 1980:11) and reveals that country cultures differ along four main dimensions, namely Power Distance Index (PDI); Individualism (IDV); Masculinity (MAS); and Uncertainty Avoidance Index (UAI). A follow-up study conducted by Chinese scholars identified a fifth dimension, Long-Term Orientation (LTO). Hofstede and Hofstede (2005) define the five dimensions of culture as follows:

- *Individualism* (IDV) "pertains to societies in which the ties between individuals are loose; everyone is expected to look after himself or herself and his or her immediate family. Collectivism as its opposite pertains to societies in which people from birth onward are integrated into strong, cohesive in-groups, which throughout people's lifetimes continue to protect them in exchange for unquestioning loyalty" (76).
- *Power Distance Index* (PDI) is "the extent to which the less powerful members of institutions and organizations within a country expect and accept that power is distributed unequally" (46).
- *Uncertainty Avoidance Index* (UAI) is "the extent to which members of a culture feel threatened by ambiguous or unknown situations. This feeling is, among other things, expressed through nervous stress and in a need for predictability: a need for written and unwritten rules" (167).

- *Masculinity* (MAS): "A society is called masculine when emotional gender roles are clearly distinct: men are supposed to be assertive, tough, and focused on material success, whereas women are supposed to be more modest, tender, and concerned with the quality of life. A society is called feminine when emotional gender roles overlap: both men and women are supposed to be modest, tender, and concerned with the quality of life" (120).
- *Long-Term Orientation* (LTO) is defined as "the fostering of virtues oriented toward future rewards – in particular, perseverance and thrift. Its opposite pole, short-term orientation, stands for the fostering of virtues related to the past and present – in particular, respect for tradition, preservation of 'face' and fulfilling social obligations" (210).

Table 5 presents a summary of the scores of selected countries across Hofstede's five dimensions of culture.

Table 5. Hofstede's cultural dimensions for selected countries/regions (Hofstede 2009). Zero represents the lowest value. See Hofstede (2009) for a complete list of all countries across the five dimensions.

Country	IDV	PDI	UAI	MAS	LTO
Arab World*	38	80	68	52	
Australia	90	36	51	61	31
Brazil	38	69	76	49	65
Canada	80	39	48	52	23
China	20	80	30	66	118
Denmark	74	18	23	16	
France	71	68	86	43	
Germany	67	35	65	66	31
Hong Kong	25	68	29	57	96
India	48	77	40	56	61
Israel	54	13	81	47	
Italy	76	50	75	70	
Japan	46	54	92	95	80
Malaysia	26	104	36	50	
Netherlands	80	38	53	14	44
Pakistan	14	55	70	50	0
Russia	39	93	95	36	
Spain	51	57	86	42	
Switzerland	68	34	58	70	
Taiwan	17	58	69	45	87
United Kingdom	89	35	35	66	25
United States	91	40	46	62	29

* Regional estimated value; "Arab World" = Egypt, Iraq, Kuwait, Lebanon, Libya, Syria, Saudi Arabia, United Arab Emirates.

Hofstede's dimensions of culture have profound implications for those who manage international, multicultural teams. Let us consider individualism versus its counterpart, collectivism. The Unites States has the highest score of any country on the individualism scale. Freedom, independence, and self-reliance are core values of the American culture. One man can fight – and defeat – an entire army; we see this scenario play itself out again and again in Hollywood movies. Americans measure success based on the individual's performance. On the other side of the spectrum, we find collectivist cultures, such as Asian and Latin American countries. A popular saying in Japan, "the nail that stands up will be nailed down," reflects the expectation in Japanese culture that an individual is subordinate to the group. Preserving harmony is paramount for collectivism-type cultures. Nevertheless, it is important that the manager of international, multicultural project teams keep in mind that these cultural differences describe *tendencies*, rather than characteristics of individuals.

Communication plan

While communication is always challenging, it can be more easily and effectively managed by establishing and using a communication plan. This plan documents what information needs to be communicated to which stakeholders, when, how often and in what format(s).

The Project Management Institute (PMI) recommends proactively planning for communication prior to launching a project. Several aspects need to be taken into consideration during communication planning. It is important to decide which meetings must be attended by everyone in person, and what decisions can be made (and/or communicated) by email or phone. It is also necessary to identify what information stakeholders require, as well as the format(s) and/or media in which they need to receive that information. These types of proactive planning are essential to managing information proliferation and keeping communication effective. In the sections that follow, we will examine the ways in which proactive planning can be applied to meetings, status reports and emails in order to improve the effectiveness of communication and to minimize the risks of information overload.

Meetings

Ineffective meetings are one of the biggest causes of frustration in the workplace. Time is limited and if people feel that their time is being wasted by ineffective meetings, they may eventually come to resent those who they see as time-wasters, including the project manager whose responsibility it is to keep meetings on track. The proper procedure for running a meeting involves having a meeting agenda, sticking to that agenda, and summarizing the key points of the meeting afterwards. Even if these cardinal rules of meeting management are followed, much time can still be lost in meetings. On the other hand, in some circumstances, meetings can actually save time. The project manager must determine at which point a meeting is warranted – or not warranted, as the case may be. When, for example, would a five-minute meeting be faster than days' worth of emailing on a topic? When would a quick email be faster than setting up and holding a five-minute meeting?

In order to get the best out of the people who are attending the meeting, it is advisable to let Extroverts talk, let Sensors present the data, let Intuitives put everything in perspective, give Introverts the agenda in advance to think things through, let Perceivers come up with multiple alternatives, and let the Judging types organize everything. When the meeting starts, Judging types will almost always be on time, and Perceiving types will usually be late. To maximize the effectiveness of a meeting, one can start on time for Judging types and begin by discussing the least important issues, and then when Perceiving types arrive, move on to the important issues. One can reduce collective stress levels by understanding that what excites and energizes one person may stress and drain another. For example, steering away from the agenda and discussing alternative options for resolving an issue will energize Perceivers because they are given freedom to explore multiple alternatives, but this will drain the energy of Judgers who want to stay on track, on time, and on schedule with the meeting. A balance has to be struck between these two opposing preferences. For meetings to be more effective, it is important to allow various points of view to be heard and different needs to be met.

Lencioni (2004) advocates two types of meetings that work well for translation and localization project managers. The first type of meeting is a quick ten-minute check-in meeting with the project team each morning. During check-in meetings, everyone remains standing and the meeting cannot exceed ten minutes in duration. If the project team is dispersed geographically, a telephone conference call or an instant messenger session can be held at the most appropriate time. The second type of meeting is a weekly project status meeting during which topics are covered in greater detail. This type of meeting has a strict agenda, including (1) old business, (2) new business, and (3) lessons learned. Any lengthier discussions can be scheduled to be included in the mid-project review or post-project review.

Depending on the project being managed, one should experiment with different kinds of meetings, such as monthly venting meetings attended by all, during which people can share their frustrations, or standing meetings held in the hallway. When holding virtual meetings of geographically dispersed teams, the latest technology should be used. If possible, a face-to-face kick-off meeting should be organized, as that might be the only chance to get the whole team together and begin building important relationships that will subsequently prove useful during the project.

The following best practices are suggested when leading meetings:

- Create an action-focused agenda.
- Ensure that everyone participates in the discussion.
- Deal appropriately with disruptive and inattentive attendees.
- Develop a climate of trust among the participants.
- Create and deliver effective presentations.
- Stay on track to achieve the goals of the meeting.
- Achieve clear communication during meetings of international teams.
- Liven up a meeting that is becoming dreary or unproductive.
- Assign action items and specify expected completion dates.
- Close meetings on an upbeat and positive note.

Status reports

Status reports are a potential source of information overload. Often people confuse a list of tasks performed, or a list of outstanding issues that need to be resolved, with a status report. In this regard, it is critical to understand what information is required by project stakeholders before creating status report templates. In most cases, stakeholders want to know what the project objectives, deliverables, and/or milestones are, and what the likelihood is that the objectives and/or deadlines will be met. If it has been decided that colored flags will be used to indicate status (red, yellow, green), it is important to define what these colored flags mean and to ensure that they are being used consistently across the organization in order to avoid possible confusion. Publishing status reports on a website from which stakeholders can pull the data is a much better solution than pushing the reports out in an email. Allow project stakeholders to look for status updates if and when they need them instead of cluttering their email inboxes with more messages. As Peter and Hull advise (1969: 63), "Never stand when you can sit; never walk when you can ride; never Push when you can Pull."

Emails

Today, the project manager cannot live with email, nor can s/he live without it. Since time and attention are finite, it is imperative that the project manager minimize to the extent possible the amount of time spent on the entire email process. Most email messages contain extraneous information that does not require immediate attention. The strong filtering capabilities of email programs like Microsoft Outlook can be used to filter and file non-critical emails. The search capabilities of one's email client can be used to retrieve these messages later. McGhee (2005) provides a number of effective strategies for limiting email-induced information overload. She recommends checking email only a few times per day, and refraining from using the email inbox like a task list. McGhee also advocates going through the inbox systematically from top to bottom and taking one of the following four actions with respect to each email message:

1. Act on it (if it can be done in 5 minutes or less).
2. Turn it into a task to do later if it will take too long.
3. File it for later reference.
4. Delete it.

These four steps are a recipe for sanity. It is also recommended that email be turned off when it is necessary to focus attention on a specific task. Humans cannot multitask, even though many of us think we can. "[T]he truth is that multitasking is neither a reality nor is it efficient," observes multitasking expert Dave Crenshaw (2008: 11). "Multitasking, when it comes to paying attention, is a myth," agrees molecular biologist John Medina (2008: 84). "To put it bluntly, research shows that *we can't multitask*. We are biologically incapable of processing attention-rich inputs simultaneously," adds Medina (2008: 85). The human brain processes information in linear fashion. When people think they are multitasking, they are in fact "switch-tasking" (Crenshaw 2008: 17). You can wash dishes and talk to someone, but you can't answer emails and listen to a speaker. No matter how fast you switch, time is lost between the switches and performance is invariably undermined. As Medina points out, "[s]tudies show that a person who is interrupted takes 50 percent longer to accomplish a task. Not only that, he or she makes up to 50 percent more errors" (Medina 2008: 87).

Turning off any beeps and/or pop-ups triggered by the receipt of new email messages also decreases the likelihood of distraction. It is advisable to log out of instant messaging programs or to display an "out-of-office" or "I'm currently unavailable" message during periods when one needs to intensely focus on something else. One can also shut the office door and request that people send an email in lieu of face-to-face communication. Responses to the emails can subsequently be sent as soon as the intensive task at hand has been completed. Making one's self available 100% of the time does not increase effectiveness – on the contrary. However, dedicating specific blocks of time – and thus, limited amounts of time – to email responses forces us to provide clearer and more concise answers to the people with whom we are corresponding.

The effectiveness of an email message is enhanced not only by clarity and concision, but also by the way in which it is composed. We recommend placing the most pertinent information or summaries at the top of the message, especially if the message includes one or more actions that the recipient is being asked to perform. Important information should be highlighted. For instance, a critical sentence can be presented in an outlined format so it will capture the reader's attention and be easier to read.

Conclusion

Communication is successful if the message that is received is the same as the one that was meant to be sent by the sender. Different personality types receive and interpret messages and information differently; it is the responsibility of the sender to communicate in the way in which the receiver is most comfortable. Perception of time, conflict resolution and problem solving are influenced by both personality type and culture. When we communicate with a person from a culture that is different from our own, it is essential that we take into consideration whether that culture has higher or lower context than ours, and proceed accordingly.

Finally, the method used for communicating, such as email, face-to-face meeting, and videoconferencing can affect the quality of the encounter. New technology can be extremely useful, but it is not a panacea for solving communication problems. Each medium has its strengths and weaknesses, and it is important to consider the possibility of information overload when selecting a medium of communication. Understanding and respecting the audience is the key to successful communication.

References

Briggs Myers, Isabel, McCauley, Mary H., Quenk, Naomi L. and Hammer, Allen L. 1998. *MBTI Manual. A Guide to the Development and Use of the Myers-Briggs Type Indicator*. 3rd ed. Palo Alto: Consulting Psychologists Press.

Crenshaw, Dave. 2008. *The Myth of Multitasking: How "Doing It All" Gets Nothing Done*. San Francisco: Jossey-Bass.

Einstein, Albert. 1938. "On the effects of external sensory input on time dilation." *Journal of Exothermic Science and Technology* 1 (9). Reproduced in Mirsky 2002.

Goodman, Michael B. 2006. *Work with Anyone Anywhere: A Guide to Global Business*. Belmont, CA: Professional Publications.

Hall, Edward T. 1959. *The Silent Language*. Garden City, NY: Doubleday.

———. 1976. *Beyond Culture*. Garden City, NY: Anchor Press-Doubleday.

Hofstede, Geert. 1980. *Culture's Consequences: International Differences in Work-Related Values*. Beverly Hills, CA: SAGE.

———. 2009. "Geert Hofstede Cultural Dimensions." http://www.geert-hofstede.com/hofstede_dimensions.php

Hofstede, Geert and Hofstede, Gert Jan. 2005. *Cultures and Organizations: Software of the Mind*. Rev. ed. New York: McGraw-Hill.

Kroeger, Otto and Thuesen, Janet M. 1992. *Type Talk at Work*. New York: Dell Publishing.

Lencioni, Patrick. 2004. *Death by Meeting: A Leadership Fable about Solving the Most Painful Problem in Business*. San Francisco: Jossey-Bass.

McGhee, Sally. 2005. *Take Back Your Life! Using Microsoft Outlook to Get Organized and Stay Organized*. Redmond, WA: Microsoft Press.

Medina, John. 2008. *Brain Rules: 12 Principles for Surviving and Thriving at Work, Home, and School*. Seattle, WA: Pear Press.

Mirsky, Steve. 2002. "Einstein's hot time." *Scientific American* 287 (3): 102.
Peter, Laurence J. and Hull, Raymond. 1969. *The Peter Principle*. New York: William Morrow.
Project Management for Development Organizations (PM4DEV). 2009. Fundamentals of Project Management for Development Organizations. 2nd ed. [Atlanta, GA: PM4DEV.]
Szalay, Lorand B. 1981. "Intercultural communication – A process model." *International Journal of Intercultural Relations* 5 (2): 133–146.
The Myers and Briggs Foundation. 2011. "The 16 MBTI® types." Excerpted from *Introduction to Type*, by Isabel Briggs Myers. http://www.myersbriggs.org/my-mbti-personality-type/mbti-basics/the-16-mbti-types.asp
Treasury Board of Canada Secretariat. 1999. *Project Plan Template*. Ottawa: Treasury Board of Canada Secretariat, Chief Information Officer Branch. http://www.tbs-sct.gc.ca/emf-cag/project-projet/ppto-pssp/templates-gabarits/project-projet/project-projet-eng.pdf
Victor, David A. 1992. *International Business Communication*. New York: Harper Collins.

Risk management in localization

Mark Lammers

> You can blame people who knock things over in the dark,
> or you can begin to light candles. You're only at fault if you know
> about the problem and choose to do nothing.
> Paul Hawken

Risk management, a set of processes designed to maximize opportunities and minimize threats, is essential to successful project management. This chapter discusses risk management in the context of outsourced localization projects. It begins by proposing a localization Risk Breakdown Structure (RBS) to categorize recurring localization project risks. It then discusses the Project Management Institute's (PMI) standardized risk management framework, which involves proactive and systematic risk identification and prioritization, response planning and monitoring. The chapter concludes by examining the application of the PMI risk management framework to localization projects and by proposing responses to common localization risks.

Why manage risks?

Risk management is as important to project management as oxygen is to life. Every action a project manager takes is an effort to decrease the potential impact of negative events and increase the potential impact of positive events in order to achieve the project goals. Without risk management, projects would fail as a matter of course.

Actually, one could say that living one's life is also managing risk. For example, making the decision to cross an intersection in one's car is done after careful inspection of the situation and consideration of the possible risks, namely other cars or pedestrians who may lie in our path and potentially prevent us from reaching our goal of getting to our destination on time and in one piece.

Project managers often manage risk instinctively, and may not even realize that they are doing so. Whether managing schedules, fixing product bugs, or adding additional resources to a project, they are mitigating potential risks that they have identified and which could prevent project success. Every time they recalculate a project schedule based on actual work accomplished, for example, they are anticipating the potential for schedule failure and reacting to normalize the results by adding more time, cutting scope or adding resources.

The fact that project managers are capable of managing risk instinctively might lead one to ask why a chapter on risk management is included in a volume on project management. However, my experience working on localization projects has led me to conclude that project managers who are not following a systematic and proactive risk management process are not as efficient or effective as they could be because they are *reacting* to risk events after they have occurred, rather than identifying them up front and trying to ensure that they do not occur in the first place.[1] Moreover, reacting to risk events after they have occurred is by definition not risk management. As the Project Management Institute (PMI) observes, "[t]he objectives of Project Risk Management are to increase the probability and impact of positive events, and decrease the probability and impact of events adverse to the project" (PMI 2004: 237), in effect, identifying risks so that one can mitigate or capitalize upon them and thus increase the potential for project success.

Managing a project without applying formal risk management is akin to navigating a boat through unknown waters in the fog and hoping not to hit anything. The set of strategies that comprise risk management could be likened to the radar, lighthouses, depth sounders and radio communication that make boat navigation possible. Without risk management, we are sailing in the dark. PMI has defined a systematic risk management framework for identifying, prioritizing and mitigating risks that can be applied to projects of any size in any industry. This chapter will discuss the PMI risk management framework and how it can be effectively applied to localization projects. This chapter will be useful for project managers of all levels of experience, as well as for translation and localization educators.

What is a project? And what is risk?

The definition of "project" used in this chapter is that proposed by PMI, namely "a temporary endeavor undertaken to create a unique product, service or result" (PMI 2004: 368). Although the term "risk" is commonly used in project management, in practice this term is not always clearly defined. PMI defines risk as "an uncertain event or condition that, if it occurs, has a positive or negative effect on at least one project objective" (PMI 2004: 373). An event is a negative occurrence, such as a missed deadline in a schedule, whereas a condition is the situation that causes or leads to the event, such as an unrealistic schedule. The effect, or impact, is the negative (or positive) result of the event, such as a missed product launch date, for example. To illustrate this definition of risk, let us consider a simple example from a hypothetical software localization project:

---

[1] A localization project is, for the purposes of this chapter, the outsourced localization into one or more languages of the user interface text and help content of a software project.

a work package (i.e., a set of files) is handed off to a translation vendor, and it turns out that the word count of these files is double the original estimate. Because of this unanticipated increase in volume (the condition), the vendor is unable to complete the translation of the package in the agreed-upon timeframe (the event), which in turn will cause delays for downstream activities such as engineering and testing and may jeopardize the software release schedule (the impact). The goal of risk management is to minimize the probability that such an event will occur and, if it does occur, mitigate the negative impact or transform it into a positive result through project planning. In other words, risk management is undertaken in order to increase the probability of project success.

Risk profile of software localization projects

Any discussion of risk management in localization projects begs the question of whether risks observed in localization projects are unique, more pervasive or more acute than in other types of projects. Localization projects are not necessarily any riskier than any other type of project in the high-tech industry. In fact, localization projects present the same categories of risks found in other projects. A Risk Breakdown Structure (RBS) is a helpful way of categorizing and organizing risks by type. Recurring localization project risks can be broken down into four main categories: technical risks, external risks, organizational-related risks and project management-related risks (see Figure 1). Each risk category can be further subdivided into more granular sub-categories, some examples of which are shown in Figure 1.

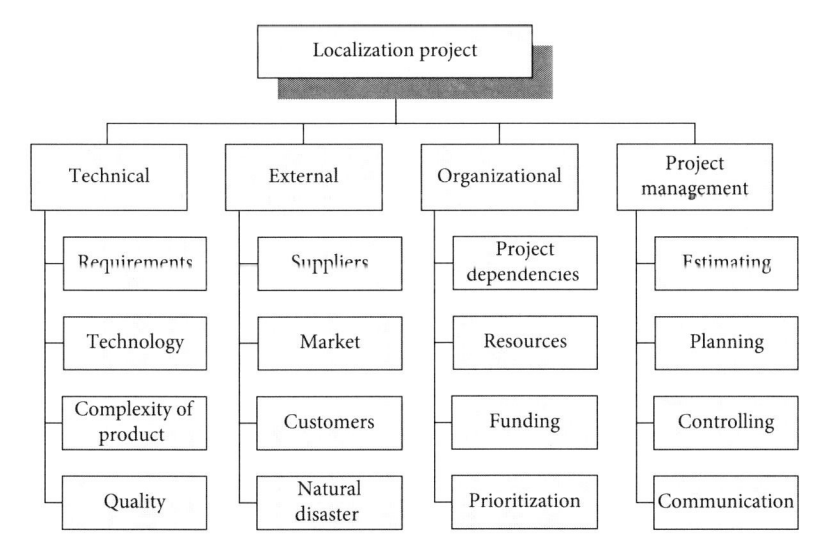

Figure 1. A localization Risk Breakdown Structure (RBS) that classifies risks typically encountered in outsourced localization projects. This figure is an adaptation of a sample PMI Risk Breakdown Structure (PMI 2004: 244).

Technical risks

Requirements-related risks
Two of the most critical requirements of any software that is destined for global markets are that it be globalized and localizable. A globalized software product is one that has been designed to support multiple languages and locales, whereas localizability describes the relative extent to which an application can be localized, or adapted to meet the needs, expectations and requirements of a given locale. Software is often designed from a U.S. perspective, and globalization knowledge among software developers in the U.S. tends to be sparse or non-existent. Consequently, the globalization or localizability requirements for a product or feature are often unfulfilled or insufficiently fulfilled. One example of a globalization requirement would be allowing multiple date or currency formats so that users from other cultures can correctly display dates or currencies in the appropriate format. An example of a localizability requirement would be designing dialog box layouts to accommodate translation-related text expansion. For example, translating into languages such as French or German can cause an increase of 20% to 30% in the length of a given text (Esselink 2000: 331). If provisions are not made during the design of the source-language software to accommodate this expansion and ensure that there is adequate space to display the translated content in the target-language dialog boxes, there is a high risk that truncation will occur. An example of requirements-related risk would be the lack of language support, or the ability to enter data written in a given human language using a keyboard; Windows Vista, for example, supports input in some 151 different languages.[2] If globalization requirements are unfulfilled, certain features may function incorrectly in the target market.

Technology-related risks
Over the past decade, the scale, scope and complexity of localization projects have increased to the point where most companies have sought to automate their file management workflows, such as the physical transfer of files between client and vendor using File Transfer Protocol (FTP) technology. However, file management workflow automation can be complicated and sometimes fails to meet the functional requirements that were originally specified. Automation that does not work as expected causes delays in the schedule due to increased task duration and can prove to be very costly to a project.

Product complexity-related risks
Highly complex software products may present a high degree of risk if their complexity makes it more difficult to fulfill globalization or localizability requirements. If a software product cannot be made readily localizable, then localization tasks may take

---

2. For more examples of globalization and localizability requirements, see Dr. International (2002).

longer than originally estimated, requiring extra work and possibly leading to schedule delays. This is not to say that localization enablement is always more difficult when creating highly complex products, only that increases in product complexity could increase localization risks in the absence of effective enablement.

Quality-related risks
Translation quality is a common type of quality-related risk in localization. Translation quality directly impacts the perception of product quality. If the translation quality is poor, meaning that the translations are either incorrect, use incorrect terminology or do not sound "natural" to native speaker, then the product will likely be perceived as being of lower quality by users in the target market. It is of paramount importance to obtain the highest quality translation services when localizing a product.

External risks

Risks related to suppliers of localization services
The use of translation and localization service providers is extremely common in software localization projects. According to Common Sense Advisory, 87% of all translation buyers outsource most or all of their translation projects (Beninatto 2006: 4). Using external service providers adds a layer of risk to localization projects: the client organization depends on the external suppliers to complete high-quality work on time and within budget, but the client organization does not have direct control over the localization production work, schedules or the testing performed by these external suppliers. From the perspective of the client organization, this lack of direct control translates into potential for schedule delays, quality issues and possibly budget overruns.

Market- and customer-related risks
In order for a product to sell well in a given market, it must meet the expectations of customers in that market in terms of features, performance, usability and affordability. If the product fails to meet expectations, customer reviews will be poor and sales will falter. However, the expectations of international customers can be difficult to capture. If the company producing a software product does not have a presence in the target market, be it a subsidiary or other local contacts, it will likely have even more difficulty understanding the expectations of customers in that market. Moreover, customer expectations can vary from market to market. Japanese customers, for example, are known to set the bar very high where product and documentation quality are concerned. If the local customer expectations are unsatisfied or under-satisfied, product sales in that market can suffer.

Risks related to natural disasters and political instability
Natural disasters such as earthquakes, floods and fires pose a risk to localization projects, as do human-created disasters such as war or political coups, albeit one of low probability. I have worked on projects during which work being done in other parts of the world by translation providers has been disrupted by flooding and by political instability. While these types of risks are of very low probability and are out of the immediate control of the project manager, they are nonetheless valid risks that need to be addressed.

Organizational risks

Risks related to project dependencies
Software localization is downstream from, and dependent upon, software feature development. For example, a feature must be developed and must be in a state of relative completeness before the user interface text can be translated into one or more foreign languages. Otherwise, changes to user interface text will require re-translation and project costs will increase. Thus, there are strong dependencies between localization project teams and feature development teams within the development organization, as the development teams must complete and test their work before localization can begin. These dependencies encompass (a) the schedule, since the overall product schedule is rarely within the full control of the localization organization; (b) internationalization of the product, since responsibility for ensuring globalization and localizability mainly falls to the core development teams; and (c) quality, since testing of the U.S. English product may include testing of pseudo-localized software or content. Such upstream dependencies increase the risk that deliverables or requirements will not be met because the corresponding work is not performed under the control of the localization team.

Resource-related risks
An example of this type of risk would be a situation in which insufficient skilled resources are available to complete the work according to the schedule. Fewer skilled technical translators are available in certain language pairs than others. Consequently, when serving the corresponding markets, finding enough skilled technical translators to work on a project and complete it within the negotiated timeframe is difficult, and can add resource-related risk to the project.

Funding-related risks
The budgets of localization divisions in major software companies are often subjected to a high degree of scrutiny because a significant proportion of such budgets consists of external spending in the form of work subcontracted to external service

providers, which is easily tracked. If localization organizations cannot justify the return on investment (ROI) on localization costs vs. sales of localized products, their budgets may be cut. This could result in the discontinuation of localized versions of the software product in one or more markets, in which case customers in the affected markets would only be able to purchase the English version. Depending on the market, the discontinuation of localized product could potentially damage the image of the company.

Prioritization-related risks
In many companies, the prioritization of localized products is determined by potential or actual revenue from the target markets. Following this logic, the largest market is typically the highest priority for the company. In this scenario, if budgets are restricted, then there is a risk that funding and resource allocation for localizing a product could be cut or severely restricted. Prioritization-related risk rises in inverse proportion to the real or projected revenue associated with the localized product.

Project management-related risks

Risks related to estimating (cost and scope)
Localization project specifications are sometimes inadequate or incomplete if the organization providing them is not experienced in providing such specifications or if the product is constantly changing. Inadequate and/or incomplete specifications in turn make it difficult or impossible to accurately define the scope of a project. If the scope definition is inaccurate or subject to constant change, there is a greater chance of schedule delays and cost overruns.

Risks related to planning
An example of a planning-related risk would be a situation in which the schedule has not been approved by all parties completing the work and is not feasible in the given time frame. The result of this planning oversight could be the failure to complete deliverables by scheduled dates and thus delays in the schedule.

Risks related to controlling
Positively controlling the factors in a project that cause the scope to change tends to be difficult since localization is undertaken following product feature development work, and since product feature development work is performed by an organization that is out of the immediate sphere of control of the localization project manager. The less control the project manager and project team have over the scope of the project, the greater the risk that the scope will increase. Scope increase, in turn, can cause budget overruns and schedule delays.

Communication-related risks
Localization project teams can be large and may comprise many members working in remote locations. In such cases, keeping the entire project team abreast of project changes can be challenging. Situations can easily arise where not all of the parties responsible for completing project work are kept informed of scope or schedule changes. The failure to communicate such changes to project team members may in turn cause work or schedule delays.

The technological, organizational and project management-related risks discussed above and presented in Figure 1 are operative in most localization projects. However, localization organizations do not always perform formal risk management, and even when they do, risk management processes are not necessarily implemented systematically. I have been involved in localization projects in which risk management was formally initiated, but incompletely executed during the course of the project. Risks were neither tracked, nor controlled, nor were new risks identified during the course of project execution. In the absence of formal, systematic risk management, project performance and outcomes usually suffer. The PMI risk management framework offers a solution to such problems.

The PMI risk management framework

The Project Management Institute (PMI) risk management framework is an effective tool that can be easily adapted to create a set of formal or informal processes for use in any localization organization (see Figure 2). The framework consists of a continuous process whereby an organization identifies and prioritizes new project risks, decides if and how it will respond to those risks (through planned risk response strategies of avoidance, mitigation, contingency planning, transfer or acceptance), monitors and controls identified risks, and seeks to identify new risks throughout the course of the project. Thus, the risk management framework is a means by which an organization can lower the likelihood that known risk events will occur over the course of the project, and minimize the impact of those risk events if they do in fact occur, thereby increasing the chances of project success.

Risk identification

Risk management begins with the identification of potential risks. Identifying project risks enables us to gain insight into the unknowns of a project and better understand what could potentially happen during a project that would negatively impact the ability to meet the project goals in terms of timeline, budget and quality. Risk identification is a process that occurs – or that should occur – throughout a project, beginning at the planning phase and continuing throughout the execution of the project.

How can one possibly know in advance what will or might happen during a project? One of the best indicators of future project events and performance is historical information on similar past projects completed by an organization. Most organizations complete project reviews or project post-mortems. The goal of the project review is to determine what was and was not successful during a given project and to document that information in the form of a set of lessons learned. Project reviews, and the lessons learned that are documented therein, comprise a project "knowledge base" that project managers can consult in order to identify the types of risks that may occur in similar future projects.

Some organizations document past project risks in the form of a risk register (spreadsheet or database) that spans multiple projects over time. Documenting this type of information is probably the most effective way for localization organizations to manage future project risks. The risk register contains the complete set of risk descriptions (conditions and risks) as well as information about probability, impacts, mitigation strategies, contingencies and "triggers" (the "symptoms" that a risk event has occurred). (These concepts will be discussed at length in the following sections). Project managers initiating a new project can consult this register to identify potential risks to their projects based on historical risks that the organization has encountered and documented in the past. The data in the risk register can also be analyzed to identify trends across the organization. In this way, overall process improvement for the organization can be informed by actual project risk data.

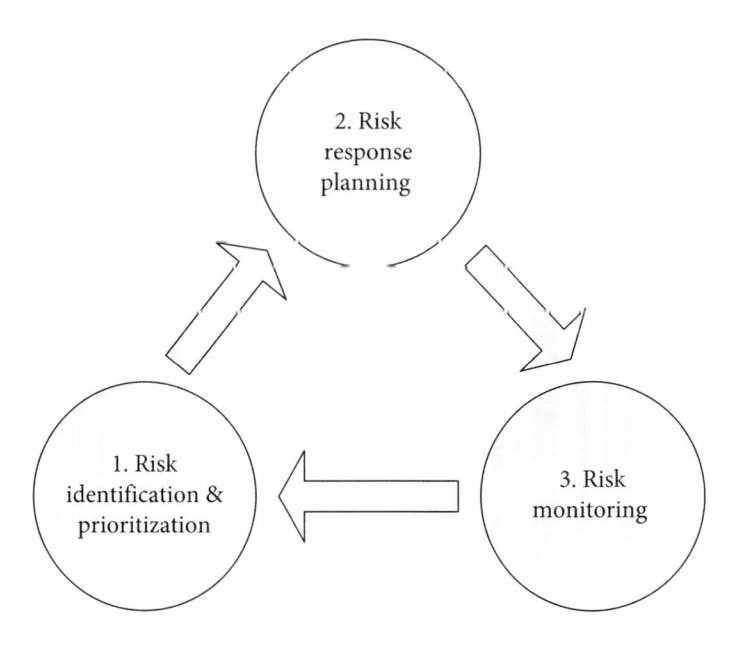

Figure 2. The PMI risk management framework (PMI 2004: 237–268).

Additional project-specific risks can be identified by consulting subject matter experts (on technology or process) who may or may not be working on the project. Such consultation can take the form of brainstorming sessions or one-to-one conversations. Soliciting expert opinion is an excellent way to uncover risks that may not be inherently obvious to non-experts and which may not have been captured in historical documentation.

It is important that project teams not get carried away in their identification of risks. Identifying hundreds of risks in a project is neither necessary, nor desirable. Mitigating hundreds of project risks would be impossible; the time required to simply plan for such an endeavor would be prohibitive. The appropriate level of risk identification detail can be determined by the organization's level of risk tolerance and the amount of time that the project team can devote to risk planning. Some organizations are very risk-tolerant, meaning that they are willing to assume a substantial amount of risk. Such organizations tend to identify risks at a high level, and generally seek to mitigate only the most serious of risks. Organizations that are more risk-averse typically track risks at a more granular level. Such organizations will commit more time to risk mitigation planning. Software development companies are often highly risk-tolerant, whereas pharmaceutical companies and medical device manufacturers tend to be more risk averse.

Risk identification is – or should be – a team effort. Some project managers may feel that because they are the people ultimately accountable for managing risks on the project, they must do all of the risk identification work. However, such thinking is itself risky: one project manager brainstorming alone cannot identify nearly as many potential risks as a complete project team that pools its collective brainpower. The more perspectives and opinions that are brought to bear during the risk identification process, the more complete the list of identified risks will be. Some organizations fail to include the entire project team in risk brainstorming. My experience suggests that this is a mistake. I have managed localization projects, for example, in which vendor and client companies both participated in the risk identification process. Soliciting input from both vendor and client perspectives exposed risks that would not have been uncovered otherwise. Vendors and clients have different perspectives on the project and therefore offer diverse opinions that can only strengthen the risk identification process.

Risk prioritization

The net result of risk identification is a list of risks that clearly defines each potential risk as a combination of a condition and an event, or "trigger." As noted above, this list of risks is often documented and maintained in the form of a risk register. The comprehensive list of risks that may impact a project is the basis of all subsequent risk management activities. However, a comprehensive list typically contains many more risks than a project team has time or resources to address. Therefore, the risks must be prioritized based on (a) the probability that the risk event will occur and (b) the impact that the risk event will have on the project if it does in fact occur. This prioritization process allows the project team to focus specifically on the risks that will cause the most damage or on those that are most likely to occur.

Probability is defined as the likelihood that a risk event will occur. A best-practice approach to probability assessment is to assign a ranking of high, medium or low to each risk. In most cases, the project team, subject matter experts, and/or historical information enable an accurate estimation of the likelihood of a given risk event. Impact is defined as the damage a risk event will cause to a project goal or deliverable if it occurs. An impact ranking of high, medium or low should also be applied to each risk. Risk prioritization is most effective when probability and impact are ranked by the entire project team at one time.

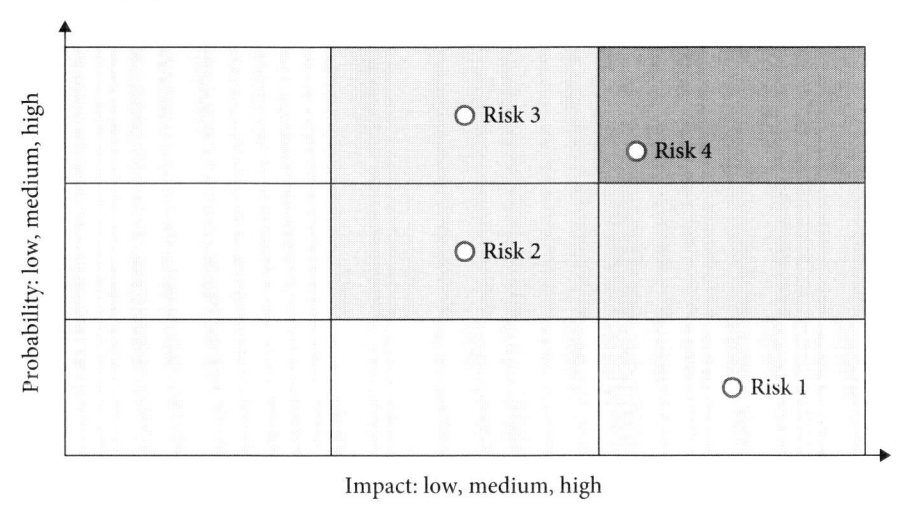

Figure 3. Sample risk probability and impact matrix.

The simplest way to prioritize risks is to plot them on a risk matrix based on assigned probability and impact values. Figure 3 presents a sample risk matrix that can be used to prioritize risks during the group probability and impact ranking activity. The matrix can be drawn on a whiteboard or on flipchart paper, and post-it notes can be used to represent individual risks. The group reviewing each risk prioritization must agree on the assignment of probability and impact of each risk. Once a consensus has been reached, the post-it note is placed in the appropriate section. The matrix can be shaded or color-coded for easier comprehension by the group. In the case of the sample risk prioritization matrix shown in Figure 3, the darkest shaded zone corresponds to risks with high probability and medium to high impact rankings, or conversely, high impact and medium to high probability rankings.

Any risks falling in the darkest shaded zone are considered to be high-priority risks for which mitigation strategies should be devised and/or contingencies made during the planning process. The darkest shaded zone should be the primary focus of the risk planning process. The lightest shaded zone in the diagram corresponds to risks with low probability and low to high impact rankings, or conversely, low impact and low to high probability rankings. Risks falling in the lightest shaded zone are considered to be less threatening risks for which contingency plans should be made or which the organization might decide to merely accept. The medium-shaded zone corresponds to risks whose probability and impact are ranked medium. One example of a medium-probability and medium-impact translation or localization risk would be terminological or product name changes occurring late in a project. The probability would be considered medium if this kind of late change had occurred once in a previous release, but the terminology to be used for this release is considered stable when the project begins. The impact would be judged to be medium if the risk event would cause extra work, but would not pose insurmountable problems resulting in missing schedule deadlines.

Some organizations become paralyzed by risk prioritization. They agonize over the probability and impact rankings and therefore the zone into which a given risk should fall. Project team members may disagree, sometimes strongly so. In such situations, a best practice is to urge participants to assign rankings based on their initial reactions, and not to over-analyze their assessments. If project team members cannot agree, then the project manager should act as a facilitator to help the team reach a consensus. If all else fails, then the team should err on the side of caution and use the higher ranking. However, the team must be careful not to rank too many risks as high priority. If every risk is ranked as high priority, the matrix loses its power to establish the relative criticality of risks: if every risk is critical, then no risk is critical. Furthermore, treating every risk as a high priority will require far more time and resources than the project team can actually devote to them. A final challenge of risk prioritization is the fact that the probability and/or impact of a given risk may change over the course of a project. In some cases, risks deemed to be a very high priority at the beginning of a project may be ranked at a lower priority in a later stage of the project.

In sum, risk prioritization is the process of examining the risk register and determining which risks warrant response planning and which do not. Once risks are prioritized, they should be assigned "owners." The risk owner will shepherd the risk through mitigation planning and continue to track it throughout the project lifecycle. The risk owner should be the person who best understands the risk and who is best qualified to determine the appropriate response strategy.

Risk response planning

After risks have been identified and prioritized, the focus of risk management turns to the determination of the appropriate risk response. Although the project manager is ultimately accountable for risk management, everyone on the project team should understand how all of the risk response methods work. The Project Management Institute proposes five strategies for responding to risk: avoidance, mitigation, transfer, acceptance and contingency (PMI 2004: 261–263).

- *Avoidance*: This strategy consists of making changes to the scope, deliverables or project management plan in order to eliminate the threat (or threats) posed by a risk. This strategy can be used to respond to risks that are identified early in a project and which can easily be handled by modifying project requirements. It can also be used for risks that are relatively critical but for which no clear mitigation strategy has been identified. To illustrate the strategy of avoidance, let us suppose that there is a risk that the translation work required to localize a particular feature or component will not be completed on time, thus delaying the release of the localized product. In this scenario, the decision to not localize the feature or component would be one example of an avoidance strategy.
- *Mitigation*: This strategy consists of a plan that will reduce either the probability or the impact of a risk in order to reduce its criticality to an acceptable level. For example, most of the risks that fall within the darkest shaded zone of Figure 4 will require the use of mitigation strategies to bring them down to acceptable levels

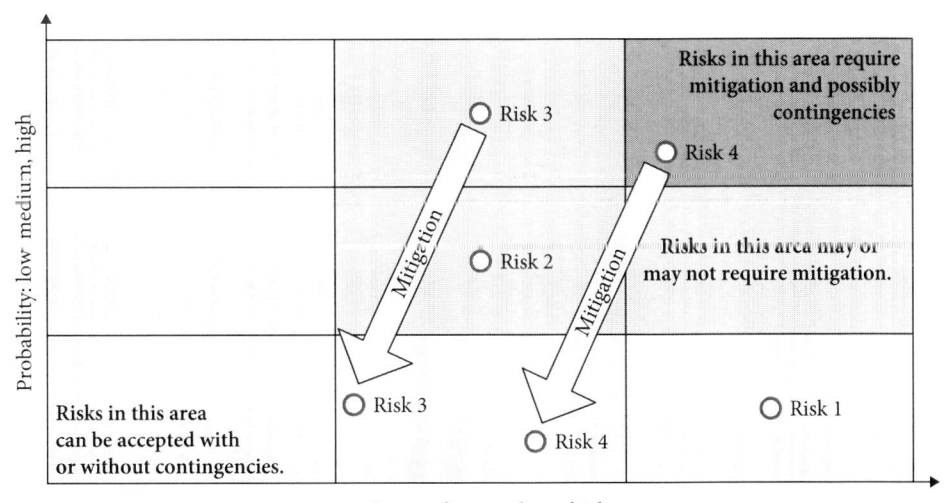

Figure 4. Risk mitigation response planning. High priority risks require mitigation, whereas lower priority risks may only require contingencies.

(i.e., to shift them into the least-shaded area of the risk prioritization matrix corresponding to the lowest level of probability and impact). To illustrate the strategy of mitigation, let us suppose that there is a risk that the localization services provider will be unable to complete the translation work in time due to public holidays in a particular market that will limit the number of working days during which the localizers can complete the work. An example of a mitigation strategy for this risk would be the hiring of additional resources in order to accomplish a given amount of work in a shorter period of time, thereby reducing the likelihood of a late delivery of the translation work.

- *Transfer*: This strategy shifts the ownership of a response as well as the impact of the threat to another party. The entire outsourcing model whereby client companies outsource translation services to external vendors is a form of risk transfer. The external vendor assumes much of the risk of schedule- and quality-related risks in this model. The purchase of insurance policies is another example of risk transfer.
- *Acceptance*: When this strategy is adopted, no action is taken to mitigate the risk. This strategy is used when a risk is minimal enough that it doesn't require mitigation. In Figure 4, any risks that fall into the least-shaded zone are acceptable, meaning that no mitigation is required. Risks that are out of one's immediate control, or which are too large to be managed effectively, such as political coups or natural disasters, must also be accepted, although in some cases contingency plans may also need to be made.
- *Contingency*: This strategy consists of the classic "Plan B" or workaround to be used if a risk event occurs. Low-priority risks whose probability is low but whose impact is high require only contingency plans, but not mitigation. An example of a contingency plan would be a workaround for a workflow automation tool in the event that the tool does not perform as expected. Risks whose probability and high impact are high may require a contingency plan in addition to mitigation, in case the mitigation strategy does not achieve the expected results.

From theory to practice: Responses to common localization risks

In order to illustrate how and when each type of response could be implemented, it will be beneficial to explore some examples of risks that are commonly encountered during localization projects (see Figure 1).

Schedule risks

- *Risk identification*: The localization project schedule is very aggressive and there is absolutely no room for error (the condition). If completed work packages are returned even a day late (the event), the schedule's critical path and the ability to

deliver the project on time will be jeopardized (the impact). (See the Appendix for a detailed discussion of the importance of the schedule's critical path in risk management.)
- *Prioritization*: This risk is deemed to be of high probability and high impact.
- *Response*:
    - *Mitigation:* One possible mitigation strategy for responding to this risk would be to hire more resources to complete the work in a shorter amount of time, thus creating a buffer in the schedule and decreasing the probability that schedule slippage will occur. Another possible mitigation strategy would be to re-negotiate the schedule so that it includes an adequate buffer to prevent missed project milestones without impacting the final delivery dates. A final mitigation strategy would be to analyze the schedule to see if there are any tasks that can be undertaken in parallel, thus shortening the critical path.
    - *Contingency plan:* If mitigation does not achieve the desired results, then the schedule will be delayed in the event that work packages cannot be completed on time. An additional contingency would be to create a communication plan with project stakeholders (higher management) so that they can be notified quickly if work packages are indeed delayed so that immediate schedule resolution can be accomplished.

Risks associated with the use of an automation tool

- *Risk identification*: New automated file management tools are being developed by a third-party company for use by the organization in a localization project. The tool development schedule is aggressive. The development company has very little experience creating such file management tools, nor does it have funds to hire testers to confirm that the tools work as expected (the condition). It is possible that, once in production, the tools will not work as expected or will take longer than expected to perform the work (the event). This could in turn cause schedule delays and potentially delay the entire project (the impact).
- *Prioritization*: This risk is deemed to be of medium probability and medium impact.
- *Response*:
    - *Mitigation:* One possible mitigation strategy for this risk would be to ensure that successful testing of the final tools is listed as one of the acceptance criteria for the final deliverables in the contract with the third-party development company. In other words, successful testing of the tools should be made a precondition for the formal acceptance of the tools developed by the outside company and for the use of the newly developed tools by the project team.
    - *Contingency plan:* A contingency plan for this risk might be to ensure the availability of an alternative or legacy tool set whose reliability has been

proven. If such a contingency plan were to be adopted, it would be necessary to train all resources on the use of the old tool set as well as the new, so that no time would be lost learning the old process if and when the plan were implemented. Another possibility would be to establish a manual workaround.

Terminology-related risks

- *Risk identification*: The organization is undertaking a project in a new target language and the terminology of certain basic hardware and software features has not yet been established. Glossaries of computer terminology do not exist for the language (the condition). There is a strong possibility that end-users of the software will be confused if the basic terminology in the software is not understandable (the event). If the target product is not easy to understand, then target users may defer to the English product, undermining target-market sales and defeating the purpose of localizing the product in the first place (the impact).
- *Prioritization*: This risk is deemed to be of high probability and high impact.
- *Response*:
    - *Mitigation*: Early engagement with target-market government entities and universities to develop basic terminology would greatly benefit this project. Community-based glossary creation would be another possible mitigation strategy. Another approach would be to conduct usability studies with end-users early in the project to gain insight into the users' relative understanding of the product.

Project scope risks

- *Risk identification*: The scope of a software localization project is defined at the outset of the project. However, during the course of the project, writing teams continue to contribute content (the condition), causing the scope of the project to grow well beyond what was planned (the event). As a result of these unplanned scope increases, the project will cost more and take longer to complete than originally anticipated (the impact).
- *Prioritization*: This risk is deemed to be of high probability and high impact.
- *Response*:
    - *Mitigation*: Establishing guidelines for scope control early in the planning process is the most effective mitigation strategy for this type of risk. In this way, all stakeholders understand that each request to change the scope of the project will have to be evaluated based its potential impact on the project schedule and budget before it is accepted.

- *Contingency plan:* One possible contingency plan would be to hire more resources to complete the additional work within the allotted time. This type of contingency plan requires contingency budgeting, so that funding is in place to hire additional resources if and when the contingency plan needs to be implemented (see Zouncourides-Lull 81–83 in this volume).

Weather-related risks

- *Risk identification*: Winter weather conditions in the Pacific Northwest of the U.S. are often poor. Wind, rain, and ice storms occur periodically from December to February (the condition). These storms have historically caused power outages in offices, and have paralyzed traffic and public transportation, preventing staff from getting to work (the event). If these events occur during a critical phase of the project they could delay the overall schedule and cause delays in releasing the product (the impact).
- *Prioritization*: This risk is deemed to be of medium probability during certain months and high impact.
- *Response*:
    - *Contingency plan:* Disaster recovery plans should be drafted. Such plans should include schedules for computer backups as well as offsite storage. Also, ensuring that staff are capable of working from home in the event of inclement weather is virtually the only mitigation strategy for this type of risk, since one cannot control the weather.

Risk response planning is essential to risk management, but it is not an exact science. Sometimes mitigation is effective, and sometimes it is not. When it comes to risk planning, there is generally no "silver bullet" or mitigation strategy that will always guarantee success. As organizations practice formalized risk management and learn from past risks, they develop an understanding of how to manage such risks more effectively in the future, thereby increasing what Apgar calls their "risk intelligence" (2006: 12–13). It is important to track and evaluate risk mitigation strategies to determine whether or not these strategies are effective as part of the continuous risk management process and to foster the development of risk intelligence.

Risk monitoring

Risk management never ends, not even once the project has been completed. After risks have been identified, prioritized, and planned for, they must be tracked and acted upon in the event that they materialize. New risks may develop that may also require action. After the project has been completed and closed, the risk information associated with that project is documented and used in future projects, and the process starts all over again. Many organizations and project managers fail to see the continuous nature of the process and stop after the initial risks have been identified and mitigation strategies put in place. This is akin to crossing one's fingers and hoping for the best, and is far less effective than a continuous process.

Known project risks can be monitored in different ways. The use of a risk register is one common method of monitoring. As noted above, the register contains all known information about the risk, including the owner and triggers. It is normally the task of the risk owner to monitor the risk throughout the course of the project and to report the status of the risk to the project manager and/or the entire project team. This can be done during project status meetings, or via status reports. The key point is that if a risk event occurs, and nothing is done about it, then that event will continue to jeopardize one or more project goals, even if risk identification and response planning have been carried out.

During the project planning phase, risk identification and response planning are (ideally) conducted using all of the information that is available at that time. As the project progresses, new information is developed, and new risks appear that may not have been apparent during the planning process. New risks may arise as result of addressing known risks. Let us suppose, for example, that the mitigation strategy for addressing a schedule risk is to increase the number of translation resources assigned to work on the project during the translation phase. While this strategy decreases the duration of the translation phase, it also increases the risk of poor quality work because the new translation resources may not be as highly qualified or as well trained as the resources that were originally assigned to the translation task. In this way, a new risk to translation quality then emerges. This risk must be prioritized and requires the creation of a mitigation strategy and/or contingency plan.

New risks can be identified in several ways. One way is to schedule periodic risk identification brainstorming sessions throughout the project, for instance when project milestones are reached. For example, one might schedule a risk review to be held when the project reaches a translation completion milestone. This risk review would provide an opportunity to examine all of the known risks, determine the relative effectiveness of the mitigation strategies and/or contingency plans developed to address the known risks, and identify new risks that could potentially impact the next phase of the project. Another way to identify new risks is to hold project status meetings. During such meetings, the project manager (or meeting facilitator) can hold a roundtable discussion during which each project team member tells the team what worries him or her most about the project, and what issues s/he see that could be potential new risks.

Continuous risk management should also include the closure of risks that do not occur over the course of a project, either because of successful mitigation planning or simple good luck. It is important for organizations to understand which risk mitigation strategies are effective and which are not. This knowledge can be then incorporated into the risk intelligence of the organization. Documenting this knowledge is especially important in organizations or industries where there is a high turnover of project managers. In the absence of documentation, departing project managers will take their accrued risk intelligence with them. Documentation enables an organization to retain and use this knowledge.

Successful risk management

Projects are by definition unique. Regardless of how much one knows and understands about localization, each project will present its share of uncertainty that could potentially endanger one or more of the project objectives in terms of time, cost, scope, and/or quality.

No project manager can afford to ignore the risks facing his or her projects. However, many project managers fail to proactively *manage* risks and instead tend to *react* to risks in an ad hoc fashion after the risks events have occurred, at which point it is probably too late to effectively address them. The application of the PMI risk management framework to any project provides an effective way to actively mitigate potential problems before they arise. Successful use of the framework can decrease the likelihood and potential negative impact of risk events during projects, and thus increase the likelihood of project success.

Most project managers agree that risk management is a good practice. Everyone I have worked with on localization projects feels that risk management should be part of localization project management. However, enthusiasm for a formalized risk management process tends to wane after teams realize how much work is going to be required to implement it properly. They feel that the process will take too long and be too costly. Such concerns are entirely understandable. In this respect, it is worth noting that risk management is both an art and a science. The challenge facing the project manager is striking a balance between the investment in time and resources needed to develop and implement a process versus the savings that the risk management process will enable. There is no one "right" way to perform risk management. Each organization and each project presents unique problems and roadblocks. The PMI framework can be tailored to meet the specific needs and requirements of a given project and/or organization. My advice to project managers and project management educators, whether they are new to the business or seasoned veterans, is to learn the risk management process so that their teams can work from a common framework and language. It is important to try things out in order to learn what works and what does not work in a given organization. Taking steps to better understand risks to projects – and proactively manage those risks – is an effective way to foster success.

References

Apgar, David. 2006. *Risk Intelligence: Learning How to Manage What We Don't Know.* Boston: Harvard University Press.
Beninatto, Renato. 2006. "A review of the global translation marketplace." Association of Translation Companies Conference, London, UK, Sep. 21. http://www.atc.org.uk/RenatoBenitatto2006.ppt
Dr. International. 2002. *Developing International Software.* 2nd ed. Seattle: Microsoft Press.
Esselink, Bert. 2000. *A Practical Guide to Localization.* Rev. ed. Amsterdam/Philadelphia: John Benjamins.
Project Management Institute (PMI). 2004. *A Guide to the Project Management Body of Knowledge (PMBOK® Guide).* 3rd ed. Newtown Square, PA: PMI Press.

Appendix
Critical path method

Identifying and understanding a project's critical path is very important in risk response planning. PMI defines the critical path method as "the theoretical early start and finish dates, and late start and finish dates, for all schedule activities without regard for any resource limitations (PMI 2004: 145). In other words, it is a way of looking at the dependent tasks in a project schedule that, if delayed, would delay the completion of the project

Viewing a schedule as a bar chart which shows all activities graphically against a calendar makes it easier to understand the concept of critical path. For example, let us suppose that we are managing a project that comprises five tasks, which are scheduled to be completed in 20 work days (see Figure 5). Let us further suppose that two sets of tasks are scheduled to be performed in parallel (e.g., Tasks 2 and 3 will be performed at the same time as Tasks 4 and 5, but by different people). Finally, let us suppose that Tasks 2 and 4 both exhibit start-finish dependencies with regard to Task 1 (in other words, Task 1 must be completed before either Task 2 or Task 4 can begin).

When two or more tasks are scheduled to be performed in parallel, the critical path is the "path" that is directly linked to the final completion of the project, in other words, the set of tasks that could potentially delay the final completion of project if their durations increase or are for any reason delayed. In the hypothetical schedule shown in Figure 5, Tasks 2 and 3 exhibit downstream dependencies with regard to Task 1, but their completion does not impact the completion date of the project as a whole. Instead the project completion date is determined by the completion date of Task 5. Thus, the critical path in our sample schedule consists of Task 1 – Task 4 – Task 5.

Risk management in localization 231

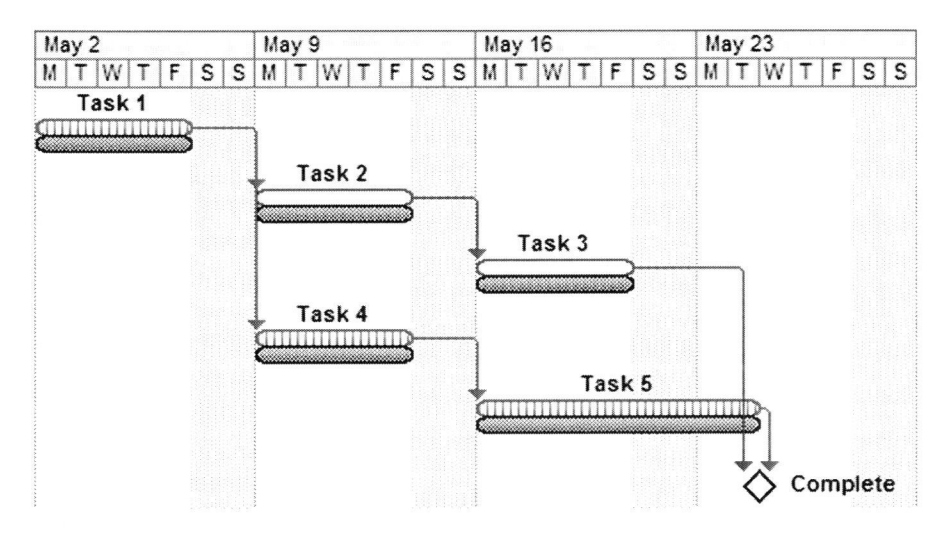

Figure 5. Any delay in a task on the critical would cause a delay in the entire completion of the project. In this example, the critical path of the project is Task 1 – Task 4 – Task 5.

In the sample schedule shown in Figure 5, a delay of 3 days in the completion of Task 4 will delay the completion of the project by 3 days (see Figure 6). Figure 6 also illustrates the fact that a simultaneous increase in the duration of Task 3 from 5 to 8 days has no impact on the project completion date, since Task 3 will still be completed before Task 5.

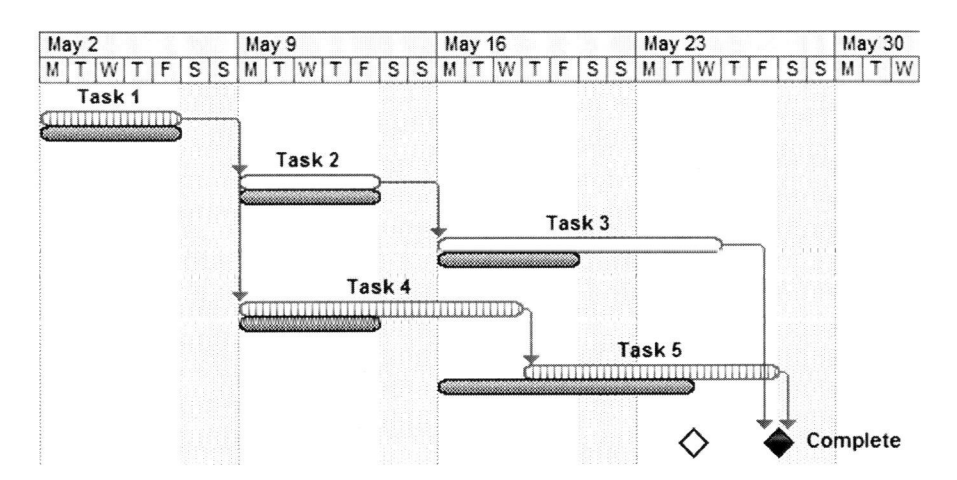

Figure 6. Any delay in a task on the critical path will cause a delay in the overall project completion date.

In some cases, delays in non-critical-path tasks can cause them to become a part of the critical path. For example, referring to the hypothetical schedule shown in Figure 6, an increase in the duration of Task 3 from 5 days to 11 days would cause Task 3 to become part of the critical path because this increase in duration would cause Task 3 to end after the planned project completion, therefore impacting the final project completion date (see Figure 7).

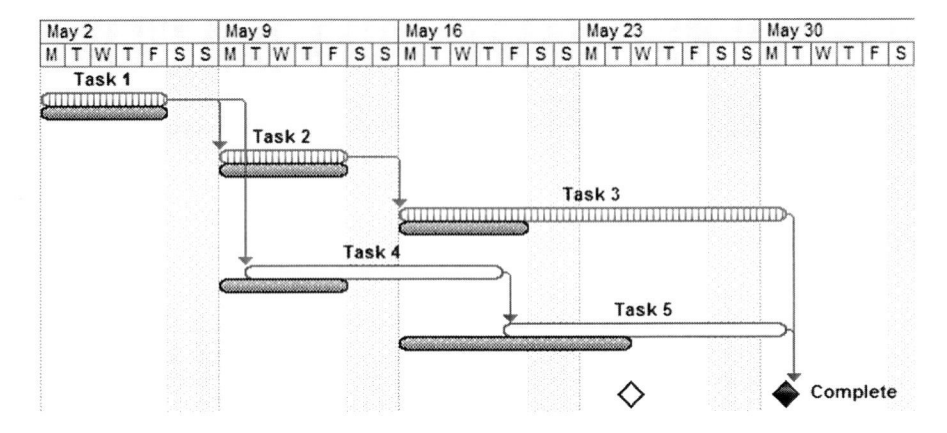

Figure 7. A delay in a task that causes changes to the critical path.

The concept of critical path is important in risk management because any risk to a task located on the critical path will have a higher impact on schedule performance than a risk to a task that is not located on the critical path. This does not mean that risks to non-critical path tasks can always be ignored; it simply means that usually such risks are of lower priority than risks to tasks located on the critical path.

PART III

Managing human and organizational factors

Rethinking the role
of the localization project manager

Richard Sikes

Many corporations do not understand the relationships and dependencies between localization, internationalization, and globalization. This state of affairs presents challenges and opportunities for localization project managers (LPMs). LPMs are well positioned to improve the integration of localization, internationalization, and globalization, enhancing their career prospects in the process, but doing so requires knowledge and skills that fall outside project management *per se* and that have not traditionally been addressed by translation, project management or business training programs or academic curricula. This chapter addresses this gap by examining knowledge and skills that LPMs need and strategies they can employ to improve the integration of localization, internationalization, and globalization and lead the corporation closer to global maturity.

Introduction: Globalization, internationalization, localization and organizational maturity

Businesses that create digital products with the intention of marketing them around the world must make use of three fundamental processes: globalization, internationalization and localization. The three processes are currently understood in the industry as follows:

– *Globalization* is the process whereby a company expands its marketing strategies to address regional requirements of all kinds.
– *Internationalization* is the process of engineering a product so that it can be efficiently adapted to meet local requirements without the need for subsequent redesign.
– *Localization* is the process of adapting digital products and accompanying materials to suit target-market locales.

Although these three processes can (and sometimes do) function effectively independently of each other, the most effective overall corporate strategies strive to integrate and to minimize the friction between them. In an ideally mature organization, the three processes are viewed as a pyramid in which globalization comprises the foundation and localization merely the capstone, with internationalization being the middle layer that ties the three processes together (see Figure 1). Attaining higher levels of localization maturity requires that this viewpoint and mental model become intrinsic to overall corporate strategy. As pointed out elsewhere, "international product development without globalization at its foundation is a recipe for failure. … globalization should be considered a mindset as much as a task-set" (Sikes 2009: 3).

A thorough understanding of the functions and relationships between the processes of globalization, internationalization and localization is a must for international or global companies in general and for localization project managers in particular. Depending on the company structure, these activities may be performed in one department, in two or three separate departments, or they may be divided along product development lines or other criteria. Any approach can be effective if the relationships between globalization, internationalization and localization are understood at all functional levels of the company and effective communication exists between all who participate and/or who are impacted by these activities. The goals, timelines, and methodologies used in each area of endeavor should also be synchronized. Such is not always the case, especially if no individual is assigned responsibility for the success or failure of the overall integration of the three processes, and for acting as a best-practice advocate across the entire matrix of corporate activities.

Indeed, most organizations have not matured to the point at which these processes are integrated. In the classic scenario, a company that is new to international markets attempts to localize without laying the necessary groundwork, and ends up making costly mistakes as it moves along a painful path from discovery of the value of proactive internationalization to research-oriented, forward-looking globalization. In recognition of this state of affairs, language industry research firm Common Sense Advisory has developed a localization maturity model that defines five levels of evolutionary maturity, as well as three levels of relative immaturity (DePalma 2006; DePalma, Beninatto and Sargent 2006) (see Figure 2).

In organizations at or below the "Reactive" stage of maturity, far more effort and expenditure are devoted to localization than to internationalization and globalization with the result that the balance between the three processes is precarious at best (see Figure 3). In less mature organizations, the three processes are typically driven less by proactive corporate strategy than by the personal efforts of a project management-oriented individual who has expertise in one or more of the processes. Often, this project manager serves as the "glue" that binds the three processes together within the company. Frequently, he or she also serves as a cross-disciplinary subject matter expert and lobbyist to ensure their viability, and sometimes their very existence as purposeful undertakings.

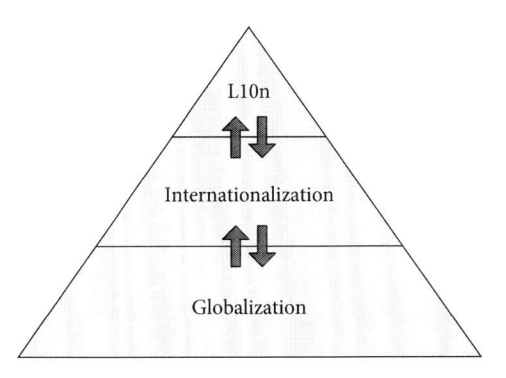

Figure 1. In a mature company, a broad globalization base provides the foundation for internationalization, which in turn supports efficient localization (l10n). Interdependencies link the three layers.

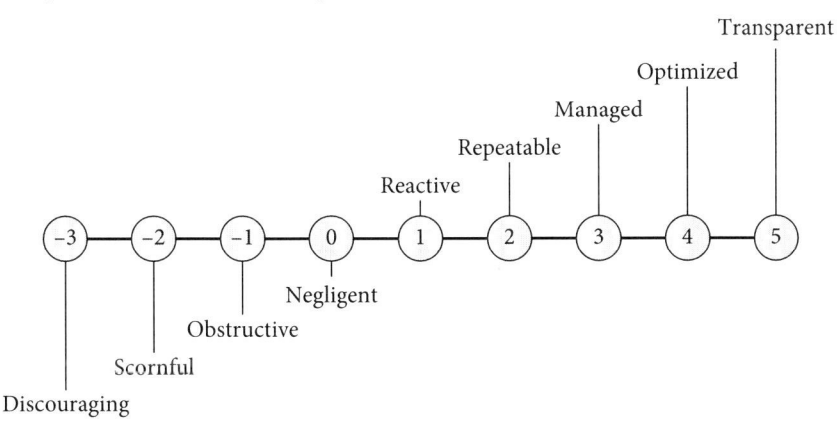

Figure 2. The phases of localization (im)maturity (DePalma 2006; DePalma, Beninatto and Sargent 2006: 13). © Common Sense Advisory.

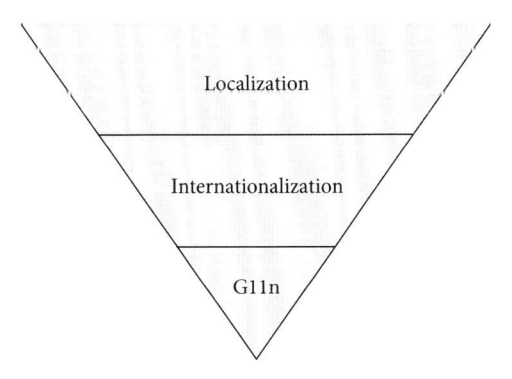

Figure 3. In companies at or below the Reactive level of maturity (see Figure 2), managing localization, internationalization and globalization is a precarious balancing act. (The numeronym "G11n" stands for "globalization.")

Localization growth pains: Challenges and opportunities

This state of affairs presents challenges and opportunities for localization project managers. On one hand, localization is only as effective as the internationalization and globalization strategies on which it is based. Indeed, senior management often asks why localization is so expensive, time-consuming, and slow, but fails to understand the chain of dependencies and the impact that its own decisions have on localization. Decisions made at the globalization and internationalization levels profoundly affect costs at the localization level, and may lead to time-to-market delays, product quality deficiencies, otherwise avoidable rework, and a myriad of other inefficiencies (see Figure 4). In other words, the LPM's ability to deliver projects on time, within budget and according to specification is largely shaped – or undermined, as the case may be – by decisions and actions taken upstream in the product development process.

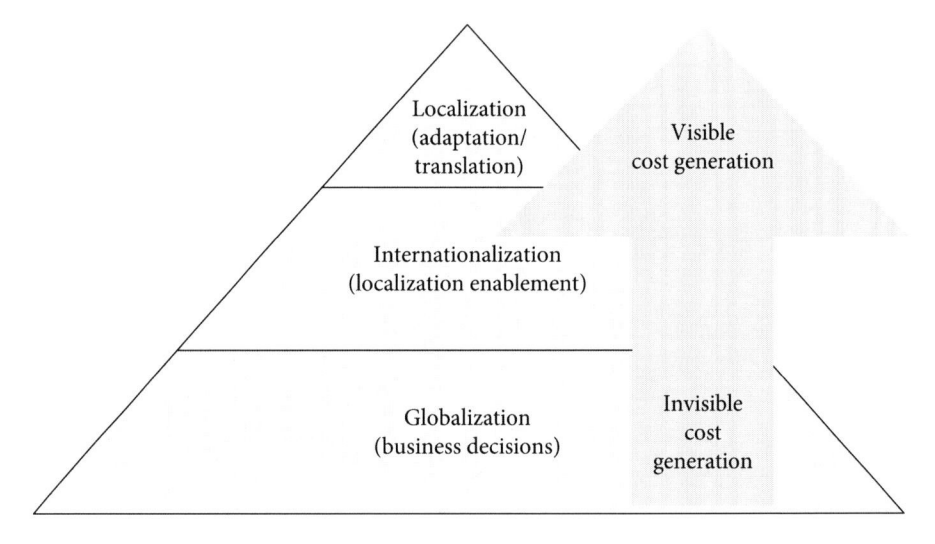

Figure 4. Poor globalization and internationalization decisions show up as excessive costs during localization. This is why localization seems (and often is) disproportionately costly in immature organizations (see Figure 2).

On the other hand, LPMs are uniquely positioned to improve the integration of globalization, internationalization and localization. Localization project managers who facilitate movement of their organization up the maturity scale toward more efficient localization significantly enhance their career prospects. However, successfully leading efforts to better integrate these three processes requires knowledge and skills that fall outside the realm of traditional project management and which are not typically addressed by project management or business training programs or academic curricula: a good understanding of the concepts of "locale," localization, internationalization and globalization, as well as the ability to act as an awareness-raising educator and advocate for best practices where each process is concerned.

This chapter proposes to address this gap. We will first examine the concepts of locale, localization, internationalization and globalization. We will then discuss strategies whereby LPMs can use knowledge of these concepts, and of the dependencies between them, to raise awareness, educate colleagues and advocate for the adoption of best practices with the goal of leading the corporation closer to global maturity. Although the localization maturity scale includes negative levels, we will focus on the positive side of the scale, that is, the continuum from the "Negligent" level to the "Transparent" level (see Figure 2). This chapter assumes that there is at least potential interest in learning how to achieve "Transparent" localization.

Locale

Before examining localization, internationalization and globalization in greater detail, it will be useful to examine the concept of locale, as it is central to the overriding goals of these three processes. A locale is not simply a country nor a language, but rather a combination of the two, reflecting the fact that some languages are spoken in multiple countries and that not all countries are monolingual. For example, French is spoken in France and in parts of Belgium, Canada, and Switzerland (counties in which is an official language), and Portuguese is spoken in both Portugal and Brazil. Another prominent example is the difference between simplified and traditional Chinese, whereby the character set serves as a kind of proxy for strongly-held political convictions rooted in relatively recent history. The concept of locale also reflects the fact that significant cultural differences may exist within or between countries in which different languages are spoken. For instance, the date 10/12/11 would be read as Dec. 10, 2011 in Ireland and Italy, Oct. 12, 2011 in the Philippines and the United States, and as Dec. 11, 2010 in Japan and South Korea. The notion of locale encompasses not only language, but also various types of data, such as date, time, numbers, currencies, weights, measurements, as well as rules for presenting and sorting those data in accordance with the cultural conventions of a given language and geographic area (Ray 2004: 116).

Problems can and typically do occur when companies attempt to enter international markets without having accounted for locale-specific requirements and/or customer expectations during product development. For example, let us suppose that a company creates a product for the North American market (i.e., United States and Canada). At some point after the product has been created, the company realizes that it has an opportunity to sell it to the Canadian federal government in addition to certain Canadian provincial governments. But, in these markets, product availability in French is legally mandated even if the product is not purchased in that language. So the company initiates a translation into French. However, if the company has not considered locale-related variables during product development, it is likely that the design of the product will not enable the currency sign to be placed after the numerical amount, as is the custom in the French Canadian locale, especially in Québec. This placement may not even be possible in the English version of the product if it is sold in that locale. If such is the case, the company will have to make some tough and expensive choices: immediately deliver a defective product and suffer the consequences, or hold up delivery while the product design is retrofitted to support the norms of the target locale and suffer a different set of consequences.

Companies can avoid these types of problems by proactively considering locale during the product development and design processes, prior to entering international markets. But a proactive approach requires knowledge and actions that fall within the realm of localization, internationalization and globalization.

Localization

The goal of localization is to adapt a product and accompanying materials to suit a target-market locale with the intent to make the product "transparent" to that locale, so that native users would interact with it as if it were developed there and for that locale alone. Localization transcends translation. In fact, localization could legitimately be viewed as imposing attributes of a specific culture on what would ideally be an internationalized, therefore culturally neutral, product. A localized product will, most likely, primarily communicate with the user in a particular language using the character set of glyphs required to display that language. Norms such as decimal delimitation, time and date, as well as currency display will be set to default to the locale setting defined for the operating system. Locale-specific technical, legal, and/or financial accounting norms may be switched on and locale-inappropriate product behavior, in other words, the way a product presents itself to the user or accepts interactions that the user initiates, may be suppressed or switched off depending on the locale.[1] Color usage and graphic symbols may be adapted. Comparative advertising may be replaced by other advertising forms. In other words, an essentially neutral product takes on attributes that are designed for and appropriate to the target locale.

Internationalization

Internationalization is a technical task that must be performed by software developers and that consists of three basic task types, each supported by numerous subtasks. The first is the removal of cultural assumptions from software design to facilitate

---

1. According to Rozendaal, Keyson and de Ridder, "product behavior captures the responsiveness of a product in relation to the actions of a user and combines both the possibilities of the product and the means in which they are manipulated" (2007: 182).

subsequent adaptation. The second is architectural separation of the presentation layer from the application logic layer. The third is implementation of support for global norms such as character sets or handling of accounting procedures. The goal of internationalization is to engineer a product so that it can be efficiently adapted to meet locale-specific requirements without the need for subsequent redesign.

Removal of cultural assumptions

Internationalization involves the removal of cultural assumptions from product behavior. A cultural assumption might be that decimal fractions are always separated from whole numbers by a period and therefore deciding to hard-code that type of numerical representation into a product. Or, it might be thinking that an image of a hand with forefinger and thumb joined in a circle with the three other fingers sticking up is a universal sign of approval. Or, it might be thinking that green is always good and red is always bad and therefore coding financial software that shows improvement in stock value in a green font and depreciation in red, not realizing that completely different colors, sometime the exact opposites, are used in Asian countries to represent these concepts.

Cultural assumptions are not confined to the user interface, and may extend to the ways in which character data is encoded, stored and processed.[2] Removal of cultural assumptions is easier said than done, however. They are not made by software developers out of malice, but rather through simple ignorance or sometimes due to time pressure. Many North Americans are unfamiliar with the norms of other countries. For example, developers trained at institutions in the United States simply may not know that much of the world represents decimal separation using commas rather than periods. Likewise, developers who have not had training in foreign languages may not know that the rules of morphology, syntax and grammar governing other languages may be very different from those of English, or that the translation of a given text may be significantly shorter or longer than the English original. Such lack of knowledge leads to the creation of irresolvable grammatical paradoxes by string concatenation and to the development of software in which text expansion is not tolerated. Unfortunately, few U.S. computer science programs teach principles of internationalization, so one can hardly fault the graduates of those programs. However, because internationalization is often poorly understood at the enterprise level, blame for localization problems caused by the failure to internationalize products properly is often assigned, erroneously, to the localization team.

---

2. For more information, see Urien, Howard and Perinotti (1993); Kano (1995); Luong, Lok, Taylor and Driscoll (1995); Deitsch and Czarnecki (2001); and Smith-Ferrier (2007).

A three-layered approach to design

Internationalization entails the architectural separation of data storage, processing and presentation. This is accomplished by creating three discrete virtual "layers" of program code. The presentation layer is what the user sees and interacts with. The business logic layer comprises the functional core of the program. In simple words, that is where the program does whatever it does. There may also be a database layer, where data is stored and from where it is retrieved. In most programs, data is transferred back and forth between these layers. Thus, developers must scrutinize the transport mechanisms between the three layers for internationalization issues as thoroughly as they do the program code that defines operations within the layers.

Implementation of support for global norms

Internationalization also involves making possible certain desirable product behaviors, and might include implementation of support for global norms such as standard language character sets or diverse international accounting principles. In other words, it is an engineering process whose goal is to enable a product to work properly in locales that differ in one or more ways from the home locale. Conversely, in some cases it might even involve the suppression of certain product attributes such as 128-bit encryption if the product will be sold in locales where that feature is prohibited. In this respect, internationalization refers to the process of making a company's products *localizable*. Internationalization need not refer exclusively to coding practices but may also apply to such tasks as allowing sufficient white space in source documentation for text expansion or designing and building a website so that localized content can easily be added.

Efficient adaptation to meet locale-specific requirements

In the context of localization, "adaptation" refers primarily to translation. However, additional reconfiguration may necessary beyond the translation of the user interface and documentation to enable the adaptation of the product for use in a different locale. Even products whose linguistic content remains untranslated may have to undergo functional modifications. Consider, for example, a product that is designed for the financial services industry in the United States, Canada, and the United Kingdom. Even if the product is not translated, it will still have to be localized for all three markets due to differences in regulations and taxation laws and in the ways that certain financial interactions are handled.

In summary, because a locale-generic product encompasses a greater range of potential functionality than one that is locale-specific, internationalization can be viewed as an *expansion* of product capability. Because few developers have formal training in internationalization, the onus for educating them about important internationalization concepts, techniques, and test strategies often falls on colleagues who are adversely affected by deficient internationalization during downstream processes, such as localization project managers. Moreover, because internationalization adds overhead to engineering efforts, it is frequently postponed or treated as a feature instead of an intrinsic aspect of core product development. Over the long term, this approach invariably leads to problems.

Globalization

Our working definition of globalization as the expansion of marketing strategies to address regional markets of all kinds reflects not just a *concept*, but also a *goal* and, as such, can be read as a company mission statement. Thinking globally has profound implications for product development and marketing, especially if it becomes a pervasive state of mind. In the sections that follow, we will explore some of these implications.

Addressing regional markets in central marketing plans and organizational strategies

Globalization begins with the organizational structure of the enterprise. Instead of striving to develop an environment that promotes a broader vision at home, many companies delegate local marketing to regional offices where relevant expertise is readily available. This delegation can result in duplication of effort across geographies, dilution of corporate identity, rogue marketing activities, and conflicting agendas. Instead, it makes more sense to concentrate global expertise at the production source where it can help build a flexible and central global product foundation. This central foundation can in turn serve as a springboard, enabling regional satellites to highlight and capitalize on their local specificities.

International market research

Many North American companies underfund or underestimate the value of international market research, and tend to design feature sets from the top down rather than from the bottom up. In this context, "top down" means innovation that emerges from a conceptual or design entity within the company that brainstorms new ways to do things or identifies problems for which their innovative new product design provides a solution. This solution is then handed over to a marketing entity, which goes about creating a market for the product. This approach may or may not work well. Consider a company that creates a new fabric softener, which obtains excellent results in the typical North American two-wash, two-rinse cycle. This product will probably not be successful in areas of the world where water is expensive or not easily accessible. Succeeding in such markets requires that the company evaluate the needs of users in that locale and create a product that requires only one wash-rinse cycle, thus saving water. Such was the approach taken by Proctor & Gamble when creating Downy Single Rinse. The product, which requires only a three step process (wash, add softener, rinse), "was a hit from the start" following its launch in Mexico in March 2004 (Lafley and Charan 38–40). The latter approach can be labeled the "bottom-up" method – examining user needs and wants in targeted geographies, and then focusing innovative energies at finding solutions that will be compelling to users there.

Along similar lines, if one thinks of a company as the inside and world markets as the outside, it also can be said that products are typically designed from the inside out instead of from the outside in. For example, during the product development cycle, an internal company entity such as Product Marketing often decides what feature set is best for the world. This approach is fine if this internal entity has sufficient input from world markets, but such is frequently not the case. Indeed, only a relatively small percentage of a company's total marketing effort, say 20% (based on the author's experience), is typically dedicated to international market considerations, which are frequently thought of as add-ons to core product concepts that originate in local (usually North American) product concepts and personalities.[3]

Product planning with the goal of serving diverse markets

Planning with a narrow geographic vision is a typically North American phenomenon. Indeed, North American businesses are often content to focus on North American markets (DePalma 2002: 18–19; Bean 2003: 12). However, taking proactive steps to avoid having to redesign and/or retrofit existing products to enable support and features that appeal to a variety of markets saves money and time in the long run. Moreover, conceptual treatment of product design for domestic markets as a subset of a generic, locale-neutral product that appeals to a wide range of locales need not be restricted to physical product design alone. It can extend to every facet of an enterprise's culture and strategy, and to the attendant marketing strategies.

Quantifiable, business-case stratification of tiered locale groupings

Every organization must set priorities. People, time and money are all finite resources. However, company priorities are frequently based more on intuition and corporate politics than on quantitative market analysis. This state of affairs arises

---

[3]. For more information about product personalities, see Norman (2004: 56–60), de Mooij (2005: 225–229) and Jordan (2002).

when companies are deal-driven, as opposed to plan-driven. In deal-driven companies, product priorities are heavily influenced by sales opportunities. Such companies are notoriously fickle and tend to switch directions *ad hoc*, careening from sale to sale (and/or from crisis to crisis) instead of working steadily towards stated and planned product goals.

In order for an organization to determine goals and to plan sensibly, a business case mentality must prevail. A business case is a document that contrasts revenue forecasts with cost forecasts, thus indicating the potential for profitability, and provides quantitative guidance for senior management's decision-making process. The preparation of business cases poses two problems. The first is that sales personnel tend to resist committing to forecasts. This is understandable, as doing so implies acceptance of a future that cannot be known. The second problem is that localization costs must also be forecast, but if the development of the product is still in flux, then localization costs cannot be known with any certainty either. However, historical trend data may enable the extrapolation of sales or cost projections.

Historical sales and cost trends may also provide a basis for classifying products and regions in groups, or tiers, in order to prioritize them. Tiers may be based on many criteria. Revenue is clearly a strong indicator, but profitability may be more important. For example, sales in Japan may generate more revenue than sales in China, but sales in China might be more profitable because Chinese localization costs are orders of magnitude lower than Japanese localization costs. One major disadvantage of using revenue instead of profitability to group products is that Sales personnel are typically compensated in proportion to the revenue that they generate, regardless of the *profitability* of that revenue. Thus, salespeople do not necessarily have an incentive to sell products in low-revenue, high-profit geographies. Cost also provides a basis on which to establish groupings. For example, a tier may reflect a combination of geographies that enable economies of scale when several product languages are localized simultaneously by one service provider (e.g., Brazilian Portuguese and Latin American Spanish).

Specialized business cases for emerging markets

Emerging markets present a unique challenge: if a company has little or no previous experience in those markets, it will have little or no historical data upon which to base objective calculations. Consequently, localization business cases for emerging markets must rely on analysis of macroeconomic data, observation of competitors' successes and failures, as well as any anecdotal input that can be obtained from people with direct experience in those markets. There is little point in using a financial threshold as a criterion for a yes-or-no localization decision about emerging markets unless the goal is to determine how much money the company can afford to lose if the chosen emerging market strategy fails to generate results.

In any event, companies must consider much more than the cost of localizing when pondering emerging markets. The choice of distribution channel(s) stands out as a primary concern. Companies must also consider how they will support the products in these new markets during the various stages of the product life cycle, i.e., introduction, growth, and maturity (assuming that the localized products prove successful), and how frequently they will update the localized products compared to new core market versions. Finally, companies must also evaluate the risk of failure and incorporate the cost of an exit strategy in case the product launch proves unsuccessful.

Tracking revenues by locale

The fundamental question that must be answered in every business case is the following: "How many more units do we believe we will sell in this locale if we localize our products than if we do not?" Since this question is the foundation of business case analysis, one would naturally expect companies to track incremental revenues that result from localized product on a locale-by-locale basis. It is surprising to learn how few companies actually implement the necessary accounting processes and infrastructure to do so. Total revenue from specific regions is often known but, unfortunately, more often than not, revenue is not broken down according to sales of source-language products versus localized products. If this information is not known, business cases will ultimately be built upon assumptions or hearsay rather than facts, magnifying both uncertainty and risk. This is not a good business practice, and would be unthinkable in other contexts such as domestic (home market) sales or acquisitions of another company.

Having examined the processes of localization, internationalization and globalization in detail, let us now consider some of the ways in which the LPM can assume the mantle of awareness-raising educator and best-practice advocate and contribute to the success of the organization's efforts in each area.

From theory to practice

Being an effective awareness-raising educator and best-practice advocate requires that project managers be able to objectively document inefficiencies and that they broaden their vision across the entire corporate matrix to better understand the root causes of problems that plague their everyday tasks, as well as potential remedies and associated trade-offs. Documenting inefficiencies and identifying root causes of problems in turn require that LPMs be able to gather and analyze relevant data. Armed with spreadsheets and an objective, interdisciplinary and solution-oriented approach, project managers optimize their chances to win the cooperation and support of upper management, make their own lives easier, and save the company money. Optimally effective LPMs not only document inefficiencies, but also provide constructive ideas for process improvement, and demonstrate mathematically such items as return on investment in technologies such as translation memory, for example. But most importantly, they clearly and compellingly demonstrate why decisions made upstream in the product development process have profound effects on downstream efficiency.

A metaphor will help to illustrate this idea. If we think of the process of creation of world-ready products as a river that flows from higher elevations of product conception and creation to empty into the oceans of the world marketplace, we can envision localization as an activity situated rather far downstream in the product development process (see Figure 5). Because the ability to successfully localize a product depends to a great extent on decisions made and actions taken (or not, as the case may be) during globalization and internationalization, the lobbying and educational activities carried out by LPMs must be oriented upstream in the process flow. This is often referred to in the industry as "upstream engagement." In other words, the LPM needs to engage the minds and wills of decision-makers who influence the process flow as close to its source as possible. This is easier said than done: much like paddling against the current in a rapidly flowing river, upstream engagement entails a great deal of physical and mental work.

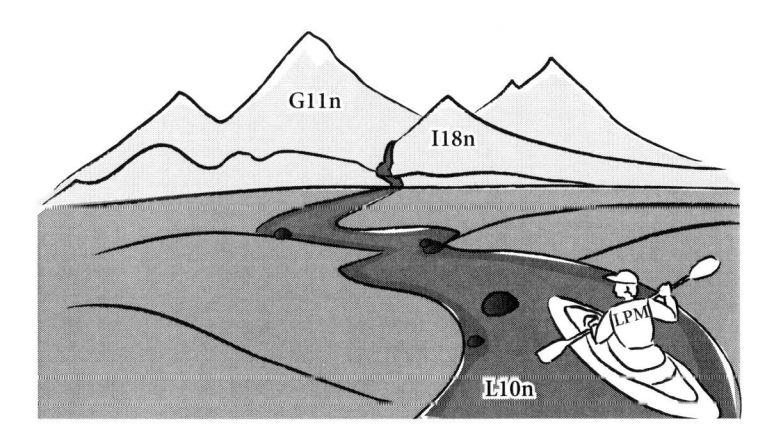

Figure 5. To address (or prevent) localization problems, it is necessary to navigate upstream from localization (L10n) to the root causes of those problems in the realms of internationalization (I18n) and globalization (G11n).

Fostering localization success

The LPM bears primary responsibility for efficient, timely, complete, and cost-effective delivery of the materials required to produce localized products. A leading factor in accomplishing these goals is the ability of the client-side LPM to establish a healthy relationship and open communication between herself and the supplier-side project manager; the success or failure of a localization project may largely depend on the strength of this relationship (see Combe in this volume). Likewise, both the client-side and the vendor-side project managers must strive to maintain open lines of communication within their respective organizations.

Prudent project managers work hard to position themselves as pragmatic advocates for their colleagues, and consistently try to generate goodwill. This can become very important when LPMs are asked to perform impossible tasks in impossible timeframes, or when they must ask their peers or colleagues to do so, a situation that is endemic in the industry.

Vendor-side project managers are responsible for ensuring that their sub-suppliers, frequently freelancers, receive materials and instructions in such a manner that their work is straightforward and their throughput is optimized. This means organizing tasks and materials in a clear, intuitive manner, being responsive to queries, and standing up for the suppliers to ensure that their time is not wasted and that they are promptly compensated for their work. If sub-suppliers see that the PM is supporting them and looking after their needs, they will often be more willing to go the extra mile when asked.

On the client side, project managers frequently chase down development personnel to get queries answered on a timely basis, push back against unreasonable demands and unrealistic schedules, and take a strong stand within their organization against the tendency to introduce last-minute changes. Furthermore, like their vendor-side colleagues, client-side project managers must continually monitor the flow of payments to suppliers to ensure that vendors who deliver materials in a timely manner are in turn paid in a timely manner. To ensure this reciprocity, the client-side LPM may need to cultivate a relationship with financial management, especially with the CFO or people close to that office.

LPMs on either the client side or the vendor side can build bridges to their company's financial management by asking to be mentored in the creation and use of cost accounting spreadsheets, business case templates, and/or project budgets. When intelligently positioned, requests for this kind of help indicate an LPM's interest in the employer's financial health, demonstrate willingness to think about the bigger corporate picture, and establish credibility that can be useful when, on a return visit to the CFO, the LPM needs to request that payment to a particular supplier be prioritized.

At the same time, any LPM who works with freelancers must teach them how to write invoices that will move quickly through their employer's financial system. Many freelance translators are primarily linguists for whom proper business practices play a very secondary role. Thus, while these linguists pay excruciating attention to detail in their translation endeavors, their invoices often lack basic information needed to ensure quick payment. Some of the best translators can be likened to craftsmen who treat their work as a vocation, not as a job. LPMs can help their subcontractors learn how to become better service providers in addition to being good translators.

Depending on the organization's localization maturity level, there may be other areas of endeavor in which LPMs can help optimize processes and consolidate linguistic assets. We will examine some of these in the sections that follow.

Overseeing localization testing

Localization testing encompasses three types of assessment: linguistic, cosmetic and functional (Esselink 2000: 150–154). Linguistic testing verifies accuracy on two levels. All text should be translated correctly and consistently so that the meaning is clear, readability specifications are met, grammar and punctuation are correct and, when appropriate, locale-appropriate dialect is employed. Such criteria notwithstanding, it is fully possible that a stylistically appropriate, grammatically correct translation will actually convey a different message from that of the source materials. Linguistic testing also entails reading the localized text and comparing it to the behavior of the localized product. Actual product behavior often changes while source text is being written, and source materials are not always revised to account for these changes before undergoing localization. In such cases, even an impeccable translation of the source will not function as designed because it does not accurately describe how the product behaves. In other words, the localized text is not *functional* because it does not fulfill its design goals (neither does the source, of course). During the localization process, alert translators who notice such discrepancies, submit queries about them, and then incorporate answers to the queries into their translations can actually produce localized texts that fulfill their design goals better than the original source materials. Unfortunately, a feedback mechanism from localization to documentation that would enable the changes to be captured and the source materials to be updated accordingly is often missing. Whether this kind of verification should be considered linguistic review, proofing, linguistic testing or linguistic functional testing may be debated but, regardless of what it is called, it must be done. This is especially important in the localization of health products such as medical devices and pharmaceutical information where an inaccurate translation could endanger users or create a liability for the product manufacturer.

Cosmetic localization testing ensures that the appearance of the product conforms to target market expectations. Products should appear pleasing to the user when operated in the target locale's language; no text should be truncated or appear squished together. If the user interface has been designed in such a way that abbreviation is unavoidable, then all abbreviations should be linguistically correct and cosmetically viable in the target language. (In theory, localization-readiness testing should eliminate such design deficiencies.) User interface elements should be separated by sufficient white space, and diagrams and descriptive text should remain together in documentation. Pagination should not be arbitrary in localized versions due to the effect of language expansion. Wherever possible, translated text should be paginated on the basis of logical units or topics. Adjustment of pagination in the translated documentation is especially important if the source text does not contain sufficient white space to meet target audience expectations and/or to accommodate translation-related expansion. Color schemes and iconography should be adapted so that they are culturally appropriate for target-market users.

Finally, functional testing should be performed to ensure that localization has not broken any functionality. If thorough internationalization testing and localization-readiness testing have been completed in the early, pre-localization phases of product development, then the number of problems uncovered by functional testing should be minimal. If there is doubt about the thoroughness of internationalization and localization-readiness testing, then each localized product version must be operated from start to finish in an environment that mimics that of the target locale.

It should be clear that it is much less efficient to perform functional testing on a plethora of localized product versions than it is to run the same types of tests, designed in a more generic manner to cover all types of localized conditions, on one candidate locale-neutral product version. This is a highly compelling notion for LPMs, because such an approach can greatly reduce the cost and lead time needed to deliver localized products to market. But it is also difficult to get core development managers to commit to this approach because it represents additional work for them. In this case, the LPM should develop a strategy to demonstrate the overall savings that the company can realize by shifting the responsibility for internationalization and localization-readiness testing from the localization group to core development teams.

Harmonizing methodologies and service providers

The localization process in a given client organization is often a patchwork of different methodologies and service providers, particularly in companies that have grown through acquisition. This heterogeneity is an obvious source of potential inefficiency that the LPM is well positioned to address. Of course, addressing such discontinuities is not without political ramifications, not the least of which may be threats to the job security of peer LPMs or even the one who takes the bull by the horns and lobbies for consolidation. There may also be philosophical disagreements about approach, and applying a cookie-cutter solution across all concerned entities could introduce greater inefficiencies than it solves, especially in complex software development environments. Given the importance of personal relationships between client-side and vendor-side project managers in localization, consolidating methodologies and/or partners is not without risk. At the very least, such changes must be explored and undertaken with great sensitivity to avoid damage to morale and/or relationships.

In addition, care must be taken to retain knowledge when consolidating methodologies and personnel. It may be that a system used in one area of a newly merged company is technically or philosophically superior to that used in another, but if personnel who are intimately familiar with the internal quirks of the inferior system or the products it serves are let go before knowledge transfer takes place, then the remaining personnel may find themselves faced with the daunting task of solving problems that they did not know existed and/or for which they are unprepared. Such a situation may arise when the acquiring company fails to perform adequate due diligence during the acquisition process. Auditors may only enquire whether or not localized products are part of the offerings of the company being acquired, instead of pursuing the inquiry to understand how those products are produced and delivered.

Consolidating and maintaining the value of linguistic assets

It is often the case that a company pays insufficient attention to the intrinsic value of its linguistic assets. Again, this is particularly true in companies that grow through acquisition. Translation memory and multilingual terminology repositories are assets for which companies pay a great deal of money. However, all too often companies neglect to maintain those assets after acquiring them. This is due in part to the nature of the assets: words are less tangible than a fleet of trucks, for example. No sensibly run company would consider operating a fleet of vehicles without regularly servicing them, changing their oil, or buying new tires, yet companies will spend large amounts of money on translations but then allow the translations and other by-products such as multilingual terminology to fall into disrepair. The LPM can lobby senior management against this tendency, making the case that it is penny-wise and pound-foolish to not maintain linguistic assets once they have been created.

Because no automated technology exists for verifying the quality and consistency of translation memories, caring for linguistic assets is an expensive, hands-on activity for which there is often little time or funding. Nevertheless, the investment in maintaining linguistic assets is worthwhile. Out-of-sync terminology can become especially problematic when products are expected to communicate with one another or are intended to be companion products. Terminological inconsistency (and by extension, conceptual inconsistency) leads to complicated paradoxes in source language products that are only exacerbated by localization.

Addressing such problems requires that the LPM be very proactive in the overall organization, interacting initially with stakeholders in the documentation process who will understand the value of consistent terminology, and then extending the scope of awareness initiatives to encompass product marketing and development. Finally, senior management must be informed about how terminological and linguistic consistency can help the company's bottom line, or, conversely, how the waste that results from lack of linguistic maintenance and control has potential negative impact. To educate senior management about such matters, the project manager can quantify costs incurred as a result of terminological or linguistic inconsistency, and then present that data to management in the form of a short white paper or presentation illuminating the cost-benefit analysis. Any such analysis should highlight how cost increase after localization is not linear but, rather, exponential in growth rate.

In preparing communications to senior management, the LPM must be aware that this is a target cohort that suffers from intense, ongoing time constraints. Any presentation should be short and to the point. Senior executives usually best understand numbers, so simple financial examples, augmented by clear graphics, are an effective medium for expressing concepts. Any presentation or white paper that gives the appearance of taking a long time to read or digest will likely be ignored. Also, logical divisions into groups of three are very effective. For example, an effective presentation could be made up of three slides, each with three subtopics. Slides crowded with bullet points can be counterproductive, as they tend to be read in narrative fashion that may obfuscate the main message. Finally, image-based metaphors such as pictures that convey concepts can be useful, but they must be used with care. The connection to the topic should be very clear, not artistically abstract.

Improving interaction with version control systems through education and credibility-building

Version control systems are commonly used by software development teams, but are less common outside such teams. Often, access by non-developers to file archives maintained within version control systems is frowned upon or forbidden outright. The irony of this kind of policy is that LPMs are frequently required to accurately manage and track a substantial multiple of the number of files that any single developer is required to maintain. While LPMs improvise their own naming conventions, directory structures, and other personal techniques to help keep thousands of files correctly catalogued, version control access remains the exclusive province of the software developer.

It is true that version control systems can be somewhat fragile, and some education is required for neophytes to understand and master their use. But using a version control system is not rocket science, and LPMs are generally no less adept at operating application software than computer programmers. They simply lack knowledge of and experience using such systems. To break through the invisible barrier and gain access to version control, LPMs must focus their efforts on convincing the system's gatekeepers to provide them with the necessary theoretical and operational grounding. Only after LPMs can demonstrate to developer colleagues that they understand and are fully capable of operating such a system will they successfully cross this important bridge.

Providing better visibility into best practices, schedules, and successes

LPMs have a tendency to just buckle down and quietly do their work. Among their peers, they sometimes complain about the lack of appreciation of their time spent, stress absorbed, and overall contribution to product delivery within the greater organization. But, overall, they tend to be self-effacing. An LPM who wishes to position her department and peers or herself in a leadership spotlight must find tasteful ways to communicate successes. Such communication may take the form of regular company-wide email announcements about localized product releases, productivity gains, adherence to schedules, and other success stories.

Alternatively, a localization department may develop its own intranet site that publishes anticipated release dates, highlights information about best practices, perhaps confers a "best friend of the month to localization" award to someone within the company, provides downloadable checklists for colleagues who may request localization services, offers a page or two of localization humor and, of course, includes a section that shines a light on localization departmental successes such as shortened turnaround times, praise from customers, etc.

Developing and applying suitable metrics

A widely held view in the realm of management is that "you can't control what you can't measure" (DeMarco 1982: 6). But the development of reliable metrics in the context of localization is difficult because throughput and productivity are shaped by numerous external factors, such as changes in source materials, shifting source delivery schedules, poor source quality, and many other variables. Nevertheless, it is essential that the LPM find a few stable trees in the chaotic forest and begin logging baseline measurements of productivity.

Seeking ways to develop localized products that better satisfy customer requirements

In the absence of adequate international product management staff, responsibility for formulating localization requirements that (ostensibly) reflect the needs and wants of customers in the target locales often falls on LPMs. For example, instructions for use for a medical device may be subject to much more regulation in some locales than in others, whereas repair instructions for a piece of machinery like a motorcycle may be subject to no regulation whatsoever. A software user interface for a large enterprise product that is installed on a server by customer personnel who are fluent in English may have very different requirements from a module of the same product that is used by rank-and-file employees who speak no English at all. At the very least, the LPM can serve as a sounding board for international product management, either by playing the role of liaison between product management and local subject matter experts, or by playing the role of devil's advocate and challenging international product management staff to re-examine their assumptions.

Contributing to internationalization efforts

One would think that the importance of maximizing localization efficiency would be obvious, but current market realities suggest otherwise. Excessive emphasis on near-term, domestic market revenues frequently causes internationalization to be postponed into an indefinite future. One direct result of the lack of effective internationalization is the need to retrofit product design after the domestic market release to enable release in other jurisdictions. But offloading costs to the future or to another department does not increase efficiency; it merely ensures that greater costs show up elsewhere when the numbers are consolidated across the entire corporation (see Figure 4). In short, postponement or offloading does not equal efficiency.

Another consequence of ineffective internationalization is that the costs of retrofitting support for localization are treated as *localization* costs, whereas these costs should never arise in the first place if the product is designed correctly. The corollary to this observation is that since retrofitting costs are caused by the development team's failure to properly internationalize the product, it is the development team that should be responsible for the additional costs. This perspective on accountability can be hard for LPMs to sell to development managers, who may have very different agendas.

LPMs can help improve internationalization efforts by researching the inefficiencies and associated incremental costs that are generated by lack of timely internationalization in the product development life cycle, quantifying the costs thereof, and presenting them to management. Such a presentation will be made much more effective by simultaneous presentation of a plan for change. Such a plan could focus on the areas discussed in the four following sections.

Defining cultural and locale-neutrality

LPMs are usually the most knowledgeable people within an organization about what is or is not a locale-neutral product or piece of documentation. The first challenge an LPM faces is defining locale neutrality with respect to the products that the company develops and sells. Key to approaching the problem is the notion that locale neutrality is an element of *core design*, not a feature or an add-on. In other words, one does not start with English and then make the product locale-neutral. Instead, one starts with a basic design for which the locale is unimportant and then develops the product in English if English happens to be the most convenient language for all concerned.

People who do not speak a second language may find it difficult to grasp the concept that locale-neutrality is a core design value, and not a feature. It is thus incumbent upon the LPM to find effective ways to express this critical concept.

Communicating the goal

After researching and defining locale neutrality with respect to the company and its product line, it is important that the LPM communicate the goal of locale-neutral design to colleagues who are in a position to contribute to change. One way to do so would be to author a comprehensive white paper that details internationalization best practices and provides pragmatic guidelines for the company's products. Although general information is available on the Internet, especially from the websites of internationalization companies, the LPM is the person best positioned to apply such information to the company's environment. One way to reach individual developers would be to distribute one-page reference documents that list best practices such as "Do not hard-code strings!" One company enclosed such a reference page in tough transparent plastic so that it was practically indestructible and then pinned the pages on the inside of every developer's cubicle. A third way to communicate internationalization goals would be to hold brown-bag lunches during which goals are explained to colleagues and discussed in a casual, friendly environment that does not eat into normal working time. Finally, one could follow the example of the company that created a prize consisting of a nicely designed certificate with a delicious foreign chocolate bar attached that was awarded once per month to the developer who had done the most to support internationalization in the product code. This recognition brought visibility to the goal.

Initiating early-stage internationalization testing

The LPM is ideally positioned to initiate a program of early-stage testing for internationalization bugs. In the software world, a visual localization tool that can generate pseudo-localized products is extremely valuable for this purpose. Pseudo-localization, a strategy often used in software development by mature companies, involves the use of specialized tools to simulate the effects of localizing a software product for a specific market (see Figure 6). For example, it might entail the replacement of source-language letters or characters with random Chinese characters to simulate localization into Chinese, or 30% expansion of the length of user interface strings to simulate the effect of translation into German or other Western European languages (see Figure 7).

Testing of pseudo-localized product builds can expose many types of internationalization and localization-readiness deficiencies early in the development life cycle, even before localization itself begins. This testing should begin as soon as product

Figure 6. A pseudo-localization of Microsoft Notepad into German created using SDL Passolo 2009.

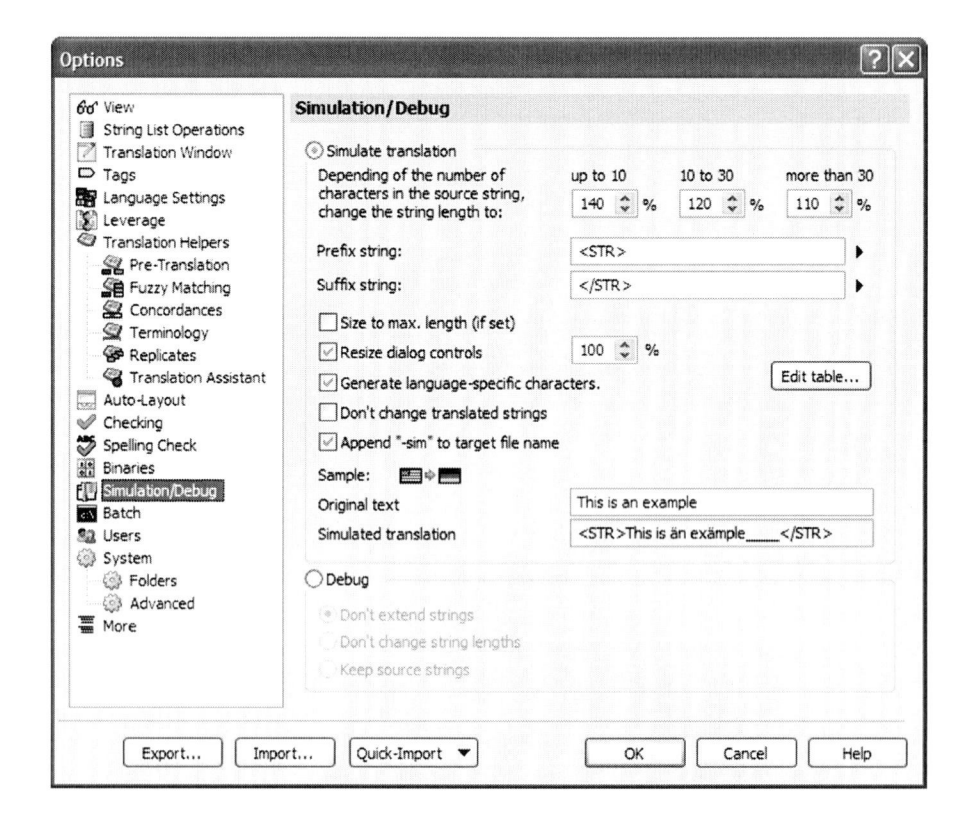

Figure 7. The SDL Passolo 2009 options used to create the German pseudo-localization of Notepad shown in Figure 5.

builds begin to contain user interaction. Ideally, it should be the responsibility of the core quality assurance team to ensure that testing for localization-readiness becomes ingrained in all team members' processes and mindsets. A bug logged by the core quality control team might, in early stages of a company's localization maturity at least, be taken more seriously than a bug logged by a localization quality control team member. This is of course not ideal, but is a reality that LPMs must take into account.

Early-stage testing should cover internationalization and localization-readiness. By "early stage," we mean that any bugs found by these two types of testing should be resolved in the core code before building the products that will be released to the market. If the company intends to ship localized product builds simultaneously with the core language build, then early stage testing needs to occur earlier in the development process to leave sufficient time for subsequent localization testing. Companies at higher levels of the localization maturity scale (see Figure 2) usually implement a policy, mandated from senior management and communicated across the organization, that part of the core development and quality control teams' job is to incorporate internationalization and localization-readiness testing into the core development cycle. However, this mandate tends to be quickly forgotten during downward economic cycles. Internationalization implementation and testing are far too often seen as expenses that can be postponed. This kind of short-term vision often boomerangs back on companies, bringing with it negative consequences and far greater expenses once the economy recovers again.[4]

In contrast to localization-readiness testing that is primarily cosmetically oriented, internationalization testing focuses on verifying successful implementation of support for any features or functionality required by targeted local markets, i.e., support for date, time, and number formatting, as well as locale-specific character sets and other attributes typical of products sold in international markets. Such support might also include building in configurability, for example, to enable the user interface skin to be changed to reflect local color and layout preferences with an eye to increasing product acceptance in target markets. Successful internationalization might also entail the suppression of functionality, such as 128-bit encryption that is legal in some markets but not in others, as noted above, or changing icons and symbols used in a product based on geolocation (i.e., built-in sensitivity to the locale in which the product is being operated). Finally, the ability of the product to correctly support entry of data in target locale character sets, transport of the data internally from module to module of the product business logic, accurate storage of data in databases so that it does not get corrupted, and correct display of data when it reappears on user interfaces are crucial to international functionality and must be tested as a core attribute of product design.

---

4. This short-sightedness is partly a side-effect of the quarterly orientation that dominates in North American business (Laverty 1996; McCarthy 2004).

Exploring new ways to improve and expand proactive international quality assurance and quality control

In the absence of knowledge about established best internationalization practices inside the company, the LPM can serve as a provider of this knowledge and as an advocate for appropriate, timely internationalization testing. The LPM may be required to research the subject matter and help create international test plans and scripts, and/or spearhead the adoption of technology to create pseudo-localized product builds. A test plan generally consists of a document that explains to all concerned, and in particular to supervisory management, *what* will be tested. In the case of international test plans, the goals of testing should be clarified, for example, to ensure that the product installs correctly on localized operating systems, or to ensure that the Japanese character set is correctly enabled throughout the application. In contrast to a test plan, a test script guides the tester, illuminating in detail *how* he or she will accomplish the goals of the test plan. The steps required to produce desired product behavior are listed, and the expected behavior is described. This allows the tester to note in detail any deviations from desired behavior that result from the steps as they are executed.

Another area of product development that the LPM can monitor is the design of a configuration management system to store, track and manage all of the files used in multilingual product builds. This will require interaction with software developers who are responsible for creating and maintaining the build system. It is critically important to proactively think through the organization of file storage locations, and to ensure identification of and access to all files requiring localization. Multilingual build environments can be complex and prone to human error, especially if they house and track component files in numerous languages. The LPM should participate in testing the multilingual build environment, ideally using pseudo-localized source files.

The LPM can also interact with development team managers and configuration management engineers to design a file naming convention that will facilitate the management of hundreds (or thousands) of files that are functionally identical but whose linguistic content differs. It cannot be assumed that software developers will be able to easily distinguish between languages simply by looking at the content of files. While Japanese may be easy to distinguish from German, even some Western languages such as Norwegian and Swedish may be indistinguishable to software developers who are not linguists. A clear file naming convention and an intuitive directory structure are thus key strategies for reducing the risk of inadvertently creating linguistically mixed product builds.

The LPM can also facilitate a secondary form of quality control to catch linguistic mixing by providing visual samples of similar languages. With some practice, quality control specialists can become quite adept at differentiating between languages, even if they neither understand nor speak them. With time, they can also learn typical user interface terms in languages that they frequently check. If the employer offers a

Management by Objectives system as part of the employee bonus calculation, quality control specialists can be encouraged by the LPM to take language courses as part of their personal development goals. This can have a synergistic effect for all concerned.

Contributing to globalization strategy

As part of their daily work, LPMs produce and monitor the cost side of international product business cases. No one in the localized product supply chain is better placed than LPMs to identify potential efficiencies that can be achieved through regional groupings or economies of scale. If for no other reason than to minimize the risk of unwelcome surprises, LPMs should proactively make contact and develop relationships with international sales personnel and actively seek early warning about requirements for products destined to be localized. International sales staff can also provide data that will be useful for advance preparation. There is no better way to impress senior management than to have risk analyses and constructive plans for solutions ready to plop down on the table the moment they are asked for.

Facilitating bi-directional information flow

Within the context of globalization as we have defined it, the most important role of the localization project manager is to foster and facilitate communication between centralized marketing staff and colleagues in regional offices. In doing so, it is important that the LPM concentrate on facilitating *two-way* information flow. For example, if an LPM puts a form-based system in place to create more thorough and region-centric marketing requirements documentation for new versions of products, then he or she has a twofold responsibility: (a) to ensure that the forms are filled out thoroughly and on a timely basis in the various regions, and (b) to ensure that the appropriate stakeholders in the central organization thoroughly understand the feature requests that are documented in the forms.

Cultivating a strong, mutually supportive relationship with content producers

The LPM is well advised to forge relationships with documentation managers, technical writers, and graphics specialists. Like localization, technical communication is directly dependent on the product development lifecycle. Consequently, documentation departments feel many of the same stresses that localization departments do. The similarity of the challenges facing localization and documentation departments presents an opportunity for LPMs to identify and build relationships with natural allies.

Becoming an advocate for initiatives that originate in foreign sales offices

Some organizations are sales-driven, some are marketing-driven, and some are development-driven. Often there exists a natural tension between these areas of the enterprise, as conflicting goals and agendas are constrained by limited resources. A localization project manager who seeks to help create and implement company strategy may be rebuffed by certain stakeholder groups on the grounds that everyone is already stretched too thin and that they cannot afford to bring the LPM up to speed. Undertaking proactive time- and money-saving research is one way to overcome this obstacle. Let us consider the example of market research. Because LPMs invest their time and energy in overseeing the delivery of products destined for regional markets, they often become a crucial contact point for colleagues in foreign offices. Because those colleagues frequently become frustrated by not being able to provide input or feedback to the generic product management team, they may seek an ally elsewhere in the organization who is sympathetic to their cause.

Becoming a sounding board and advocate for initiatives that originate abroad can be both an opportunity and a burden for the project manager. If she is able to take on the additional responsibility and has the communication skills required to represent foreign points of view, then she may be able to augment product marketing activities in constructive ways that save the core marketing team time and provide greater insight into offshore market needs. Participation in such initiatives can be synergistic, both for the company as a whole and for the individual LPM. However, performing this role too well can also become a distraction from the localization project manager's primary responsibility, which is to deliver projects on time, on budget, and with the specified level of quality. If these activities prove successful, demands on the LPM's time may increase dramatically as other international entities seek to undertake their own initiatives. The localization project manager must be careful to establish well-defined ground rules for such initiatives to avoid taking on too much responsibility at once.

Listening, learning, and synthesizing

By acting as a communication facilitator, the project manager can gain insight into the ideas and creativity of numerous locations and synthesize them to create a cohesive whole. The localization project manager can also provide early warning to central marketing if she senses dissatisfaction in the regional offices that might lead to rogue activities such as unsanctioned regional websites, dilution of corporate identity, or agendas that conflict with central marketing plans. On the other hand, as an advocate for regional needs, tastes, and legal constraints, the LPM can explain these needs, tastes and constraints to personnel in the central entity who may not otherwise be aware of them, thus helping to educate headquarters staff and broaden their horizons.

Furthermore, the LPM's position at the nexus of numerous regions means that she or he is ideally situated to help design product release roadmaps as well as synchronized international marketing initiatives that are adaptable to a variety of target markets, thus saving the organization time and money. Finally, given that marketing activities frequently precede actual product releases, the LPM is well advised to adopt a proactive stance vis-à-vis terminology and verbiage that is developed in the marketing department. At the very least, capturing marketing terminology in mono- and multilingual glossaries or termbases for use in subsequent localized product releases is a useful practice. Doing so can create further demonstrable savings of time and money downstream. Even better, if possible in the corporate environment from a political point of view, is direct involvement in the creative process so that potential downstream rework can be avoided at the concept design stage.

Steadfastly advocating plan-based discipline

Successful LPMs strive to the extent possible to impose a certain degree of corporate discipline by insisting on a plan-based approach to decision-making as opposed to a reactive, emotional, deal-driven approach. One way for LPMs to support a plan-based approach is to work proactively with corporate accounting to obtain revenue information for localized and non-localized products being released in international locales. People tend to be flattered when colleagues in other departments show interest in their work, and those who work in corporate finance are no exception. They are nearly always open to mentoring project managers about financial matters and, after knowledge-based relationships become established, a great deal of trust and information-sharing can be achieved.[5] LPMs can use information and concepts gleaned from corporate finance to write white papers about the advantages of plan-based globalization versus the costs of deal-based efforts, or about the risks of launching into globalization without thinking through all of the ramifications, as previously discussed. Most importantly, it is up to the LPM to educate whomever, wherever, and whenever greater corporate awareness is required.

---

5. This approach has proven to be both viable and fruitful at several companies where I have worked. Likewise, a number of attendees at the Localization Managers Roundtable, organized annually by the Localization Institute, have successfully adopted this strategy. The ability of the project manager to develop relationships with corporate accounting is of course contingent on many factors, including the size of the company, geographic distribution (i.e., it is harder to establish this type of relationship remotely) and even personality types. As a generalization, however, it can be said that staff in corporate accounting departments react in a positive and supportive manner to project managers who seek to develop greater knowledge about fiduciary responsibilities.

Implications

Project management knowledge, skills, tools, and techniques and the ability to apply them correctly in projects are necessary but not sufficient to be a successful project manager in organizations at lower levels of localization maturity (see Figure 2). As the preceding discussion demonstrates, the ability of the localization project manager to deliver projects on time, within budget and according to specification is shaped to a great extent by decisions and actions taken upstream in the product development process, before localization projects even begin. This type of situation, in which different functional units work independently and fail to communicate with each other has for the past two decades been commonly referred to in both the literature and in industry as the "silo effect" (Barabbam and Zaltman 1991; Twomey 1993).

Problems in localization and translation projects are often blamed on the silo effect (Hoffman and Mehnert 2000; Rockley, Kostur and Manning 2003; Swisher 2010). The existence of functional and information silos in many companies does undoubtedly make for more difficult projects. However, the longevity and pervasiveness of the silo effect are symptoms of other problems. On one hand, they can be read as evidence of a widespread failure on the part of senior management to define and implement a clear, coherent strategy in many companies. On the other hand, they can also be read as evidence of a lack of skills, knowledge and understanding of what happens before and after localization and of overall global strategy on the part of localization project managers and other localization team members.

This situation is rather ironic. Because their work touches and depends upon many areas of a company's activities, LPMs occupy a unique position in the company hierarchy. Their position affords them a virtually unparalleled perspective on the various functional silos that comprise the productivity matrix (see Figure 7). Practically no other position in corporate organizational structures, with the exception of certain positions in senior management, offers such a broad view of the corporation as a co-ordinated (or sometimes uncoordinated) functional entity.

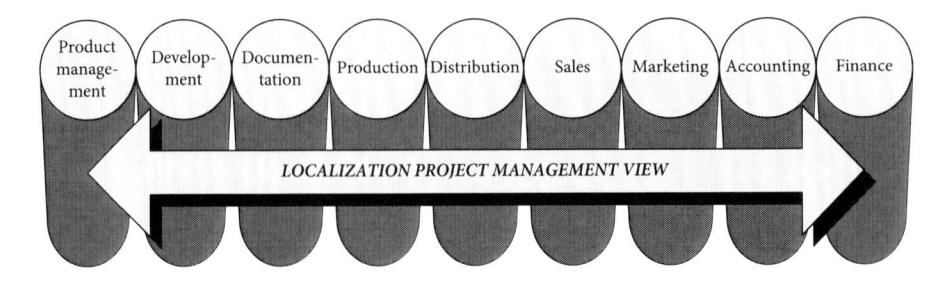

Figure 8. The localization project manager must understand, at a high level at least, the activities in many corporate silos.

Improving their performance requires that LPMs understand the methodologies and issues of the various functional areas of corporate endeavor, and that they be able to proactively convince decision-makers in those functional areas to adopt practices to foster successful localization, internationalization and globalization. This chapter has outlined some of the knowledge required and strategies that can be employed by LPMs to do just that. It is the author's hope that this chapter will begin a dialogue between industry and academia about the role of the localization project manager and the knowledge and skills that LPMs need to succeed in today's economy.

Thanks to their interaction with units that span the full range of corporate activities, LPMs are in a unique position to observe and analyze dependencies between diverse activities and agendas, and then to formulate and advocate measures to improve understanding and cooperation between corporate silos that will ultimately benefit not only the company as a whole, but also the individual LPMs. By thinking through and then promoting an integrated approach to the corporate processes of localization, internationalization and globalization, by implementing modest measures that cross the boundaries of corporate silos, and then using those success stories to further promote improvements on a global, holistic level, LPMs can help the company move beyond the silo effect towards greater localization maturity, while learning and growing personally as individual contributors at the focal point of the corporate matrix.

References

Barabbam, Vincent P. and Zaltman, Gérald. 1991. *Hearing the Voice of the Market: Competitive Advantage through Creative Use of Market Information*. Boston, MA: Harvard Business School Press.
Bean, James. 2003. *Engineering Global E-Commerce Sites: A Guide to Data Capture, Content, and Transactions*. San Francisco: Morgan Kaufmann.
Deitsch, Andrew and Czarnecki, David. 2001. *Java Internationalization*. Sebastopol, CA: O'Reilly.
DeMarco, Tom. 1982. *Controlling Software Projects: Management, Measurement & Estimation*. New York: Yourdon.
de Mooij, Marieke K. 2005. *Global Marketing and Advertising: Understanding Cultural Paradoxes*. 3rd ed. London: SAGE.
DePalma, Donald A. 2002. Business without Borders: A Strategic Guide to Global Marketing. New York: John Wiley & Sons.
———. 2006. "Localization maturity model." *GALAxy Newsletter*. Globalization & Localization Association. http://www.gala-global.org/articles/localization-maturity-model
DePalma, Donald A., Beninatto, Renato S. and Sargent, Benjamin B. 2006. *Localization Maturity Model*. Lowell, MA: Common Sense Advisory, Inc.
Esselink, Bert. 2000. *A Practical Guide to Localization*. Amsterdam/Philadelphia: John Benjamins.

Hoffman, Cornelia and Mehnert, Thorsten. 2000. "Multilingual information management at Schneider Automation." In *Translating into Success: Cutting-Edge Strategies for Going Multilingual in a Global Age*, Robert C. Sprung and Simone Jaroniec (eds), 59–79. Amsterdam/Philadelphia: John Benjamins.

Jordan, Patrick W. 2002. "The personalities of products." In *Pleasure with Products: Beyond Usability*, William S. Green and Patrick W. Jordan (eds), 19–47. London/New York: Taylor & Francis.

Kano, Nadine. 1995. *Developing International Software for Windows 95 and Windows NT*. Redmond, WA: Microsoft Press.

Laverty, Kevin J. 1996. "Economic 'short-termism': The debate, the unresolved issues and the implications for management practice and research." *Academy of Management Review* 21 (3): 825–860.

Luong, Tuok V., Lok, James S. H., Taylor, David J. and Driscoll, Kevin. 1995. *Internationalization: Developing Software for Global Markets*. [New York]: John Wiley & Sons.

McCarthy, Brian F. 2004. "Instant gratification or long-term value? A lesson in enhancing shareholder wealth." *Journal of Business Strategy* 25 (4): 10–17.

Norman, Donald A. 2004. *Emotional Design: Why We Love (or Hate) Everyday Things*. New York: Basic Books.

Ray, Julian J. 2004. "Business-to-business (B2B) electronic commerce." In *The Internet Encyclopedia*. Hossein Bidgoli (ed.), Vol. 1, 106–120. New York: John Wiley & Sons.

Rockley, Ann, Kostur, Pamela and Manning, Steve. 2003. *Managing Enterprise Content: A Unified Content Strategy*. Indianapolis, IN: New Riders.

Rozendaal, Marco, Keyson, David V. and de Ridder, Huib. 2007. "Product behavior and appearance effects on experienced engagement during experiential and goal-directed tasks." In *DPPI 2007 – Proceedings of the 2007 International Conference on Designing Pleasurable Products and Interfaces*, Ilpo Koskinen and Turkka Keinonen (eds), 181–193. New York: ACM.

Sikes, Richard. 2009. "Localization: The global pyramid capstone." *Getting Started Guide: Localization*. Supplement to *MultiLingual* 20 (3): 3–6. http://www.multilingual.com/downloads/screenSupp103.pdf

Smith-Ferrier, Guy. 2007. *.NET Internationalization. The Developer's Guide to Building Global Windows and Web Applications*. Upper Saddle River, NJ: Addison-Wesley.

Twomey, Daniel F. 1993. "Organizational competitiveness: Building performance and learning." *Competitiveness Review: An International Business Journal incorporating Journal of Global Competitiveness* 12 (2): 1–12.

Urien, Emmanuel, Howard, Robert and Perinotti, Tiziana. 1993. *Software Internationalization and Localization: An Introduction*. New York: Van Nostrand Reinhold.

Swisher, Val. 2010. "Content silos." Content Rules blog. May 22. http://www.contentrules.com/blog/localization-and-translation/content-silos/

Project as a learning environment
Scaffolding team learning in translation projects

Elena S. Dunne

> Learning is not compulsory; neither is survival.
> W. Edwards Deming
>
> The word "experienced" often refers to someone who's gotten away with doing the wrong thing more frequently than you have.
> Laurence Gonzales

The process of learning is fundamental to project success. In translation projects, learning is not confined to aspects of the text being translated (such as the domain, topic and text type) or to pragmatic text-related variables (such as the purpose of the source and target texts and the target audience). It extends to the project itself, encompassing the processes and tools to be used, the expectations held by various stakeholders, as well as the requirements that the project must fulfill. Empirical research shows that project managers can increase the likelihood of project success by managing the learning process for their teams and for themselves. This chapter proposes the use of the pedagogical technique of scaffolding as one way to manage learning in project teams.

Introduction: Survival, projects and learning

On January 23, 1945, a B-17 bomber of the U.S. Eighth Air Force was hit by anti-aircraft fire over Dusseldorf and its left wing was blown off.[1] Unlike the rest of the ten-man crew, pilot Federico Gonzales survived the fall in the crippled plane and regained consciousness after the crash only to see a German farmer point a gun at his head and pull the trigger. The gun misfired. Despite having fallen 27,000 feet (8,200 meters) without a parachute and broken most of the bones in his body, Gonzales survived the crash, near-execution and subsequent internment in a German prison camp.

Inspired and intrigued by this miraculous survival story, the pilot's son, Laurence Gonzales, has studied the behavior of people in life-or-death situations in an attempt

---

1. The information in this paragraph is drawn from Gonzales 2003 (9–12, 262–269).

to understand why some people survive and others do not. The resulting book, *Deep Survival*, draws on numerous examples to illustrate the fact that having relevant equipment, training and experience does not necessarily translate into survival in extreme situations (2004:15). Survival entails more than being prepared. The qualities that play a decisive role in survival include determination, humility, open-mindedness, and the ability to adapt to a constantly changing environment.

At first glance, life-or-death situations might seem to have little (if anything) in common with projects. However, if we equate "survival" with "project success" the analogy becomes clearer. The Standish Group's *CHAOS Summary 2009* report offers sobering statistics in this regard:[2]

- In 2009, only 32% of the projects examined by Standish Group were successes (delivered on time, on budget, with all required features and functions);
- 44% were challenged (delivered late, over budget, and/or with less than the required features and functions);
- 24% were failures (cancelled prior to completion, or delivered and never used).

The finding that less than one-third of projects succeed is not the only reason why survival is a relevant concept for project managers. Both extreme situations and projects are characterized by change, uncertainty, and the critical need to adapt. Indeed, at a fundamental level, the purpose of a project is to *create change*. The Project Management Institute's *A Guide to the Project Management Body of Knowledge (PMBOK® Guide)* defines a project as "a temporary endeavor undertaken to create a unique product, service, or result" (PMI 2008:5).[3] In other words, a project can be considered a state change: "A project is all about achieving some goal. The universe is in one state before the project, a different state afterwards, and the difference is the goal" (O'Connell 2001:2). The fact that a project is unique means that the product, service or result being created is in some ways unlike any other. It follows that every project presents an element of uncertainty and no two projects are ever identical. A new project may involve the creation of a product similar to one that already exists, or the delivery of a service similar to one that has already been provided. Nevertheless, the new project will inevitably present new variables, such as the inclusion of one or several new project team members, the use of a new version of a software program or hardware platform, and so forth. The presence of new variables in an otherwise

---

2. Since 1994, The Standish Group has conducted research on project success and failure and published the results in the *CHAOS Report*, which is generally held to be the most widely quoted source of such statistics, although it must be noted that Eveleens and Verhoef (2010) have recently questioned the validity of the CHAOS data.

3. All references to the *PMBOK Guide* in this chapter are to the fourth edition (2008), which has been recognized as an ANSI standard (ANSI/PMI 99-001-2008) and is the most recent version available as of this writing.

familiar project model introduces uncertainty. Of course, the project will present an even greater degree of uncertainty if the project model is unfamiliar or if the product, service or result is entirely unlike any other.

One of the consequences of uniqueness and uncertainty is that the characteristics of the product to be created or the service to be provided are not known in detail in advance, and thus must be defined and refined progressively over the course of the project. As new information becomes available, estimates are revised and the project plan and other project documents are updated, thus improving their accuracy and completeness throughout the project. This form of adaptive learning, known as *progressive elaboration*, is an essential aspect of project management.

Finally, the project takes place in an environment that is itself in a constant state of flux, and as such, a source of potential uncertainty and change:

> Heraclitus said that every time you step into the river, it's a different river. Every time you walk on Mount Hood, it's a different mountain. To use the technical terms, it's a boundary condition, a phase transition zone. And because of that, even if you are intimately familiar with its subtleties of character, it can make a mockery of the most thoughtful plans. ... And when the environment changes, you have to be aware that your own experience might be inappropriate.
>
> (Gonzales 2003:118)

Given the risk of failure and the challenges posed by uncertainty and change, it is clear that successful project performance and management, i.e., project "survival," requires not only appropriate training and experience, but also the ability to adapt and learn. As Gonzales puts it, "Survival is adaptation, and adaptation is change, but it is change based on a true reading of the environment. ... Those who avoid accidents are those who see the world clearly, see it changing, and change their behavior accordingly" (2003:280). It is to enable precisely this type of adaptation and learning that best-practice approaches to project management recommend the use of some type of "lessons learned" documentation process throughout the project, along with a retrospective post-project review.

While learning is critical in all projects, it is of particular importance to translation projects.[1] This chapter begins by examining why and how learning occurs in translation projects. It then discusses whether learning can be managed, and if so, how. Finally, it considers scaffolding of the learning process as a strategy to facilitate translation project management and to improve the project experience for everyone involved.

---

4. The concepts discussed in this chapter are relevant for translation projects in general and outsourced projects in particular, due to the distributed and often virtual nature of outsourced project teams.

The role of learning in translation projects

It is important to distinguish between translation as a *project* (an undertaking whose goal is to create a translation) and translation as an *activity* (the task by which that creation occurs). Although a translation project may involve a variety of activities, translation is necessarily one of them, and is often the primary one. The questions of what comprises the translation task and what competencies, subcompetencies or knowledge are required to successfully perform that task have been the object of scholarly inquiry for decades.

Historically, translation scholars have focused primarily on the linguistic aspects of the translation task. The linguistic approach helps us understand the product of the translation process, but not the translation process itself. In other words, the linguistic approach provides a framework within which to analyze the features of translation products, but sheds little light on the process whereby those products are created. The linguistic perspective does not enrich our understanding of the competencies or knowledge required to perform the translation task beyond knowledge of the source and target languages. In the 1970s and 1980s, a growing interest in pragmatics shifted the focus of translation research from language alone to typologies and pragmatic factors. Reiss's text typologies (1981) and work on Skopos theory by Reiss and Vermeer (1984), translational action Holz-Mänttäri (1984), and later, Nord (1997) on functionalism, demonstrated the importance of the pragmatic aspects of translation, such as text type and genre; the function of the translation and its purpose; the target audience; the time, place, and medium of text transmission; and the motive for carrying out the translation. Like linguistic theories of translation, these functionalist approaches have been criticized for their lack of empirical grounding (Lörscher 1988; Koller 1995; Pym 1996). Nevertheless, the ideas that the translator plays an active role in translation and that external factors impact the translation process are supported by research in other areas, such as descriptive translation studies and, perhaps surprisingly, in cultural approaches to literary translation. Scholars have explored the position of translated literature in the literary system (Even-Zohar 1978); patronage, poetics and ideology (Lefevere 1992); the asymmetry of power relations and politics (Niranjana 1992; Spivak 1992; Brisset 1996); and the translator's concept of his or her role (Venuti 1986, 1995), among other aspects. This work underscores the fact that the context shaping translation extends well beyond the immediate linguistic confines and the pragmatic situation of the source and target texts. Indeed, the work of scholars in both literary and pragmatic translation highlights the multiplicity and the complexity of the variables that impact the decisions the translator makes during translation. As Lefevere acknowledges, "language as the expression (and repository) of a culture is *one* element in the cultural transfer known as translation" (Lefevere 1992: 57; emphasis added).

Nevertheless, understanding the variables that impact the translator's task is not sufficient for understanding *how* the translator performs the task, or by extension *what knowledge* is required to do so successfully. Thus, researchers in translation studies have begun to examine these problems from a cognitive perspective (e.g., Séguinot 1989; Jääskeläinen 1989; Dancette 1997; Danks and Griffin 1997; House 2000; Shreve and Angelone 2010). Shreve (2002:156), for example, observes that translation requires at a minimum the following five types of knowledge:

- Linguistic knowledge (receptive competence in the source language and productive competence in the target language)
- Textual knowledge (knowledge of appropriate textual forms in the source and target cultures)
- Transfer knowledge (procedures and strategies for performing message transfer between the source and target cultures)
- Subject knowledge (knowledge about the subject matter or field with which the text deals)
- Information knowledge (knowledge necessary for concept formation, e.g., learning specialized vocabulary and terminology). Information knowledge can also include instrumental (tool-using) competency

In theory, when someone is asked to perform translation work during a project, that person is selected because she or he has the appropriate knowledge in each of these five areas. However, in practice this is not always possible. Moreover, it is not even *probable* for a translator to have all of the precise knowledge needed to carry out the translation in a specific project. The sections that follow will examine some of the reasons why.

All projects are unique, and so are all translations

As noted above, uniqueness is a fundamental project characteristic. Thus, every translation project involves the creation of a new translation. If an acceptable translation of a given text that meets the project requirements already exists, then that text will not need to be translated. Conversely, if a project involves re-translation of a previously translated text, then the principle of uniqueness holds that one or more aspects of that project must be new compared to the project which produced the existing translation. In other words, new requirements have arisen that the existing translation does not meet, or the existing translation does not fulfill the existing requirements.

Text-related and pragmatic variables are unique to each project

The choices that the translator makes during the translation process are impacted by pragmatic factors and by text variables, such as type and genre. Since every project situation is unique, so too are the operative pragmatic factors and text variables in each project. Because these factors and variables change from one project to the next, they must be elicited anew for every project. Translators can often identify many of them when they analyze the source text (e.g., type or genre). However, one should not assume that the factors which shaped the production of the source text are automatically valid for the target text. Doing so can lead to mismatched expectations (in the event that the intended purpose of the translated text is different from that of the source, for example).[5] On the other hand, expecting that the requestor will provide a clear description of all the necessary characteristics of the target text is unrealistic, since he or she does not necessarily possess the expertise needed to do so. Eliciting the necessary information requires that the translator and translation project manager engage in a collaborative process with the requestor to identify:

- Who wrote the source text (the author)
- Whom the source text was written for (the source audience)
- Why the source text was written (the purpose or intended use of the source text)
- Why the translation is needed (the purpose or intended use of the target text)
- Who the translation is being provided to (the target audience)
- Where (place), when (time) and how (medium) the translation will be made available to the readers/users

Stakeholder expectations must be defined and managed

Accounting for text-related and pragmatic variables during translation is necessary but not sufficient to ensure project success. Even if the translation is linguistically correct, culturally appropriate and fit for the intended pragmatic situation, the project may still be a failure in the eyes of the requestor. For example, suppose that a project involves the documentation of a technical manual, that multiple equivalents exist in the target language for many of the source-language terms in the manual, and that the requestor has specific preferences about the specific target-language equivalents that should be used when these terms are translated. If the usage in the translation does not reflect these preferences, there is a risk that the requestor will be dissatisfied.

Thus, the *PMBOK Guide* advises project managers that "[i]t is critical for project success to identify the stakeholders early in the project, and to analyze their levels of interest, expectations, importance and influence" (2008: 246). Moreover, it is a mistake to assume that the phrase "project success" holds the same meaning for everyone involved in the project. For instance, success for the project manager might mean delivering the translation to the client on the agreed-upon date, without exceeding the allotted budget. For the third-party reviewer involved in the project, success might

---

5. Nord (1997) addresses this problem by distinguishing between equifunctional, heterofunctional and homologous types of translations, depending on the degree of functional invariance. See also Dunne 175–180 and 182 in this volume.

mean ensuring that the translation reflects his/her terminological and stylistic preferences, and meeting the timeline may be seen as irrelevant. For the requestor, success might mean not receiving complaints from the reviewer, nor receiving requests from the project manager for additional time or budget to complete the project.

Although it is the job of the project manager (PM) to identify all stakeholders and their expectations, to balance and manage those expectations, and to ensure that they are met (to the extent possible), it is obvious that stakeholder expectations directly or indirectly impact the translator's task. If the authority for evaluating project success is vested in a third-party reviewer and that reviewer prefers the use of specific target-language terms, then the translator must be able to learn about those preferences and account for them in the translation to maximize the chances of project success. The translator must also be prepared to rationalize and justify translation decisions in the event that those preferences cannot be satisfied due to technical or other constraints. If the translator is unable or unwilling to learn about such preferences and account for them in the translation, there is a higher risk of rework and of project failure.

Most translators are generalists

Most translators have a background in language, culture or translation studies. Consequently, while they may specialize in a certain area, such as oil/gas engineering or accounting, translators are typically not subject-matter experts (Goetschalckx 1979; Wilss 1992; Woyde 2001; Zielinski and Ramírez Safar 2005). This reality underscores the importance that learning holds for translators. Diminishing the gap that separates them from subject-matter experts requires that translators undertake a concerted and sustained effort to educate themselves about their field(s) of specialization. Moreover, this learning must be an ongoing process. Even if they have extensive knowledge of the specialized concepts and of the stylistic and formatting conventions of the domain, translators must continuously educate themselves if they wish to remain abreast of new developments in the field.

Such is also the case for true subject-matter experts who become translators. Time spent translating is time not spent continuing to develop expertise in the area of specialization. Experts-turned-translators learn about new developments in their field within the framework of translation projects in which they participate, thus developing expertise in the area of specialized translation rather than in the specialty itself. Once a scientist becomes a translator, for example, the development of his or her *scientific* expertise gives way to the development of *scientific translation* expertise.

Finally, translators need to keep up with trends in general usage in both the source and target languages. This is particularly important for translators who emigrate. Languages, like the communities that give rise to them, are inherently dynamic. Translators whose usage ceases to evolve end up producing translations for audiences that no longer exist. Consider the following example of client review feedback discussed by Kelly, Beninatto and DePalma (2008: 14):

> When our internal reviewers looked at one project, the feedback was that it sounded 'cheesy'. The person was using terms that were outdated. We found out that the person who did the translation had lived outside of the country for the last 30 years, and was no longer up-to-date on terminology. So yeah, she was a native speaker, but she was out of touch, and was using language from an older generation.

Translators must continuously learn about new concepts and usage in both their field(s) of specialization and in general language. If their knowledge and usage does not evolve in parallel with the field and with society as a whole, their translations risk being seen as outmoded and substandard.

The number of qualified translators is limited

Given the advent of the Internet and the proliferation of Web-based freelance translator directories (e.g., GoTranslators.com, Proz.com, TranslatorsCafe.com, etc.), one might think that finding qualified translators should be easy. Nothing could be further from the truth. Although estimates of the number of full-time and part-time freelance translators worldwide range from approximately 300,000 (Allied Business Intelligence 1998; Allen 2006) to as high as 700,000 (Beninatto and DePalma 2008), and despite the fact that searches for translators in a given language pair can return hundreds or even thousands of candidates, the requirements for a given project can dramatically reduce the size of the potential resource pool. For example, simply specifying the language pair, subject matter and translation tool to be used may shrink the number of ostensibly qualified translators from hundreds to a dozen or so, even in language pairs characterized by high volume and large numbers of service providers. Availability and the requisite level of expertise further diminish the size of the resource pool. These problems are magnified when the project involves less translated languages, or unusual language pairs or directionality. An example will help to illustrate these issues. A search for translators who work from English into Thai and whose native language is Thai on Proz.com returns 434 results, whereas a search for Thai into English translators (with English being the native language) brings only 57 results. If the search is filtered using criteria such as area of specialization, years of experience and CAT tool usage, the number of results drops even further. Because the number of expert translators is limited, the project manager may have to select translators who do not meet all of the required criteria and who have significant gaps in their knowledge and/or skills, especially in highly specialized projects. In such cases, compromises will be necessary when deciding which translators to hire, and provisions will need to be made to give the translators learning opportunities so that they can fill in their knowledge gaps.

The subject field or combination of subject fields can exacerbate the knowledge gap

New areas of research are emerging continuously, and companies are in constant competition to develop new and unique products, technologies and services. As a result, translators may find themselves translating documentation for equipment or technology that is unique in the world and for which no reference material, nor parallel texts from which to extract terminology exist. Because translators cannot translate that which they do not understand, they may need to educate themselves about specific concepts or aspects of any source text to be translated. The scope of the required learning effort increases considerably when the project involves one-of-a-kind products or services.

Moreover, the gap between required and available knowledge is often magnified by the fact that certain types of translation projects, such as software localization, require expertise in multiple subject areas and familiarity with multiple text types and genres. For example, translation of the user interface of a Windows-based project management software application would require that the translator be familiar with (a) general software concepts; (b) Windows terminology; and (c) project management concepts. In addition, the translator would also need to acquire a certain level of understanding of the way that particular application functions, and would need learn how to locate specific strings in the running application to be able to determine their meaning.

Project process requirements may be specific to a given service provider or client

In addition to the factors discussed thus far, projects may involve specific tools, processes or logistics with which translators are unfamiliar. For example, a requestor company (i.e., a translation service provider or a direct client) may require (a) the use of a portal for accessing/downloading project files and uploading deliverables; (b) the use of a proprietary translation or terminology management tool; and/or (c) the completion of specific steps in a process, e.g., submitting a completed checklist with the deliverables, providing a translation log, following a specific process for query or invoice submission, etc. These too must be learned.

Learning: A core translation competency

Given the complexity of the real-world environment in which translation occurs and the number of factors which shape that environment, it is clear that learning must occur on some level during every project to enable translators to close the gaps between the knowledge they possess and the knowledge they need to successfully complete the project. This observation has larger implications for translation project managers. Learning is not only critical for translators or for translation tasks; *all* project team members must engage in the process of learning at some level. Thus, a localization engineer who will be compiling a Help system in MadCap Flare may know how to use Flare and how to compile a Help system in a specific language, but will still have to learn how a specific Flare project is structured, which types of outputs are needed, and so forth. The project manager himself or herself is a professional learner: the technique of progressive elaboration at the heart of project management is essentially an iterative learning process. Moreover, learning is a prerequisite to core project management processes, such as scope management and risk management. One cannot manage the project scope without having first determined what precisely comprises the scope; likewise, risk management requires that the project team ascertain where uncertainties lie in the project in order to identify potential sources of risk.

Managing learning as a process within the project environment

The reality of the market economy is such that all of the companies and individuals participating in it are in competition with one another. This competitive environment is not static. Individuals who do not update their skills and expertise risk being overtaken and displaced by those who do. Likewise, companies that do not continuously improve will eventually lose market share to competitors, no matter how successful they may be at the moment. As American humorist Will Rogers aptly observed: "Even if you're on the right track, you'll get run over if you just sit there." Companies and individuals must continually adapt to survive, and ideally, thrive in the competitive environment.

Empirical research on project teams demonstrates that actively managing learning can enhance team performance. For instance, an observational study performed on surgical teams found that "the most successful teams had leaders who actively managed their teams' learning efforts" (Edmondson, Bohmer, and Pisano 2005: 140). Another study, which focused on the effectiveness of multinational teams by examining the effects of group structure and electronic communication patterns on the performance of 18 multinational teams over an 8-month period, identified membership, communication, trust, identity, and learning as the five top predictors of team performance (DeSanctis and Jiang 2005).

Managing the learning process within a project team should be part of the larger knowledge and information management strategy that many organizations are currently developing. As Drucker wrote more than two decades ago in his prescient article "The Coming of the New Organization" (1988), the evolution of the economy, and especially developments in information technology, dictate that businesses become information-based. In the information-based organization, knowledge resides within the minds of specialists who do the work, rather than in mid-level or top management, as is the case in classic hierarchical, functional organizations. In a project-based organization, this means that the project manager must be able to structure a team learning environment in such a way as to enable the exchange and documentation of knowledge and information required by team members to make the right decisions and to complete their tasks successfully. Receiving the right information at the right time or learning a more efficient way of carrying out a task for any team member may make the difference between successfully completing the task at hand and not completing that task correctly (or not completing it at all).

Even if project team members are highly motivated and aware of the importance of the learning process, the constraints imposed on them in a given project may prevent them from engaging fully in that learning process. As Sense observes, "an opportunistic and unstructured approach to learning may indeed limit the quality and the quantity of learning activity situated within the context of projects" (2007: 411). Conversely, the quality and the quantity of learning will likely increase, and by extension, the quality of a product or service being produced or delivered by the team will likely improve in a structured environment that seeks to facilitate learning. For example, during a multilingual translation project, a translator working into one language may ask a question that did not occur to translators working into other languages, or may discover a factual error in the source text that the other translators overlooked. Once the author has clarified the ambiguity or corrected the error in the source text, the project manager should provide this information to the entire translation team. If this information is only provided to the specific translator who asked the question or discovered the error, there is a risk that translators working into other languages will misunderstand the text and introduce a mistranslation, or that they will replicate the source-text error in the target text.

The development and implementation of a framework for managing the learning process within the project team thus allows the project manager to enhance the team's performance and to mitigate or eliminate certain project risks. The teaching methodology of scaffolding can be used to create just such a framework.

Scaffolding project team learning

The concept of 'scaffolding' was first introduced in developmental psychology and education by Jerome Bruner in the late 1950s. However, the origins of this concept date back to the first half of the twentieth century and to Vygotsky's notion of the *zone of proximal development* (1935). A zone of proximal development is the transitional zone between what a student knows and what he/she does not yet know. Reflecting on Vygotsky's influence on developmental psychology and education, Bruner created the metaphor of scaffolding, which he reconstructed from Vygotsky's works and other sources. Bruner agrees with Vygotsky that "there is at least one deep parallel in all forms of knowledge acquisition – precisely the existence of a zone of proximal development and the procedures for aiding the learner to enter and progress across it" (1987: 78). As an instructional strategy that is used to assist the learner in the zone of proximal development (Roehler and Cantlon 1997: 9), scaffolding plays an important role for social constructivist theoreticians and practitioners in cognitive and developmental psychology, and in education. From being defined as "a process that enables a child or a novice to solve a problem, carry out a task, or achieve a goal which would be beyond his unassisted efforts" (Wood, Bruner, Ross 1976: 90), the process of scaffolding has been generalized to classroom-based student learning, including learning by adult students,[6] and also discussed outside of student-teacher interaction (see, for example, the discussion on peer scaffolding in Lai and Law 2006).

Both Vygotsky and Bruner refer to language acquisition as the most compelling example of a learning activity in which a scaffolding strategy should be used, in recognition of the fact that one cannot learn the language without "borrowing" the knowledge of the language instructor/tutor (Bruner 1987: 76). However, the metaphor of scaffolding takes us beyond the notion of *borrowing* to that of *building*. In construction, scaffolding is a temporary structure that allows for a building to be constructed one story at a time. Instructional scaffolding works in a similar way. It is a temporary framework created by the instructor to help the learner acquire specific knowledge or skills and to meet specific educational objectives.

In a classroom, the instructor is the person who is most competent and who is providing the knowledge to the students, or assisting in the acquisition of knowledge by the students. In a project environment, each team member is competent in his or her own area, but a knowledge asymmetry often exists between the team members. More critically, knowledge asymmetry often exists between the project team and the creators of the materials being translated. Thus, while translators may be experts in the translation of texts from a given domain, they likely do not possess the same degree of knowledge about the content being translated during a specific project as the authors who created that content. In addition, the translators are in all likelihood not users of the product/service, and are probably unfamiliar with the jargon used within the company where the author or authors work (especially in outsourced translation projects). In such cases, the bulk of the knowledge about the content being translated and the expectations with respect to the translation reside within the minds of the content authors and of subject-matter experts. Such knowledge asymmetry must be resolved if the project is to succeed. Thus, the project manager, much like the instructor in a

---

6. For instance, Keller and Werchan (2006: 407) and Taylor (2006: 209) discuss scaffolding in the construction of knowledge or self-scaffolding.

classroom, can assist the team by scaffolding the acquisition of knowledge. Holton and Clark argue that scaffolding is "a social process whereby a learner is supported in their [sic] construction of knowledge" (2006: 128). It follows that the project manager can support and manage the process whereby the team acquires knowledge that it lacks by scaffolding that process.

There can be different types of scaffolding. Holton and Clark (2006) distinguish between expert, reciprocal scaffolding and self-scaffolding. They also distinguish between conceptual and heuristic domains of scaffolding. Conceptual scaffolding promotes conceptual development and heuristic scaffolding allows for development of heuristics (i.e., strategies, methods or techniques for problem solving and learning). All three types of scaffolding and both domains are applicable to translation projects.

Expert scaffolding involves an expert who can act as a guide during the learning process. In a translation project, such scaffolding takes place when subject matter experts interact with the team to provide information on specific concepts or advice on the resolution of specific problems. For example, when translating user interface strings during a localization project, translators must be able to view the strings in context in order to understand them. But given the reality of outsourcing, the pressures of simultaneous shipment ("simship") of multiple language versions and ever-decreasing translation prices, it is increasingly difficult for translators to spend the time necessary to gain a thorough understanding of how the application functions and how to (easily) find specific strings in context. Moreover, if the content is over-internationalized and translatable content is completely isolated from the context in which it appears, there may not even be any easy way to map each string or message to its location. In such cases, the project manager can work with the development team and/or a subject-matter expert (SME) to provide a basic introduction to the application via a webinar or on-site training. Such training must be targeted specifically at the needs of translators (as distinct from general-orientation training) and should answer questions such as the following:

1. What is the high-level structure of the application?
2. How can the translator determine which sections, files, sets of strings and messages map to which application modules, sections and functionalities?
3. What are the most common operations that users perform?
4. If any strings are subject to concatenation, is there a key enabling the translators to rebuild the structure of the complete composite sentences and to view them at runtime?

Alternatively, or in addition to the training, the SME can provide a script to be used to access the core functions in the application. During software upgrades, providing a script that contains information on ways to access only the new functionality can serve as the scaffolding that helps the translation team to quickly understand what is new in the application. In addition, because the script enables the translators to see strings in context, it allows them to avoid having to translate sight unseen, thus reducing the risk of comprehension errors and mistranslations. This in turn will enhance the time- and cost-effectiveness of subsequent quality checks.

In reciprocal scaffolding, two or more people work collaboratively. "Because of the different skills that [peers] bring to the work, each may provide a contribution that is a form of scaffolding," observe Holton and Clark (2006: 136). Reciprocal scaffolding takes place during translation projects in which team members are able to collaborate with each other. All too often translation projects are carried out using a waterfall approach in which steps and phases are completed in sequence, without any kind of collaboration or feedback loops (see Dunne 162–163 and 168–171 in this volume). The introduction of feedback loops, for instance by carrying out editing on a rolling basis and allowing and encouraging editors to provide feedback to the translators over the course of the project, provides opportunities for the translators to improve the quality of future output, to prevent incorrect or unnecessary edits, should any happen to be introduced by the editor, and to exchange conceptual subject-matter knowledge and/or knowledge of the product. In addition, such scaffolding allows the project manager to balance skills within the team. For example, if a translator has an excellent understanding of the subject matter but not of the product being localized, an editor who has knowledge of the product can provide the necessary guidance. Conversely, if the translator has a deeper understanding of the product being localized than the editor, then the editor can be directed not to make any changes to user interface terminology.

Finally, self-scaffolding takes place when an individual "is able to provide scaffolding for her(him)self when any problem or concept that is new to the individual is being tackled" (Holton and Clark 2006: 136). While self-scaffolding is internally motivated and constructed, "learning to learn" (Bickhard 2005: 171) is a skill that is developed within a social environment and from interaction with others. As Kelly Washbourne suggests, the ability to self-scaffold is itself a competence, and certainly is a huge step toward self-directed learning (autonomy); while not every team member might be able to self-scaffold, those who can probably can scaffold for others (personal communication).

Although the project manager cannot control self-scaffolding, he or she can proactively engage in expert and reciprocal scaffolding to increase the efficiency of the learning process within the translation team. By creating a learning environment and implementing processes that enable expert and reciprocal scaffolding, the project manager can improve the project team's understanding of the project itself, thus enhancing the process of progressive elaboration, while simultaneously facilitating knowledge exchange and acquisition between project team members and even between the project team and client-side stakeholders.

Creating scaffolds to facilitate the learning process in translation projects

Making the transition from theory to practice requires that we map the characteristics of scaffolding to areas of project management application. McKenzie (2000: 155–160) identifies eight essential characteristics of scaffolding: (1) clear directions; (2) clarification of purpose; (3) keeping learners on task; (4) assessment to clarify expectations; (5) worthy sources; (6) reduction of uncertainty, surprise, and disappointment; (7) efficiency; and (8) momentum. The following sections discuss each of these characteristics in turn as they can be applied to translation projects.

Clear directions

Providing clear instructions is often one of the more challenging tasks for a translation project manager. While information about basic characteristics, such as locale and target audience, is relatively easy to obtain, translators frequently do not ask for such information. Likewise, clients who are new to translation or new to working with my company, for instance, often fail to understand why such information should be necessary. "Why do you need that?" they often ask. "Can't you just translate?" However, it is through the process of discovering these details, which will later become important for the client, that the project manager creates the project specification. The intentional process of discovering and identifying project requirements enables the translation project manager to create clear directions for the translation team. The team, in turn, uses these directions to create the final product, thus ensuring that it conforms to the requirements identified by the project manager.

However, specifying pragmatic variables such as the purpose and audience of the target text does not necessarily suffice to ensure a successful outcome. Every word in the translation reflects the translator's conscious (or automated) decisions driven by his or her unique background, experience and expertise in terms of languages, cultures, translation and the domain. It follows that in any given instance of translation, there is a risk that another person (i.e., an editor, client reviewer, etc.), drawing on different expertise and knowledge, will make a different decision. Both decisions could be correct; after all, there is often no single correct translation, but rather multiple possible translations. Determining whose decision will be retained in the final version is a challenge for the project manager who is trying to make the client happy while also maintaining the peace in the translation team.

Scaffolds can be put in place to facilitate this decision-making process. Addressing certain features of the future translation (e.g., terminology, stylistic requirements, etc.) and agreeing on them before the translation is created is a way to minimize the risk of problematic disagreements. In addition, it is important to educate stakeholders who have the final say in the process, such as editors or client reviewers, about the range of acceptable solutions and to put a structure in place to enable them to conduct their portion of the project work without encroaching on the decision-making responsibility of other team members. Specifically, an editor can be asked to compare the source with the target to identify and correct spelling, grammar, punctuation errors, as well as missing translation and inconsistent terminology, but not to make any changes to the approved terminology. Or, the client reviewer can be asked to review proposed target-language terminological equivalents to ensure that they reflect company-specific usage and to correct any terms that do not, after which the translation team will not be able to modify the approved terminology, hence limiting the range of translation decisions they make. From a technological perspective, the project manager can select (or create) and maintain infrastructure (tools, platforms) to facilitate the process of setting up and complying with the project requirements. Thus, working in a flat file such as a word processing or spreadsheet document might suffice to meet the requirements of a project involving a limited number of terms and one target language, while a project involving multiple languages and/or an extensive collection of terms might necessitate that the use of a centralized depository for storing, accessing and reviewing term equivalents.

Clarification of purpose

Functionalist approaches to translation studies generally advocate the use of what has become known as a "translation brief," which includes information about the readership and purpose of the target text (Nord 1997: 30), among other things. While it is important that the requestor, project manager and translator(s) understand and agree on the purpose of the target text, such understanding and agreement is not sufficient to ensure project success. It is project manager's responsibility to identify the overall purpose of the project. In project management terms, the purpose is the highest-level determination of project scope: where the final deliverable will be used, who will comprise the target audience, what the target document should achieve, and above all what the customer is trying to accomplish by doing the project in the first place. All too often, when asked for a quote, translation companies provide just that – the price and turnaround – without bothering to ask the question of how the project fits into the big picture of the requestor company's strategy.[7]

No author would start writing without having a clear understanding of the target audience, the purpose of the document, and the time, place and medium of publication or distribution. In this respect, and at this stage of the process, there is absolutely

---

7. This statement is based on my experience participating in competitive bids for translation projects. In many cases, at the conclusion of the bidding process, the customer has indicated that the company for which I work (Advanced Language Translation Inc.) was the only vendor to ask questions about the purpose of the project, the intended use of the translation, and so forth.

no difference between writers and translators: both must understand the purpose of what they are about to write. The fact that the ideas that technical writers communicate are in the heads of developers or managers, whereas the ideas that translators communicate are in the form of a source text, is beside the point. Clarification of purpose must precede the creation of clear and detailed directions for each of the team members and project stakeholders.

Keeping students on task

While the title "project manager" implies that PMs manage *projects*, in reality, they manage *people who perform project work*. To keep the translation team on task, the PM should set up the schedule at the project planning stage; inform all translation team members of the schedule and milestone dates; indicate which deadlines are flexible and which are not; and finally, monitor the schedule, adjusting it if necessary to increase the team's effectiveness while meeting the defined standards of the required final output.

Assessment to clarify expectations

By creating a framework within which the purpose of the project is specified, reference materials are provided, preferred terminology and style are defined and approved, and clear instructions are provided, the project manager indirectly creates the framework within which the final translation can be assessed. The criteria on which the assessment can be performed may include but are not necessarily limited to using approved terminology; following an approved style guide; adhering to specific formatting requirements; converting measurements using a specific converter; using fonts required for specific languages; and performing QC checks using provided scripts. By identifying parameters that the client and/or end user deems important, the project manager moves from the realm of unidentified needs (or expectations) to identified needs (or requirements), increasing the likelihood that the project will satisfy the client's expectations. However, one must keep in mind that in most cases, receiving a clear list of specifications from the client is impossible. Some purchasers of language services may be high enough on the translation/localization maturity scale (DePalma 2006) to be in position to provide clear requirements, but the vast majority are not (Txabarriaga 2009: 1). It is for this reason that the PM and LSP must engage in a collaborative and often iterative process with the requestor to elicit the necessary information, as noted above. Indeed, in a survey conducted by Fraser, only 12% of the translators reported that they received information about the target audience on a regular basis and only 21% were told the purpose of translation (2000: 54).

Worthy sources

Providing any reference material that illustrates desired terminology or style, that clarifies the object and purpose of the translation, and that is recommended (and ideally, approved) by the end client or end user,[8] allows the project manager to focus the translation team's attention on a single set of approved sources, rather than letting them wander about "like prospectors on the desert" (McKenzie 2000: 157). Selecting a list of reference materials in addition to any legacy translations that may exist and obtaining formal approval from all stakeholders to use those reference materials is a simple but effective translation scaffolding strategy.

Reduction of uncertainty, surprise, and disappointment

This is the essence of managing risk and stakeholder expectations, and is a normal part of any project manager's duties.

Efficiency

By front-loading critical terminological and stylistic decisions, translators, editors and the client no longer need to wonder which term or which formulation of a string (or tagline) should be used in the target text. This approach increases the translation team's efficiency by eliminating the more difficult barriers that the team may encounter. This front-loading strategy also significantly decreases or even eliminates the risk of costly and inefficient fixes at the tail end of the project, as there is far less likelihood that a terminological or stylistic decision will diverge from the reviewer's or end-user's preferences.

Momentum

By providing strong support for the translation team in all critical areas (terminology, style, communication framework, etc.), the translation project manager allows the team to shift its attention away from project logistics and focus on the task at hand, thereby creating momentum.

---

8. The client may not necessarily be the end user of the translation. For example, suppose a software development company is localizing a piece of software and the accompanying documentation for subsequent sale to customers. In this scenario, the software development company that purchases the translation/localization service is the end client, whereas those who buy the localized software are end users.

Alternate views on scaffolding

Although McKenzie's model of scaffolding enjoys widespread currency in the literature, alternative views have been proposed. Applebee and Langer (1983, 1986), for example, frame scaffolding in terms of (1) intentionality; (2) appropriateness; (3) structure; (4) collaboration; and (5) internalization. Applebee and Langer's model is not incompatible with McKenzie's; rather, these two models represent slightly different perspectives on the same object. Moreover, both models can be applied to translation project management. Thus, *intentionality* combines both instructions and the purpose of the translation, which together constitute the foundation of project scope definition. *Appropriateness* takes a different twist in the project management environment compared to education. In instruction, tasks pose problems that cannot be successfully solved by the students on their own, whereas in translation it is the project itself that cannot be "solved" by any one person by and requires *collaboration* between translators, editors, the project manager, localization engineers, technical writers, developers and/or others, depending on the project. Besides the framework for collaboration that the project manager creates, the source text itself is in a way a *structure* or blueprint on the basis of which the text is re-created in the target language. That is, the source text contains information that must be communicated by the translator, but it is up to the translator to decide how that information can be most effectively communicated in the target language on the denotative, connotative, pragmatic and other levels. Finally, *internalization* occurs throughout the project. The more the project team internalizes, the less directed involvement is required of the project manager.

Conclusion

Learning plays a fundamental role in translation project success. Proactive management enables the creation of an environment in which learning occurs in a structured way despite the challenges of the typical translation project. Scaffolding the process of learning helps the project manager to uncover the scope of the project through progressive elaboration, develop the team, manage stakeholders' expectations and balance the strengths and weaknesses that exist within the team.

Translation project managers must understand the core principles of project management, the challenges that translation poses for project management, as well as the importance of being able to clearly see and communicate the vision of the final product to the translation team. In other words, project managers must understand both project management and the nature of translation.

On their end, translation team members must understand that no single person possesses all the knowledge required to achieve successful project outcomes. Therefore, translation team members, and especially translators and editors, will need to know how to identify and acquire the knowledge that they lack.

Project participants cannot successfully perform their tasks without understanding the big picture, the ways in which the various pieces of the project fit together and the impact that each person's task can have on the quality of the end product and on the success of the project. Requestors must understand that translation projects (or any project for that matter) cannot simply be thrown over the wall. If clients want their projects to be successful, they must be prepared to actively participate and contribute to project success by communicating and conveying the big picture to the project manager and project team.

Learning is essential in projects not only because of knowledge asymmetry, but also because of the nature of projects themselves, which are characterized by change, uncertainty, and the critical need to adapt. Success in today's dynamic business environment requires that project teams embrace change. As project management expert Robert Wysocki observes, "[we] need an approach that is built around change – one that embraces learning and discovery throughout the project life cycle. Moreover, it must have built-in processes to accommodate the changes that result from this learning and discovery" (2009: xlv). Without the ability to learn and thus to adapt to the ever-changing project environment, the team, the project manager, and the project itself cannot "survive" to its completion. Scaffolding the process of learning and discovery is one way to create a framework in which the team can learn and stay attuned to the changes and uncertainty inherent in projects.

Finally, creating scaffolds, such as lists of approved terms (or even comprehensive termbases), and defining general requirements for translation (e.g., purpose, audience, etc.) in a structured way, has the added benefit of creating information and knowledge assets that can later be used in similar projects, related projects or in the training of new team members for such projects. From this perspective, scaffolding does not just allow PMs to manage the learning process, but also provides a structure for managing the knowledge acquired during projects.

References

Allen, Jeff. 2006. "Number of translators who use CAT TM tools." TranslatorsCafe.com, April 28. http://www.translatorscafe.com/cafe/MegaBBS/thread-view.asp?threadid=6473&messageid=86440#86440

Allied Business Intelligence. 1998. *Language Translation: World Market Overview, Current Development and Competitive Assessment*. Oyster Bay, NY: Allied Business Intelligence, Inc.

Applebee, Arthur N. and Langer, Judith A. 1983. "Instructional scaffolding: Reading and writing as natural language activities." *Language Arts* 60 (2): 168–175.

———. 1986. "Reading and writing instruction: Toward a theory of teaching and learning." *Review of Research in Education* 13: 171–194.

Beninatto, Renato S. and DePalma, Donald A. 2008. "The top 25 translation companies and some really big revenue numbers." *The Global Watchtower* [Common Sense Advisory blog], June 20. http://upgrade.globalwatchtower.com/2008/06/top-25-revenue-08/

Bickhard, Mark H. 2005. "Functional scaffolding and self-scaffolding." *New Ideas in Psychology* 23 (3): 166–173.

Brisset, Annie. 1996. "The search for a native language: Translation and cultural identity." In *A Sociocritique of Translation: Theatre and Alterity in Quebec, 1968–1988*, Trans. Rosalind Gill and Roger Gannon, 162–194. Toronto: University of Toronto Press.

Bruner, Jerome. 1987. *Actual Minds, Possible Worlds.* Cambridge, MA: Harvard University Press.

Dancette, Jeanne. 1997. "Mapping meaning and comprehension in translation: Theoretical and experimental issues." In *Cognitive Processes in Translation and Interpreting*, Joseph H. Danks, Gregory M. Shreve, Stephen B. Fountain and Michael K. McBeath (eds), 77–103. Thousand Oaks/London/New Delhi: Sage.

Danks, Joseph H. and Griffin, Jennifer. 1997. "Reading and translation: A psycholinguistic perspective." In *Cognitive Processes in Translation and Interpreting*, Joseph H. Danks, Gregory M. Shreve, Stephen B. Fountain and Michael K. McBeath (eds), 161–175. Thousand Oaks/London/New Delhi: Sage.

DePalma, Don. 2006. "Localization maturity model." *GALAxy Newsletter.* Globalization & Localization Association. http://www.gala-global.org/articles/localization-maturity-model

DeSanctis, Gerardine and Jiang, Lu. 2005. "Communication and the learning effectiveness of multinational teams." In *Managing Multinational Teams: Global Perspectives*, Debra L. Shapiro, Mary Ann Von Glinow and Joseph L.C. Cheng (eds), 97–123. Amsterdam: Elsevier.

Drucker, Peter F. 1988. "The coming of the new organization." *Harvard Business Review* 66 (1): 45–53.

Edmondson, Amy, Bohmer, Richard and Pisano, Gary. 2005. "Speeding up team learning." In *Harvard Business Review on Managing Projects*, 190–197. Boston, MA: Harvard Business School Press.

Eveleens, J. Laurenz and Verhoef, Chris. 2010. "The rise and fall of the Chaos Report figures." *IEEE Software* 27 (1): 30–36.

Even-Zohar, Itamar. 1978. "The position of translated literature within the literary polysystem." In *Literature and Translation: New Perspectives in Literary Studies*, James S. Holmes et al. (eds), 117–127. Leuven: ACCO.

Fraser, Janet. 2000. "The broader view: How freelance translators define translation competence." In *Developing Translation Competence*, Christina Schäffner and Beverly Adab (eds), 51–62. Amsterdam/Philadelphia: John Benjamins.

Goetschalckx, J. 1979. "EURODICAUTOM." In *Translating and the Computer: Proceedings of a seminar*, B. M. Snell (ed.), 71–75. Amsterdam: North-Holland.

Gonzales, Laurence. 2003. *Deep Survival: Who Lives, Who Dies, and Why.* London/New York: W. W. Norton.

Holz-Mänttäri, Justa.1984. *Translatorisches Handeln: Theorie und Methode.* Helsinki: Suomalainen Tiedeakatemia.

Holton, Derek and Clark, David. 2006. "Scaffolding and metacognition." *International Journal of Mathematical Education in Science and Technology* 37 (2): 127–143.

House, Juliane. 2000. "Consciousness and the strategic use of aids in translation." In *Tapping and Mapping the Processes of Translation and Interpreting*, Sonja Tirkkonen-Condit and Riitta Jääskeläinen (eds), 149–162. Amsterdam/Philadelphia: John Benjamins.

Jääskeläinen, Riitta. 1989. "Translation assignment in professional vs. non-professional translation: A think-aloud protocol study." In *The Translation Process*, Candace Séginot (ed.), 87–98. Toronto: H. G. Publications.

Keller, Heidi and Werchan, Anne. 2006. "Culture, learning, and adult development." In *Handbook of Adult Development and Learning*, Carol Hoare (ed.), 407–430. Oxford: Oxford University Press.

Kelly, Nataly, Beninatto, Renato S. and DePalma, Donald A. 2008. *Buyer-Defined Translation Quality: Illuminating the Customer's Perspective on What Good Language Services Mean*. Lowell, MA: Common Sense Advisory.

Koller, Werner. 1995. "The concept of equivalence and the object of translation studies." *Target* 7 (2): 191–222.

Lai, Ming and Law, Nancy. 2006. "Peer scaffolding of knowledge building through collaborative groups with differential learning experiences." *Journal of Educational Computing Research* 35 (2): 123–144.

Lefevere, André. 1992. *Translation, Rewriting, and the Manipulation of Literary Fame*. London; New York: Routledge.

Lörscher, Wolfgang. 1988. "Modelle des Übersetzungsprozesses: Anspruch und Wirklichkeit." *Fremdsprache lehren und lehrnen* 17: 62–83.

McKenzie, Jamie. 2000. *Beyond Technology. Questioning, Research and the Information Literate School*. Bellingham, WA: FNO Press.

Niranjana, Tejaswini. 1992. *Siting Translation History, Post-Structuralism, and the Colonial Text*. Berkeley, CA: University of California Press.

Nord, Christiane. 1997. *Translating as a Purposeful Activity: Functionalist Approaches Explained*. Manchester: St Jerome.

O'Connell, Fergus. 2001. *How To Run Successful Projects III: The Silver Bullet*. 3rd ed. Harlow, UK: Pearson Education.

Project Management Institute. 2008. *A Guide to the Project Management Body of Knowledge (PMBOK® Guide)*. 4th ed. Newtown Square, PA: Project Management Institute.

Pym, Anthony. 1996. "Material text transfer as a key to the purposes of translation." In *Basic Issues in Translation Studies. Proceedings of the Fifth International Conference*, Albrecht Neubert, Gregory M. Shreve and Klaus Gommlich (eds), 337–346. Kent, OH: Kent State University Institute for Applied Linguistics.

Reiss, Katharina. 1981. "Type, kind, and individuality of text: Decision making in translation." Trans. Suzan Kitron. *Poetics Today* 2 (4): 121–131.

Reiss, Katharina and Vermeer, Hans J. 1984. *Grundlegung einer allgemeinen Translationstheorie*. Tübingen: Niemeyer.

Roehler, Laura R. and Cantlon, Danise J. 1997. "Scaffolding: A powerful tool in social constructivist classrooms." In *Scaffolding Student Learning: Instructional Approaches and Issues*, Kathleen Hogan and Michael Pressley (eds), 6–42. Cambridge, MA: Brookline.

Séguinot, Candace. 1989. "The translation process: An experimental study." In *The Translation Process*, Candace Séginot (ed.), 21–53. Toronto: H. G. Publications.

Sense, Andrew J. 2007. "Structuring the project environment for learning." *International Journal of Project Management* 25: 405–412.

Shreve, Gregory M. 2002. "Knowing translation: Cognitive and experiential aspects of translation expertise from the perspective of expertise studies." In *Translation Studies: Perspectives on an Emerging Discipline*, Alessandra Riccardi (ed.), 150–171. Cambridge: Cambridge University Press.

Shreve, Gregory M. and Angelone, Erik. 2010. "Translation and cognition: Recent developments." In *Translation and Cognition*, Gregory M. Shreve and Erik Angelone (eds), 1–13. Amsterdam/Philadelphia: John Benjamins.

Spivak, Gayatri. 1992. "The politics of translation." In *Destabilizing Theory: Contemporary Feminist Debates*, Michèle Barret and Anne Phillips (eds), 177–200. Stanford, CA: Stanford University Press.

Taylor, Kathleen. 2006. "Autonomy and self-directed learning: A developmental journey." In *Handbook of Adult Development and Learning*, Carol Hoare (ed.), 196–218. Oxford: Oxford University Press.

The Standish Group. 2009. "CHAOS 2009." The Standish Group. http://www1.standishgroup.com/newsroom/chaos_2009.php

Txabarriaga, Rocío. 2009. *Best Practices for Client Review Processes*. Lowell, MA: Common Sense Advisory.

Venuti, Lawrence. 1986. "The translator's invisibility." *Criticism* 28 (Spring): 179–212.

———. 1995. *The Translator's Invisibility: A History of Translation*. London/New York: Routledge.

Vygotsky, Lev Semyonovich. 1935. Умственное развитие ребенка в процессе обучения [Mental Development of the Child During the Learning Process]. Moscow/Leningrad: Государственное учебно-педагогическое издательство [State Educational-Pedagogical Press].

Wood, David, Bruner, Jerome S. and Ross, Gail. 1976. "The role of tutoring in problem solving." *Journal of Child Psychology and Psychiatry* 17 (2): 89–100.

Wilss, Wolfram. 1992. "The future of translator training." *Meta* 37 (3): 391–396.

Woyde, Rick. 2001. "Managing quality translations." LISA Forum USA, Chicago, IL, Aug. 31. Localization Industry Standards Association Knowledge Archive: Forum Presentations. Retrieved Jan. 6, 2011. http://www.lisa.org/Chicago2001.631.0.html

Wysocki, Robert K. 2009. *Effective Project Management: Traditional, Adaptive, Extreme*. 5th ed. Indianapolis, IN: Wiley.

Zielinski, Daniel and Ramírez Safar, Yamile. 2005. "Research meets practice: T-survey 2005." *Translating and the Computer 27: Proceedings of the Twenty-Seventh International Conference on Translating and the Computer, 24–25 November 2005, London*. London: ASLIB. http://fr46.uni-saarland.de/download/publs/sdv/t-survey_aslib2005_zielinski.htm

Global virtual teams

Willem Stoeller

Global virtual teams are project teams whose members do not work together at the same physical location, but who collaborate across geographic, national, temporal, cultural and/or linguistic boundaries. Over the past decade, most organizations have begun using global virtual teams; they are particularly prevalent in the translation industry. Due to the distance, language and time differences that typically separate their members, global virtual teams raise a number of unique challenges for translation and localization project managers. These challenges are compounded by cultural differences that impact communication, decision-making, mutual trust and common vision. The first part of this chapter describes strategies to best deal with the above challenges. Additionally, since communications technologies are important enablers of virtual teams, the second part discusses the applicability of those technologies in the context of the translation industry.

Introduction

Over the past two decades, the commoditization of the personal computer, smart phones and the advent of the Internet have combined to usher in an era of unprecedented global connectivity. This global interconnectedness has revolutionized the creation and dissemination of knowledge, and has profoundly transformed the global supply chain for services and manufacturing (Friedman 2005). Today, thanks to the expansion of information and communication technologies, distributed work has become easier, faster and more efficient than ever before. Faced with the increasing velocity of change and intensified competition of the global on-demand economy, companies are decentralizing and globalizing their business processes, and creating global virtual teams that collaborate across geographic, temporal, cultural and/or linguistic boundaries to advance the goals of their organizations.

The localization industry has not escaped this trend. On the contrary, it could be argued that outsourced translation and localization work, which dates back to the 1980s, is one of the earliest examples of widespread usage of global virtual teams, and that virtual teams are the foundation on which localization has established itself as an industry. Despite their critical importance in the industry, virtual teams have to date been mostly overlooked as an object of analysis by scholars of translation and localization.

This chapter proposes to fill this gap in the literature by examining the most relevant aspects of global virtual teams in the context of localization project management. The chapter begins by proposing a definition of global virtual teams and discussing the different forms such teams can take. It then examines the impact of global virtual teams on project management in general, and on localization project management in particular. The chapter then proceeds to discuss the ways in which cultural differences manifest themselves in global virtual teams, and proposes strategies for managing these differences. Finally the chapter explores the tools of the trade used by global teams today.

What is a global virtual team?

For the purpose of this chapter, our working definition of a virtual team is that of Lipnack and Stamps (1997: 6–7):

> A virtual team, like every team, is a group of people who interact through *interdependent* tasks guided by *common purpose*. Unlike conventional teams, a virtual team works across space, time, cultural and organizational boundaries with links strengthened by webs of communication technologies. (emphasis added)

In fact, global virtual teams are impossible without the Internet and other advanced communication technologies.

Types of global virtual teams

Cascio and Shurygailo (2003) identify four forms of virtual teams based on two primary variables, namely the number of locations and the number of managers: a telework team is based at one location and reports to one manager, whereas a remote team is distributed at multiple locations (see Figure 1). Telework and remote teams each report to one manager, whereas matrixed teams report to more than one manager.

		Managers	
		One	Multiple
Locations	One	Teleworkers	Matrixed teleworkers
	Multiple	Remote team	Matrixed remote team

Figure 1. Forms of virtual teams (Cascio and Shurygailo 2003: 364).

To illustrate telework team participation, let us consider the example of the technical writer who telecommutes most days from home. Through the Internet, this writer has access to all necessary information at the corporation for which he/she works, often using a Virtual Private Network (VPN) in order to penetrate the corporate firewall and for increased security. He or she also has access to all of the company's communication facilities via Voice-Over IP (VOIP) telephone, instant messaging (IM) and email. The same Internet allows sharing of calendars, documents and schedules. Once a week the writer will participate in face-to-face meetings in the office. This day in the office helps to maintain better contact with other team members, resulting in trust and a common vision. Another example of telework team collaboration would be the freelance translator who works from her home in the French Alps far from any major city. The availability of fixed wireless broadband means that the translator still has a reasonably fast connection to the Internet. She interacts with her clients through VOIP, IM and email. Documents are transferred by means of email, FTP or some collaborative environment such as Google Docs or Documentum eRoom. In some cases our translator might use an online workflow system such as Lionbridge's Freeway or the Lingotek Collaborative Translation Platform. The freelance translator participates most often in several independent teams. Most of her interactions will be with Localization Project Managers and possibly client reviewers. In this situation the translator is not an employee of the corporations for which she is working; instead she is a contracted partner. This means she will have to negotiate different corporate cultures, which can complicate communication and the development of mutual trust. It is up to the Localization Project Manager (LPM) to provide a vision and work towards a trusted relationship, especially since our freelance translator will typically never meet with her clients face to face.

To illustrate remote team participation, consider the example of a software company in California that has merged with a similar software company in Dublin. Now the development teams of these two formerly separate organizations work together on common projects even though they are separated by thousands of kilometers and by eight time zones. Although English is the working language at both locations, cultural differences are substantial and may initially be overlooked. Through the Internet developers from both locations have access to the same development environment and source control software. The teams communicate weekly through tools such as GoToMeeting or Adobe Acrobat Connect, which allow sharing of desktops while streaming telephone-based audio to participants via VOIP. Face-to-face meetings are infrequent, but recommended to address cultural differences. Another example of remote team collaboration would be the Fortune 500 company headquartered in Silicon Valley that is conducting planning meetings with in-country marketing and sales managers. In this case, the corporate marketing and sales team needs to engage with sales and marketing managers in over twenty countries. Because of the spread in time zones, some participants will need to stay up very late or get up very early in order to join in the meeting. However, using telepresence tools makes it possible to conduct effective virtual meetings during which body language remains an important part of the communication (see Figure 2). Face-to-face meetings are infrequent due to the high cost of travel.

A final example of a remote team would be the crowd of Facebook members who participate in the translation of the Facebook site and applications using the Facebook Translations application. In this case the virtual team is very large and loosely connected. There is no longer a contractual connection with monetary awards binding the team members to the organization on whose behalf the project is being completed. In this scenario, the Localization Project Manager is a facilitator and does not directly control deadlines or quality. Team members share an emotional commitment to Facebook and a common desire to provide access to Facebook in languages other than English. The interactions between the team members are limited to Facebook communications. In crowdsourced projects such as the Facebook project, the team members often only know each other through their avatars (i.e., the graphical representations that they have chosen to portray themselves).

Figure 2. A virtual team meets via Cisco TelePresence. Courtesy of Cisco Systems, Inc. Unauthorized use not permitted.

Today, many organizations execute localization projects using global virtual teams. Some of the common ways in which global virtual teams are used include the following:

- Performing localization project work across geographically and/or temporally dispersed resources in the wake of acquisitions or mergers that result in distributed localization staff
- Outsourcing localization or testing to contractors or employees located in lower-cost areas such as India, Vietnam, Thailand, China, and Eastern European countries
- Outsourcing specialized work to specialized resources independent of location, in particular translators, editors and desktop publishing specialists working remotely
- Crowdsourcing translation to a community of volunteer power users or developers, an example of which would be the translation of Moblin by its community of open source developers[1]

Challenges posed by global virtual teams

Leading a project team can be challenging under any circumstances. However, global virtual teams pose unique challenges. Chief among them are the risk of communication breakdowns due to geographical distance, language, cultural, and time differences, and the risk of loss of trust and/or shared vision due to cultural differences and to the fact that most team members have never met in person.

Cultural differences manifest themselves via widely varying styles in communication, negotiation, decision-making and meetings. Even our view of ethics is heavily influenced by our own culture. Western cultures are more concerned with absolute values, while many Asian and Latin American cultures have a more relative view of values and focus on obligations to family and society. In the sections that follow, we will examine these issues in greater detail. However, before doing so we must situate global virtual teams within the context of localization project management.

---

1. Moblin is an optimized Linux platform that provides a modern, engaging user experience for mobile devices, such as netbooks, mobile Internet devices (MIDs), and in-vehicle infotainment (IVI) systems. Moblin has a common core of application and user interface services as well as application programming interfaces (APIs), which provide application developers a rich and consistent development environment across multiple device form factors. For more information, see www.moblin.org. In 2010 Moblin became MeeGo! MeeGo is an open source, Linux project which brings together the Moblin project, headed up by Intel, and Maemo, by Nokia, into a single open source activity.

The impact of global virtual teams on localization project management

Generic project management

The Project Management Institute's *A Guide to the Project Management Body of Knowledge (PMBOK® Guide)* provides a generic framework as well as a set of tools and techniques for managing projects without regard to the domain in which those projects will be performed (e.g., construction, software, or translation).[2] The *PMBOK® Guide* is a *de facto* international standard, as well as a *de jure* American National Standards Institute standard (ANSI/PMI 99-001-2008).

Localization project management skills

To understand how the *PMBOK® Guide* is relevant to the Localization Project Manager, let us take a closer look at the skills required to successfully manage localization projects (see Figure 3). These skills can be grouped in three categories:[3]

1. Technical localization and internationalization skills
   a. Localization processes, activities and tools
      i. Processes for the localization of software, multimedia, websites, training and marketing materials
      ii. Localization activities such as translation, localization engineering, desktop publishing (DTP) and quality assurance (QA)
      iii. Tools such as Trados and other translation memory (TM) systems, content management systems (CMS), globalization management systems (GMS, e.g., SDL Across, Lingotek), project management tools
   b. Internationalization concepts
      i. Encoding, fonts and language support
      ii. Externalization of user interface (UI) components
      iii. Locale support
      iv. Global English and writing for an international audience

---

2. PMI is the world's leading not-for-profit membership association for the project management profession, with close to half a million members and credential holders in 185 countries. PMI's Project Management Professional (PMP) certification is the world's most recognized professional credential for individuals associated with project management with nearly 300,000 credential holders worldwide.

3. This list is not exhaustive.

2. Industry and product knowledge
   a. Understanding the client's industry (e.g., software, medical, automotive, etc.)
   b. Understanding the product to be localized
      i. Product objectives and especially the target users, who are often overlooked
      ii. UI and functionality
      iii. Product components
      iv. QA issues
3. Last but not least: Project management skills
   a. Analytical skills
      i. Scope definition and management
      ii. Scheduling and resource management
      iii. Quality management
      iv. Risk management
   b. "Soft" (people-oriented) management skills
      i. Managing stakeholder expectations
      ii. Developing team motivation and trust
      iii. Using good human resource management skills

The author's experience suggests that non-industry-specific knowledge, skills, tools and techniques described in the *PMBOK® Guide* comprise approximately two-thirds of the skills and knowledge required to successfully manage large localization projects (see Figure 3). Knowledge of localization and of the client's industry (and by extension, the product to be localized) comprises the other one-third.

According to the *PMBOK® Guide*, project management encompasses five major processes. In the following section, we will briefly examine the major processes of the PMI project management methodology as they apply to localization project management.

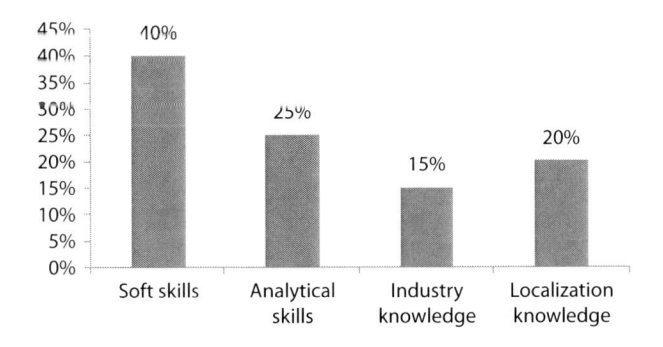

Figure 3. Project management skills needed to manage large localization projects.

Project management processes

According to the *PMBOK® Guide*, project management comprises five high-level processes: planning, initiating, executing, monitoring and controlling, as well as closing processes (see Figure 4). During the Initiating and Planning processes, all project documents are created. During the Executing process, the project documents are used to complete the work. In the Monitoring and Controlling process project documents are updated and distributed based on progress made, issues to address and changes in risks. Finally, in the Closing phase, project documents are archived and a post-mortem document is created and added to the archive.

Initiating involves the following activities:

- Obtaining approval of the Statement of Work (SOW) from the client
- Issuance of a Purchase Order (PO) by the client
- Finalizing the project start date
- Finalizing the project requirements, including delivery format details
- Determining the project approach and workflow

Planning involves the following activities:

- Identifying and assigning resources to project activities
- Finalizing the project schedule and budget
- Training the team on tools and project processes as needed
- Holding a kick-off meeting with the client
- Obtaining approval of project glossaries from the client
- Identifying major project risks and determining risk response strategies

Executing involves the following activities:

- Keeping the client informed of project progress
- Obtaining resolution of queries about terminology and/or content from the client

Monitoring and controlling involves the following activities:

- Measuring actual project budget usage vs. planned (i.e., scheduled) usage: is the project over budget, under budget, or on target?
- Measuring actual project progress vs. planned (i.e., scheduled) progress: is the project ahead of schedule, behind schedule, or on target?
- Measuring actual task completion versus planned task completion: have all phases in the workflow been completed?
- Managing changes and adjusting the schedule and/or budget in the event of scope changes
- Tracking and resolving issues

- Monitoring and managing project risks to determine if any risks have changed (in terms of their impact or probability), if our risk response strategies need to be changed and/or to add any new risks that have been identified

Closing involves the following activities:

- Obtaining formal acceptance of the project deliverables from the client
- Holding a post-project meeting with the client
- Documenting lessons learned during the project
- Archiving project deliverables and project metadata, i.e., project documents used to execute and monitor/control the project such as progress reports, requirements definitions, scope statements, quality statistics, etc.

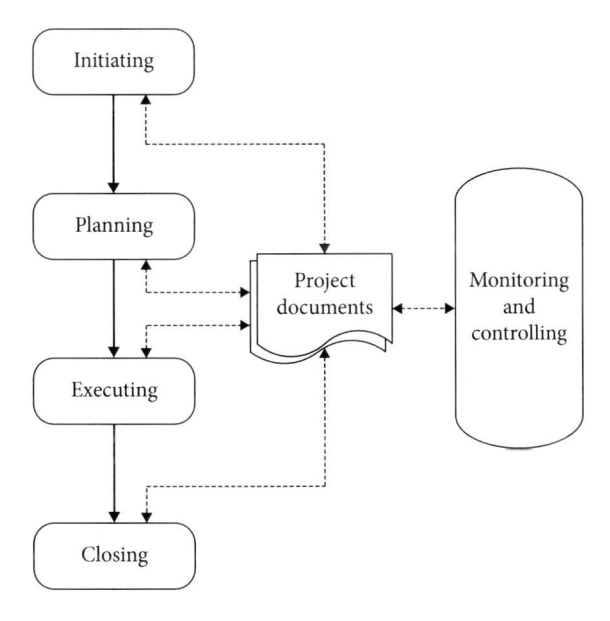

Figure 4 The major processes of the PMI project management methodology.

PMBOK knowledge areas impacted by global virtual teams

The *PMBOK® Guide* groups the requisite analytical and people skills needed to manage projects in nine knowledge areas:

1. Project Integration Management
2. Project Scope Management
3. Project Time Management
4. Project Cost Management

5. Project Quality Management
6. Project Human Resource Management
7. Project Communications Management
8. Project Risk Management
9. Project Procurement Management

Of these nine areas, the following are impacted by the unique challenges of global virtual teams:

- Project Integration Management
- Project Communications Management
- Project Human Resources Management
- Project Quality Management
- Project Procurement Management

Project integration management
Project Integration Management includes the processes and activities needed to identify and coordinate the various project management activities in the different process groups:

- Creating a Statement Of Work
- Developing a business case, taking into account corporate global objectives
- Creating and obtaining approval for a localization contract
- Creating a budget, schedule and quality plan
- Creating staffing and procurement plans
- Creating a communication plan

The budget will be impacted by additional hardware/software resources needed to support a global virtual team (groupware, teleconferencing, telepresence, etc.). Moreover, human resource costs and third party service costs will vary from country to country.

The schedule will be impacted since global virtual teams usually present a higher degree of slippage (project delay) risk than conventional, non-distributed project teams because of reduced communication and common vision. The schedule needs to contain buffers to account for this risk. Staffing, procurement plans and contracts will take more time for resources and third parties located in other countries due to different legal, financial and human resource requirements in the countries of the team members.

The decision to use a global virtual team will most strongly impact the communication plan due to geographic, time zone and cultural differences. However, the primary challenge for the manager of a global virtual team lies in the impact of cultural differences that affect communication, negotiation, decision-making and meeting conduct. These issues will be discussed in greater detail below.

Project communications management
Project communications management includes the processes required to ensure timely generation, distribution and storage of project information:

- Identifying stakeholders and managing their expectations
- Planning project communications: reporting, meetings, means of communication, escalation processes
- Distributing information, in particular progress information

Managing stakeholders, one of the most important tasks of a localization project manager, is far more challenging if those stakeholders come from different cultural backgrounds. The process of planning project communications is (or should be) shaped by time zone, geographic and cultural differences. Tight standards are needed for turnaround time on emails and voice mails. If team members do not return messages promptly, project communication will crash. Finally, the distribution of information in global virtual teams should be accomplished using collaborative groupware.

Project human resources management
Project human resources management involves staffing, training and monitoring the project team. Project human resources management also includes monitoring the team environment, geographical location of team members, addressing cultural issues, managing internal/external politics, as well as professional/ethical behavior.

Both training and monitoring are far more challenging when team members have different cultural backgrounds. These challenges are compounded in the absence of face-to-face meetings.

Project quality management
Project quality management involves the definition of the level of quality required to meet or exceed customer expectations, quality assurance (auditing quality control processes) and quality control itself (testing, reviewing, etc.). The goal is to *plan for and manage quality* throughout the project, not obtain it through end item testing and multiple reviews.

Because it is far more challenging to communicate with a global virtual team than with a conventional, non-distributed project team, quality management in projects performed by virtual teams require more exhaustive documentation than do projects executed by co-located teams. The need for documented specifics is amplified by cultural and language differences.

Project procurement management
Project procurement management includes the processes necessary to purchase or acquire products and services that cannot be provided by the project team. This involves selecting, contracting and monitoring the third parties that provide these products and services.

The technology products and/or services needed to maintain communication within the global virtual team and with associated stakeholders must be accounted for as part of the project procurement management in terms of both budget and time. For those accustomed to conducting business in Western Europe or North America, the process of acquiring services in other countries (for example hosting software with a Chinese ISP) can be daunting and slow.

Global virtual teams and cultural differences

Globalization is a reality today, and intercultural communication is becoming the norm rather than the exception. In an era of globalization, it is critically important to understand how culture influences business behavior. It is a known fact that people from different countries do things in different ways; culture enables us to understand some of the reasons why. Thus, before we examine how (and why) cultural differences affect ethics, decision-making, communication, negotiation, decision-making and the management of teams in a multi-cultural environment, it will be useful to first briefly discuss culture and cultural differences.

Understanding different cultures

According to renowned social scientist Geert Hofstede, culture consists of shared "mental programs" that condition individuals' responses to their environment (Hofstede 2001: xix; 1–7; Hofstede and Hofstede 2005: 3–5). In the late 1960s and early 1970s, Hofstede conducted extensive survey-based research (involving more than 100,000 questionnaires) that explored differences across national cultures in more than 50 countries. Based on the results of this research, Hofstede identified four dimensions that structure the value systems in the countries that comprised the study and which affect the ways in which people from those countries tend to think, feel and act. Subsequent research conducted by Michael Harris Bond in the 1980s revealed another dimension, long-term orientation, which Hofstede later adapted as the fifth dimension of his model. Hofstede's research has been updated and extended over time, and has been much criticized, but few alternative theories have been presented. One notable exception is Shalom Schwartz's Value Theory (Schwartz and Bilsky 1987, 1990; Schwartz 1992), which posits a set of ten different motivational types of values as the variables that shape behaviors and attitudes.

Because a detailed analysis of cultural differences is beyond the scope of this chapter, we will focus on Geert Hofstede's five dimensions to examine cultural differences and their impact on global virtual teams. These five dimensions are as follows:

- *Power distance index (PDI)*. This dimension measures "the extent to which the less powerful members of institutions and organizations within a country expect and accept that power is distributed unequally. Institutions are the basic elements of society, such as the family, the school, and the community; organizations are the places where people work. Power distance is thus described based on the value system of the *less* powerful members". (Hofstede and Hofstede 2005: 46)
- *Individualism index (IDV)*. "Individualism pertains to societies in which the ties between individuals are loose; everyone is expected to look after himself or herself and his or her immediate family. Collectivism as its opposite pertains to societies in which people from birth onward are integrated into strong, cohesive in-groups, which throughout people's lifetimes continue to protect them in exchange for unquestioning loyalty". (Hofstede and Hofstede 2005: 76)
- *Masculinity index (MAS)*. "A society is called *masculine* when emotional gender roles are clearly distinct: men are supposed to be assertive, tough, and focused on material success, whereas women are supposed to be more modest, tender, and concerned with the quality of life. A society is called *feminine* when emotional gender roles overlap: both men and women are supposed to be modest, tender, and concerned with the quality of life". (Hofstede and Hofstede 2005: 120)
- *Uncertainty avoidance index (UAI)*. This dimension measures "the extent to which members of a culture feel threatened by ambiguous or unknown situations. This feeling is, among other things, expressed through nervous stress and in a need for predictability: a need for written and unwritten rules".
(Hofstede and Hofstede 2005: 167)
- *Long-term orientation (LTO)*. Long-term orientation is defined as "the fostering of virtues oriented toward future rewards – in particular, perseverance and thrift. Its opposite pole, short-term orientation, stands for the fostering of virtues related to the past and present – in particular, respect for tradition, preservation of 'face' and fulfilling social obligations". (Hofstede and Hofstede 2005: 210)

Hofstede's model assigns numerical values for the various cultural dimensions to the countries in the study (Hofstede 2001, Hofstede 2010, Hofstede and Hofstede 2005), thereby enabling comparative analysis (see Figure 5). However, it is important to note that the cultural differences revealed by Hofstede's work describe *averages* or *tendencies* across nations and *not* characteristics of *individuals* within those nations. Moreover, subsequent research suggests that cultures and therefore cultural dimensions change over time. Finally, although this chapter focuses on cultural differences between nations, it is important to keep in mind that regions and ethnic groups within any nation can have a very different culture. For example the cultural values of First Nation (American Indians) are very different from those of the rest of the US and Canadian population.

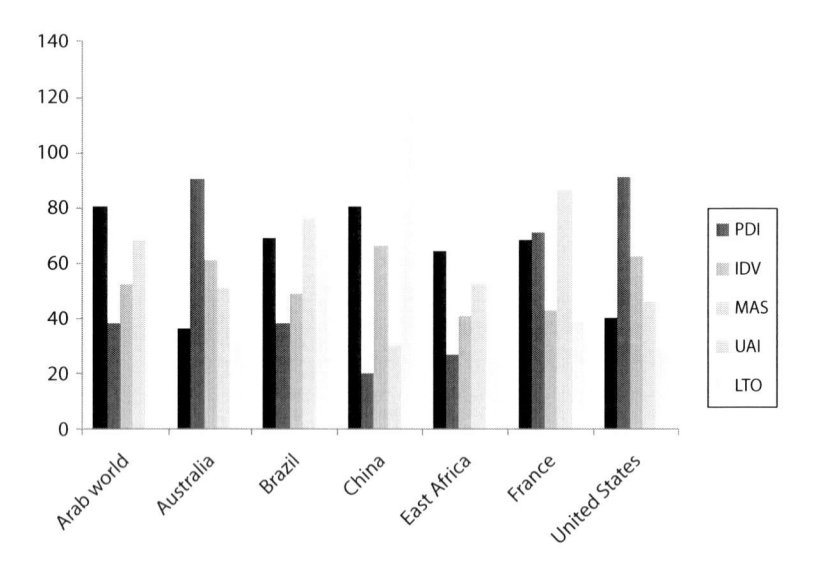

Figure 5. Sample comparison of cultural dimensions (Hofstede and Hofstede 2005: 43, 78–79, 120–121, 168–169, 211; Hofstede 2010). No long-term orientation (LTO) data is available for the Arab World.

Having examined the impact of global virtual teams on localization project management knowledge areas and processes, and having explored Hofstede's dimensions of culture as a framework within which to analyze cultural differences, let us turn our attention to the ways in which cultural differences typically manifest themselves in global virtual projects, namely via different approaches to and attitudes toward decision-making and ethics, communication, negotiation, team leadership and meetings.

Decision-making and ethics

The cultural aspects of ethics need to be discussed before addressing the process of decision-making. After all, nearly every business decision has an ethical dimension. For example outsourcing work to countries with lower labor cost raises the ethical issue of reducing job opportunities in the home country and possible exploitation of workers abroad (sweat shops). A similar example is outsourcing production to countries with looser environmental regulations, which brings up the ethical dilemma of actions that bring harm to the environment and people for larger profits. Finally in the translation industry translation vendors often send presents to their major clients at Christmas time: is this bribing or simply good human relationship development? Often it is difficult to reconcile one's own ethical standards with local practices, especially since many business decisions are themselves ethically ambiguous.

People make ethical decisions using different rules. For instance, some people determine the choice that produces maximum benefit for everyone, the underlying idea being that striving for profit is good for everyone. Because of the narrow and subjective interpretation of benefit, many people reject decisions made using this rule. Other people rely on some fixed set of moral rules (often derived from religion). This approach results in blanket rejection of anything that is not in line with those moral rules and leaves no room for moral rules from other cultures. Finally, others may apply cultural relativism, which results in the adoption of moral rules from other cultural environments. This rule could lead to the acceptance of reprehensible behavior in violation of basic human rights (e.g. honor killings, known locally as Karo-Kari, of women in Pakistan). The best approach for addressing the ethical dimensions of decisions seems to be a reasonable combination of a limited set of fixed moral rules such as those in the Universal Declaration of Human Rights (UN OHCHR 1998) and careful application of cultural relativism.

Culture shapes not only the ethical framework within which decisions are made, but also the process of decision-making itself. Most people who grow up in Western countries are culturally conditioned (or "mentally programmed," to borrow Hofstede's term) to make decisions using a very *rational* model:

1. Define a problem.
2. Generate alternative solutions.
3. Apply systematic analysis, using pre-defined criteria, to the potential solutions.
4. Based on the analysis, select the best alternative.

However this seemingly rational process is imperfect. Identifying and analyzing all possible alternative solutions is in most cases prohibitively time consuming and therefore a subset of all possible alternatives is used, resulting in a sub-optimal decision. In particular people tend to focus on alternatives that are in line with their mental programming (experience) and therefore do not think outside of the box or engage in lateral thinking (de Bono 1970). In addition, the criteria on which analysis process is based are often unclear or incomplete. This problem is compounded by the fact that heuristics, i.e., references to common practices or rules of thumb, are often used to simplify the analysis. Finally, in systems involving people, rationality is often replaced by emotions. People frequently become biased towards one of the alternatives early in the decision-making process and then use the rational selection process as a means of justifying their decision, a strategy known as "satisficing" (Simon 1957). Culture dictates what criteria should be used in the rational analysis of alternative solutions in the context of virtual teams. For example nepotism is frowned upon in most Western civilizations, but in China and Russia it is considered fully acceptable because trust is one of the highest-ranking criteria in those cultures, and in this context, there is no one more trustworthy than one's own relatives and family.

The preceding discussion sheds light on the reasons why many rational decisions are of lesser quality, but another dimension to decision-making needs to be considered when managing global virtual teams, namely acceptance of the decision. If a decision is not well accepted, project team members will feel little or no commitment towards that decision. This lack of commitment will in turn lead to problems at implementation time. Culture has a strong influence on perceptions of the acceptability of decisions. For example, the selection of a woman for a position of high public status tends to be met with very little acceptance in Japan due to that country's high Masculinity index value (Hofstede 2010). Likewise, any decision that conflicts with religious taboos can lead to acceptability problems (e.g., ankles in the Victorian British Empire, women's hair in parts of the Middle East, or nudity in the United States).

Collectivism, masculinity and power distance all have a strong impact on the decision-making process. For example, in Latin America and Japan decisions tend to be made collectively by the team instead of unilaterally by the team leader. Therefore it is important to understand the motivations of the team members (motives, cultural values, traditions and habits) before a project manager can make decisions.

Communication and negotiation

During human face-to-face communication, meaning is conveyed by both verbal and non-verbal behavior. In a pioneering study on the inference of attitudes from non-verbal communication, Mehrabian and Ferris (1967) found that when observers were judging whether a speaker liked his or her listener, 55% of their inference of the speaker's attitudes and feelings was based on communication via the facial channel (i.e., body language), 38% of their inference was based on communication via the vocal channel (tone of voice) and only 7% of their inference was based on communication via the verbal channel (words).[4] Figure 6 clearly illustrates the extent to which our ability to infer the feeling and attitudes of others is undermined when we switch from face-to-face to phone communication. Mehrabian's and Ferris' findings strongly suggest that other forms of communication would likewise be significantly impacted by the switch from face-to-face to phone communication. A move from spoken to written communication would presumably have an even more dramatic impact on communication.

These observations have profound implications for communication in the context of multilingual, multicultural, international virtual teams, as language, language conventions, gestures, facial expressions and other body language are all culture dependent.

---

4. It is important to note that the research conducted by Mehrabian and Ferris focused on communication of attitudes and feelings, and not on the relative importance of these three channels of communication in human cognition. Consequently, although Mehrabian and Ferris found that observers rely predominantly (93%) on non-verbal communication when inferring the feelings and attitudes of others, it does not follow that 93% of *all* communication necessarily occurs non-verbally.

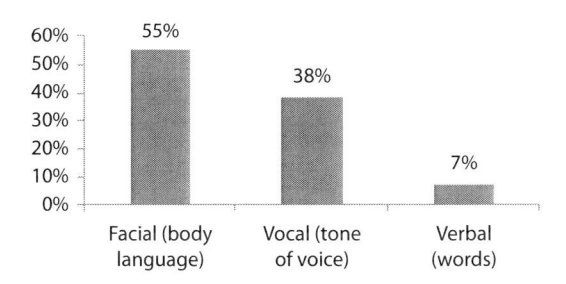

Figure 6. Decoding of face-to-face communication of feelings and attitudes via facial, vocal and verbal channels of communication as measured by Mehrabian and Ferris (1967: 252).

Language is the primary potential barrier to communication. In the absence of a common language, it is almost impossible to communicate ideas. While it is true that English has become the major language of business, those who learn English as a second language often learn only the basic language but not its dialects, slang, jargon and idiomatic expressions. Additionally voice tonality in English may be very different from voice tonality in other languages; therefore that facet of non-verbal communication may be lost on non-native speakers of English.

It is thus important when a project manager communicates with people for whom English is a second language to refrain from using jargon, slang, euphemisms (for example "he passed away" instead of "he died") and idiomatic expressions (for example "going to bat for someone," "the greatest thing since sliced bread" and "not being on the same wavelength") and to speak slowly and clearly. It is good practice during meetings to ask participants, if at all possible, to write down in their own words what they have understood of the objectives, mission, etc., in order to confirm that the intended messages have been properly understood. A direct, yes-or-no question such as "do you understand?" or "do you have any questions about anything?" may not suffice to reveal comprehension problems. For example, members of Asian cultures who are concerned with loss of face may indicate that they have understood even if they have not.

Culture also shapes non-verbal communication, including body language, gestures, and facial expressions, which may mean very different things in different cultures. For instance, nodding one's head is widely understood to be a way of indicating agreement or assent. However, this meaning is not universal: in some cultures (e.g., Bulgaria), head nodding indicates disagreement or dissent. Along similar lines, head shaking (or nodding, as the case may be) are not the only ways of expressing disagreement non-verbally. For example, raising one's eyebrows is as a polite way of saying "no" in Turkey.

The cultural dimension of individualism impacts attitudes toward directness of speech. Cultures that rank highly on the individualism index, such as the United States and Western Europe, tend to express use low-context communication: the meaning of the message is conveyed primarily by the literal meaning of the words themselves. Conversely, in collectivistic cultures that do not rank highly on the individualism index, such as Latin America, Korea, Japan and China, people use high-context communication: the receiver relies more on the context than on the literal meaning of the words that comprise the message. In high-context cultures, the receiver is expected to discover the meaning in a message that uses indirectness and metaphor.

Many cultures in Asia are reserved and sensitive in their communication, while North American and Middle Eastern cultures tend to be far more aggressive and loud in their communication. These differences can easily lead to cultural misunderstandings. For example the verbal communication from a U.S. project manager with a Chinese translator might be perceived by the translator as rude and aggressive, while the reply from the Chinese translator might cause him or her to be perceived as not interested and/or evasive by the U.S. project manager.

Negotiation is a special form of communication in which the objective is to overcome conflicting interests and reach a mutually satisfactory outcome. Negotiators from individualist cultures such as the United States and Western Europe typically focus on trying to persuade each other and reaching an agreement through concessions. Negotiators from collectivistic cultures such as Latin America and Eastern Asia tend to focus more on first establishing long-lasting relationships and exchanging information, and also prefer bargaining to concessions.

In cultures that rank highly on the power-distance index, it is expected that a higher-level authority figure will impose a decision on both parties; this approach is common in Japan. Another alternative negotiation model involves the use of detailed policies and procedures; this bureaucratic approach eliminates most negotiation, and is popular in Germany for example.

In sum, effective cross-cultural communication requires that one learn about different conventions and cultural dimensions, observe and pay attention to context and conventions when communicating or negotiating, and adapt behavior to different conventions. It is important to note, however, that excessive adaptation may foster suspicion or invite ridicule.

Leading global virtual teams

Leading global virtual teams involves leading the team in meetings, collaborative tasks, decision-making and negotiation. Not only must the Localization Project Manager her/himself be aware of cultural differences and be flexible with respect to other conventions, but she/he also needs to educate *all team members* on the existence of cultural differences, and on the importance of being mindful of those differences and of being willing to adapt to other conventions when working with team members from other cultures. For example team members from collectivistic cultures such as Japan need to accept that there are required deadlines for coming to a decision, whereas members from individualistic cultures such as the U.S. and Western Europe need to understand that decisions require team involvement and acceptance. A combination of a collectivistic culture with high power distance and English as a second language makes it very difficult for a Chinese person to contribute in a team dominated by members of Western countries. The Localization Project Manager needs to be sensitive to this fact and take steps to help the team members bridge the cultural distance that separates them in order to foster trust, cooperation and collaboration.

Building trust and establishing a common vision are real challenges for the leader of a global virtual team. As Lipnack and Stamps observe, "in the networks and virtual teams of the Information Age, trust is a 'need to have' quality in productive relationships" (1997: 225), while according to Platt, "relationships based on trust are essential to a virtual team because these teams do not have everyday interaction, and the potential for losing trust is much higher" (1999: 41). High-trust teams communicate face-to-face where possible, have regular synchronous computer-mediated communication (e.g., via GoToMeeting, Adobe Connect, or Live Meeting) and engage in social interactions. The latter allows for the development of relationships that are a critical precondition of trust in many cultures.

Leaders of global virtual teams must take special care to avoid focusing too heavily on the *tasks and deliveries* of the team and not enough on the *processes* used by the team to complete those tasks. Cultural differences result in very different views on what processes the team should use. It is particularly important at the beginning of the project (during the Initiation and Planning processes) that the team leader set time aside to explore the processes to be used and negotiate a set of processes that are acceptable to all team members and are appropriate given the mission of the project. In localization projects, the topic of processes needs to be covered in detail during the project kick-off meeting

In order to build trust, the team leader also needs to encourage the team to engage in social interactions. One way to do so is to start each team meeting with an "icebreaker" to set the tone (Lipnack 2010). The team leader can also encourage the use of Facebook or Twitter to foster social interactions between the team members.

It is true that the management of international, multilingual virtual teams presents a number of unique cultural challenges. However, this does not mean that the management of a linguistically and culturally homogenous is free from cultural issues. On the contrary, project teams can develop negative processes such as "groupthink" (Janis 1972), where no out-of-the-box thinking occurs because all team members have similar backgrounds and characteristics. Another negative process that the project manager must guard against is "social loafing" (Latané, Williams and Harkins 1979), where team members do not make much contribution to the team because it is expected that other team members will make up for them. People from individualistic countries tend to present a higher risk of "social loafing," while team members from collectivistic cultures present a higher risk of "groupthink."

A word of warning is again in order here. As noted above, Hofstede's cultural dimensions describe patterns that characterize national cultures, but the cultural conventions of individual members within a given national culture may vary greatly. It is also important to remember the existence of sub-cultures within nations with value orientations that may differ markedly from those identified by Hofstede for the nation as a whole.

Technology

Without technology, especially the Internet, global virtual teams would not be able to function. While technology can help people in disparate locations connect, communicate and collaborate, the use of technology does not necessarily guarantee improved results

For example, a few years ago when I was working for a global LSP, we attempted to implement a global virtual team management process using Microsoft's SharePoint Server combined with Project Server. The idea was to store all information to be shared on SharePoint and to track availability and tasks of all resources in Project Server. This endeavor failed for several reasons. Because the implementation involved the adoption of a commercial off-the-shelf system, the requirements were not gathered and defined as exhaustively as they might have been if the project involved the design of a new system from scratch. Consequently, ease of locating project and client data was not identified as a critical requirement until the system had been deployed. In addition, tracking the availability of 300+ resources proved to be a very-labor intensive task. Finally, the focus on task completion in Project Server resulted in diminished involvement in and commitment to high-level customer service. This project demonstrated that one must plan the use of technology as thoroughly as possible, and most importantly that an assembly-line approach to localization results in high productivity but low quality. In an assembly-line scenario, team members to tend to rapidly switch from project to project to complete individual tasks, therefore there is less commitment to the quality of the final deliverables (one does not see the big picture) and less of a service commitment to individual clients.

This example should serve as a cautionary tale to those who believe that technology offers a solution to human-related project issues. It is true that the availability of collaborative technology has exploded over the past five years. These collaborative tools have also leveled the playing field: small companies and localization providers can now afford very good collaboration and communication tools at minimal cost and overhead. Furthermore, the trend towards "cloud" (Internet-based) computing reduces the need for in-house servers and IT support. Nevertheless, it is important to always keep in mind that technology is not a panacea for communication problems. A global virtual team will become dysfunctional very quickly if the team members do not commit to answering emails, voicemail and other communications. If such a scenario occurs and the team members cannot easily meet face to face, then team communications will be at risk of breaking down completely.

With that in mind, let us turn our attention to the tools of the trade of virtual teams.

Email, instant messaging and social networks

Email is fast, simple, bi-directional and asynchronous. People can read and answer emails when they want; therefore time zone differences have less impact on this form of communication than on others (such as phone calls). Email also lessens the risk of miscommunication in global virtual teams insofar as non-native speakers usually express themselves more effectively in writing than speaking. Finally, recipients of emails can translate email with readily available free machine translation to get the gist of a message.

However, email also presents a number of problems. In the current business environment, many people receive hundreds of emails each day; the consequences of this information overload include delayed responses and important emails that go unnoticed in the avalanche of incoming messages. Unanswered emails result in communication breakdowns and frustration.

Ironically, most email clients are not ideal for storage of the information sent and received via email. Effective storage that facilitates subsequent retrieval requires text search capabilities, the creation of smart mailboxes and the identification of discussion threads in email clients. For these reasons, it is preferable to create discussion threads in discussion boards or Wikis in groupware rather than using an email client for project information storage and retrieval. Server-based email systems such as Lotus Notes and Microsoft Exchange that offer such capabilities require substantial IT support and dedicated servers. Cloud-based options such as Google Apps offer reduced cost and administrative overhead, although offsite, third-party hosting may raise questions about corporate control and security, particularly in large corporations and publicly traded companies subject to Sarbanes-Oxley reporting and auditing requirements.

In addition, the asynchronous, disembodied nature of email communication makes it too easy to be abrupt or even rude. One should never respond in the heat of the moment by sending insulting or derogatory messages or other forms of emotionally fueled "flame" mail. Team members need to know when to switch from email to another means of communication such as a phone call, and under what circumstances a problem should be escalated to a supervisor (e.g., in the event of disputes involving team members from high power-distance cultures). It is difficult to build relationships via email, but very easy to damage them.

Email communication is shaped by dimensions of culture, as is any other form of communication. Team members from high-context cultures will have a hard time with the direct communication style of emails from teammates from low-context cultures (mainly Western); conversely, their own emails will seem imprecise and obtuse to team members from Western cultures. Notions about the number of recipients to which an email message should be sent are also shaped by culture. Team members from collectivist cultures will tend to send copies of messages (cc) to numerous colleagues, while team members from individualist cultures will tend to limit email distribution on a need-to-know basis. It is important that team members understand what types of email responses are expected and considered appropriate in the context of project team communication. Depending on the cultural composition of the project team, the project manager may decide to avoid email altogether. Team members from collectivistic cultures may well consider email to be too cold and impersonal a form of communication, preferring conference calls or face-to-face meetings instead. Requiring that such team members communicate exclusively or even primarily via email could prove counterproductive.

Chat via an instant messaging (IM) client is an excellent way to communicate informally with team members. Unlike email, chat is synchronous communication. It is ideal for asking a quick question and receiving a prompt answer, but is not a suitable medium for conducting meetings. Time zone differences make one-to-many chatting across a global team more difficult; it is better suited to short one-on-one communication. In the author's previous employment at a large LSP, all project managers in the US and Europe used IM to chat with staff in China. The staff in China felt far more comfortable communicating via chat than on the phone due to their limited verbal proficiency in English.

Instant messaging need not be confined to communications with the project team. Certain clients prefer a quick chat session to discuss progress and project issues. When IM is used for such purposes, it is important to save the chat history for future reference or follow up the IM session by sending a summary of conclusions, active tasks and decisions in an email or similar means. Today, instant messaging is a relatively mature technology. Not only are many IM clients available for free or at very low cost (e.g., Windows Live Messenger, Skype, AOL Instant Messenger, Google Talk, etc.), but there are a number of clients (such as Pidgin and Trillian) that support all or most of the commonly used chat protocols. Using chat in combination with social networks such as Facebook, LinkedIn, Plaxo, Twitter, and L10NCafe is an effective way to maintain relationships within the team. Moreover, participation in localization-focused discussion groups on LinkedIn is a good way to communicate and network with members of the localization industry at large.

Finally, the fact that much of the email and chat/IM traffic now takes place over smart phones means that team members can be highly mobile while still remaining connected.[5] However, let us not forget the importance of body language and in-

---

5. On March 23, 2010 Ericsson issued a press release in which it announced that "mobile data surpassed voice on a global basis during December 2009" according to company "measurements from live networks covering all regions of the world" (2010).

tonation in communication. Because email and chat convey neither body language nor intonation, they are inherently limited forms of communication. To the extent possible, it is highly preferable for team communications to be conducted by phone and conference calls followed up by email summarizing the conversations, especially when communicating with team members from collectivistic cultures.

Teleconferencing

Teleconferencing is an ideal tool for LSPs and their clients if face-to-face meetings or video conferencing are not feasible. Although telephone conferencing can be confined to conversation over the phone, the value of the communication can be greatly enhanced when used in combination with document- or desktop-sharing tools such as Webex, Live Meeting, Adobe Connect or GoToMeeting, which enable remote participants to view whatever the presenter is displaying on his or her screen, be it a document, a presentation, or the demonstration of a software application, to cite but three possible examples.

To maximize the effectiveness of a teleconference meeting, it is essential to send an agenda to all team members prior to the meeting and then follow up by sending minutes to all attendees after the meeting has concluded. Meetings can be distributed to attendees via groupware, such as Google Apps, or email. Groupware is preferred as it obviates the need to send email messages, and the document remains accessible to all team members at all times via a browser. Team members need to be comfortable with the language used during the conference: all team members need to be reminded to speak slowly and to avoid using slang, jargon, and idiomatic expressions. In order to create a welcoming team environment for team members from collectivistic cultures and those who tend to rely on high-context communication, it is important to start the teleconference with relationship-based "small talk" before jumping into the business at hand. One effective approach is to use icebreakers. For example, the project manager might begin each teleconference by having one of the team members share a personal experience. Time zone differences make setting up teleconferences with a global virtual team a challenge. Shared calendars can help facilitate the process by enabling the person handling the logistical arrangements to see when each participant is and is not available. Finally, one of the worst scenarios for a teleconference is having a mostly local team conferencing with a few remote team members. In such situations, the remote team members will often feel left out and they will miss much of the communication between the local team members. One way to handle this issue is to force everyone in the meeting to call in from his or her office or cubicle.

Video conferencing and telepresence technologies

Basic videoconferencing tools such as Skype (which only supports one-to-one video conferencing), Adobe ConnectNow, and Tokbox use standard webcams and broadband connections and allow a limited number of simultaneous users see and listen to each other. This type of videoconferencing augments ordinary telephone conferencing with limited body language and facial expression. However, because of the limited resolution and the fixed placement of webcams, which are usually built into laptops and flat panel displays, this type of videoconference cannot replace a face-to-face meeting.

Telepresence tools such as Cisco's TelePresence (see Figure 1) provide the closest approximation of live face-to-face meetings, but require expensive specialized video conferencing equipment and very high bandwidth. Therefore their use is confined primarily to large corporations and organizations that are able to rent public telepresence rooms. The cost of in-house installation is currently prohibitive for most language service providers, but public telepresence rooms can be rented for less than USD 1,000/hour.

Video conferencing is particularly useful for communicating with team members from a collectivistic culture that use high-context communication. However, the benefits of video conferencing can be significantly undermined by the technical limitations of the media, which can include poor quality audio and video reception and transmission delays that cause the audio to be out of sync with the image. Likewise, video conferencing is of limited benefit if the team members participating in the meeting are not confident in the use of the language chosen for the meeting; and if the team is dispersed over multiple time zones, it may be difficult to find a meeting time acceptable to everyone.

Language service providers can use basic video conferencing tools for informal, small team meetings either internally or with client staff. For very large projects a public telepresence facility could be used for major milestones such as a kick-off meeting or post-project review.

Groupware

Groupware as discussed in this chapter consists of server-based software that can be accessed by traditional operating systems or application software ("fat" clients), slimmed-down application software that relies on the server-based software to perform the majority of the data processing (light clients), or, increasingly, browser-based clients. As its name suggests, groupware allows users to share documents and multimedia content. Most groupware systems also allow collaborative creation and maintenance of those documents and rich media. Of particular interest are features that have potential project management applications such as team schedules and shared calendars. In addition, groupware often provides discussion boards that can replace many project-related emails.

The past five years have witnessed a transition in industry from expensive systems that are installed and maintained in house, such as Documentum eRoom and IBM's Lotus Notes, to low-cost, cloud-based (Internet-based) systems such as Google Apps for sharing and collaborating on documents, email, instant messaging and sharing calendars, or Basecamp for project management.

The use of groupware is *essential* for global virtual teams in the localization industry. Groupware can facilitate collaboration during the processes of gathering and defining user requirements, scheduling, defining team member responsibilities, tracking and resolving project issues, creating and executing test plans and/or localization processes and tracking project progress.

Specialized examples of groupware that can be used in the localization industry include the following:

– Localization client portals through which files can be transferred and critical metrics displayed via dashboards
– Translation management systems consisting of workflow automation and sometimes online translator/reviewer workbenches, the details of which are beyond the scope of this chapter
– Crowdsourcing or community translation platforms such as the Lingotek platform or Facebook's Translations application

Technological constraints

By far the most significant constraint on the use of the aforementioned technology by global virtual teams is latency, that is, delays in sending and receiving data due to limitations in communications bandwidth and/or country-specific controls (e.g., the "Great Firewall of China"). Most of the technologies discussed in this chapter here are *unfeasible* if the project team members do not have access to a broadband Internet connection that is, a high-speed, always-on connection (see Figures 7 and 8).[6] Some exceptions are email, chat and social networking applications, which work well with more limited bandwidth connectivity. Figures 7 and 8 illustrate the fact that average connection speed and availability of high speed connections vary substantially from country to country.

---

6. The Organisation for Economic Co-Operation and Development (OECD defines broadband as a connection that offers speeds of "at least 256 kbits/s, or 256,000 bits per second" (OECD 2010). The US Federal Communications Commission (FCC) defines broadband service as "data transmission speeds exceeding 200 kilobits per second … in at least one direction" (FCC 2010b). One of the stated goals of the FCC's proposed National Broadband Plan is that "at least 100 million US homes should have affordable access to actual download speeds of at least 100 megabits per second and actual upload speeds of at least 50 megabits per second" (FCC 2010a).

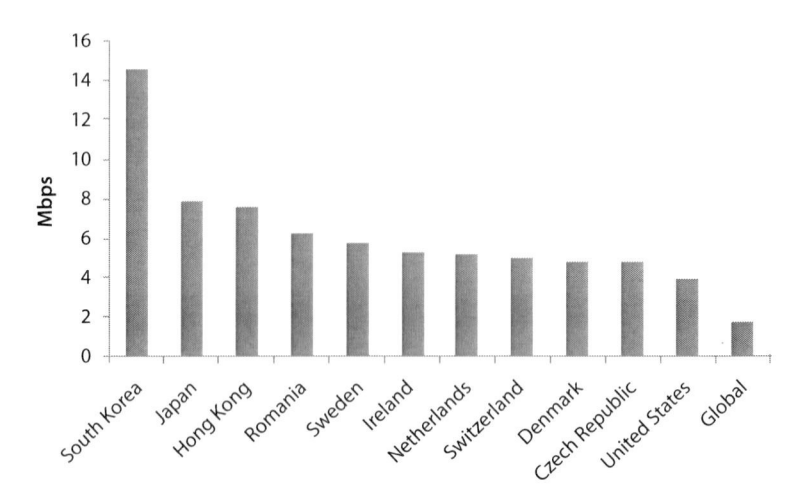

Figure 7. Average measured connection speeds of the top ten countries plus the United States during the third quarter of 2009 (Akamai 2010:10).

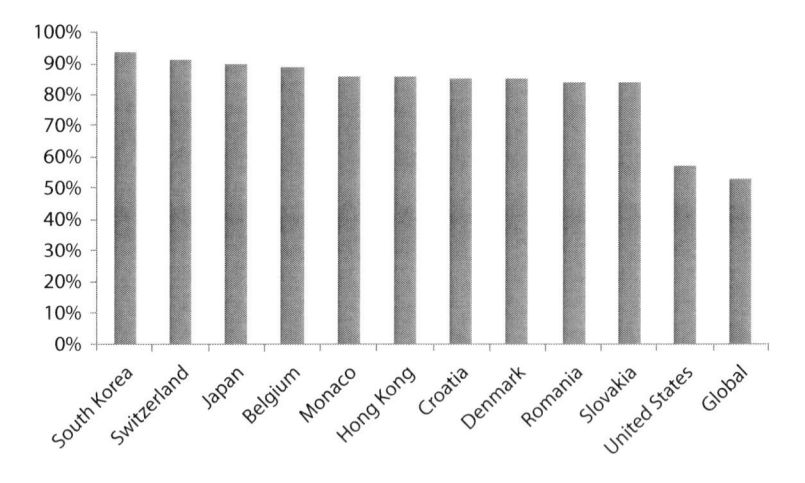

Figure 8. Global broadband connectivity: percentage of connections that exceed 2 Mbps bandwidth in the top ten countries plus the United States, third quarter 2009 (Akamai 2010:19).

Wireless technologies (also referred to as "Wi-Fi") offer an alternative to DSL, cable and fiber access, especially in countries whose legacy telecommunications infrastructures cannot support extensive development or deployment of DSL or cable connectivity. More and more people are conducting business using wireless technologies via smart phones, laptops and net books. 3G and 4G cellular networks allow use of IM, social networking, VOIP (if allowed by the cellular provider), very low-resolution video, transfer of low-resolution photos and generally slow Internet access. Wi-Fi provides low to medium-bandwidth broadband connections.

The following technologies work well even with modest broadband Internet connections (< 3,000 kbps):

- Email, IM and social networking (e.g., Facebook, Plaxo and LinkedIn)
- VOIP telephony using Skype in either one-to-one or conference mode (requires bandwidth of approximately 100 Kbps)
- Access to most groupware for simple viewing of text content or uploading/downloading of small files (less than 10 Mb)

The following technologies require medium- to high-speed bandwidth connections (3,000 kbps to 15,000 kbps):

- Video conferencing using Skype or other tools with low-resolution video, which may not provide the level of quality required for formal presentations, but which may be acceptable for informal or social communications
- Access to groupware using multimedia, highly interactive cloud based applications and uploading/downloading of large files (less than 100 Mb)
- Teleconferencing combined with sharing of presentations, documents and/or desktop (e.g., Live Meeting or GoToMeeting)
- VPN access for file transfers and modestly interactive cloud-based applications

The following technologies require very high-speed broadband connections (>15,000 kbps):

- High-resolution video conferencing or telepresence (requires bandwidth of greater than 15 Mbps in both directions)
- Transfer of very large files (greater than 1 Gb) using VPN or other secure data paths

China presents two challenges: latency and access. China's infrastructure, combined with the "Golden Shield Project," known colloquially as the "Great Firewall," results in unacceptable latency for applications hosted outside of China. It also limits access to websites hosted outside of China from official networks such as those located in universities. In order to make groupware and other applications available and usable in China, it is necessary to host those applications in China using a well-connected ISP.

Conclusion

The management of global virtual teams presents many challenges, some of which can successfully be addressed using technology. Distance complicates collaboration on documents, scheduling and team communication; groupware such as Google Apps offers a low-cost, collaborative solution to such problems. Communication can be facilitated using email, teleconferences and IM, while social contact between members of the team can be enhanced through the use of a social network such as Twitter or Facebook. If the means are available, video conferencing or better yet telepresence technologies enable verbal and non-verbal dimensions of communication that email, teleconferencing, chat and social networking do not.

Time zone differences make synchronous communication more difficult in global virtual teams. Synchronous communication can be partly replaced by asynchronous communication via tools such as email, IM and groupware. However direct synchronous communication using phone calls and teleconferences is essential to the proper functioning of the team. This means that some team members need to participate in calls outside of normal working hours.

Language is a particular problem. If team members do not speak the same language, then only the non-verbal dimension of communication is left. Because English has become the generally accepted language of business, many people speak it as a second language. However dialect, slang and jargon can be very difficult to understand for people who speak English as a second language. In the case of email or instant messaging, on-the-fly machine translation can be used to better understand international teammates' written communication, but verbal communication via an interpreter is usually not an option because of the logistical difficulties and cost involved.

Decision-making, team participation, trust and motivation are all critical to successful project management, and all are highly culture-dependent. Power distance (accepting hierarchy and authority), collectivism versus individualism and low versus high context communication all play an important role in the correct functioning of a global virtual team. Technology cannot help manage these variables of cross-cultural communication; to do so the project manager must have a good knowledge of cultural dimensions and be mindful of different values, motives and traditions. This by far is the most complex aspect of working with global virtual teams.

References

Akamai. 2010. "The state of the Internet." 2:3 (3rd quarter 2009). Retrieved January 13. http://www.akamai.com/dl/whitepapers/Akamai_State_Internet_Q3_2009.pdf?curl=/dl/whitepapers/ Akamai_State_Internet_Q3_2009.pdf&solcheck=1&ver=1&
Cascio, Wayne F. and Shurygailo, Stan. 2003. "E-leadership and virtual teams." *Organizational Dynamics* 31 (4): 362–376.
de Bono, Edward. 1970. *Lateral Thinking: Creativity Step by Step*. New York: Harper & Row.
Ericsson. 2010. "Mobile data traffic surpasses voice." Press release, March 23. http://www.ericsson.com/thecompany/press/releases/2010/03/1396928
Federal Communications Commission [of the United States of America] (FCC). 2010a. "The National Broadband Plan: Connecting America." Retrieved March 29. http://www.broadband.gov/

———. 2010b. "What is broadband?" Retrieved March 29. http://www.fcc.gov/cgb/broadband.html

Friedman, Thomas L. 2005. *The World is Flat*. New York: Farrar, Strauss and Giroux.

Hofstede, Geert. 2001. *Culture's Consequences: International Differences in Work-Related Values*. 1980. 2nd ed. Beverly Hills, CA: SAGE.

———. 2010. "Geert Hofstede Cultural Dimensions." http://www.geert-hofstede.com/hofstede_dimensions.php

Hofstede, Geert and Hofstede, Gert Jan. 2005. *Cultures and Organizations: Software of the Mind*. Rev. ed. New York: McGraw-Hill.

Janis, Irving L. 1972. *Victims of Groupthink: A Psychological Study of Foreign-Policy Decisions and Fiascoes*. Boston: Houghton Mifflin.

Latané, Bibb, Williams, Kipling and Harkins, Stephen. 1979. "Many hands make light the work: The causes and consequences of social loafing." *Journal of Personality and Social Psychology* 37 (6): 822–832.

Lipnack, Jessica. 2010. "Virtual teams." *NetAge Endless Knots* [blog]. March 7. http://endlessknots.netage.com/endlessknots/virtual_teams/

Lipnack, Jessica and Stamps, Jeffrey. 1997. *Virtual Teams: Reaching Across Space, Time and Organizations With Technology*. New York: John Wiley & Sons.

Mehrabian, Albert and Ferris, Susan R. 1967. "Inference of attitudes from nonverbal communication in two channels." *Journal of Consulting Psychology* 31 (3): 248–252.

Organisation for Economic Co-Operation and Development (OECD). 2010. "OECD broadband subscriber criteria." Retrieved March 29. http://www.oecd.org/document/46/0,3343,en_2649_34225_39575598_1_1_1_1,00.html

Platt, Lilly. 1999. "Virtual teaming: Where is everyone?" *The Journal for Quality & Participation* 22 (5): 41–43.

Project Management Institute (PMI). 2008. *A Guide to the Project Management Body of Knowledge (PMBOK® Guide)*. 4th ed. Newton Square, PA: Project Management Institute.

Schwartz, Shalom H. 1992. "Universals in the content and structure of values: Theoretical advanced and empirical tests in 20 countries." *Advanced in Experimental Social Psychology* 25: 1–49.

Schwartz, Shalom H. and Bilsky, Wolfgang. 1987. "Toward a universal psychological structure of human values." *Journal of Personality and Social Psychology* 53 (3): 550–562.

Simon, Herbert A. 1957. *Models of Man, Social and Rational: Mathematical Essays on Rational Human Behavior in a Social Setting*. New York: Wiley.

United Nations Office of the High Commissioner for Human Rights (UN OHCHR). 1998. "Universal declaration of human rights." United Nations Office of the High Commissioner for Human Rights. http://www.ohchr.org/EN/UDHR/Pages/Language.aspx?LangID=eng

Relationship management
A strategy for fostering localization success[*]

Karen R. Combe

Localization success depends largely on activities which precede localization, performed by groups outside the localization function that may be unaware of their role as stakeholders in the localization process or may even refuse to acknowledge that role. Consequently, localization project managers must manage relationships with stakeholders in other functional units (and even in other organizations) to obtain what they require to ensure successful project outcomes. Thus, this chapter examines the management of outsourced localization projects through the lens of relationship management. It contrasts the variables that shape localization project management in client organizations versus vendor organizations, proposes relationship management strategies for addressing these variables, and concludes by examining a number of tools that can be used to facilitate relationship management in outsourced localization project management.

The paradox of localization project management: Project success depends largely on activities that precede localization

Localization project managers (LPMs) all perform a certain number of common activities, and all are responsible, in varying degrees, for the scope, budgets, and schedules of localization projects. However, localization project managers also share a common constraint: their ability to achieve successful project outcomes depends to a greater or lesser extent on a number of important preconditions for success over which they often have no direct control. These preconditions result from the fact that localization is only one part of a much larger process – the development of an international product. Furthermore, localization occurs downstream from a number of activities that comprise preconditions for success:

---

[*] This chapter focuses primarily on outsourced localization projects, but the concepts are applicable to outsourced translation projects as well.

- Collection of requirements for local markets
- Internationalization
- Establishment of a testing plan
- Formulation of a global publications strategy
- Inclusion of localization milestones in the master product release schedule

Paradoxically, although each of these preconditions plays a significant role in shaping the context that leads to successful localization, each falls under the responsibility of a group that is outside the purview of the localization function. Thus LPMs must manage relationships with colleagues in the groups that perform these activities to obtain what they require to ensure successful project outcomes.

Collection of requirements for local markets

The Project Management Institute (PMI) defines project requirements as "the quantified needs and expectations of the sponsor, customer and other stakeholders" and notes that requirements are the foundation on which cost, schedule and quality planning are all established (2008: 105). The importance of documenting requirements as clearly and comprehensively as possible cannot be overstated. Requirements for local markets are typically provided by a function that may be variously called Product Management, Technical Marketing, Product Marketing, or even Sales. In many companies, decisions about local markets are based strictly on ROI (Return on Investment) analysis, and local product launches are followed by rigorous revenue and cost analyses. New languages are adopted based on the company's global business strategy, which encompasses (or should encompass) product localization, marketing, a sales organization or value-added reseller relationships, product distribution mechanisms, and legal and accounting infrastructure. However, the people who establish requirements and make decisions about what to localize often lack clear decision-making criteria and either make random decisions or fail to make a decision in a timely fashion. In the absence of clear and/or timely requirements decisions, the project manager (PM) may find himself or herself in the position of soliciting requirements from stakeholders who may not know what decision to make and who are therefore reluctant to commit to a decision, in which case the PM must manage the relationship to obtain the necessary information.

Internationalization

Internationalization is the exclusive province of the development team. This team is in charge of developing a product that can function in any targeted locale and that can be efficiently localized. Internationalization does not happen spontaneously or automatically. In general, it is mandated from the top of the organization and reinforced at the bottom. The role of the localization project manager in this context depends on the position of Localization in the company. During the localization of the user interface (UI), translators may bring to the attention of the PM files that present any number of common internationalization problems, such as string concatenation or improper use of variables. Development may or may not be willing to fix such problems, depending on the importance of international markets in the company, and by extension, the amount of institutional clout wielded by Localization. Recalcitrant developers can delay internationalization remediation work in a number of ways, such as marking a bug as not critical for the product release. However, if the localization department is in a position to positively influence Development by raising awareness about internationalization standards and engaging in proactive internal consulting, it can prevent many localization problems from arising in the first place. If not, the PM will likely encounter difficult projects.

Establishment of a testing plan for localized products

Quality assurance for localized products includes three forms of testing: (a) internationalization testing, which precedes localization and is designed to ensure that the localized product supports all of the target locales, languages and writing systems; (b) localization testing, which includes linguistic validation of the translation and verification that the UI elements are properly formatted; and (c) functional testing, which follows localization and is designed to ensure that nothing has been broken during the localization process and that the localized products work correctly in the locale-specific operating environments, which may encompass operating systems, browsers and/or other software. Either the core (source) development team or the quality assurance (QA) team should test any product that will be localized to ensure that it is in fact properly internationalized. Since localization QA requires language expertise, it is generally performed not by the core development or QA team, but by an in-house localization QA team, by a vendor, or even by local technical field personnel. Functional testing of the localized versions is performed by the core QA team or by the localization QA team, typically using automated tools that replicate the testing performed on the source version of the software.

Regardless of who performs the QA steps, Localization depends on Development and the core QA team to participate in the establishment of a testing plan for the localized products that clearly specifies who is responsible for testing what and when. For example, localization testing should not start until the core product has reached a certain level of stability. Otherwise, localization testers may find defects in multiple localized products at the same time as the core QA team finds them; this will result in several bugs being reported and filed for the same problem. If these various bug reports all use slightly different descriptions to characterize the problem, then the amount of effort that the development team must expend will increase in direct proportion to the number of duplicate bugs, since the team will need to assess each one individually to determine whether or not it is a duplicate. Therefore, at a minimum, the localization project manager requires status communication from the core QA team. A localization QA team may also need to receive test cases and training on new functionality from the core QA team, or integration with test management systems, or may need to work with the core QA team in order to develop an automated test strategy that will work for all languages. Since the core QA team members often consider such requests from Localization to be outside the scope of their job descriptions, the localization PM may need some leverage to ensure that what needs to be done to ensure successful localization is in fact done.

Implementation of a global publications strategy

Publications teams tend to choose authoring and publishing tools and processes based on the ability of the tools to create the desired output(s) in the source language. Encounters with localization departments may persuade them that such decisions must be made jointly, but more often than not the degree of collaboration (or mutual accountability) depends on the relative positions of the departments in the organization. In the typical scenario, Publications makes authoring and publishing decisions independently, and Localization figures out how to cope with the consequences of these decisions. For example, if the publications team invests in an authoring tool that does not entirely support Asian languages, then the localization team working into Japanese and Simplified Chinese will need to find workarounds, or perform manual work, to compensate for the lack of Asian language support. In such cases, the organization would benefit from the formulation of a global publications strategy to optimize productivity and user experience in *all* languages. A global publications strategy would ensure that the publications and localization teams collaborate on the choice of both tools and their implementation and perhaps even a style sheet that would serve all languages. They might together consider and decide upon the process and mechanism by which the language of the online help is chosen or changed by the user.[1] If a localization department is well positioned in the company, it may spearhead the adoption of this type of collaborative strategy because the impact of a bad tool or process tends to be more immediately apparent when working in multiple languages.

---

1. In the absence of a global publications strategy, such decisions are often made by individual developers or development teams, to the detriment of a common user experience across products and possibly to the detriment of the non-English user.

Inclusion of localization milestones in the master product
release schedule

Whether or not a company simultaneously ships the source and localized versions of a given product (a process referred to in industry as "simship"), localization milestones should be included in the master product release schedule. Inter-departmental milestones and hand-off dates may initially be established based on a handshake between individuals, but the localization project manager may subsequently have problems enforcing the agreement if it is not formalized. The localization project manager must seek to influence the release management function to recognize these inter-departmental dependencies, in order to facilitate the success of all teams. Release managers may hold the title of project manager, program manager, or even release manager and are likely to be part of the development organization. They plan and track the schedule and the release, based on the requirements from Product Management and the resources of Development.

Although it is possible to successfully complete a localization project if the preconditions discussed above are not met, it is significantly more difficult to implement best project management practices in such cases and the project manager may be forced to devise ad hoc solutions to overcome the resulting problems.

Identifying dependencies and raising stakeholder awareness through relationship management

Because requirements for local markets, internationalization, a testing plan for localized products, a global publications strategy and the inclusion of milestones in the master product release schedule are preconditions for successful localization project outcomes, the groups that perform these activities are by definition localization project stakeholders:

> Stakeholders are persons or organizations (e.g., customers, sponsors, the performing organization, or the public), who are actively involved in the project or whose interests may be positively or negatively affected by the performance or the completion of the project. *Stakeholders may also exert influence over the project, its deliverables, and the project team members.*   (PMI 2008: 23; emphasis added)

The problem for the localization project manager is that the functional groups responsible for performing these activities may not recognize or acknowledge their influence over localization. In such cases, the localization team can state what it requires from other groups for the project to be successful; but if those groups are not formally identified as project stakeholders, the PM may have little leverage with which to gain commitments from them. These problems are compounded by the fact that even if these groups are unaware of or do not acknowledge their roles as stakeholders in the localization process, these dependencies remain.

Relationship management offers a solution to problems of stakeholder engagement and tensions caused by competing objectives. As MacDonald (2008:169) observes:

> Relationship management is more than communicating, solving problems and managing conflict. As critically important as these skills are, they are like a saddle and bridle – very important for riding and steering but they won't take you anywhere without a horse. Relationship management is like that. To go places we need to engage with people. This includes working within our organization to clarify goals and objectives, develop strategies and work out tactics and project details. It also involves working with our external relationship partners to think through a problem, analyze an opportunity or take advantage of our collective creativity and thought power.

It is essential that the LPM identify dependencies between Localization and other functional units and engage decision-makers in those groups to raise awareness to lead them to realize that they are in fact localization stakeholders and that they must provide deliverables to Localization at agreed-upon times and in an agreed-upon condition. If such a commitment can be secured, then the success of those groups will be judged by management at least partly in terms of their ability to hand off required materials to the localization team on the agreed-upon dates. However, if this situation is not managed properly and one or more groups on which localization depends fail to deliver required materials when they are needed, causing project delays, it is the localization personnel who will be seen as being late or having missed their deadlines. It is for such reasons that experts agree that "[p]artnership with key stakeholders must be built and nurtured" (Kerzner 2003:21) and that "actively managing stakeholder relationships from the very beginning of the project all the way through is [one] of the core success strategies in project management" (Dobson 2003:106).

Outsourcing extends the scope of localization dependencies and relationships

Translation and localization projects require extensive resources but typically last only a few weeks or months. When a project is concluded, a significant amount of time may elapse before a new project is undertaken, depending on the length of the organization's product development cycle and the frequency of product version updates, for example. Faced with peaks and troughs of demand for translation and localization services – intense projects of relatively short duration followed by periods of little or activity – and given the fact that translation and localization are not one of their core competencies, most organizations choose to outsource their projects to external service providers. Indeed, the translation and localization market research firm Common Sense Advisory reports that 87% of translation buyers outsource most or all of their translation projects (Beninatto 2006: 4).

The outsourcing process establishes an inter-organizational client/vendor relationship, sometimes referred to as the buyer/seller relationship, defined as "an ongoing, long term linkage between an outsourcing vendor and customer arising from a contractual agreement to provide one or more comprehensive … [business] services with the understanding that the benefits attained by each firm are at least in part dependent on the other" (Goles and Chin 2005: 49). In the context of sourced translation and localization services, the client and vendor project managers are the primary actors in this relationship.

The vital importance of relationship management to successful outsourcing initiatives is amply documented in the literature (Konsynski and McFarlan 1990; Fitzgerald and Willcocks 1994; McFarlan and Nolan 1995; Quinn 1999; Kern and Willcocks 2001; Stading and Altay 2007: 29; Farn and Huang 2008). Thus, the lens of relationship management can provide insights into the respective roles of the client-side and vendor-side project managerst.

Environmental factors and their impact on localization project management

Aside from the specific preconditions discussed above, localization project management is also shaped at a more fundamental level by the environment in which localization is performed, i.e., the inherent dependency between development and authoring on one hand, and localization on the other hand. After all, the products of development and authoring are the raw materials of localization. Consequently, the role of the localization project manager in the client organization is particularly challenging because the PM needs to understand not only localization processes but development and authoring processes as well, and also how they intersect with localization in terms of integration and testing.

Development

Most software companies adhere to a formalized development methodology, whether it is the more traditional waterfall model, Agile or other iterative methodology (see Dunne 164–168 and 181–184 and Zhou 372–376 in this volume), or some combination thereof. The localization PM who does not understand the development lifecycle will be unable to engage and interact with other groups as an informed, credible partner. Localization cannot reasonably make demands of Publications without understanding that group's constraints. For example, the documentation cannot be complete, or accurate, if the product itself continues to change, so it makes little sense for Localization to demand that Publications respect a hand-off date if the publications team is itself experiencing delays due to slippages in the development schedule. Likewise, Development cannot commit to a code freeze (i.e., a date beyond which no further changes to the source code are permitted) if Marketing modifies the functional requirements in response to changing market conditions. To be an effective partner and team player, the localization project manager needs to know and understand the product development cycle from start to finish.

It is important that a project manager working in localization understand the major issues associated with various development environments, the stages of the software development cycle, and the specifics of the development of a given product being localized. Different development environments and programming languages give rise to different internationalization issues. For example, consider the example of apostrophes in Java: if apostrophes are not handled properly, they may either disappear from the localized version of the product or appear in duplicate.[2] At a minimum, the PM must be able to elicit information from Development about the specific processes, tools, and programming languages used in the creation of the product, and must convey this information to the Localization Service Provider (LSP), so that they in turn can select appropriate tools or filters.

Integration

The integration, or build, process varies from company to company (and may even vary from product to product). The build team consists of a group of developers who write the scripts and manage the processes that integrate the pieces of code from individual programmers into a complete, running product. In most cases, online help and other forms of documentation are also included in the product build. In some companies, integration of the localized product is performed by the localization department, while other companies have one central integration department that produces all the builds. Generally there are cut-off dates for builds, as well as a cycle leading up to the final production build. In any event, the localization PM should understand how the translated software files fit into that larger process: when to start submitting files, how the builds may be affected by the translated files, whether errors in localization

---

2. This problem stems from differences in the way apostrophes are handled by two string formatting methods in Java, PropertyResourceBundle and MessageFormat (Sun Developer Network 2010). In the PropertyResourceBundle method, an apostrophe is treated as a normal character and displayed whenever it appears. In the MessageFormat method, an apostrophe is treated as a special character and ignored for display purposes; it is thus necessary to enter a apostrophe in duplicate ('') to ensure the display of a single apostrophe in a MessageFormat string. If the apostrophe is not entered in duplicate, none will display. Conversely, if a double apostrophe is used in a PropertyResourceBundle string, two apostrophes will display.

could break the build, and so forth. The LPM may not need to know the engineering issues in detail, but knowledge of the primary constraints is certainly imperative. For example, Integration teams typically do not want to receive large numbers of files or large volumes of content late in the release cycle, because the greater the changes to components of the build, the more likely it is that something will break during the build process. However, in simship projects, Localization is often obliged to make large submissions late in the release cycle, since by nature the localization process follows the creation processes (development of code and authoring of documentation). Regardless of the specific project configuration, the localization PM can work with Integration to set expectations and minimize risk of disruption to the release.

Testing

The localization PM should understand the types and extent of internationalization testing performed prior to localization, which could include a pseudo-localization process supported by the localization department involving the use of localization tools. Even though Development is responsible for internationalizing the product, it is Localization that will feel the pain of incomplete or ineffective internationalization. Consequently, the localization PM needs to understand the types and extent of internationalization testing to gauge the internationalization risks to the project. For example, if pseudo-build testing has not been performed prior to localization, there is greater risk of string length problems, concatenation problems, incomprehensible variables, or even character display issues in the localized product. The localization PM should warn the translation team to be alert for such issues, and may also want to increase the allotted time for localization testing to discover and fix related bugs.

The platform on which the localized product will run may or may not be the same as the one most commonly used in the source language. For instance, users of the company's products in China may prefer the IBM platform to Windows, whereas users in Japan may rely on Windows to the exclusion of all other operating systems. Such local preferences must determine the testing priorities.

The localization PM is likely to be assigned the responsibility for tracking and overseeing the resolution of localization-related software defects through a bug reporting system. It is therefore important that the PM understand that system, including the life cycle of a software defect and the criteria for determining whether, and when, the defect should be fixed in a particular release. For example, any kind of submission to the build, whether it is a piece of code or a translated string, may be restricted once the final QA stage of the release has begun. In such cases, the restrictions in place may lead to the refusal of a submission. The localization PM might want to request an exception to this practice if a very serious translation error were identified, and would need to be able to argue knowledgeably.

Authoring and publishing tools and processes

Much as different development environments and programming languages give rise to different internationalization issues, different authoring and publishing tools and processes give rise to different translation and localization issues. Some translation tools, for example, do not parse index markers correctly if they are not all grouped at the beginning or end of a paragraph. Some authoring tools cannot alphabetically sort text, which can cause problems when creating a target glossary. The localization PM needs to know what tools are used in the authoring and source publishing processes in order to be able to convey appropriate information to the LSP or to whoever will produce the localized documentation.

Many companies choose to leave parts of their localized documentation in the source language, if that language is English. For example, if the administrators who will be installing and configuring the software are expected to read and understand English, then the administrator documentation and installation documentation will most likely be left in English. In such cases it is possible that there may be a mixture of English and localized content in the same help system, or a mixture of localized and non-localized sets of documentation on the final product CD, depending on how the documentation is presented to the user. If the online help system contains topics written in two or more languages, a decision must be made about the Table of Contents: Should each title be listed in the language in which the corresponding topic displays in the Help, in which case the Table of Contents will present a mixture of English and translated titles? Or should all of the titles be translated even if the some topics are not localized? Alternatively, should a parenthetical translation be provided for topics that are not translated? The localization PM needs to understand what the customer will actually receive in the package in order to know what questions to ask on the user's behalf. It is unfortunately true that Product Management or Marketing (whoever is in charge of product requirements) often does not have sufficiently detailed knowledge of the localized product to foresee and address such issues as part of the product requirements, or they may simply not think about the ways in which non-English-speaking users experience the product. The localization PM can act as an advocate for non-English-speaking customers and bring such issues to the attention of the appropriate decision-makers.

Summary

Localization PMs on the client side need to understand how to function in an environment in which localization is not the primary activity, but rather depends for information and requirements on groups that are upstream in the development process and that often occupy a position closer to the top of the organizational hierarchy. In order to work effectively, the PM must understand the development process to be able to participate as an informed, credible partner in cross-functional teams and to be able to convey the proper information to LSPs.

Organizational structure and its impact on localization project management

By and large, the relative position of Localization in the hierarchy of the client company determines the ability of localization project managers to obtain what they need from teams in other functional units. The relative position of localization in the corporate hierarchy, in turn, is largely determined by the depth of the company's localization experience. In the following paragraphs, we will examine where and how localization fits in to the structure of a typical company, and how the position of localization changes over time as the company gains experience in and mastery of the localization process.

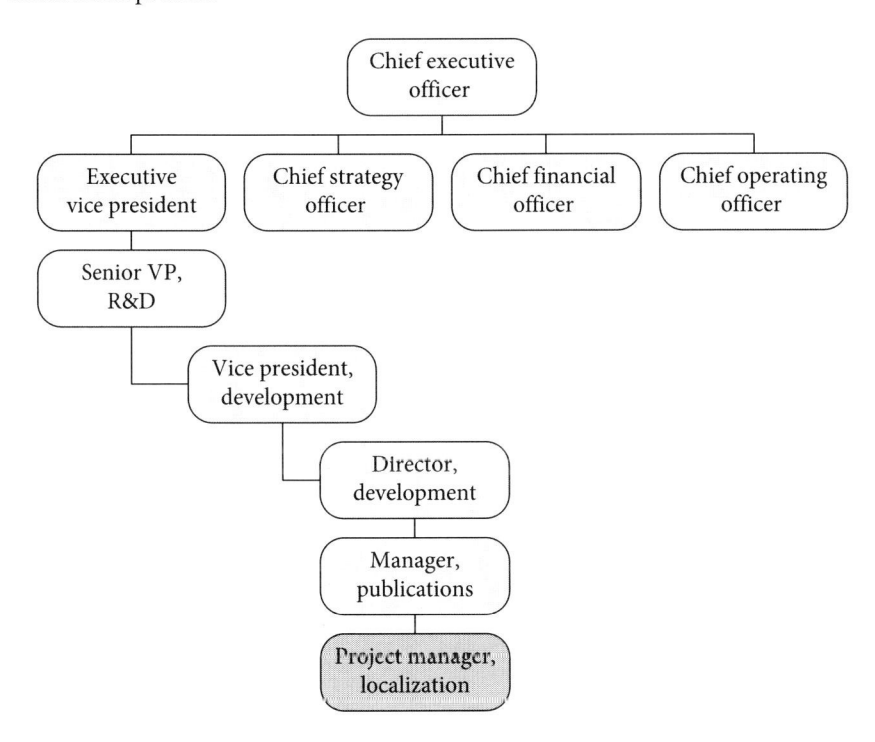

Figure 1. The structure of a company that has little or no localization experience.

Typically, in a company that is a newcomer to localization, the publications department is authorized to hire someone to focus on translation and localization, and a localization project manager is brought on board. (This may occur after some unfortunate writer has tried to do the job part time.) In this scenario, the new localization PM is often relegated to the bottom of the corporate pecking order, where she or he has little power to influence decision-making at higher levels of the company (see Figure 1). The localization PM may attempt to educate decision-makers at higher levels, but as the hierarchical structure shown in Figure 1 makes clear, the localization PM has no leverage with which to compel the publications team or the development team to change their behavior. The bottom line is that problems encountered by the localization PM are his or her responsibility, even if such problems ultimately stem from the actions (or inaction) of other groups higher up the ladder. The best chance to improve localization conditions hinges on the project manager's ability to convince the publications manager that costs and time can be reduced by making changes in Publishing and/or Development, and that it is in the best interest of the client company as a whole to make such changes. The publications manager is thus motivated to pass suggestions one level higher to the development director and in so doing demonstrate commitment to increasing productivity and reducing costs. This is the first step towards establishment of standard processes that will allow the localization project manager to plan and execute projects in a repeatable, predictable fashion.

Eventually, localization evolves to the point that it can be performed in a repeatable and predictable fashion and requires department-level status and management (see Figure 2). Once Localization has moved up to the same level as Publications in the corporate hierarchy, directly underneath Development, the localization manager is in a position to formulate requirements for successful project outcomes and provide them to the development director. Typically, managers assume some level of responsibility for the success of the people and groups that report to them, so the localization manager has a reasonable chance to be heard. In addition, the managers of publication and localization departments may be able to exert greater leverage by formulating shared requirements. For example, let us suppose that the company is undertaking a project that involves the simultaneous shipment of the source version of a product and one or more localized versions. In this scenario, both Publications and Localization need the development team to specify a user interface (UI) freeze in the master schedule if they are to complete their work with a reasonable level of accuracy by the deadline.

Depending on the corporate organizational structure, Localization may report to Development, Marketing or Product Management. Nevertheless, the closer the localization function is to upper management in the corporate hierarchy, the more visibility it has and the better able it is to effectively promote, across the development groups, the standard processes that enable a mature global product strategy (see Figure 3).

Regardless of their relative position in the organization, localization project managers need to manage relationships with their colleagues in units located in other departments. As a general rule, the PM is more likely to be successful by stating the localization case objectively, setting clear goals and striving to achieve them. For example, in order for Localization to ensure that translated files will be submitted for inclusion in the product build by a given date Y, Publications must hand off the files to Localization by date X. It is not the PM who requires that Publications hand off the files by this

Relationship management in localization

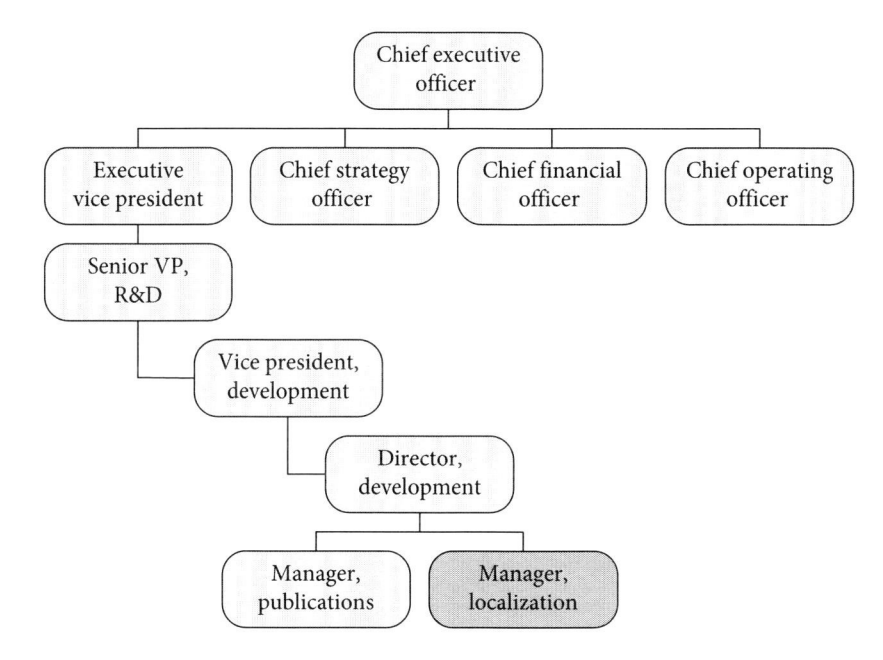

Figure 2. The structure of a company in which localization requires dedicated management.

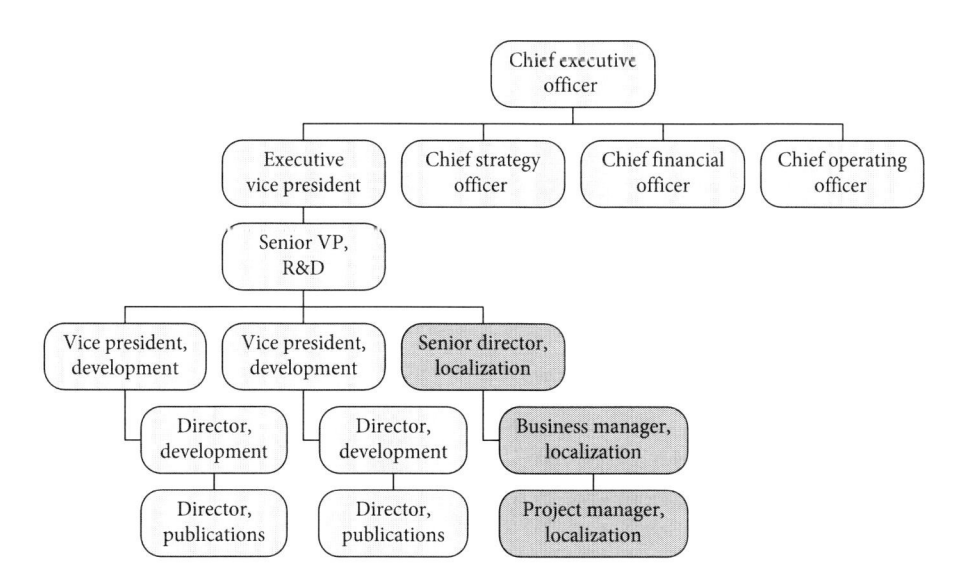

Figure 3. The structure of a company in which localization has reached maturity.

particular date, but the process. Trade-offs and alternative dates should be discussed in terms of the relative risks associated with various alternatives and their potential impact on the project and/or process, rather than in terms of the inconvenience that schedule changes may cause to the localization department. People outside of localization tend to be unaware of the localization industry and its standard practices. The localization PM can take advantage of the body of industry knowledge and practices to explain the requirements for a particular project. Even a simple explanation may suffice. For example, the PM may need to educate colleagues about the requirement that a certain amount of time be allotted for translation in the schedule based on the conventional wisdom that professional translators can translate approximately 2,000 source-language words per day, or that high translation quality can only be achieved by limiting the total number of translators involved in a given project. The important point is that PMs must present themselves as knowledgeable professional practitioners.

Paths to success: Building relationships across departments

Localization PMs may raise awareness about the logical dependencies between Localization and other functional units, and the important role that these units play in helping shape the conditions that enable successful localization project outcomes, by educating colleagues in the other units about internationalization, by establishing shared requirements in tandem with other departments, and by conducting post-project reviews.

Cross-functional teams

In cross-functional teams, each group has the opportunity – and the obligation – to state what it requires for the project or release to be successful. Participating in cross-functional teams provides the localization PM with the opportunity to educate colleagues from Publishing, Development and other units about specific internationalization issues. For example, it is well known that the concatenation of software strings at runtime tends to make translation difficult, and depending on the grammatical and syntactic assumptions on which the concatenation is based and the grammatical and syntactic rules of the target language, the strings may even be untranslatable as written. Generally speaking, translators cannot know without receiving detailed explanations from the developers which strings will appear together at runtime. In the absence of a concatenation mapping scheme, ensuring that all of the target string combinations are grammatically and syntactically correct becomes an impossible task. The localization PM can explain this problem fairly easily to the development team and require a resolution from them. Along similar lines, after creating the project schedule, the LPM can confirm with colleagues in Publications and QA the dates of handoffs from those teams that will enable timely project completion. In this way, the dates of handoffs from Publications to Localization and from QA to Localization can be specified and tracked as part of the cross-functional team's work.

Establishing shared requirements

The localization PM can look for natural allies to establish shared requirements. For example, Quality Assurance, Publications, and Localization all depend on the development cycle: a stable user interface is required in order to perform testing, create documentation, and/or undertake localization. Since all three groups rely on a code freeze date to finalize documentation and enter the final QA phase of the release cycle, they can all work together with the release management or program management function to establish UI and code freeze milestones in the master release plan that will allow all groups to be successful.

Post-project review

Most companies undertake some sort of post-project review, whether it is called "lessons learned," "retrospective" (popular in the Agile environment), or "post-mortem." Post-project review offers the localization project manager another opportunity to call attention to issues that may have prevented an optimal localization process during the completed project and to suggest specific changes for the next release or project. Such project reviews are of little value if no action is taken in response to the suggested corrective actions. The localization PM will most likely need to take responsibility for following up on these actions and may even need to form a task force or other ad hoc working group to resolve difficult problems.

Outsourcing magnifies the importance of relationship management

As noted above, the vast majority of companies outsource their localization work. However, in solving staffing problems caused by peaks and troughs in internal localization demand, companies that outsource localization risk compounding the problems discussed in the preceding sections. Vendor-side PMs are subject to all of the client-side environmental and process-related dependencies discussed above, but as external subcontractors they have even less leverage or influence over localization stakeholders than client-side PMs. Clients take a hands-off approach to outsourcing and to relationships with vendors at their peril. As Jim Leto, president and chief executive officer of the program management consulting company Robbins-Gioia, observes: "Just because you outsource something … doesn't mean you can abdicate responsibility for it. The quality of management provided by the client is one of the most important factors in whether the relationship succeeds or not" (quoted in Santana 2004).

Outsourcing thus magnifies the importance of relationship management. Wise clients and vendors will realize that "[t]he mutual dependence between [outsourcing] participants makes the management of relationships a key issue in harnessing the benefits" (Meier 1995: 137) and that "astute relationship management in the value chain has become a competitive imperative" (McIlvor 2005: 10) because "[a] contract on its own is neither self-enforcing nor self-adjusting" (Kern 1997: 52). Unfortunately, in reality "clients and vendors have a strong tendency not to plan and resource sufficiently their relationship management arrangements prior to outsourcing" (Kern and Willcocks 2001: 357). Greaver (1999: 269) concurs and offers the following guidance for organizations that seek to outsource one or more business processes:

> To build the relationship effectively ... the [outsourcing] organization should be active in monitoring and evaluating performance and addressing issues. If this doesn't occur, the provider's performance is likely to suffer. This might happen because the provider takes shortcuts that are not caught and corrected. But the provider's performance is more likely to suffer because the provider cannot get answers to questions (causing delays or inappropriate assumptions to be made) or the provider's suggestions for organizational improvement (that affects the provider's performance) are not implemented. It takes time to manage the relationship.

Having examined localization project management in the client organization, let us now turn our attention to localization project management in the vendor organization.

The role of the localization project manager in the vendor organization

While the role of the PM on the client side depends largely on the *position* of Localization in the company, the role of the localization PM on the vendor side depends on the *size* of the company. In a small company the project manager is likely to be a jack of all trades who is knowledgeable about file formats, software localization, desktop publishing, and who may even have a background in translation. As localization service providers grow in size and capability and their internal company functions become more stratified, the role of the localization PM becomes more specialized, focusing on the primary project variables of cost, quality and time. This PM in a larger LSP may not know as much about engineering processes or desktop publishing tools or requirements for Asian languages as his or her colleague in a small LSP, in which case he or she relies on the expertise of the Production team for such information.

Intra-organization dependencies

Much like client-side LPMs, vendor-side localization PMs are also dependent on other groups. Aside from the relationship with the client-side PM, on whom the vendor-side PM depends for project information and requirements, arguably the most critical relationship for the vendor-side localization PM is with Sales, which engages with potential customers and writes proposals long before the localization PM becomes involved. In the classic project management nightmare scenario, a Sales person sells a project to the client that only a superhero PM and project team can deliver. Sales may agree to timelines that are too short on the grounds that projects always change and there will be opportunities to alter the schedule later. Or, in an effort to win the business over competing bids, Sales might agree to a price that is so low that the localization PM will certainly exceed the budget. The disconnect between those who sell projects and those who must subsequently perform the project work and deliver the agreed-upon product or service is a well known problem in project-oriented organizations:

> The traditional account manager has probably sold something and left it to others to install and bring this service on behalf of the client. The traditional project manager is used to receiving an order sold by an account manager who, in the project manager's view, has no concept of the difficulty of the installation or the timescales needed for the work. The professional respect that the traditional account manager and the traditional project manager hold for each other is often very low. (Davis and Pharro 2003: 103)

In a company in which Sales can sell a project that is likely (or even certain) to fail, the localization PM is best served by adopting a strategy of professional presentation to management of localization-related options and risks. Projects are shaped by three interdependent variables: time, cost, and quality (see Figure 4).[3] Modifying one variable will impact one or both of the other variables. For example, if the timeline is too short, then quality can only be maintained by paying rush fees to the preferred translators or agencies or by hiring additional translators or agencies with equivalent resources (assuming such are available). Either of these options will result in an increase in the cost of the project. Along similar lines, if the price agreed upon with the client is too low then the laws of supply and demand suggest that quality will suffer unless the timelines can be extended sufficiently to secure the scarce, less expensive resources who nonetheless do good work. Due to the interdependency among the three variables, conventional project management wisdom holds that the customer can prioritize any two of the three variables; attempting to maximize quality while minimizing cost and time will inevitably lead to project failure.

---

3. As a general rule, the project scope is assumed to be fixed as far as the LSP is concerned. LSPs generally bid upon, and are awarded, projects that require the creation of a specific set of deliverables of pre-defined scope. In practice, scope can and often does in fact change.

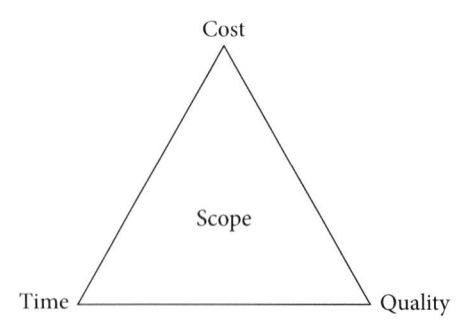

Figure 4. The project management triangle, also known as the law of triple constraints.

The solution to such problems is for sales and project management personnel to collaborate on promising prospects, and in fact, this is what happens in many LSPs. For example, the PM may participate in critical meetings with the prospective customer to hear and respond to their particular concerns, or to discuss scheduling constraints. This cooperation supports the sales process by exposing good project management and problem-solving skills to the potential client and also helps to ensure that the company sells projects that can be completed successfully.

Aside from Sales, the other critical relationship for the vendor-side localization PM is with Production (if there is a dedicated production department that controls engineering, translation and desktop publishing personnel), or with the person in the company who is responsible for carrying out engineering, translation and desktop publishing tasks. One of the biggest challenges for localization service providers is the management of human resources through peaks and valleys of demand. In principle, LSPs develop systems and processes to ensure that the PMs assign human resources in an orderly fashion, but in fact the PMs sometimes find themselves in competition with each other for access to critical personnel:

> In many organizations, resources are shared or spread across multiple project teams…. These days … more and more companies [are] trying to 'do more with less.' As a result, there are often severe constraints on key resources, which may be spread across three, four or even five projects. In these types of environments, PMs will be competing against each other for the resources they need at the time that they need them. (Mersino 2007: 112)

When demand for one or more people outstrips their availability, schedules may have to be adjusted or quality may suffer.

Inter-organization dependencies

Like client-side localization PMs, vendor-side localization PMs must understand the development process. However, the challenges that vendor-side LPMs face are compounded by the fact that they typically work with a number of different client companies, each of which may have its own process. Because each client may do things differently, knowledge of the business side of localization and knowledge of localization processes, including the various ways in which projects may be configured, ultimately plays a larger role in project success than knowledge of development. The vendor-side localization project manager may need to act as an advisor and educator to the client, as someone who is capable of providing solutions when the client needs to delay or change delivery of project components to the vendor but cannot change the final completion date.

A software localization project typically involves the creation of target versions of three main components, namely the software, online help and documentation.[4] In the course of the average project, the software is localized first, followed by the Help and/or the documentation. However, it is important to note that because of time pressures, the Help translation almost always begins before localization of the software is completed. In any event, the individual tasks that must be performed to create the localized versions of the three main components constitute the moving parts of the project. The localization PM can sequence these tasks in various ways, with greater or lesser degrees of risk to quality, depending on the needs of the client. For example, if client-side delays result in a tight schedule, then it may be necessary to capture screens for the documentation before the localization of the interface has been completed. But in that case, a corresponding task should be inserted in the project schedule prior to the final desktop publishing stage to track changes to the localized software and re-capture screens as needed to reflect UI updates. Re-capturing screens is likely to result in additional cost, so the PM may need to persuade the client that this billable task is necessary, for example by noting that the quality of the final product will suffer if some of the screen captures in the documentation do not reflect the actual user interface content.

Ultimately, localization PMs achieve success by acting as facilitators. As their job title suggests, the primary responsibility of project managers is the management of *projects*, not *employees*. PMs seldom have any employees who report directly to them. Thus, even though the LPM may be allotted production personnel for a particular project, it is the production manager (or translation manager or engineering manager) who manages those individuals' priorities and schedules, not

---

4. Documentation refers to all of the content written to support (document) the product. Today, documentation consists primarily of online help and what were formerly printed books but now are mostly delivered as PDF files.

the localization project manager. So the PM has to set clear project goals, and find ways to resolve unforeseen problems. For example, if an engineer is assigned to work on the PM's new project, but is unavailable when the project starts because his previous project has been extended, what should the localization PM do? If an alternative person cannot be assigned to the task, the PM may need to re-schedule the whole project, use up project buffer time, or find a way to make progress on the project without the engineer, perhaps by assigning a translator to assess UI files for translatability problems instead.

Summary

The role of the localization PM on the client side depends largely on the size of the organization. But as on the client side, the localization project manager typically leads without direct authority and thus must communicate, negotiate and effectively manage relationships with stakeholders to obtain what he or she needs. The vendor-side PM achieves success through the optimal configuration of the process building blocks within the constraints imposed by project scope, time, quality and cost.

Paths to productive relationships

An ongoing healthy relationship between the client and vendor localization project managers and their stakeholders is critical to the success of any outsourced localization project. A schematic representation of the relationships that client and vendor project managements must typically maintain is shown in Figure 5. Certain relationships, such as those with upper management or with personnel from the finance and legal departments, are similar on both the client and vendor sides. For example, the client-side PM may need to interact with Finance to ensure that purchase orders are issued and that invoices paid. She or he may also need to provide monthly or quarterly reports on the status of work done measured against purchase orders, and may even need to interact with a purchasing entity that qualifies and selects localization vendors. Likewise, the vendor-side PM needs to interact with Finance to ensure that the vendor company receives purchase orders (POs) and credits them to the correct project, and must confirm that invoicing is done according to agreed parameters. The PM must also report on work completed so that the company can accurately track revenue for recognition and accounting purposes. Although some relationships are similar on the client and vendor sides, others are specific to the organization in question (e.g., relationships with cross-functional project teams on the client side and those with sales representatives or resource allocation staff on the vendor side).

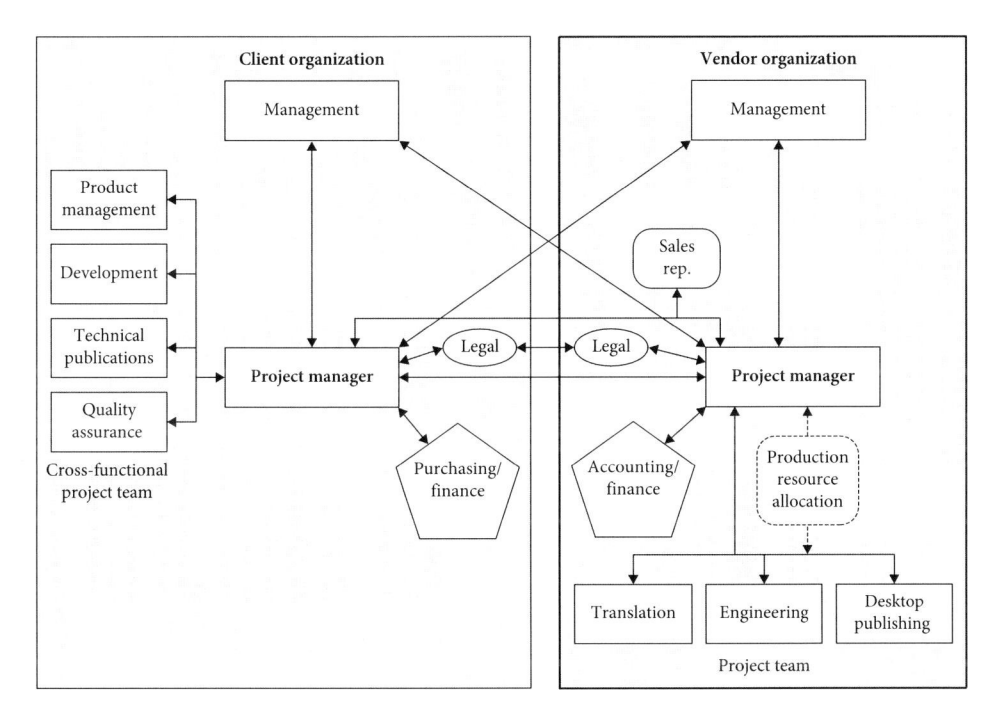

Figure 5. The web of relationships: The various functional groups with which project managers interact in client and vendor organizations.

Tools for relationship management

Having positioned localization project management with respect to certain preconditions for success, discussed some of the reasons why it is critical to manage relationships in outsourced localization projects and examined some examples of those relationships, let us look at some of the tools that can be used to facilitate relationship management in outsourced localization project management. Such tools include, but are not limited to, project definition documents, budget baseline documents or spreadsheets, kick-off meetings, status reports and change management processes.

RFQ/Project definition document

Defining the project is the first critical step in the relationship between client and vendor project managers. It is crucial that they understand what they are going to work on together and what the value of the project is. A request for quote (RFQ) or project definition document is extremely important in this regard. It typically includes scope information, including a list of components, along with word, page, and other counts if they are available, as well as costs, deliverables, and often timelines. If this document includes imprecise specifications, such as a deliverable described as "final software files," there is a risk of trouble at some point in the project, most likely at the end. But if this document formulates clear definitions of work to be done and project deliverables, the project managers have a strong foundation for their project.

Budget baseline

Along similar lines, although projects often change, a project cannot (should not) start until and unless the vendor accepts a purchase order, which must specify the amount that the client will pay the vendor to complete the project. That amount is based on an agreement between client and vendor about the components of the project and their corresponding costs. The budget may be presented in the form of a spreadsheet or via a web-based tool, or even as a Word document. It may be called the budget or the statement of work. Regardless of its name, this document should be signed by authorized representatives of both the client and the vendor organizations as it will become one of the legal documents that define the relationship between the two parties.

Kick-off meeting

The kick-off meeting, whether it is virtual or face-to-face, provides the opportunity for the stakeholders to review the project specifications, to call attention to critical information (such as a particularly tight timeline or entry into a new market), to state risks and discuss the plan to manage them, and to get to know one another. The kick-off meeting typically includes a review of the localization kit, which includes the files to be localized, specifications on tools and processes to be used, reference materials, and any related instructions. Reviewing the localization kit enables the client and vendor project managers to ensure that they have a common understanding of the files to be translated and the instructions that must be followed. The kick-off meeting also provides an opportunity for the project managers to furnish project background information to the team members and to begin to build team spirit. Perhaps this project represents the client company's first venture in the Japanese market, or perhaps the essential goal is to get a ground-breaking product to market before competitors. It is the task of the project managers to familiarize the team with the larger goals and objectives in such a way that they become a source of supplemental motivation while the project is underway and a source of pride when the project has been successfully completed.

Status reporting

Some project managers find status reports to be superfluous and bothersome, since frequent communication by email can provide a written record of issues and resolutions. However, emails can be lost or misfiled. Rigorous written reports of status and issues, including resolutions, milestones, deliveries, and budget changes prevent misunderstanding and obviate the need to rely on memory. It is usually the responsibility of the vendor localization PM to provide status reports to the client PM.

Change management

Many fledgling localization relationships have foundered on scope changes. Changes to project scope usually require that the vendor perform more work, and thus entail an increase in the project budget. Scope changes can lead to budget problems when the client organization does not plan with the vendor in anticipation of such potential changes. Budget problems can be avoided with relative ease by relying on two principles. First, any changes to the scope beyond the budget baseline should be controlled by a mutually agreed-upon process as soon as they have been identified. For example, let us suppose that the vendor finds that the word counts in the files provided by the client for localization are higher than the figures provided in the original RFQ. In this case, the change management process might be as simple as the vendor localization project manager notifying the client localization project manager by email. The PM on the client side would then execute a formal change process. (The increase would also be noted in the next status report provided by the vendor PM to the client PM). Second, the vendor should never perform any work that has not been formally approved, either as part of the project scope baseline, or as part of a change process. In the United States, the provisions of the Sarbanes-Oxley Act of 2002, and more specifically, the rules adopted by the Securities and Exchange Commission to implement the provisions of section 302 of Sarbanes-Oxley, require full financial reporting by publicly traded companies. In order to comply with this rule, many public companies have strict guidelines that explicitly prohibit vendors from working out of contract. Even though many LSPs are not publicly traded, they can protect themselves from potential disagreements with their clients over payment by following a clear, mutually agreed-upon change management process. The change process should include the following steps:

- Checking the purchase order to see if it covers the additional work. If it does, formal guidelines are satisfied, since the PO represents the contract.
- Amending the budget to include the additional amount.
- Initiating an approval process that ends with the vendor receiving authorization to perform the work.

Even if a new purchase order is not required to cover additional work, the change process outlined above will allow the client-side and vendor-side project managers to ensure that their respective scope and budget figures remain identical over the course of the project.

Post-project review

Sometimes things go wrong in a project due to factors beyond the control of either the client-side or vendor-side project manager. The post-project review provides an important opportunity to review both positive and negative aspects of a project in an objective framework in order to improve processes and avoid at least the same problems in future projects. It is also important that both the client and vendor project teams recognize and celebrate their successes.

Measuring success: Reporting

Good project managers produce post-project reports. The PM solicits input from the various stakeholders and compiles a report that captures the essential data about the project and summarizes what went well and what did not go well. Some project managers provide a great deal of detail about what could be improved, and suggest specific corrective actions for future projects. Most managers consider a project successful if it is on time, on budget, and delivered to the agreed-upon level of quality, despite some problems along the way. In addition to these high-level indicators of project success, a number of additional metrics allow the PM to provide a more detailed view of project performance to upper management.

Schedule performance

It may be instructive to see a table of milestone deliveries, both from the client to the vendor and from the vendor back to the client, that shows planned versus actual delivery dates and illustrates any variances. The actual deliveries might deviate from the plan for various reasons; these variances can be analyzed and summarized in the report.

Cost performance

Likewise, it is useful to compare planned versus actual costs. The budgets of most large projects are revised at some point after the baseline is defined, and ideally these changes will have been planned. It should be a goal of client organizations to estimate the project scope, and therefore project costs, as accurately as possible and to improve the accuracy of these estimates over time. Managing change as efficiently as possible to minimize disruption should be a goal of both the client and vendor organizations. A comparison of planned versus actual costs can help to measure the success of these efforts and diagnose the causes of problems (if any).

Quality performance

Quality may be measured in detail or at a more general level. On the client side, quality may be measured during in-country review. It may be possible to capture the number of comments made or errors identified by the reviewer compared to the total number of words reviewed. The vendor organization can be asked to capture this information as part of its implementation of the reviewer's feedback. If the client tests the product within the localization organization, it may be possible to capture the number of defects of various types that are identified, such as translation, internationalization, or functional problems. Many vendors have a process in place for evaluating translations performed by sub-contractors or freelancers. Comprehensive evaluation of all translation is prohibitively time-consuming and expensive, and is performed only in industries where the consequences of translation failure would be catastrophic (i.e., pharmaceuticals and medical device manufacturing). Thus, assessment processes tend to involve spot-checking or sampling. For example, if a subcontractor translates 20,000 words of content, a 500-word or 1,000-word passage may be chosen at random and assessed, and the result treated as being representative of the whole. The PM can document the number of translation defects per X number of words in the final project report.

Volume

The PM can easily track the volume of the project components, which constitute a significant portion of the costs. Component-related statistics include numbers of languages, words, help topics, pages of documentation, or dialog boxes in software – whatever can be counted for costing purposes. In this way, the PM can help quantify the total volume of localization work completed by his or her department or business unit per quarter, year or other fiscal reporting period.

Senior management in client organizations generally understands little about the localization process. But senior management understands numbers. The project manager in a smaller organization can demonstrate business acumen by gathering, recording and reporting project metrics to show positive results, or even to show how better results can be achieved in the future. Larger client-side localization departments track and report such metrics on a regular basis; the vendor-side project manager can provide the base-level information from which the department data are derived, and any client-side PM appreciates a vendor who compiles and presents project performance metrics consistently as part of the working relationship.

Conclusion

Although they share the same title, localization project managers on the client and vendor sides often have quite dissimilar roles. On the client side, the PM often masters multiple parts of the localization process, including translation, use of translation tools, desktop publishing, and even engineering. But the ability of the PM to control the project assets and hand off files to the vendor in a timely and orderly fashion depends on the recognition by stakeholders in other functional units of their obligations and commitment to schedule milestones. On the vendor side, depending on the size of the company, the PM focuses on scope, budget and schedule and relies on other groups in the company for expertise in product of the localization artifacts and for resources to do the work. By understanding their respective positions and constraints, these PMs can work successfully together with the aid of rigorous relationship management tools and processes. Each PM depends on the other, after all, to achieve the desired outcome – projects completed within budget, on time, and to the agreed-upon level of quality.

References

Beninatto, Renato. 2006. "A review of the global translation marketplace." Association of Translation Companies Conference, London, UK, Sep. 21. http://www.atc.org.uk/RenatoBenitatto2006.ppt

Davis, Tony and Pharro, Richard. 2003. *The Relationship Manager: The Next Generation of Project Management*. Burlington, VT: Gower.

Dobson, Michael Singer. 2003. *Streetwise Project Management: How to Manage People, Processes, and Time to Achieve the Results You Need*. Avon, MA: Adams Media.

Farn, Cheng-Kiang and Huang, Li-Ting. 2008. "Exploring determinants of industrial customers loyalty on service providers in the e-business environment – the perspective of relationship management." In *Proceedings of the 7th WSEAS International Conference on E-ACTIVITIES*, Azami Zaharim, Nikos Mastorakis and Ioannis Gonos (eds), 60–67. N.p.: WSEAS.

Fitzgerald, Guy and Willcocks, Leslie. 1994. "Contracts and partnerships in the outsourcing of IT." In *Proceedings of the Fifteenth International Conference on Information Systems: December 14–17, 1994, Vancouver, British Columbia, Canada*, Janice I. DeGross, Sid L. Huff and Malcom C. Munro (eds), 91–98. Victoria, BC: ICIS.

Goles, Tim and Chin, Wynne W. 2005. "Information systems outsourcing relationship factors: Detailed conceptualization and initial evidence." *The DATA BASE for Advances in Information Systems* 36 (4): 47–67.

Greaver, Maurice F. II. 1999. *Strategic Outsourcing: A Structured Approach to Outsourcing Decisions and Initiatives*. New York: AMACOM.

Kern, Thomas. 1997. "The gestalt of an information technology outsourcing relationship: An exploratory analysis." In *Proceedings of the Eighteenth International Conference on Information Systems, December 15–17 1997, Atlanta, Georgia*, Kuldeep Kumar and Janice I. DeGross (eds), 37–58. [N.p.]: ACM.

Kern, Thomas and Willcocks, Leslie. 2001. *The Relationship Advantage: Information Technologies, Sourcing, and Management.* Oxford/New York: Oxford University Press.

Kerzner, Harold. 2003. "Strategic planning for a project office." *Project Management Journal* 34 (2): 13–25.

Konsynski, Benn R. and McFarlan, F. Warren. 1990. "Information partnerships – Shared data, shared scale." *Harvard Business Review* 68 (5): 114–120.

MacDonald, Hugh. 2008. *The Arts of Influence: Soft Power and Distant Relationships.* Victoria, BC: Trafford Publishing.

McFarlan, F. Warren and Nolan, Richard L. 1995. "How to manage an IT outsourcing alliance." *Sloan Management Review* 36 (2): 9–23.

McIlvor, Ronan. 2005. *The Outsourcing Process: Strategies for Evaluation and Management.* Cambridge, UK: New York: Cambridge University Press.

Meier, Johannes. 1995. "The importance of relationship management in establishing successful interorganizational systems." *Journal of Strategic Information Systems* 4 (2): 135–148.

Mersino, Anthony C. 2007. *Emotional Intelligence for Project Managers: The People Skills You Need to Achieve Outstanding Results.* New York: AMACOM.

Project Management Institute (PMI). 2008. *A Guide to the Project Management Body of Knowledge (PMBOK® Guide).* Newtown Square, PA: Project Management Institute, Inc.

Quinn, James Brian. 1999. "Strategic outsourcing: Leveraging knowledge capabilities." *Sloan Management Review* 40 (4): 9–21.

Santana, Joe. 2004. "Decision support: Outsourcing relationship don't stop at negotiations, part 2." *TechRepublic* (Feb. 11). http://articles.techrepublic.com/5100-10878_11-5140304.html

Stading, Gary and Altay, Nezih. 2007. "Delineating the 'ease of doing business' construct within the supplier-customer interface." *Journal of Supply Chain Management* 43 (2): 29–38.

Sun Developer Network (SDN). 2010 [1999–2001]. "Bug ID: 4293299 RFE [Request for Enhancement]: Need better handling/documentation of single quotes in MessageFormat." Sun Developer Network Bug Database. http://bugs.sun.com/bugdatabase/view_bug.do;jsessionid=5d9bbe21b6cb37b7c3ff/11812460?bug_id=4293229

PART IV

Translation and localization project management in action

Managing the challenges of game localization

Ping Zhou

This chapter describes the unique challenges posed by game localization projects. It begins by examining the various activities that comprise a typical multi-platform game localization project. It then situates the localization function in a game publishing corporation and discusses the composition of game localization teams, as well as the respective roles and responsibilities of the team members in a typical game localization project. Next, it examines the relationship between the development and localization functions and discusses the two main approaches to game localization today, namely post-release and simultaneous shipment ("simship") projects. Finally, it explores four project management processes that are especially critical to the successful management of game localization projects: communications management, scope management, risk management and change management.

Introduction

Game localization is a complex endeavor. It typically involves many different media, including text, graphics, video, and audio. Aside from the challenges of localizing the user interface, the storyline and content may need to be modified or even re-created to account for cultural and legal issues. The goal of localizing a game is to provide players in the target market with the information they need to successfully accomplish their interactive journey to the game's conclusion, and to do so seamlessly. Game localization requires a highly organized, flexible and daring team to make each localized title a work of value that helps achieve the company's business objectives.

Game localization projects

Before discussing the challenges of managing game localization, we need to first examine what precisely constitutes a game localization project. A typical multi-platform full game localization project involves the translation of text, modification or re-creation of audio, integration of localized materials into the game, quality assurance, submission to manufacturers, and project administration (see Figure 1).

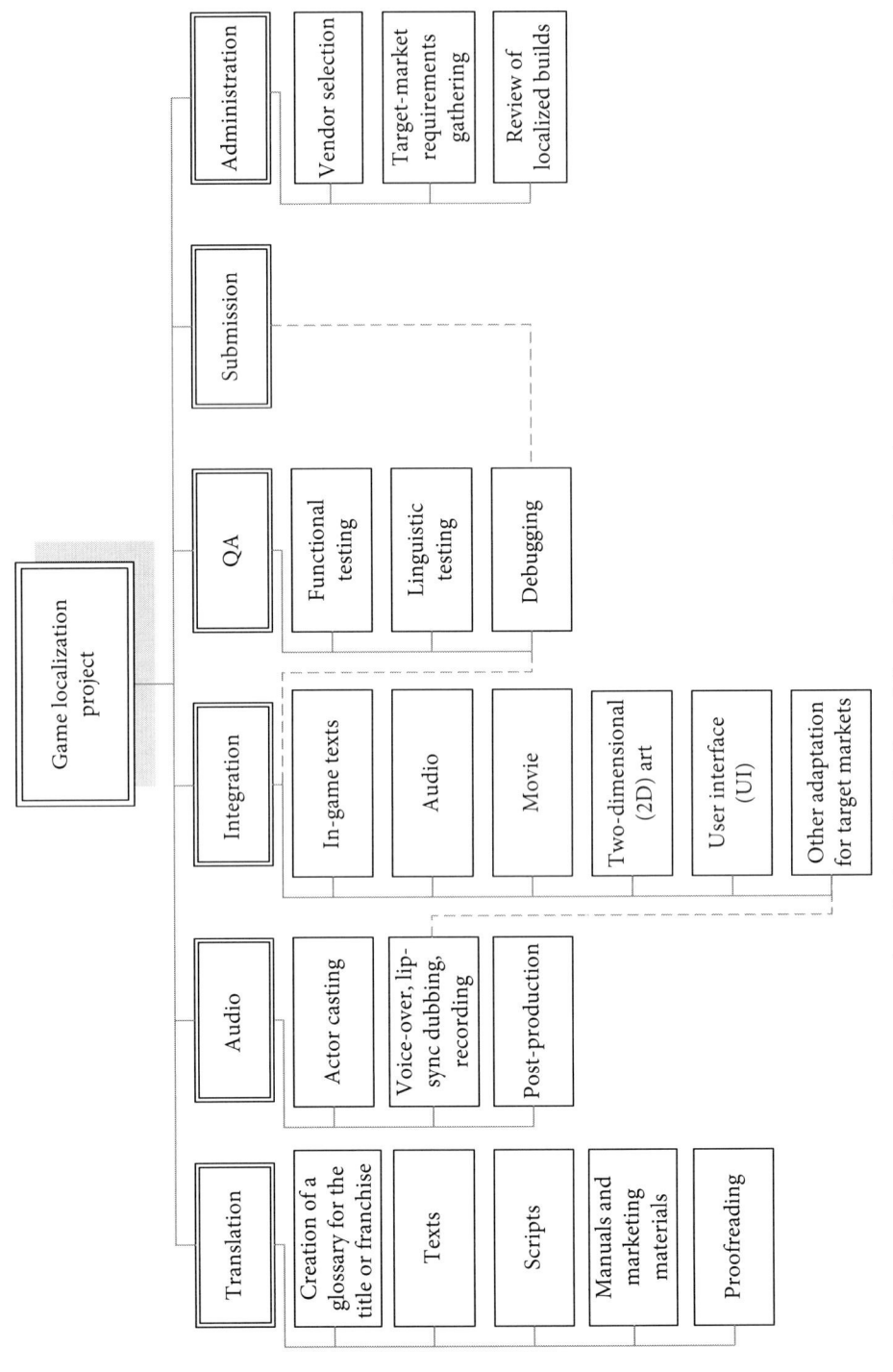

Figure 1. A work breakdown structure (WBS) of a multi-platform full game localization project.

Translation is a central task in game localization. The goal of translation is two-fold. On one hand, it must convey the meaning of the source text accurately in order to provide players with the information they need to navigate through the game. On the other hand, it also needs to convey the experience and atmosphere fostered by the source-language text. "Games create alternate worlds whose relationship to the real world can range from extreme realism to utter fantasy," as Dietz notes (2006: 122). In the case of fantasy games, for example, maintaining the appropriate tone in the target-language text may require translators to "dig deep in the folklore and mythology of the target culture to find an emotional equivalent" for a given term (Dietz 2006: 124). If the text is a script of dialogue spoken by in-game characters, the words used in the translation will need to be chosen carefully to facilitate lip-syncing. Translation is sometimes outsourced to external translation companies. In such cases, localization project managers (LPMs) typically create a glossary for the game title or franchise to help the external vendors ensure accurate and consistent translation.[1] This glossary can be used during both translation and proofreading.

Full game localization projects also involve the modification or replacement of audio files. For example, the dialogue spoken by each source-language character must be re-recorded by an actor (sometimes referred to as "voice talent") performing in the target language to enable target-language narration and dubbing of in-game movies. Usually, the localization project manager (LPM) collaborates with the country specialist to cast actors according to the character requirements and game information provided by the development team in the game design guide. Sometimes voice recording takes place in an external studio. In such cases, the studio outputs the voice files in the required format. Once the voice recording and lip-syncing work has been completed, the audio files enter a post-production phase, during which they are re-mixed with music and/or sound effects (if applicable). Finally, artwork may also require modification for use in localized versions, e.g., if it contains embedded text that requires translation.

Integration involves the merging of all assets that comprise the localized title, including translated texts and localized audio files, movies, artwork and user interface, into the game. If other requirements have been identified for specific target markets, they are addressed and completed during integration.

Following the integration of translated texts and localized audio, QA (also referred to as testing) is performed on the localized version(s) of the game. In many cases, both functional testing and linguistic testing are necessary to ensure that the localized versions of the game are bug-free and of high quality. The goal of functional testing is to confirm that localization has not introduced any problems that prevent successful game play, whereas the goal of linguistic testing is to detect and correct translation errors.

---

1. A franchise may include several titles developed from stories and characters involved in the same plot set, or prequels/sequels developed from the first released storyline.

Following integration and QA, submission is required in the case of console games localization. Console manufacturers such as Sony, Nintendo, and Microsoft require games to be submitted for approval before authorizing their release and use on game machines. Each manufacturer has specific requirements that developers must follow. The console manufacturers perform their own QA to assess the quality of the games and determine whether their own requirements have been met by the game company. If not, the manufacturers will reject the submission and send it back to the localization team to fix bugs or problems. This process continues until the manufacturers are fully satisfied with the game. If a console manufacturer requires separate submission for each target market, then functional testing is performed by the console manufacturers or their designated representative(s) on the submitted localized versions.

Finally, the localization project manager may also be responsible for vendor selection and target-market requirements gathering (in collaboration with the country specialists). In the case of virtual teams, the LPM will also manage the review of the localized game builds. Last but not least, any game localization project also includes daily and routine administrative tasks such as budgeting and invoicing.

Organization of the localization function in a game publishing corporation

In a multinational game publishing and development corporation, a typical localization group is staffed with project managers, country specialists, and localization engineers (see Figure 2). Occasionally, the localization team may include internal graphic artists, translators and testers to supplement external vendors on urgent projects and to solve problems on the fly. The team members are usually located around the world and work remotely.

Localization project manager (LPM)

The localization project manager (LPM) orchestrates and oversees the deliveries of all of the different localized versions of the title. Often the LPM is responsible for several titles. She or he takes on the challenges of planning, scheduling, budgeting, actor and voice talent casting, vendor management, quality assurance, and technology support for each title to be localized. The LPM is the single point of contact for external and internal stakeholders and sponsors for all issues and decisions concerning the various localized versions of the title(s) that he or she is managing. Given the trend in the industry to release games in an increasing number of locales worldwide, the LPM sometime contributes to the development of global strategy with respect to titles.

Managing the challenges of game localization 353

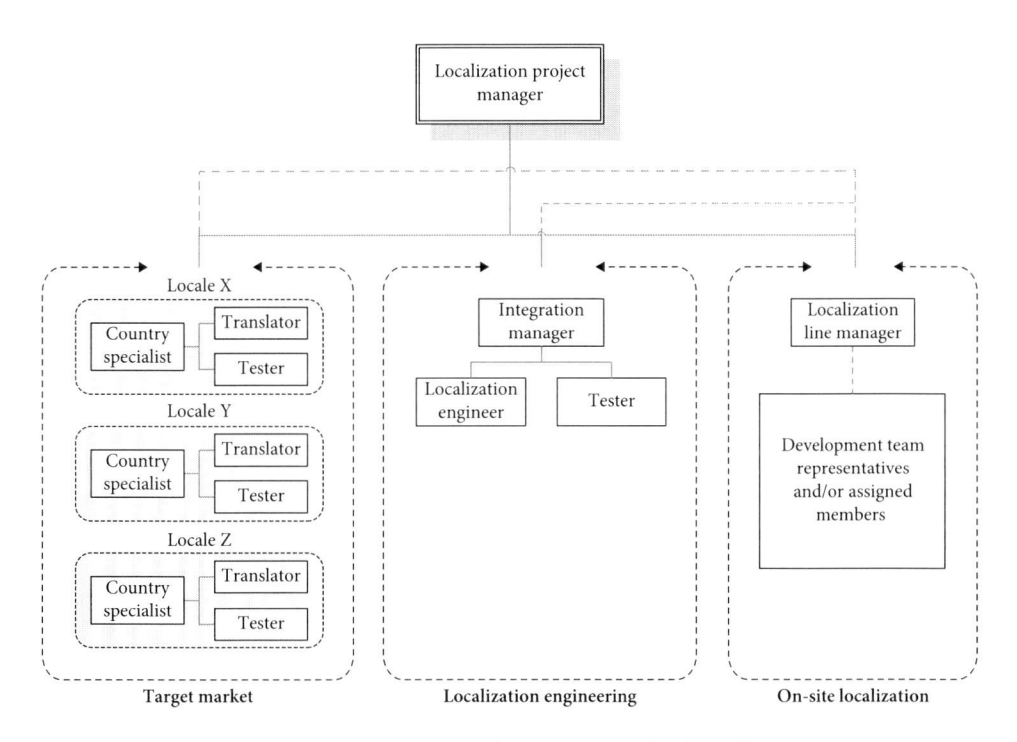

Figure 2. Composition of a typical game localization team. The dotted lines represent both functional differentiation and spatial distance, as the three groups have different roles and work in different locations.

Country specialist

The country specialist is a secondary project manager who coordinates the language versions to be released in his or her country or territory. She or he usually resides locally and is the designated expert on local language, culture, legal and regulatory requirements, as well as events happening in that country or territory. She or he may specify certain requirements accordingly. For example, it may be difficult to obtain approval to release a game in Japan when the plot involves a North Korean missile launch and real-world tensions are building between the two countries. Such was the case with the title *Tom Clancy's Ghost Recon 2*.[2] The FIGS (French, Italian, German, Spanish) versions of the title were released in November, 2004 and the Japanese

---

2. In August 1998, North Korea tested a long-range missile that flew over Japanese territory without Japan's permission, provoking an international furor and causing profound anxiety in Japan. These tensions were exacerbated by a major North Korean military buildup in the first half of 2000.

version was ultimately released in August 2005. To take another example, Japanese players might view the introduction of *seppuku* (a form of ritual suicide by disembowelment that was part of the samurai honor code) into a modern plot involving Japanese characters as an anachronistic, comical or ridiculous depiction of contemporary Japanese culture. This issue arose during the localization of titles in the series *Tom Clancy's Splinter Cell*.

The country specialist arranges the translation of user interface strings, messages, scripts for spoken dialog and other non-screen content, as well as proofreading, testing, local actor casting and voice recording. The country specialist also ensures that the content is appropriate for the target country and that the quality of the localized version meets the standards set for the title.

Localization engineer

The localization engineer solves technical issues (which are generally related to the user interface), integrates localized assets, and releases localized builds.[3] When country-specific localization requirements necessitate modification of core game technologies, the localization engineer may need additional support (i.e., staff assistance) to implement the necessary changes. If the country-specific requirements are approved, the LPM will likely have to recruit resources from the development team to make up for the shortage of specialized engineering talent on the localization team. Since not all localization sites are staffed with game development personnel, some companies gather the localization engineering team in one or several fixed locations that include a game development studio and a development team. Doing so is efficient as it allows the companies to avoid duplication of work needed to support the various localized versions.

Usually, the country specialist and the localization engineer each report to their own functional managers. On project matters, they may report either to the LPM or to their direct managers, who coordinate and oversee all ongoing projects. The workflow, responsibilities and roles of the country specialist and localization engineer may vary depending on the type of localization process adopted for the project.

Integration manager

The integration manager oversees multiple localization projects that require technical solutions. The integration manager is responsible for ensuring that all translated texts, localized audio files, movies and artwork can be successfully built into the

---

3. Wikipedia (2010b) defines a build as "the process of converting source code files into stand-alone software artifact(s) that can be run on a computer, or the result of doing so. One of the most important steps of a software build is the compilation process where source code files are converted into executable code."

localized versions of the game. In addition, if country specialists request additional modifications to the game, the integration manager investigates whether it is feasible to implement these changes. A multinational game company may designate several sites located close to development teams and target markets as integration centers. These centers can leverage technology produced by offshore development teams and/or benefit from their cultural proximity to the target markets.

Development and localization

Games are comprised of content and the technology that presents the content to players and that controls the sequence of the game. Content is created by graphic artists, audio designers, animators, as well as game and level designers, and may take the form of game levels, characters, animations, and movies.[4] Technology is the executable code that is read by the computer (or console or other device) on which the game is played. Executable game code is created using programming languages or scripts, and developed by engineers in order to bring characters to life, assemble content and enable players to progress logically through the game storyline, scenes and levels (scenes) of the plot as designed. The code is not modified unless a target market requires the implementation of specific features or changes to specific features. Thus, the majority of localization tasks focus on content. Once the development of the source version of a game is nearing completion and it is agreed that no additional changes will be made to the source code, the title is said to be "code complete." The title undergoes release to manufacturing (RTM) when all of the source files have passed final testing and are deemed ready for distribution to resellers and customers, whether on CD, on DVD, or via download. The final deliverable sometimes takes the form of a so-called "gold master" disc that is used for mass production.

Post-release and simship localization

Localization projects that start after the gold master of the source version has been created are called "post-release" projects. Conversely, localization projects performed in parallel with the source version development to enable the simultaneous shipment of the source and target versions are called "simship" projects (see Figure 3).

When localized versions are shipped simultaneously with the original, the game development team integrates localization into the development plans and typically implements support for the localized versions as "features." In this scenario, the

---

4. Wikipedia (2010a) defines a game level as "a discrete subdivision of a video game's virtual world or set of challenges."

356   Ping Zhou

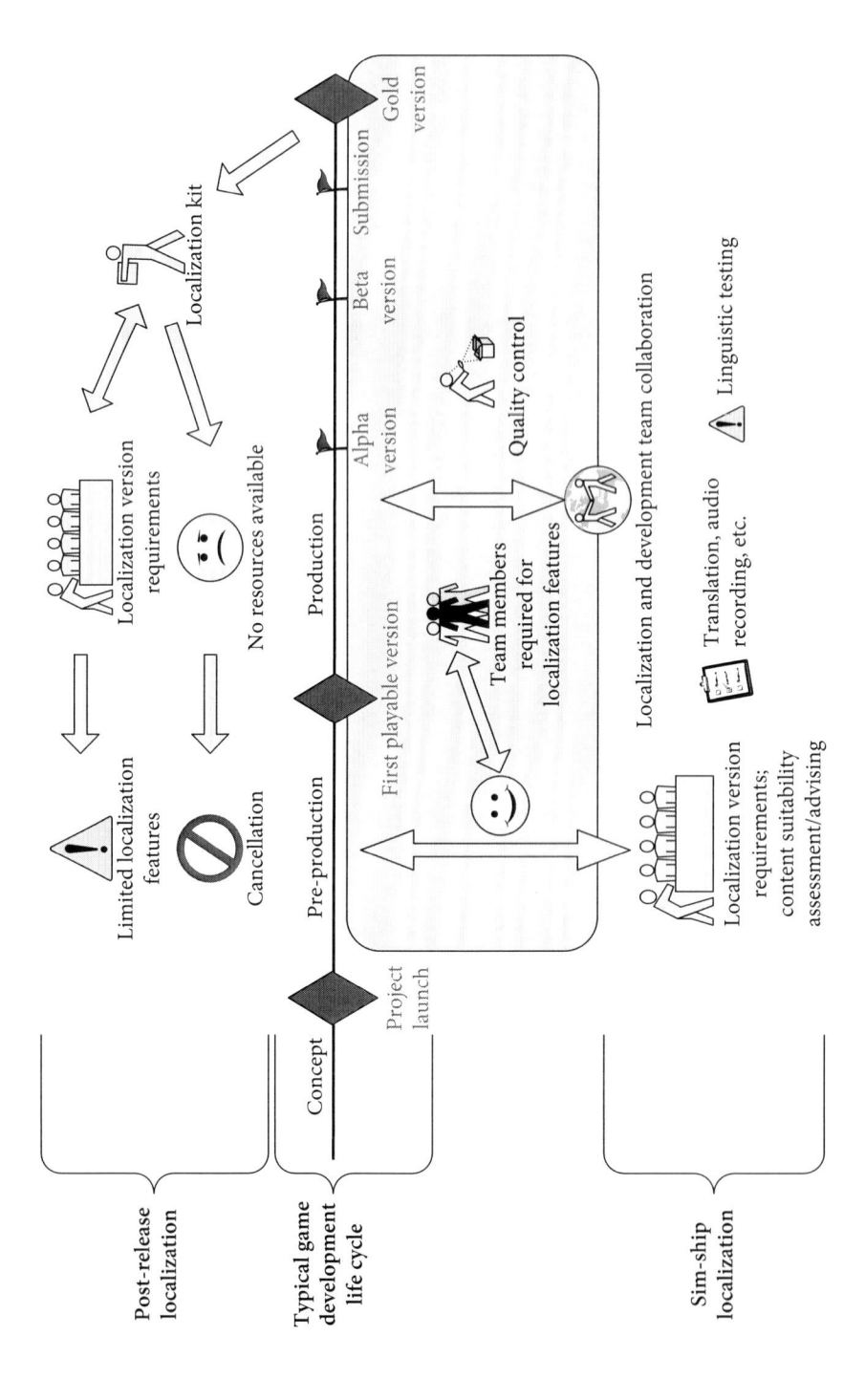

Figure 3. Simship localization is performed in parallel with the development of the source version, whereas post-release localization follows development.

localization team is a functional entity unto itself within the larger organization, much like Art, Engineering, Design, and QA, and the localization project schedule will share many project milestones with the development schedule.

Post-release localization
In a post-release scenario, the localization kit is created from the gold master of the game. The localization kit serves as the foundation for all of the different localized versions. In a post-release localization project, it is difficult to alter anything that would require changes to the design of the game or artwork or to add features requiring modifications to the game technology because the development team has moved on to other projects by the time localization begins. The development team's schedule typically leaves very little room for country specialists to request locale-specific enhancements; in similar fashion, the localization team is generally left to its own devices when it comes to resolving problems. If the localization team discovers errors in the source materials, or content that would be culturally inappropriate for one or more of the target locales, the localization schedule will need to be modified to give the team sufficient time to make the necessary modifications to the materials. In a worst-case scenario, the discovery of such issues may force the cancelation of the project. As a general rule, the ability of the localization team to successfully and smoothly create the target versions depends first and foremost on the quality of the localization kit and the adaptability of the original game. A country specialist may identify a significant number of enhancements for the product to be released in a given locale, but if the localization team has to rely on its own engineering and creative capacities to fulfill country-specific requirements, it is likely that those requirements will be unfulfilled or at best partially fulfilled. Publishers may invest into promising language versions by retaining necessary development team resources to work on the localization project for a while. However, post-release is not the optimal approach to complicated localization projects because it forces the localization team to address problems when it is often too late to effectively resolve them.

Simship localization
The simultaneous release or simship approach addresses some of the disadvantages of post-release localization. In a simship scenario, the LPM works with the producer at an early stage of the development project even though localization will not begin until after the completion of the Alpha milestone (defined as the point at which all content has been completed and game can be played through without major bugs).

If the LPM is responsible for managing the localization of several titles simultaneously and if she or he does not work at the same site as the development team, an additional on-site localization line manager may be assigned to work with the development team in the LPM's stead and oversee the simship versions of the franchise or title (i.e., the product "line") (see Figure 2). The on-site manager has a better chance of influencing the development team and convincing the producer to consider and implement localization requirements during development because he or she is able to communicate with these stakeholders face to face. Support for both fundamental and market- or locale-specific localization requirements can be built into game technology more easily before the development of the technology has been completed than after.[5] In this way, localization engineering can be shifted to the development team, and the localization team can focus on linguistic and cultural issues.

The game development team can also benefit from the presence of an on-site localization line manager. For example, if the game has multiple plots and country- and/or culture-specific requirements, e.g., a non-player character (NPC) speaks a local dialect, the development team can seek prompt support from the on-site localization manager. Adopting a simship approach to localization and development enables high production value and high quality in all localized versions of the game.

In theory, the simship process allows for the release of multiple language versions at the same time. However, in practice, human and financial resource constraints often limit the number of versions that a publisher can release simultaneously. In such situations, publishers typically prioritize the development of the various localized versions based on the commercial importance of the corresponding markets. For example, let us suppose that a producer considers the EMEA region (Europe, Middle East and Africa) and the United States to be the most important markets. In this case, in order to ensure that the versions for the most important markets are shipped safely under resource constraints, the producer may decide that the initial simship release will include only English, French, German, Italian and Spanish, and will exclude other versions from the initial development scope, which specifies how many languages will be supported as well as the relative priority of each. This does not mean that the LPM has to adopt a post-release process when localizing the remaining versions, e.g., Japanese, Chinese, etc., which are planned but deemed to be a lower priority. The LPM can still schedule the localization of these versions to be done in parallel with the core simship versions, for example by assembling an off-site team that is not comprised of development project personnel to work on the remaining versions simultaneously. Although this team will not have direct access to the development team, the on-site localization manager can effectively provide the latest game content assets, like in-game texts, scripts, and the newest compiled builds, as well as immediate status updates to the off-site team. If managed well, the remaining versions still can be shipped together with the source and core simship versions or shortly thereafter.

---

5. Fundamental localization requirements refer to capabilities that the game technology must possess to be deemed localizable. Unicode support and the externalization of linguistically and culturally bound content from source code are two common examples of fundamental localization requirements. Market- or locale-specific localization requirements refer to aspects of the content, such as the prohibition against addressing certain subjects in a given country to avoid potential censorship problems.

The discussion of the localization function and processes thus far has focused on some of the ways in which the LPM and the localization team interact with *internal* project resources and stakeholders. The LPM or country specialist also needs external vendors for translation of user interface content, voice dubbing, and linguistic testing. Vendor management begins with the selection of appropriate external partners. The LPM may define general or global criteria for vendor selection for all projects. Vendors that meet these criteria can be added to a vendor pool. The LPM can then select appropriate vendors for a given project based on the specific requirements of that project. For example, in the case of a military simulation, the LPM might search for a vendor that has military translation experience. After selecting the vendor, the LPM needs to develop a process to ensure problem-free receipt of rolling deliveries. If working on a simship project, the LPM should consider integrating the vendor workflow in the internal process.

Managing game localization projects is extremely challenging. However, by implementing proper project management processes, the LPM can overcome these challenges and successfully complete complex, demanding projects. Four processes are particularly important: (a) communications management; (b) scope management; (c) risk management; and (d) change management. In the sections that follow, we will examine each of these processes in turn.

Communications management

A LPM reports to both his or her business unit manager as well as to the producer of the title(s) being localized. Conversely, multiple people report to the LPM, including country specialists and localization engineers, the number of whom may increase in proportion to the number of projects the LPM is managing. The LPM also interacts with producers, upper management, and vendors. Managing communication in such an environment can be a complicated and challenging process. However, the use of certain tools can facilitate communication within a localization team.

Localization wiki

The creation of a localization wiki enables the in-house localization team to share information with other groups in the company as well as team members working remotely.[6] When working on a simship project, the development team's project wiki can be used

---

6. For information on setting up a wiki, see wikiHow (2010). In addition to wikis, an increasing number of companies are using Microsoft Sharepoint as a collaboration platform. Note that as a general rule, the LPM does not actually set up the wiki site, but merely maintains it and adds localization-related information as it becomes available.

to address project-specific localization issues and can serve as the foundation for a localization knowledge base. A localization wiki can be used to store schedules, staffing plans, design documents, status reports, updates on target-country regulations, policies, news, pop culture, history and any other information deemed useful by the localization team. This resource is accessible to all team members and stakeholders 24/7 regardless of their geographical location, and can be updated on a rolling basis so that it always contains the most recent information. A localization wiki can also help the development team learn about the target markets in which their game is going to be released. Along similar lines, the wiki can serve as a reference for game designers to help them avoid creating content that will be challenging or even impossible to localize. In sum, investing in the creation of such a resource offers immediate benefits during a given project by enabling decentralized, on-demand information transfer via a centralized platform. On the other hand, a localization wiki also offers benefits to localization efforts over time as the scale, scope and volume of material in the wiki expand, and as more and more of the knowledge captured in the wiki is put to use by development teams.

Reporting

In addition to creating a passive resource such as a wiki, the LPM can manage communications by sending weekly or bi-weekly reports to project stakeholders and sponsors. Such reports may include highlights of project status, risks, deliveries, emerging trends as to whether the project is ahead of or behind schedule and/or over or under budget, as well as information about and news from the target market. For busy people, important information can be provided in graphical or summarized format so that it that takes little time to read but still brings them up to speed on the project status.

A mailing list can be created to expedite information exchange between team members. Likewise, specific mailing lists can also be created to enable prompt communication with project stakeholders and/or sponsors. The creation and use of different project mailing lists for different stakeholder groups facilitates directed communication and shortens the localization process.

Written communication is a particularly effective way to stay in touch for teams and stakeholders that are dispersed around the world. In some countries, people feel more comfortable communicating in writing. In addition, many game localization team members and stakeholders are not native speakers of English, and in this respect, written communication offers a major advantage over spoken communication in that it is devoid of accent interference. However, when an urgent situation arises, written communication may not enable the sender to reach the receiver(s) quickly enough, so the project communication plan should not be confined merely to written communication.

Indeed, written communication connects team members that are geographically dispersed, but there are limits to the connections that can be forged in writing.

As the project progresses, it will be necessary to carry out team building activities in order to foster camaraderie and to further develop the team. Likewise, clients and upper management may at some point require more than written status reports, and may request a face-to-face meeting and/or debriefing. So in addition to providing written communication, the LPM can proactively anticipate these interactive real-time communication needs by arranging to hold phone or video conference calls to discuss project status, schedules, issues and resolutions with clients and management, and in so doing, reassure them. Similar meetings can also be an effective way of managing vendors' progress. The LPM, being in the position of client, can conduct face-to-face reviews with vendors. If some localization team members and stakeholders are in different locations, the LPM can also use conference calls to kick off the project, formally present team members to each other and explain their respective roles and responsibilities. Subsequent conference calls enable the LPM to obtain project status updates, discuss risks and risk response strategies, as well as issues and resolutions, and so forth.

Game localization requires that communication be intensive and detailed, but also diplomatic and proactive throughout the project lifecycle. Establishing communication on such a level can help LPM successfully manage the constant changes that characterize simship projects and help sponsors and stakeholders understand the nature of the difficulties that may arise during post-release localization projects, such as censorship due to the inclusion of inappropriate content.

Scope management

According to the Project Management Institute, project scope management "includes the processes required to ensure that the project includes all the work required, and only the work required, to complete the project successfully" (PMI 2008:103). Complete and proper scope definition can make or break a project. If the scope is not defined with sufficient precision, if the LPM, management and client do not confirm their shared understanding of the scope, if uncontrolled changes are made to the project scope (a phenomenon known as "scope creep" in industry), or if the scope is unmanageable to begin with, there is a strong risk that what is delivered will fail to meet management's and/or the client's expectations. Most project failures ultimately stem from a flawed scope definition and/or scope management failure.

First and foremost, when defining the project scope, the LPM should collaborate with all stakeholders. This will require working with target market representatives, usually country specialists, to gather and document requirements on specific content and linguistic needs and to reach agreement on the final deliverables. All concepts must be clearly defined and all needs clearly identified. The acceptance criteria for project deliverables should be agreed upon by all stakeholders, and everyone should share the same vision of the result to be created and the work to be done in order for the project to be deemed successful.

Second, the goal of scope definition should be to capture *needs*, not the *implementation* of the solution for meeting those needs. For example, displaying target market publisher credits is a need. Adding the names of all the people who worked on the game to the original credits movie is the implementation. As the project goes on, it might be discovered that the source file for the credits movie either does not exist or cannot be edited, but that a new one can be created to display the names. Either way – modification of the existing credits movie file or the creation of a new one – allows the display of the new credits. Identifying needs rather than implementation allows the LPM to understand and define fundamental requirements.

Third, needs must be described concisely and unambiguously. Let us consider the example of displaying target market publisher credits discussed above. The LPM probably wants to specify in the scope statement where the localization team credits should be added (but, as noted above, not *how* they should be added), i.e., before, after or in the middle of the development team credits, as doing so will prevent unnecessary arguments about the location of the added credits at the time of delivery.

Lastly, it is necessary to identify internal and external constraints and assumptions that may have an impact on the scope and potentially result in changes to the deliverables, e.g., regulations, standards, laws, and other factors. Although the identification of such factors is technically the domain of risk management, it provides insight into the potential for scope creep and should be included in the formal project scope document. Otherwise, the LPM may face a never-ending project.

As discussed above, game localization deliverables typically include in-game text and audio, subtitles, user interface (UI) strings, graphics, and movies (see Figure 1). In addition, the printed game manual and marketing materials may be part of the deliverables. When defining the scope of a game localization project, the project manager must decompose the deliverables to (a) identify and estimate the volume of translatable text and other localizable content, (b) assess the cultural appropriateness of the content, and (c) determine whether localization will require modification of the core game technology. Determining the relative volume of work in these three areas will help the project manager better understand the degree of complexity of the project.

Scope definition and localization complexity

As part of the scope definition process, the LPM should ask probing questions of the development team producer, product manager, marketing manager, country specialist, and localization engineer. The relative degree of complexity will give an experienced LPM a good general idea of the needs of these stakeholders. Thayer and Kolko (2004: 482) propose a three-tiered scale for classifying game localization projects according to their relative degree of complexity and cost:

1. *Basic localization:* The game retains its original GUI and icons, leaving only the text to be translated.
2. *Complex localization:* The GUI and icons must be translated along with the text.
3. *Blending:* The story itself is rewritten, and the graphics are recreated to match the requirements of a different culture.

The scale proposed by Thayer and Kolko is a useful starting point. However, there is not a significant difference in the complexity of what they term "basic" and "complex" localization projects, provided that the source files have been properly internationalized and contain no hard-coded strings. Today, hard-coded strings are generally a non-issue when localizing titles produced by mainstream game publishing companies. From the perspective of game localization project management, complexity is more accurately gauged by assessing whether localization will require functional modifications to the game, such as the addition and/or removal of features, changes to multimedia content, and so forth. Thus, for the purpose of this discussion, we will differentiate between only two types of game localization projects: basic localization projects, which do not entail functional modifications, and complex projects, which do.

Basic localization
Basic localization typically focuses on text translation with the goal of fulfilling the same informative purpose as the original. Care must be taken, however, to not translate any text whose entry is required for game functionality. For example, if a text message pops up and tells the players to enter the word "lion" to open a trap door, the word "lion" should not be translated into the target language. Otherwise, if the word is translated, the game engine will not recognize the target-language input as the key word "lion," and thus will not execute the required action, preventing the players from progressing any further in the game. (Such errors that effectively end game play are referred to as "showstoppers.") The translation should maintain the same style and "feel" as the original text, while at the same time being adapted for the target market culture. For example, if one is localizing a medieval real-time strategy (RTS) game, the reference to an army officer of a specific rank can be replaced with an analogous reference to a rank in a military hierarchy from the target country, using terms and idiomatic expressions from that time period as well. The players may feel close and/or become attached to the story and the action that the game tries to sell. The voice-over should match the character's facial animation. When translating the script, one must strive to enable a sequence of target-language mouth movements that replicate as closely as possible those of the source dialogue while also ensuring that the text remains informative.

Complex localization
Complex localization requires that both content and functionality be altered to bring the game culturally closer to the target market. The game technology must support such alterations. Such support is not confined to double-byte character enablement

or Unicode support for the user interface, but can potentially expand to every area of the source code if features need to be altered or added. Complex localization projects sometimes require major re-work. The LPM can fully rely on the team to handle basic localization engineering tasks, but if major rework is required that exceeds the scope of localization engineering, additional development resources may need to be recruited. So when defining the scope of complex localization projects, it is important to evaluate the availability of development resources. If the LPM is working on a post-release localization project, the development team usually has already been assigned to other projects by the time localization begins, as noted above. Absent a jack (or jill) of all trades on the localization team, the lack of available development resources may jeopardize the team's ability to complete work on some of the game functions. For example, if subtitles are required for the target market but the source version of the product does not support subtitles, an event triggering mechanism (or other means of enabling subtitles) will need to be retrofitted into the architecture of the game. In such cases, the LPM may need to arrange an Artificial Intelligence (AI) engineer, an audio engineer, and a level designer to enable the implementation of subtitles. The LPM and the team members can study the localization kit and play the game to help them decide whether the localization team can perform the necessary functional modification without in the use of external resources. Once a determination has been made, the LPM should discuss it with the stakeholders and finalize the scope.

Simship is better suited to complex localization projects than the post-release approach. The LPM should hold discussions with the game producer at the development stage so that localization needs can be identified and be included in the scope of the game development project. In a simship project, the scope of the game is not yet completely defined at the beginning of the development phase. Consequently, the LPM can only provide a rough overall estimate of the localization scope at the beginning of the source development project. However, as the development progresses and the scope of the game is clarified and finalized, the LPM will gradually develop a more precise understanding of the game and can progressively update the localization scope definition. If the localization scope is included in the development project, the implementation of adapted target game features and content will be simpler.

Finally, once the scope has been defined, a scope change management process should also be defined. Change management is one facet of risk management, which will be discussed in the following section.

Risk management

Risk management, which is typically planned during the project initiation phase, is a systematic, proactive and ongoing process that aims to manage project uncertainty (Wideman 1992; Stoeller 2004). The goals of risk management are to minimize or eliminate the negative impact from threats and maximize the positive influence from opportunities. Making risk management an integral part of project activities throughout the duration of the project offers numerous benefits. Risk management can help the project manager improve the probability of achieving project objectives, namely completing the project within budget, on time, and according to pre-defined quality requirements. During game production, unforeseen tasks often need to be completed due to the creative nature of the project, the frequency of change during game development, as well as the complexity of the cooperation between the technology, art, and design teams. The degree of uncertainty is such that teams must often perform extra work beyond what was originally planned to meet defined milestones. The period the precedes milestones and especially the final delivery has come to be known colloquially in game development circles as "crunch" time, during which everybody works harder, faster and longer in order to achieve the milestone. Risk management can maximize the chances of successful milestones and project deliveries, and can also help the project manager create a more confident and happier team by reducing the likelihood of crunch time and situations in which the team members are constantly putting out fires. By demonstrating successful risk control strategies, the project team can earn the trust of stakeholders and sponsors.

Regardless of whether the target versions of the product are to be delivered simultaneously or after the original version has already been released, risk management is crucial to the successful introduction of the localized titles into the target markets. In some cases, risk management may also be critical to the achievement of the financial goals defined for the title and the implementation of the overall global strategy of the title. Certain risk factors, such as the cultural appropriateness of the game content for the target market, might affect critical decisions, such as project launch or cancelation determinations, budgets, and staffing. It is the project manager's responsibility to formulate and present a practical and sufficient localization-related risk plan to the stakeholders during the early phases of the project.

In a simship project, because localization is integrated into the development plans and the localization team is treated as a functional entity unto itself similar to Art, Engineering, Design, and QA, as noted above, the localization team will be invited to participate in risk planning meetings, during which localization-related issues will be recorded. The localization team will be assigned the responsibility for localization-related risk mitigation by the producer. Since the producer is in charge of risk management for the entire project, she or he plays a critical role in determining how the identified localization risks should be addressed. One of the more important responsibilities of the LPM during simship projects is to produce a risk plan and discuss it with other team leaders and members early in the project, and proactively develop the preliminary plan in order to assist the producer with development of an accurate and realistic project risk plan.[7]

---

7. Team leaders (often referred to as "team leads") are members who represent a given specialty within the game development team, such as artificial intelligence, game play, etc. Unlike project managers, team leaders do not manage schedules.

By way of contrast, during a post-release project the game development team is usually not involved in the production of localized versions of a title, as noted above. The game's producer may be knowledgeable about the target countries, but she or he will not consider localization part of the project scope, or at most will treat localization-related issues as a lower priority. Thus, in a post-release localization scenario, the requirements and potential risks for the target-language versions will most likely not have been addressed during the development of the source version of the product. In post-release projects, the LPM will begin drafting a risk management plan when she or he receives the initial localization kit and will work closely with marketing and product managers to manage risks throughout the project.

Risk management processes include risk identification, analysis, planning, monitoring and controlling.

Risk identification

The goal of risk identification is to reveal uncertainties that exist in the project. To identify risks in a game localization project the LPM may consider looking at variables such as technology, content, resources, team morale, budget, planning, communication, scope, quality requirements, submission requirements, the vendor organization, regulations, the target culture, the political situation in the target market, and current events. The identification of risks in some areas (i.e., target culture) may require specialized, in-depth knowledge, and thus consultation with experts. The identification of certain risks may involve more assumptions and/or estimates than others. Some risks may be identified before the localization kit is received, whereas other may only be identified after the localization kit has been received and assessed. The LPM can encourage the team to brainstorm to identify risks. The LPM can also review "lessons learned" reports created during previous projects to identify potential risks. Although projects are unique, similar types of game localization projects present similar types of risks. By gathering as much information as possible from stakeholders, the LPM can avoid overlooking significant activities during risk identification and overlooking risks as a result. The output of the risk identification process is a comprehensive risk list for subsequent analysis.

Risk analysis

The purpose of risk analysis is to classify each risk in the list by identifying its root cause, evaluating the probability that the risk event will occur, determining the severity of the impact if the risk event does in fact occur, and finally, ranking risks in terms of their priority (see Figure 4). (See Lammers in this volume for a detailed discussion of risk management.) The LPM and team should approach risk analysis from different angles to more thoroughly evaluate and understand the individual risks.

Risks are not necessarily negative: risks that share the same root cause may bring both threats and opportunities. For example, let us suppose that an in-game character setting is deemed inappropriate and subjected to censorship in the target market. Adapting the setting after the fact to resolve this problem will cause a schedule delay. Extra tasks and resources will need to be added to the schedule in order to create a replacement for this character. However, this problem also represents an opportunity to attract local players by replacing the existing "foreign" character with one that is familiar in the target market.

Risk matrix		Probability		
		HIGH	MEDIUM	LOW
Impact	MAJOR	1 (critical)	3 (high)	6 (medium)
	AVERAGE	2 (high)	5 (medium)	8 (low)
	MINOR	4 (medium)	7 (low)	9 (low)

Figure 4. A sample risk matrix.

Risks can stem from both external and internal factors. Internal risk factors are risks that are theoretically within the company's power to control. An example of an internal risk would be the creation of a project schedule that requires extensive or continuous team overtime, posing a threat to team morale. Frequent changes to the schedule made in response to shifting requirements or timelines provided by stakeholders outside the localization team requiring extensive or continuous overtime would be another example of an internal risk. This latter risk is quite common in simship projects. Conversely, external risk factors are risks that are theoretically not within the company's power to control, such as political turmoil, power failures and natural disasters. A high quality evaluation with priorities and classification is valuable for effective risk response planning if it is based on thorough analysis performed from a variety of perspectives, reflecting the concerns of various stakeholders.

Risk planning

Risk planning involves deciding what should be done about the identified risks and implementing strategies to carry out those actions. Several strategies can be employed to reduce risks, such as transfer, avoidance, mitigation and contingency planning.

When risk is transferred, it is shifted to a third party. This strategy is used by an LPM when the team does not have adequate resources or lacks certain expertise. For example, moving the functional implementation of localization-specific requirements from the scope of the localization project to the scope of the development project would be an example of transfer, as it shifts the responsibility for meeting these requirements from the localization team to the development team.

As its name suggests, risk avoidance involves taking steps to avoid encountering risks during the project lifecycle. Examples of this strategy would include the termination of a project if the risk would preclude successful project completion, or changing vendors if they do not possess the requisite technical skills.

Mitigation entails the acceptance of risks and the identification of ways to reduce their impact. An example of this strategy would include the selection of backup vendors who meet the project qualification criteria to address unforeseen problems whose resolution would require more work than the project team is able to perform. In a post-release localization project, this might entail the selection of vendors who are able to add features required for localization in the event that in-house development specialists are unavailable to perform the work. This would enable the project manager (and by extension, the organization as a whole) to avoid releasing a final product that is less attractive to users in the target market(s).

Contingency planning involves "the development of a management plan that identifies alternative strategies to be used to ensure project success if specified risk events occur" (Field 2002). An example of a contingency plan would be the identification of additional or backup vendors. In the event that a selected vendor is unable to complete the project, the LPM can implement the contingency plan and assign a backup vendor to the task.

Once the risk response strategies have been identified, the LPM can assign an owner to each risk. Ownership assignment identifies not only who will implement the strategy and carry out the requisite task(s), but also who will pay the bill for implementing the strategy. Let us suppose that a change to the design of the game requires re-work on a voice-over recording. In order to meet the original milestone, the LPM must request that the team and the vendors work overtime. This overtime will in turn require additional budget to pay for the overtime. This extra budget should be accounted for in advance.

Another important aspect of risk management is efficient risk-related communication. First, the risk owners need to know their responsibilities. Second, the team and stakeholders need to be aware of the risks in order to help reduce their impact and also to avoid reporting duplicates when identifying new risks. A best-practices approach is to include risk topics in the project communication plan, add risk review to team meeting agendas, and/or include a risk dashboard in weekly reports. When the risk plan is ready, continuous tracking and iteration can be started. It is important to note here that although the project risk management plan may identify dozens of risks, only critical risk events, such as an increase in the project budget or a delay in project milestones, should be communicated to project sponsors.

Risk monitoring and controlling

Risk monitoring and controlling is the process of ensuring that existing risks are being tracked and addressed appropriately and also that any new risks identified over the course of the project are being managed as well. Tracking *risks* differs from tracking *tasks*. Risk tracking focuses on the current situation and risk trends that become apparent, but ignores the status of the tasks associated with those risks. Risk monitoring and controlling seeks to answer a number of questions: Has the risk disappeared? Have mitigation strategies reduced the threats? In so doing, have they also created secondary risks? Has the priority ranking of the various risks changed? Has the estimated impact of the risks changed? By answering these questions and updating the risk management plan, the localization project manager will have a clear view and good control of the various identified risks as the project progresses.

The whole risk management process may at first look quite complicated. However, it is quite a straightforward practice in game localization projects. The LPM can schedule periodic risk meetings. The LPM can ask each attendee to identify their top three new risks prior to the initial meeting. During the first meeting, the LPM can complete the initial processes of identification, analysis and planning together with the rest of the team members, and a risk matrix similar to the one in Figure 4 can be used to prioritize risks identified by attendees. The LPM can then request that risk owners review the status of their risks and identify new risks prior to subsequent meetings. During the subsequent meetings, the team can discuss and address any new risks, and perform monitoring and controlling as well. Advance preparation will save everyone time during these meetings.

The LPM can create a spreadsheet in which to log risk identification, prioritization, planning, monitoring and controlling information. The document should be made accessible to all stakeholders on a shared network or through a wiki, and should be used during the risk meetings. The file can include but is not necessarily limited to the following information:

- Source of each risk (i.e., technology, content, resources, the vendor organization, budget, target market regulations, scope, quality, submission, etc.)
- Risk description
- Ranking from the risk matrix (see Figure 4)
- Analysis
- Response plan
- Priority
- Monitoring frequency
- Owner
- Status

- Date of the first identification
- Date of the most recent assessment
- Deadline for a decision about the strategy to be adopted or for the implementation of that strategy

After the meeting, the LPM should distribute the spreadsheet to the team members and other stakeholders. Alternatively, a separate report can be written highlighting the new risks and the most critical existing risks that includes a link to the complete risk log. When preparing weekly reports for sponsors, the LPM should include information about the most important risks, status information, and risk-related deadlines. The aforementioned strategies enable the effective management of risks associated with game localization projects.

Change management

Change is inevitable in any type of project, but is especially prominent in game localization. In the realm of game development, upper management almost always defines innovation as *the* key strategy. As customers are exposed to ever more options in the marketplace, a game company must evolve constantly and rapidly to stand out from the crowd. In order to stay competitive and meet customer expectations, development projects face constant change pressure that begins at project inception. As the project progresses, the scope, resources, plans, cost and/or quality requirements may all change. Changes are usually interrelated and tend to set off chain reactions. For example, suppose that a new feature is added to the original product specification. The project manager needs to revise the schedules and resource plans in order to implement this new feature. In the meantime, specialists from the team are also asked to investigate the amount of time, resources, and technology needed to determine whether it is feasible to implement the feature. The project manager may subsequently identify several solutions: (a) add resources; (b) delay the delivery date; (c) remove less important features; or (d) simplify or remove final "polishing" steps that aim to make the final set of features as flawless as possible. No matter which solution is selected, the project manager cannot implement it without consulting with key team members, senior managers or customers and enlisting their support. Because the proposed change ultimately impacts management and areas of customer concern such as the project budget, financial goals, staffing, or quality, it is necessary that a proper change control process be established to ensure effective communication between the many parties involved and to support them in their decision-making.

Change control process

The change control process often consists of three major activities: initiation of a formal change request, review of the request by the change control board, and change execution (assuming the request is approved, of course). A change request can be initiated by team members, customers, sponsors, or other stakeholders with the goal of introducing enhancements to the game. Change requests often focus on physical aspects of project components, as in the hypothetical request to add a new feature to a product discussed above. The project manager may also receive process-related requests, such as a workflow optimization proposal from the team members. Change requests are submitted to, and reviewed by, the change control board, which is a group that represents the project team, customers, and sponsors. This board reviews change requests and decides whether to reject or approve them. If a change request is rejected by the change control board, then the change case is closed. If a request is approved, then the change will be executed and the project manager will work further to update the project plan, resources, budget, and so forth.

In order to make the change control process manageable and ensure that it does not interfere with the team's ability to complete their scheduled tasks in a timely fashion, some project managers delay the process for certain period, allowing for a two-week turnaround between the submission of a change request and the announcement of the change board's decision. This delay may sometimes render certain change requests irrelevant as the project progresses and self-correction occurs.

The challenge for the project manager stems from the fact that she or he cannot control every change. Sometimes a team member will implement whatever change he or she thinks is necessary or good for the project without telling others. The project manager has to be aware of this risk and prevent team members from acting unilaterally, as the implementation of uncontrolled changes may in turn cause milestone slippage. Team members typically do not have a clear understanding of the overall development process in all its complexity, nor of the dependencies between individual tasks, and thus they are ill-positioned to understand the full ramifications of changes that may wish to make. In the absence of a formalized and carefully managed change control process, innovation and customer satisfaction are much more difficult to achieve.

Change management in post-release localization projects
Depending on the type and complexity of a game localization project, the change control process may vary. If the LPM is in charge of a basic game localization project, i.e., the post-release localization of a title in which there is little likelihood of product functionality changes, then she or he can use the change control process described above. In a basic game localization project, a comprehensive localization kit

is provided by development team. This kit includes detailed guidelines for texts, game dialogue scripts, and building the localized versions. Usually there is no need to replace assets or alter the design of the game, and any necessary code changes tend to be simple. Using this kit, the localization team can complete the project with minimal or no consultation with the development team. Normally, there will not be much iteration across the various localization project phases and a simple change control process is adequate.

Change management in simship localization projects
If the LPM handles a complex localization project involving simship or online titles that require periodic updates, the change process discussed above may not suffice and the LPM may simply have to accept the high pace of change of the source development project, which reflects the dynamic nature of the game development process and the collective creativity of the team members. As mentioned previously, when the localization team works on a simship project, it is part of the development functional team and will share the same project goals as the development team. Consequently, the localization team will have to accept and adhere to whatever change process is adopted during the development project.

Change management in the development process
Whereas change management is critical to localization, it can prove crippling to the game development process. In the real world, it is difficult to manage game development effectively using the change control process described above. Games are a synthesis of technology and art. The look and feel of a game play an essential role in immersing players in the game world and helping them to successfully complete the game. Developers cannot judge whether the art, animations, interactions, and effects will appear and function as expected until they have viewed them on the screen and experienced them through play. Sometimes the developers have no clear goal in mind and just want to explore different approaches. When they see the results on the screen, new ideas occur to them, which they typically want to implement in the game immediately. A few weeks later, after implementing other new ideas and evaluating the progress that they have made, they may feel that certain old ideas no longer fit and want to modify them.

Such frequent changes and intensive iterations occur throughout most of the game development life cycle. Because the aforementioned change control process cannot address requests quickly, formal change requests are either postponed or rejected outright. This inability to react rapidly to change requests has a negative impact on creativity, which is an essential component of game development.

Instead of *controlling* changes, many game projects use Agile development processes and Scrum methodology to *embrace* changes. These approaches represent a sea change compared to the traditional waterfall methodology, which emphasizes repeatable processes and results, as Highsmith (2004: 51–52) observes:

> [T]he word "repeatable" isn't in the agile lexicon. Implementing repeatable processes has been the goal of many companies, but in rapidly changing environments, repeatability turns out to be the wrong goal; in fact, it turns out to be an extremely counterproductive goal. Which brings us to the critical difference between reliable and repeatable. Repeatable means doing the same thing in the same way to produce the same results. Reliable means meeting targets regardless of the impediments thrown in your way – it means constantly adapting to meet a goal.

How does the adoption of agile development methodologies impact the localization team and localization projects? Localization requires completed content. Localization usually starts after the Alpha milestone has been reached, at which point, by definition, no content or major code changes are made. So in theory no changes should be made to content or code in a localization project after the Alpha stage. Does real-world practice reflect theory?

To answer this question, let us take a closer look at the Scrum development methodology. Instead of having the development team wait until the design has been finalized and technology has been implemented to make changes, the Scrum methodology allows features, art, and technology to emerge throughout the project. Scrum is an iterative and incremental process that allows changes to the product being developed at any time, even in the final stages of development. Scrum projects comprise repeated short development cycles, called iterations:

> The heart of Scrum lies in the iteration. The team takes a look at the requirements, considers the available technology, and evaluates its own skills and capabilities. It then collectively determines how to build the functionality, modifying its approach daily as it encounters new complexities, difficulties, and surprises. The team figures out what needs to be done and selects the best way to do it. This creative process is the heart of the Scrum's productivity. (Schwaber 2004: 6)

In Scrum projects, product and technology features identified as requirements do not constitute a formal specification *per se*, but rather comprise a list that is referred to as the "product backlog" (see Figure 5). The individual iterations during which Scrum project work is accomplished and features are created are called sprints. During every sprint, which can last from two to four weeks, functionalities and contents are delivered iteratively and incrementally based on priorities. The features and content to be developed during a given sprint are called the sprint backlog, and comprise a subset of the product backlog. Sprint planning takes place throughout the project until a satisfactory game has been delivered.

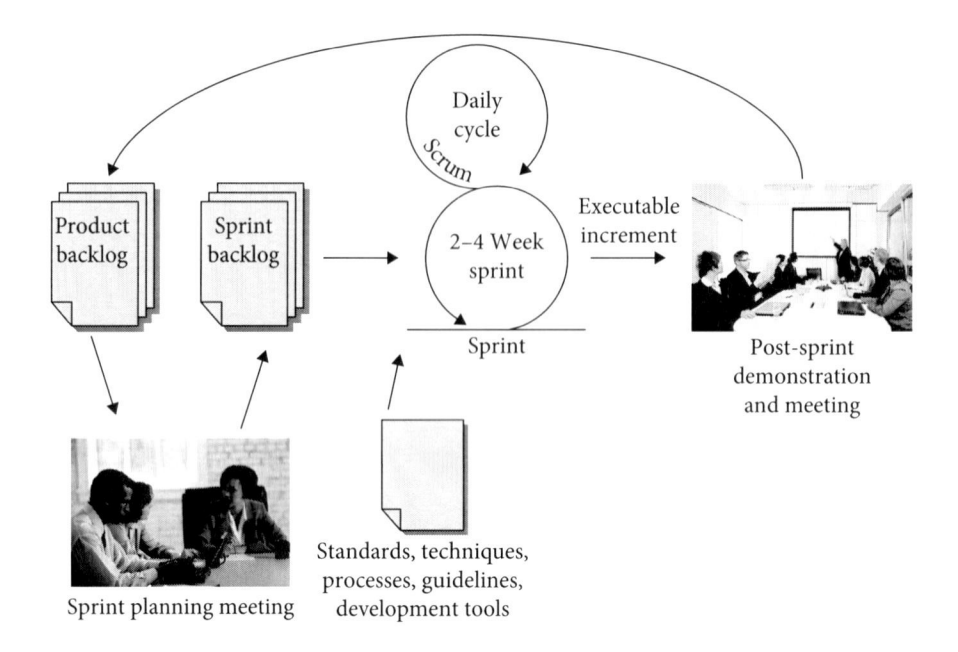

Figure 5. The overall Scrum process (adapted from Highsmith 2002: 243).

The Scrum methodology is not without its drawbacks, however; chief among them is the risk that the lack of a fixed deadline will lead to a never-ending project. For this reason, many game development teams use a hybrid waterfall-Scrum process, in which the major milestones such as alpha and beta releases are pre-scoped, the project deadline is predefined, and the project proceeds through major phases and milestones in a linear, sequential fashion. However, there is no guarantee that the content will not change between the Alpha milestone and the creation of the gold master. Integrating Scrum into the traditional waterfall methodology is an effective way for the development team to embrace changes and bring them under control in a timely and effective manner.

This atmosphere of innovation, experimentation and constant change is the creative crucible in which new games are forged. However, constant change creates enormous challenges for localization, which does not involve the creation of a new title from scratch but rather the translation and adaptation of materials created by the development team. One major advantage of the Scrum process is that it allows the team to self-organize, as Highsmith (2004: 64) points out:

> In a self-organized team, individuals take responsibility for managing their own workload, shift work among themselves based on need and best fit, and participate in team decision making. Team members have considerable leeway in how they deliver results, but they are accountable for those results and for working within the established flexible framework.

In a game development project, a Scrum team is cross-functional and comprises approximately seven people who are able to transform the sprint requirements into an interactive artistic experience. The team has sole responsibility for the delivery. This gives the localization team a chance to play a constructive, participatory role in development. If there are localization requirements, the project manager can ask the producer to address them during the sprint planning process, especially technologies that must be built into the game engine to enable localization or tools that must be created for subsequent use during the localization process. When the sprint starts, people from the localization team will be part of the Scrum team and will define the localization features to be delivered. The LPM can also identify features whose development will indirectly influence localization tasks later, and can ask the producer to assign her or him to the Scrum team to be able to contribute feedback to the development team about the impact of various features on the localizability of the product earlier rather than later. Even if the LPM cannot join the Scrum team, she or he still can monitor and learn about features that may potentially impact localization from the outside. This investment of time helps the LPM to develop knowledge that will prove useful to the localization team during later tasks. If the LPM sees that one or more features developed during a sprint may negatively impact the localization project, she or he can propose corrections to the producer for the next sprint (or a subsequent sprint).

In the traditional waterfall development methodology, it is usually difficult to draw attention to localization issues during the development process. There is almost no localization team involvement in the development process before the Alpha milestone. The localization project manager may be invited to attend routine meetings and will be consulted for some localization issues. However, during development, localization requirements will usually be assigned a lower priority and when the development project gets hectic, localization requirements will likely be omitted altogether. If localization is deemed to be a low priority, development leads will not communicate localization-related issues to their team. Most of the time, the development team members are not even aware of the existence of localization requirements, especially those members who have no experience with localization. Ignoring the needs of localization may result in a product in which architecture- or content-related localization requirements are unfulfilled or only partially fulfilled. When the localization project subsequently starts, the failure to build in localization support may leave the team little room to maneuver, requiring the use of workarounds to overcome obstacles and sometimes resulting in imperfections remaining in target language versions.

Even though the Scrum process entails far more changes and complicated development iterations than the waterfall approach, it nevertheless enables the localization team to manage change efficiently and promptly, and also to influence development and to proactively address potential localization problems by using the same methodology as the development team. Although Scrum is highly challenging, it does ultimately enable the localization team to help the development team create a final product that is as localizable as possible. Scrum is particularly well suited to simship projects and can potentially enable the delivery of a greater number of localized versions with desired features to target markets than traditional development methodologies. It can also be used to manage online games that involve constant content updates. It is completely flexible and thus can accommodate each development team's unique cycle.

Critical facets of development in successful game localization

Three facets of development play an especially critical role in enhancing (or undermining) the likelihood of successful localization efforts, namely the game design, the user interface and the game's audio. To be able to release a localized game to target markets on time, on budget, and with no last-minute changes or rework, the LPM must closely monitor these three facets of development, and must also ensure that the development team understands their importance.

Game design

Game designers may borrow cultural elements from various countries to enrich the game's narrative. However, if their knowledge of those countries is not based on personal experience but rather is drawn from literature or films, there is a risk that the characters or settings that they create may be perceived as dated, awkward or unrealistic by players from the corresponding locales. The LPM should identify such problems during the development phase. A similar but far more serious issue can arise if the content portrays a sensitive historical or political event in a way that is deemed inappropriate. In such a case, the game may be prohibited in the target country. The political climate in target markets changes constantly and the LPM needs to remain alert to cultural and political risks at all times and provide prompt feedback to the development team whenever potential problems are identified (as in the case of the North Korean missile launch in *Tom Clancy's Ghost Recon 2* discussed above). When game development and/or localization are offshored, cultural and political risks in the offshore locales must also be considered. For example, if the development of a new game involves plot elements or content that the offshore team finds offensive or objectionable, the studio may modify those elements to avoid potential problems and maintain a good relationship with the local staff and government.

User interface

The development of the user interface should be followed closely as well. If one asks a group of developers which function of the game they think will change the most during development, nine out of ten will probably identify the UI. Because the UI is the most directly accessible and highly visible component of the game, it is typically subject to the highest degree of scrutiny. UI design work and changes continue until the very end of some development projects. Although localization engineering can handle most UI issues, such as expansion and truncation of translated text, the LPM still should make sure that the development team uses icons and symbols in the game UI that will not be confusing or offensive to players in target markets.

Audio

The challenges of audio development mainly involve quality, cost and time concerns. When preparing simship versions, the first batch of audio source files received is often incomplete and changes may be made to the files at any time. However, the fact that the source files may be in flux does not change the reality that the LPM has firm deadlines to meet. The LPM needs to coordinate external vendors for translation, casting, recording and linguistic testing. In addition, level designers and AI engineers may need to be involved to add dialogues to the game. Even slight changes will be costly in terms of time and money, and will require extensive external and internal communication. The creation of audio materials is a complicated process and should be carefully followed in order to deliver the desired results on time.

Conclusion

There is no well defined methodology or process that can be applied universally to game localization projects. Simship localization projects pose a different set of challenges compared to post-release projects, as do complex versus basic projects. Nevertheless, some generalizations can be made about best practices in game localization project management. Given the strategic importance accorded to innovation in the game publishing industry, change is a fact of life. In this fast-moving, dynamic environment, it is critical to keep an open mind, proactive attitude, and long-term approach to manage changes. In addition to proactive change management, effective scope, risk, and communication planning along with innovative project integration management to coordinate all of the components of each unique project are the keys to successful game localization projects.

References

Dietz, Frank. 2006. "Issues in localizing computer games." In *Perspectives on Localization*, Keiran J. Dunne (ed.), 121–134. Amsterdam/Philadelphia: John Benjamins.
Field, John C. ["Buck"]. 2002. "Glossary C." Field Operative Project Management. http://www.fieldoperative.com/Tools/Glossary/Glossary%20c.htm
Highsmith, Jim. 2002. *Agile Software Development Ecosystems*. Boston: Addison-Wesley.
———. 2004. *Agile Project Management: Creating Innovative Products*. Boston: Addison-Wesley.
Project Management Institute (PMI). 2008. *A Guide to the Project Management Body of Knowledge (PMBOK® Guide)*. 4th ed. Newton Square, PA: Project Management Institute.
Schwaber, Ken. 2004. *Agile Project Management with Scrum*. Redmond, WA: Microsoft Press.
Stoeller, Willem. 2004. "Risky business! Risk management for localization project managers." TranslationDirectory.com http://www.translationdirectory.com/article462.htm (Orig. pub. *The Globalization Insider* 3.7, http://www.lisa.org/globalizationinsider/2003/09/risky_busines.html)
Thayer, Alexander and Kolko, Beth E. 2004. "Localization of digital games: The process of blending for the global games market." *Technical Communication* 51 (4): 477–488.
Wideman, R. Max. 1992. *Project and Program Management: A Guide to Managing Project Risks and Opportunities*. Drexel Hill, PA: Project Management Institute.
wikiHow. 2010. "How to start a wiki." http://www.wikihow.com/Start-a-Wiki
Wikipedia. 2010a. "Level (video gaming)." http://en.wikipedia.org/wiki/Game_level
———. 2010b. "Software build." http://en.wikipedia.org/wiki/Software_build

Project management for crowdsourced translation
How user-translated content projects work in real life

Donald A. DePalma and Nataly Kelly*

The community or "crowdsourcing" project model presents opportunities for organizations to translate content that might otherwise not be financially feasible to offer in other languages. In this chapter, the authors find that relying on the voluntary labor of the community raises a variety of traditional and new project management issues. They describe the challenges faced and solutions chosen by four commercial pioneers of community translation: Facebook, Microsoft, Plaxo and Sun Microsystems. Each of these companies recognized the existence of a community willing to volunteer time and expertise in return for some benefit other than direct compensation. Then, the companies actively invested in developing the community, refining processes, incorporating technology, and managing the work.

Introduction to crowdsourcing in translation

When Common Sense Advisory published the first report on what has been called community, collaborative, or "crowdsourced" translation (Howe 2006) in December 2007 (Beninatto and DePalma 2007b), there were few examples to reference. In that original research, we explained how collaboration tools, open sourcing concepts, and a new vision of working processes could increase translation efficiency and replace the synchronous, step-wise procedures that mimic industrial manufacturing and which we have referred to as "translation Taylorism" (Beninatto and DePalma 2007a) (see Figure 1).

---

* The authors would like to acknowledge the generous support of the innovators in crowdsourcing translation who contributed their knowledge to this research. They are Ghassan Hassad and Kate Losse of Facebook, Britta Simon and Sara Nicolini of Microsoft, Regina Bustamente (formerly of Plaxo), and Janice Campbell (formerly of Sun Microsystems, now at Adobe). We would also like to thank Merle Tenney who helped us with the initial documentation of these cases.

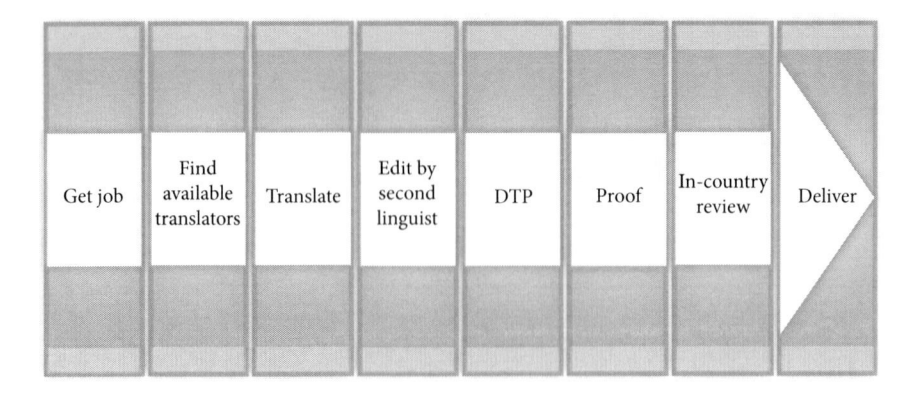

Figure 1. Timeline for traditional translation: Each step waits for a hand-off. Source: Common Sense Advisory, Inc.

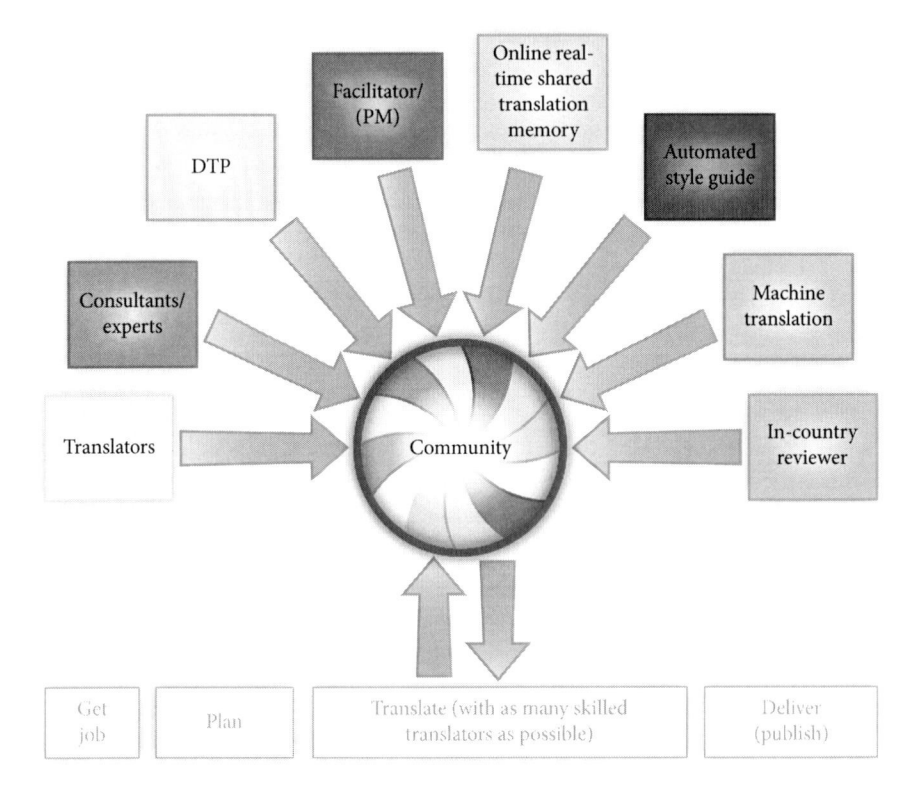

Figure 2. Timeline for collaborative translation: No wait time between activities. Source: Common Sense Advisory, Inc.

Our discussion focused on the collaborative part of the process and how such projects would proceed. We contended that a community approach could replace the traditional waterfall process known as T-E-P for "translate, edit, proofread." With collaboration, translation itself and revisions of translated work proceed in parallel with source content creation and editing, greatly reducing the lag between development and authoring, on one hand, and completion of a localized product and publication of translated content, on the other hand (see Figure 2). The community sits at the crux of every tool, process, and participant in the collaborative translation process.

Since the publication of our initial report, we have seen both suppliers and buyers of language services use this new model in controlled environments to execute large projects in short bursts or as part of systematic translation and localization efforts. This model provides real potential for collaboration to increase value and reduce turnaround time. However, these benefits come at a price. At the very least, community translation involves an overhaul of the traditional sequential translation process and has implications to the sourcing of people, the use of technology, and the form of translation output. In all cases, it involves some fundamental rethinking about the ways in which projects are managed and where this management takes place.

In this chapter, we present primary research on four pioneers in crowdsourced translation. We describe what they did, how they did it, what tools they used, and what project management tactics they used for "crowd control."

Crowdsourcing applies a known model to translation

The move toward more asynchronous, geographically dispersed translation projects involves multiple, concurrent translators collaborating via the Internet. These translators employ Web 2.0 services and concepts, with web-based translation memory tools and servers operating in real time. Buyers expect to benefit from an increased speed of translation and perhaps to increase their ability to deal with greater volumes of content at the same or lower costs.

Open-source communities have long applied the collaborative modus operandi to localizing offerings such as the Ubuntu operating system with tools like Launchpad. Then Google and Sun Microsystems took up the practice with volunteer localizers for search and NetBeans, respectively. In early 2008, Facebook launched sites in Spanish and German using translations that were provided free of charge on a volunteer basis by its own members and rapidly added new languages based on that approach.

Definitions of terms associated with crowdsourcing

As often happens during transitions, the creation of words to describe this new phenomenon has lagged behind the technological innovations responsible for its emergence. When we discuss translation that is generated of, by, and for the people, we think of three core elements that combine to shape a new way of thinking about translation and localization:

- *Community translation* (or social translation) is performed, usually on a volunteer basis, by members of a group or by people with common goals or interests. As we will see with the case studies in this chapter, these groups can be technology-focused, interested in accessing information in their own language, or just plain linguistic aficionados.
- *Collaborative technology and processes* let the community that forms around a project work together on the same content and code. Community members can check and correct each other's work as they go. We also use the term collaborative translation to describe the work of *professional* translation teams working as a "swarm" – where multiple translators interact with the same document or source content simultaneously using advanced translation memory tools.
- *Crowdsourcing* opens a translation project to teams comprised of any mix of volunteer translators, employees, contractors, or language service providers (LSPs). It leverages the power of the swarm to accomplish much more than a single translator or even an LSP alone could do. Crowdsourcing requires both technology and a business process to induct ad hoc resources and then manage them as users within a collaborative online environment. In some cases, it refers to the business strategy of eliciting volunteer or paid labor from external, commercial resources.

These three concepts have already begun to overlap, to the point the boundaries between and among them have become blurred. For the sake of consistency, we will refer to these phenomena collectively as "crowdsourced translation."

Case: Facebook applies social networking to translation

In August 2007, when Common Sense Advisory examined 505 top websites in 15 different countries, Facebook was a flop from the globalization perspective. We measured the site by the two criteria that we use to determine the popular and economic potential of any Internet property GDP: (1) its "availability quotient" (AQ), a metric that we developed to objectively rank the proportion of the total worldwide online population that can access a given website, with a maximum value of 1,000; and (2) the percentage of the world's online gross domestic product (GDP) represented by that site's total available audience, a number that we characterize as the "online GDP" or e-GDP (Sargent and DePalma 2007).

Because the August 2007 instance of Facebook was available in English only, it had a very low availability quotient (AQ) rank of 277 and an e-GDP score of 48.4% (Sargent and DePalma 2008: 32). The latter score is a measure of the economic potential of online language populations, with Facebook addressing less than half of what we call the "world online wallet" (that is, the world's online GDP). Facebook's community translation project began in December 2007. In February 2008, the company announced the launch of a Spanish version, and by the end of 2008 the site had 63 languages in various stages of development. By September 2009, Facebook had 65 languages in production and more than 40 in development.

When we reviewed Facebook's AQ and e-GDP rankings in August 2008, it had 20 languages in production. It had increased its scores to 851 out of a maximum 1,000 for the AQ and access to 90.7 percent of the world's e-GDP, a much more favorable comparison to Google and Microsoft, which had AQ scores of 989 and 921, respectively, and e-GDP factors of 100 and 99.9 percent, respectively.

How did a company with just US$150 million in revenue in 2007 become a leader in website globalization by 2008? The company blended its initial reliance on translation agencies with the linguistic skills of an enthusiastic community that wanted Facebook in their languages and evolved a four-step translation process:

1. *Translation.* Facebook users translate strings and sentences in the interface and help files. Because the site has many members, it is possible that multiple translations may be provided for the same English text.
2. *Voting.* Members of the community vote on the proposed translations. Popular translations rise to the top of the selection pool. Facebook maintains a leader board that shows who's who among the volunteer translators. Facebook members can override the most popular translation, but only with a compelling justification – these end users are the de facto experts.
3. *Collaboration.* Facebook's user-translators review and solve trickier or more difficult translations on discussion boards.
4. *Review.* Professional translators review all translations. They see which community members generate the most popular translations and the scores they receive. Facebook sometimes skips this step, but designates the language as "beta" if it is launched without a review.

An application development platform makes translation easier

Facebook provides a platform for developing applications that site members can install and run. Facebook used this same capability to deliver the Translations application, the application that underlies its collaborative translation process. The Translations application works as a homepage and staging point for the translation community. It highlights Facebook's three major localization steps – glossary creation, content translation, and testing and verification – and indicates the progress of each.

For example, if we log into the Translations application and select Irish (Gaelic), the screen reveals that the glossary creation phase is complete, the translation phase is in progress, and the voting and verification phase has not yet begun (see Figure 3). The screen also indicates that there are 80 translators working on the Irish translation, 39,179 translated phrases, and 10,975 phrases yet to be translated. The status report remains even after translation is complete, so that users can participate in maintenance.

The Translation application has two modes: in-context and bulk translation:

– *In-context translation.* The community's translators work in the partially localized version of Facebook. User interface (UI) elements that have been localized are underlined in green, whereas those that have not are underlined in red. The translator may offer a target-language equivalent for any untranslated element. One major advantage of working in this mode is that content to be translated is displayed in context, which minimizes the risk of mistranslation. Another advantage is that translation is prioritized based on frequency of usage, as the most frequently used UI elements are encountered and translated first. Facebook's

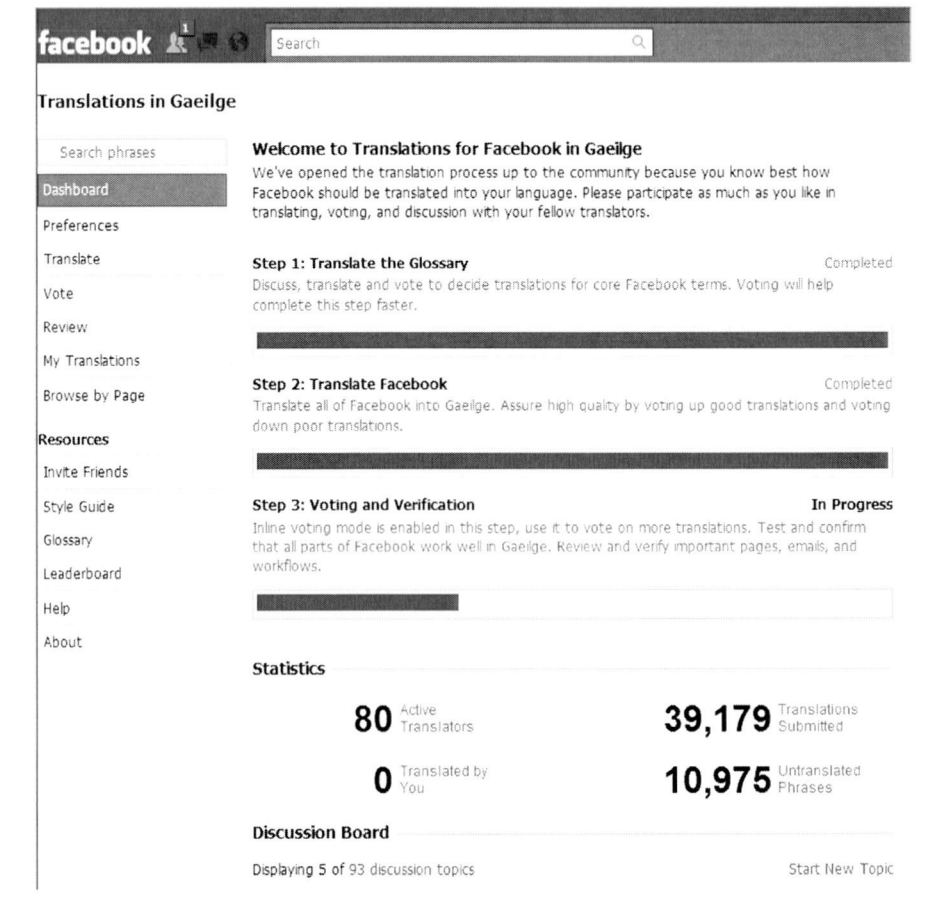

Figure 3. Facebook Translations Application homepage for Irish Gaelic.
Source: Facebook, Inc.

crowdsourced translation creators caution that the site is very dynamic, and as a result, it is not possible to display all possible text on a given page at one time. In order to address this situation and minimize the risk that translatable content will be overlooked, the in-context mode also has an option called "see more phrases from this page." This option provides access to a list of additional strings that may potentially display on the page.
– *Bulk translation.* This model employs a more conventional translation framework that is separate from the Facebook runtime environment. It presents content elements one after another. Translators can select tabs that let them cycle through different sets of UI elements – untranslated units, their own translations, and elements from the most popular pages.

Facebook built several quality control mechanisms into the Translations application: (1) it automatically presents glossary entries with definitions and approved translations for the technical terms found in each translated element; (2) it generates tokens as placeholders for variable elements in strings; and (3) it verifies that capitalization and punctuation conform to style specifications for different element types. Professional reviewers use the same application as the community translators.

Strategic categorization of content and languages

Determining what content to translate and into which languages can be a daunting challenge for any company. To focus its planning efforts, Facebook added two triage steps to its decision-making process:

– *Prioritizing content for translation.* Facebook began by determining which content assets had to be offered in other languages. Its analysis identified 300,000 words of content that required translation, including 125,000 words in user interface elements, another 125,000 in legal and help content, and 50,000 words of miscellaneous content. These categories reflected top translation priorities, with user interface text as the first – and in some cases, the only – content to be translated. As of late 2009, the number of translatable words had grown to nearly a half million – 250,000 for the main user interface, 200,000 for legal and help content, and the balance for miscellaneous functions.
– *Targeting the languages that matter most.* At Facebook, not all languages are equal. Each receives a level of support based on its strategic importance, determined largely by the number of Internet users. Supported languages get full internal support. Unsupported languages get lower levels of support or no support at all. Common Sense Advisory has long advised companies to focus on the languages and content that make the most sense for its business objectives, and to use information about online language populations in order to make localization decisions based on the size of online populations. Facebook did exactly that.

Three motivators: Speed, quality, and reach

Facebook wished to achieve three specific goals through its community translation initiative. Notably, cost reduction was not among the factors.

1. *Speed.* Deliver localized sites in a fraction of the time required with conventional methods.
2. *Quality.* Localize using the terminology that is preferred by the target users.
3. *Reach.* Bring Facebook to more communities around the world. Using its collaboration tools aggressively with top-priority languages enables Facebook to test and fine-tune them so that they can be used reliably with unsupported languages when and if the company chooses to add them.

Collaborative translation satisfies the need for speed

Facebook found that collaborative translation delivers dramatic improvements in speed. Initial discussions with LSPs revealed that traditional processes would enable the completion of the first translation in a matter of months. With a collaborative translation model, the company believed the turn-around time could be reduced to days or weeks, depending on the size of the community that it could energize.

Facebook's organizers were right. Using collaborative translation, volunteers completed the Spanish and German localizations in just one week, while the French team took just 24 hours to produce its language variant. Even with the added incentive of rush charges, most LSPs would struggle to produce a 300,000-word human translation project in a week, let alone within a day – unless the service provider, too, adopted a similar crowdsourcing model.

End-user involvement in the translation process boosts quality

The Facebook translation system brought together a unique combination of people, processes, and technology. The company needed translators with linguistic skills and subject-matter expertise, both of which could be found in its user community. Facebook found that collaborative translation offered significant quality benefits because its community provided it with expert reviewers. The resulting translations met the company's requirements: they were clear and unambiguous and conveyed the meaning of the original, but they did not sound unnatural or forced.

Facebook devised a system that included many conventional translation steps, such as style specification, glossary development, and linguistic quality control. The organizers added two important elements – immediate feedback and correction. Facebook also wanted to simplify the job for its volunteer translators, so its software platform eliminated the need for manual processing beyond translation.

A collaborative approach extends the company's global reach

Thanks to collaborative translation, Facebook was able to extend the benefits of localization to a larger international community. More Facebook users can now interact with the service in their own languages; the process itself was conducive to creating greater brand awareness through social networking and word-of-mouth marketing. For example, a U.S.-based member working on a translation project for Colombian Spanish could easily invite friends in other countries to join the network and participate in the translation project.

Application developers also benefited from Facebook's foray into international markets. The company gave Facebook members who are interested in localizing their own applications access to the same technology, language assets, and processes that it used for its own localization efforts.

Building a strong community – what Facebook does best

Facebook applied its vision and expertise in social networking to mobilize communities of user-translators. Four facets of its program stand out:

– *What happens in the community stays in the community.* While a language is in the being-translated phase of the process, only those members working as user-translators on that translation project can actually see what is going on with the target language.
– *Country- and language-specific content stays specific.* Facebook offers multiple variants of Latin American Spanish. This approach not only customizes the content for the distinct user groups, but reduces the chances of community infighting that can occur when one nationality dictates the fate of the terminology and idioms that other members would have to live with.
– *Facebook tracks translation in real time.* The company monitors the translation process closely, keeping this information in front of translators as a way of marking progress and keeping participants focused on the tasks at hand. It also gives great visibility to the volunteers who do the most to make translation happen.
– *Contributors are recognized.* Each language has a leader board that monitors progress and recognizes the leading contributors by displaying the total number of winning words and phrases they have submitted and the number of votes they have received.

One volunteer, Fernando Pérez Chercoles, dominated the leader board for the first six months of the Spanish for Spain project with his translation of 36,824 winning words. This means that Señor Pérez provided approximately one word in eight of the total community-translated output during that period. Would he have been as motivated if his contributions were known only to him? Not likely. For volunteer-based contributions, recognition is the coin of the realm, so community engagement and real-time progress updates are an essential part of the successful Facebook collaborative translation formula.

Community translation offers old and new challenges

The Facebook project uncovered some new problems and older challenges in a new guise:

- *Community interest.* Facebook needs to keep its user-translators interested and engaged at each stage of translation and maintenance. It has to ensure availability of sufficient contributors, especially for unsupported languages.
- *Motivation of contributors.* Sabotage via bad translations has been an issue, testament to the fact that not all volunteers are virtuous or altruistic.
- *Technical challenges.* Any networked multi-user platform invites problems, including access control, scalability, and security issues.
- *Traditional translation issues.* Any translation project must deal with quality assurance concerns, re-use and leverage, and linguistic complexity. Given their highly dynamic nature, Web 2.0 sites compound these issues.
- *Scalability and growth.* The large and growing number of languages requires a continuous re-design of the Translations application and re-evaluation of the language selection process. It also requires the implementation of more error checking and reporting in order to make sure that translators fluent in more than one language do not mix them up and to give professional paid linguists the ability to identify and resolve issues.

Facebook also faced criticism of its user-based translation effort, primarily from observers who viewed the initiatives as a form of doing translation on the cheap. However, Facebook realized minimal or no cost savings; its large investment in technology offset most of what it saved from getting translations from its members. It did benefit financially from translating unsupported languages, automating the localization process, and prioritizing text segments to be translated, so that localized sites can be operational sooner.

Finally, commercial language service providers (LSPs) translate more than half of Facebook's content into supported languages – under more traditional paid service agreements. Facebook uses the LSPs to evaluate the work of its volunteer translators. However, perception is reality, and every group attempting a community translation project will face the criticism that it is merely adopting a crowdsourcing approach just to squeeze out LSPs.

Case: End-user passion guides Microsoft community

Microsoft has undertaken two language initiatives as part of its community outreach efforts. One of these, the Microsoft Language Portal (http://www.microsoft.com/language), provides general language resources, such as searchable terminology databases and downloadable language style guides. It also supports community involvement in the form of a tool that enables users to provide feedback about the terminology used in different language versions of Microsoft products.

Microsoft constructs a community forum for terminology

The company's Language Excellence Committee sponsors the Microsoft Terminology Community Forum (MTCF, http://www.microsoft.com/language/mtcf/mtcf_default.aspx), an initiative that benefits end users and helps improve the company's products (see Figure 4). Aspects of the forum include the following:

- *Open community discussions.* MTCF enables community members to develop, discuss, and approve new terminology for Microsoft products. It also allows product groups and individual localization teams to obtain user feedback on legacy and new terminology.

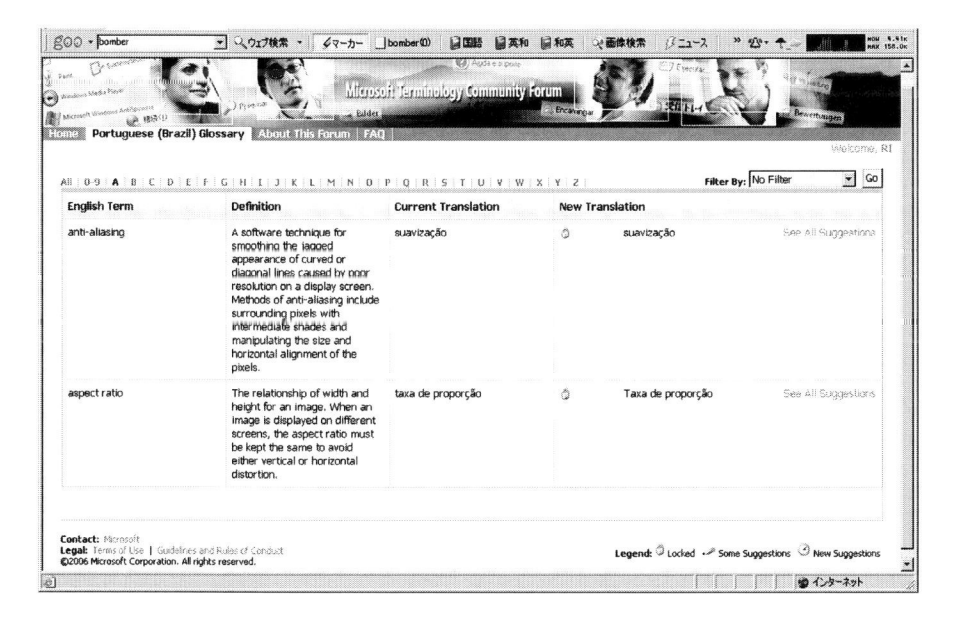

Figure 4. Microsoft Terminology Community Forum. Used with permission from Microsoft.

- *Restricted or unrestricted access.* The forum's organizers can open the MTCF portal on microsoft.com to the general public or limit it to a subject-matter expert community on an invitation-only basis. MTCF has been translated into 12 languages.
- *Corporate communication vehicle.* The forum incorporates the voice of the community in localizing Microsoft products, and highlights the fact that Microsoft listens to its users. Engaging the user community in terminology for future products also helps raise visibility for upcoming product launches.
- *Quality and consistency of existing terminology.* The MTCF platform leverages the expertise of local subject matter experts and customers. This approach validates the terminology and increases consistency.
- *Enhanced development of new terminology.* MTCF facilitates terminology development for new products in all languages. It also helps expand terminology in less widely supported languages for existing products.

MTCF translation projects follow a clearly defined process

Microsoft engages its MTCF community through a series of scheduled, focused projects. Depending on the audience and the specific user community of the product – which can range from consumer software to highly technical server systems – Microsoft may open the project to the general public or limit participation to a smaller community of invited local subject-matter experts. Microsoft's Windows 7 and Office 2010 products are currently localized into more than 90 languages, all of which are candidates for community work. The community process includes four basic steps:

1. *Glossary creation.* Source language terms, source term definitions, and target language terms are added to the project glossary. Localized term definitions and screenshots may also be incorporated into the glossary.
2. *Community building.* Microsoft identifies a local community and invites them to join the effort.
3. *Translation and voting.* Users can contribute alternate translations, comment on existing and proposed translations, and vote for their preferred translations. Community projects usually stay open for about four weeks.
4. *Finalization.* Terminologists, engineers, and marketing experts review translations. Then they choose the final terms based on the popularity of the suggested translation, either the original translations or alternative suggestions from the community.

Once these steps are complete, Microsoft updates the master terminology database that is leveraged by all product groups and localization teams, and hands off the modified glossaries to LSPs.

Challenges in running a successful community project

An MTCF-based project requires a substantial commitment from Microsoft. A program manager must first define the specifications of the MTCF processes and site. A web developer then designs and builds the site. Development, testing, and localization engineers maintain the site after it is launched, and a project manager runs the forum. Term changes must be agreed on by all affected teams and implemented in the user interface (UI) and user assistance (UA) of existing products. Once terminology changes are accepted, someone must record them in the appropriate databases.

Microsoft considers MTCF to be an overall success, but it does acknowledge some lingering questions about these community initiatives:

- *How should it establish consistent terminology?* Many terms presented for community feedback are inherited from existing applications or shared across products. For software already released in the market, Microsoft's ability to make changes to reflect community preferences is limited. Along similar lines, shared terminology cannot easily be updated to mirror community preferences without compromising terminological consistency and the overall usability of localized products. This reality leads to a difficult trade-off between implementing a community preference and keeping an existing term for purposes of usability and backward-compatibility.
- *How can it assess community engagement levels?* Microsoft has found that it is difficult to gauge the relevance of specific user feedback. Part of the difficulty lies in determining whether the level of participation is adequate, statistically relevant, and truly reflective of the wider end-user community being targeted.
- *How can it increase local market participation in all markets?* Minimal participation in some locales makes it harder to build communities and plan advertising for upcoming projects.
- *How can it minimize red tape?* Participants must agree to and sign legal statements, which can slow down the process and create barriers to participation. Requiring volunteers to sign a statement makes some less eager to participate.

Microsoft uses community feedback to test terminology

Collaborative translation gives Microsoft the means to understand whether the terminology used in its products differs from the terminology established by specialized communities on the web. To verify this, the Windows Live team undertook a case study in early 2008. This terminology community project helped the team ensure that market expectations were met and that product terminology closely reflected the local culture. The reasons why this close engagement with customers was so helpful include the following:

- *Fertile ground for neologisms.* Social networking applications like Windows Live Messenger and Windows Live Spaces represent a rich source of both general vocabulary and Internet jargon. Such terms can evolve very quickly in the interactive, integrated environment of email, instant messaging, blogs, and other user communications on the web.
- *User preferences reign supreme.* Users in some markets, such as Germany, Russia and Brazil, unanimously preferred Anglicisms. However, no pattern was found as regards the usage of the English term "online" in the local markets, but it was indeed useful for validation. For example, in other countries, including Italy where "online" is widely used, the term received only one vote.
- *Improved source terminology.* Community projects can provide feedback on outdated terminology or unclear definitions. Source terms that are ambiguous or difficult to grasp can generate discussion in many languages. For example, for "appear offline," more than six languages preferred the direct translation "invisible."
- *Access to many languages.* Microsoft launched MTCF for the entire Windows Live language set, comprising 35 Western European, East Asian, Eastern European, and bidirectional languages. The MTCF website for Windows Live is has been localized into Arabic, Brazilian Portuguese, Simplified Chinese, Traditional Chinese, Dutch, French, German, Italian, Japanese, Korean, Spanish, and Russian.
- *Fast-tracked development.* Windows Live products follow an agile development model, with three to four releases per year. That means the associated MTCF processes must be focused and efficient from day one. The company opened MTCF for Windows Live on 31 March 2008, flipping on the switch to allow user terminology feedback. Just two months later, Microsoft had received enough valuable user suggestions to begin evaluating the feedback. The terminology changes approved from this community feedback were implemented in the next release, and the cycle began anew.

If you build it, they may or may not come

The Windows Live localization team needed to find effective ways to recruit users to the forum. Although Microsoft conducts MTCF launch campaigns and ongoing public relations efforts in all applicable markets, the company still faced the following challenges in getting the word out:

- *Lack of integration.* Because MTCF is a standalone website, it was not integrated with the Windows Live products themselves. As a result, many Windows Live users were unaware of the MTCF initiative.
- *Local staff priorities.* Much of the MTCF public relations responsibility was assigned to local subsidiaries that needed to juggle the MTCF announcements and ongoing campaign support with their other work duties. Sourcing the correct point of contact in up to 35 different markets can be time-consuming.

Engagement levels are encouraging despite challenges

Bearing in mind that its MTCF implementation is still quite recent, the Windows Live team found the level of participation encouraging and has decided to continue offering opportunities for proactive customer feedback as part of the localization process. Microsoft believes this closer engagement with its customers is important to help the company meet market expectations by using terminology that more closely reflects the local culture. Languages for some traditionally smaller markets, such as Bulgarian, Croatian, and Romanian saw especially active participation and engagement.

Based on its experiences with community translation, Microsoft concluded that successful crowdsourcing requires active company involvement in the following three ways:

- *Invest in the project.* Do not underestimate the effort required to support community engagement initiatives and to provide quality assurance in the process. The commitment and dedication needed to select the best term candidates and to implement them requires the attention of localization experts, linguists, and local marketing representatives.
- *Promote the effort.* Establish the public relations framework during the planning phase. Customize awareness-spreading efforts for each market, because users in different markets may respond differently to the same campaigns.
- *Recognize participants.* Develop a recognition module for the users who have taken part in giving feedback to demonstrate that their feedback is being implemented in the actual product.

Case: Community experience facilitates Plaxo's translation

Plaxo's networked address book and social networking platform, Pulse, enables users to share content from multiple social media sources. Plaxo, which is naturally inclined toward community engagement, had several goals in kicking off its project:

- *Community building.* Collaborative translation enables Plaxo to produce translations while reinforcing the fundamental message that its site is a social construct in every sense. Participants feel a great sense of ownership of the translation, which also makes them feel as if they are contributing to the community itself.
- *Market penetration.* Plaxo's community translation efforts have allowed it to expand into markets beyond those in which vehicular European languages are spoken by enabling access to the site in less widely spoken vernacular languages such as Hrvatski (Croatian).

- *Subject-matter expertise.* Collaborative methods improve translation quality. Plaxo's volunteer translators regularly use Pulse and presumably other Web 2.0 sites as well, so they are already acquainted with the basic concepts of social collaboration and subscribe to accepted behaviors.
- *Speed.* Community translation at Plaxo has enabled quicker completion of small web updates.

Translation Portal serves as a central gathering place

The Plaxo website includes 65,000 words, not counting help text. The primary goal of this collaborative translation project is to translate the messages used on the site. During the first phase of Plaxo's collaborative translation effort, the company organized its efforts around a Translation Portal (see Figure 5). This Portal facilitates translation work by providing a central workspace to all community participants – translators, moderators, and administrators. During the first phase, Dutch was the only language translated.

Roles make the Portal useful to diverse team members

The portal offers customized functions to the various collaborative project team members based on their role in the project. The portal also enables translators to communicate one-to-one with administrators and moderators and one-to-many with the whole translation community.

- *Translators.* Individual translators are drawn either from the pool of volunteers or from the ranks of professional linguists supplied by commercial LSPs. Translators can scroll through a list of messages within a given project, view existing translations and compare them to the glossary and to matches found in other messages. They can then rate the translations and/or propose translations of their own (see Figure 6), even if the messages have already been translated.
- *Administrators.* This group, comprised of Plaxo globalization engineers, handles all community privileges, such as enabling and disabling user access, granting and revoking moderator privileges, and so forth. Administrators also manage translation memories and internal community dashboards that provide details on project status, translation ratings, and translator contributions.
- *Moderators.* Each language has moderators, who are either volunteers or professional linguists. The Translation Portal gives moderators access to functions for overseeing translation quality, which is important when many translators have contributed to a project or when volunteer translators provide the bulk of translations. As their name suggests, moderators also monitor and preside over discussions on community forums and, if necessary, address unacceptable behavior by contributors.

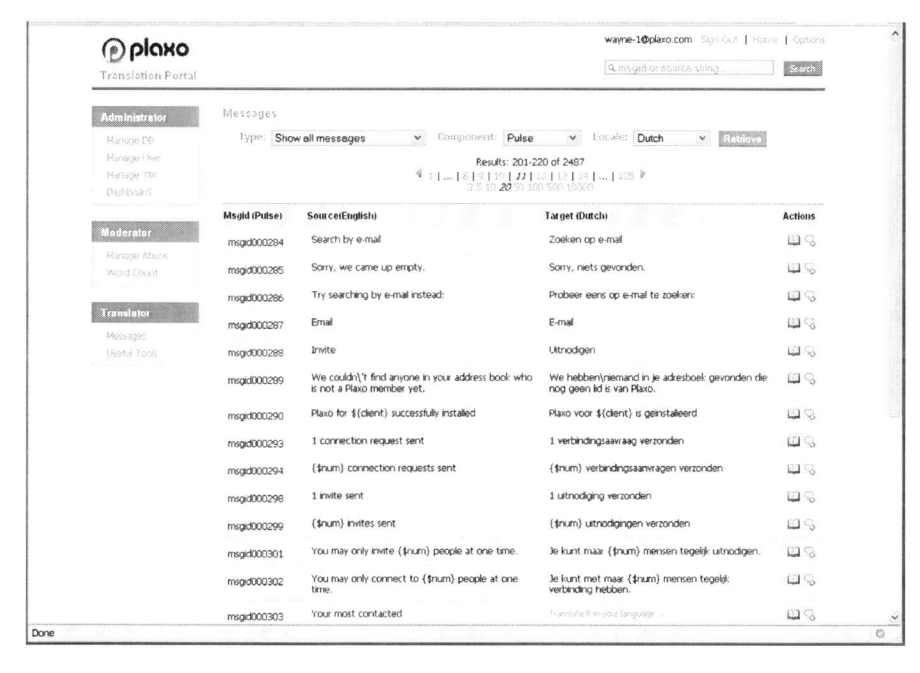

Project management for crowdsourced translation 395

Figure 5. Plaxo Translation Portal. Source: Plaxo, Inc.

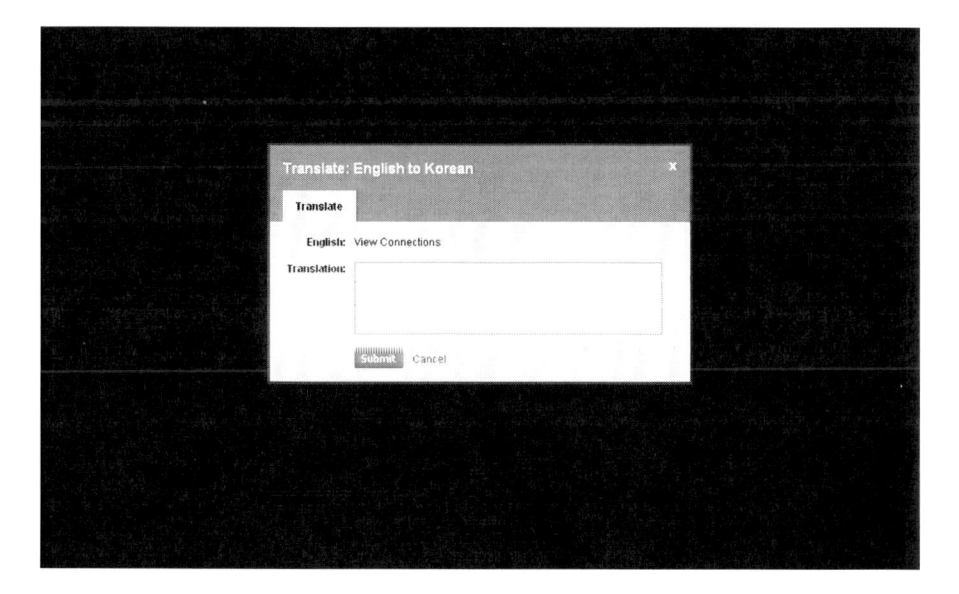

Figure 6. Plaxo in-line translation. Source: Plaxo, Inc.

- *Vendors.* Vendors are language service providers (LSPs) that perform work for hire. LSPs performed the bulk of the translation work and were a critical part of the initial phase of the project. They were also involved in testing and improving the Translation Portal.

Users suggest future Translation Portal feature enhancements

What's next for Plaxo's Translation Portal? Its volunteer translators and language service providers have suggested an array of improvements, some of which the company plans to build into its next-generation core technology:

- *Translation memory support.* Plaxo currently loads TM matches before it imports translation resources to the Translation Portal. Users would prefer a real-time connection between the translation Portal and the translation memory manager.
- *Contextualization.* Volunteers would like better contextual information about the messages that they translate. They have told Plaxo that they can translate more accurately and more quickly if they can see the context in which a message displays rather than just reading a glossary explanation of how and where it is used.
- *Improved dashboards.* Plaxo's commercial translation vendors have asked for workflow management and project dashboards. For example, they would like a dashboard that shows project status for a single language and, ideally, status indicators for multiple languages in the same display.
- *In-context editor.* Plaxo will implement a translation editor directly within the Plaxo Pulse site, moving away from a dedicated, standalone translation environment toward an integrated approach. The new editor's AJAX-based application programming interface will allow it to mash up with the existing Pulse platform. The Translation Portal will continue to exist as a standalone translation tool, but it will also provide back-end functionality for the new in-context translation editor.

Integrating the in-context translation editor within Plaxo's production user interface has not been a simple exercise, which is why the company pushed it into its next development phase. Because the UI has to enable updates to approved and published content, the company currently generates the user interface from a database. Plaxo engineers are investigating ways to minimize the impact of the new in-context translation tool on the production source code.

Major questions that Plaxo faced

As in the case of other pioneering companies, the collaborative translation experience at Plaxo generated many questions and required a great deal of discussion. Three queries consumed much of the organizers' attention:

- *Which languages will it support?* Plaxo has yet to determine the full set of target languages that it will support. However, it has defined a strategic translation priority scale: Pulse (the personal news page) will always be the first component to be translated by the community, followed by the address book and calendar. Plaxo has also decided to exclude from this community effort corporate webpages such as terms of service and the privacy policy.
- *How will commercial vendors participate?* Plaxo has decided that select LSPs will play an important role in its community translation effort. These providers will help to develop glossary entries and provide contextual explanations of terms. They will be responsible for project management and for scheduling reviews of crowdsourced translations. They will also bear the primary responsibility for translating significant volumes of content from Plaxo's corporate website.
- *Does this make financial sense?* Plaxo has begun calculating its cost savings compared to the traditional LSP outsourcing model. While it is too soon to tell, the company expects to save some money on the cost of updating its first six localized sites, which currently amounts to about US$150,000 per year. Plaxo also expects to see savings in the cost of bulk translations for new languages, currently about US$30,000 per language.

However, it will incur other costs for regular vendor monitoring and other activities associated with the new translation model. It is estimated that two person-months of work will be necessary to bring the quality of the new in-context translation editor to the level of a Beta release. Even though it may sound like Plaxo is expending a great deal of effort to achieve minimal cost reductions, the benefits of this initiative transcend costs. Thanks to its collaborative translation efforts, Plaxo now has the ability to move more quickly into other markets.

What Plaxo concluded from its experiments

While crowdsourcing offers great promise for translation, Plaxo's crowdsourcing organizers determined that not all projects lend themselves to a community approach. They concluded that:

- *Brand may override member involvement.* Community translation may make less sense in larger corporations with established brands that need to be protected and/or writing styles and terminological conventions that need to be followed.
- *Recognition trumps compensation.* Crowdsourced project participants are not motivated by traditional forms of compensation. Organizers of these projects need to pay careful attention to how they organize, recognize, and reward participants in their community translation projects.

- *Community projects do not stand alone.* Their success depends on other engagements, corporate quality models, and the commitment of participants to the project and to each other (that is, their emotional investment).
- *Sponsors must be hands-on managers.* Community translation demands continuous and efficient translation filtering by the organizing company. In-house project managers must manage contributions, sort the good from the bad, and address any appropriate behavior in a timely and cost-efficient way.

Case: Sun develops a virtual translation community

Sun's Web 2.0 localization model disrupts every aspect of the traditional translation and localization model. The principal participants in Sun's model are customers, communities, partners, and vendors. Some of these carry over from the traditional model, but simply work in new ways. The tools and processes used at Sun are inspired by the Web 2.0 world and differ in fundamental ways from the tools and processes of the T-E-P model. They include discussion lists, file-sharing, wikis, chats, and special tools, such as Pootle for translation projects and the Community Translation Interface (CTI) for collaborative open-source efforts (see Figure 7).[1]

Community projects are only as good as their members

The leaders of a community translation effort in a sponsor organization are often given the responsibility for recruiting participants. Community leaders must determine whom they should recruit and among them, who is most likely to be interested in the community or product. Logical target groups may include developers, customers, end users, developers, professional linguists, and university students. Once Sun identified the target group, it had to define strategies to recruit from these communities and engage them on an ongoing basis.

---

1. Pootle is an open-source web-based translation portal that can be deployed as an Internet or Intranet site. See http://translate.sourceforge.net/wiki/pootle/index?redirect=1 for more information. Pootle can be used in conjunction with the Translate [sic] Toolkit, a set of file conversion tools and application programming interface for translation and localization projects. The Translate Toolkit enables the use of a single file format, and thus a single translation editor, across an entire project. See http://translate.sourceforge.net/wiki/toolkit/index for more information. CTI is a web-based translation tool that lets users translate user interface strings of the NetBeans IDE (integrated development environment) via a web browser. See http://wiki.netbeans.org/TFGetStartWithCTI for information.

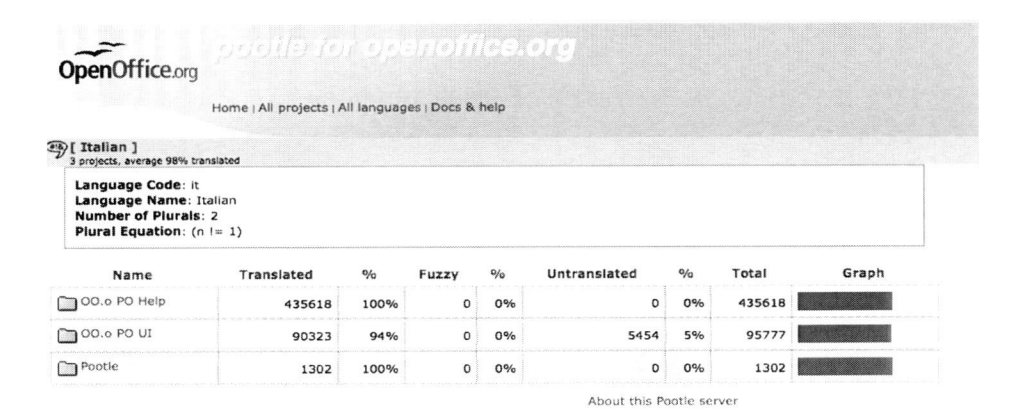

Figure 7. Sun community translation monitoring via Pootle.
Source: Sun Microsystems, Inc.

Motivations of sponsor and participants differ

Sponsors and participants in translation communities have different goals and motivations.

- *What the sponsor seeks.* As the organizer, Sun focused its attention on improving translation quality across the board, generating feature requirements from its NetBeans user community, increasing the customer base, expanding marketing, and gaining support for unfunded, less economically significant languages.
- *What drives participants.* Many things might motivate people to volunteer their time and expertise. In Sun's case, it was enthusiasm for a product that they wanted to see used more broadly. Some wanted to share their expertise, while others looked for greater professional recognition, networking opportunities, and career advancement. Altruism spurred some to join the fold, while support for open-source development motivated others.

Sun keeps community translation project members engaged

Once a translation community is up and running, Sun strives to keep its participants involved and motivated. It focuses positive attention, particularly in the form of recognition and rewards, on community members. For example, Sun highlights what project members have produced, shows participants how their contributions have been used, and recognizes community members publicly with websites, events, announcements, newsletters, and blogs.

Translation communities require hands-on management

In Sun's experience, building the community is just the first step. Giving them the tools to succeed is the next. Sun found that certain technologies were essential to the success of its communities of volunteers:

- *Collaboration tools.* The community needs a project landing page that serves as a home for all of the activities of the community. Collaboration tools that such as wikis, discussion lists, and chat rooms meet that need.
- *Development tools.* If the community is localizing a software application, it needs software development tools. Applications such as database management systems, code and resource editors, workspaces, version control systems, file format converters and scripts, file filters, verification scripts, and bug tracking systems support the software development life cycle.
- *Management tools.* Project management software and other tools for working with community participants and leaders help to facilitate communication and workflow. Complementing these systems are knowledge bases with how-to guides and instructions. Sun wanted to make it easy for all volunteers to contribute to these repositories, but found that quality was higher when contributions were not anonymous. To make participation more visible for recognition purposes and to filter out people who were not serious about the task at hand, Sun asked its volunteers to subscribe to a mailing list, register to use the collaboration tools, or sign a contributor agreement.
- *Translation tools.* Community translation projects frequently use conventional translation tools such as terminology management systems, style guides, translation workflows, and translation editors. These tools, optimized for synchronous T-E-P environments by individual translators laboring in small workgroups, are not well suited for use in a crowdsourced translation project. However, Sun supplied open-source CTI and Pootle to various translation communities – on their own, volunteers do not proactively develop their own tools, and communities prefer not to use proprietary or commercial tools for translation activities.

Sun uses quantitative metrics in community projects

For tracking and reporting progress, Sun measures total costs, including infrastructure costs, and total time expended. It also tallies the effort required to provide tools, information, project instructions, localization kits, bug fixes, rework, test builds, and management. Sun also evaluates the level of involvement in its translation community, using a variety of quantitative measures (see Table 1).

Table 1. Quantitative measurements of community translation success. Source: Sun Microsystems, Inc.

Metric	What the metric reveals
Number of subscribers to the localization project	Size of the community
Number of postings in localization mailing lists	Levels of community activity
Number of hits on localization webpages	Community interest and activity patterns
Number of localization contributors	Community growth pattern
Percentage of Sun vs. community contribution to the localization project	Contribution volume

Crowdsourcing requires effective project management

The crowdsourced translation pioneers who shared their experiences with us shared one major characteristic: they were all experienced in the business practices of translation or localization. Thus, they could apply their experiences with traditional globalization processes to this new model of translation.

They each followed a very similar path, recognizing the existence of a community willing to volunteer its time and expertise in return for some benefit other than direct hourly or per-word compensation. Then, they actively invested in developing the community, refining processes, incorporating technology, and managing the work.

Throughout these efforts, we see parallels between crowdsourced translation and the typical path companies take on their way to establishing localization as an integral component of their business strategies (DePalma, Beninatto and Sargent 2006). Their journey begins with planning in reaction to the offer of a group of volunteers willing to help; continues with efforts to make crowdsourcing a more repeatable exercise through community development and nurturing; and proceeds to initiatives to better manage the activities both with technology and with the integration of other resources.

Step 1: Plan for crowdsourced translation

Each community translation project began with a "eureka" moment when a company realized that its website, product development, or content infrastructure attracted technology users, site visitors, or members of a social network who might be interested in volunteering their time and expertise. With that realization came some hard thinking and project planning about what should come next. At this stage, it is important to:

- *Identify the community.* Face-to-face conversations, email threads, interactions at conferences, and online surveys led the organizers we interviewed to believe that they might aggregate their user communities into a force for localizing websites or translating content. It is up to you to determine community members' reasons for volunteering their labor and expertise on your organization's behalf. Once you understand their motivations, you must figure out how to satisfy their expectations.
- *Determine your goals.* Wanting to support languages that otherwise might not make the cut, planning to increase the amount of information you translate, maybe including user-generated content (UGC), or thinking about speeding up market entry are three sound business reasons for engaging a community in translation. Ignore the comments of observers who focus on the words "free translation" or "free labor."
- *Define the task clearly.* Choose the content and code well – not every translation or localization project lends itself to community involvement. While a community approach might be appropriate for translating things like text blocks and externalized strings in the user interface, UGC, and terminology, it is advisable to reserve branding elements, help, frequently asked questions, legal text such as terms and conditions, hands-in-the-code localization, and final review and quality assurance for an in-house team and commercial language service providers.
- *Allocate management time and resources.* Don't think that community translation will run itself. Project Management 101 teaches us that every project has a beginning, a number of discrete tasks, an end, and a post-mortem analysis. Crowdsourced translation is no different: Dedicate a project manager to your volunteer team. Then, make sure that you can dedicate sufficient in-house resources to support the work. Finally, given the division of labor on the task, brief your LSP partners on how you intend to use volunteer labor and where you will engage the LSPs to support your initiative.
- *Establish ownership of the resulting work.* From the beginning, let everyone know who owns what. With employees and contractors, "work for hire" clauses establish that any work done while in the employ of a company belongs to that company. Volunteers might think otherwise. Some projects require volunteers to sign contributor agreements, some ask them to sign their rights over to the company, while still others require less control. Whatever is ultimately decided should be reviewed with corporate counsel.
- *Figure out the how and where.* The initial project likely reflects the ad hoc nature of a nascent community, organizational uncertainty about how to proceed, and the cobbled together state of technology. Once a decision has been made about what content will be translated, it is necessary to present the content to the members of the community, assign jobs, accept input, measure quality, and otherwise manage

the process. Most companies will adopt collaborative tools such as email threads, wikis, instant messaging, Google Docs, and rudimentary check-in/check-out as they ramp up crowdsourcing efforts. Open-source translation tools like OmegaT and Pootle support online translation, work assignment, statistics collection, and volunteer contributions.

Step 2: Build and support the community

A common characteristic of the four companies we profiled is their expertise in working with existing communities. Microsoft and Sun already had large groups of people who congregate online to discuss their products and services. At Facebook and Plaxo, membership constitutes a vital piece of the very platform and value proposition that the companies offer to their users. In each case, these firms developed a community and then followed common principles to manage and grow them.

Principles for managing crowdsourced community translations
The success of a community translation initiative derives from the quality, depth, and comprehensiveness of its management. We identified five practices that characterize good crowdsourcing project management:

1. *Be transparent.* Foster an atmosphere of open communication. Be open, honest, and transparent at all times. The goal should be to build a sense of trust, which is vital for every virtual community.
2. *Enable mentoring.* Seek out leaders and talented contributors and allow the experienced members to train the newcomers. This approach helps develop relationships, reinforcing the notion that the community itself is trustworthy.
3. *Engage participation.* Allow volunteers to learn and be involved in the crowdsourcing processes. Help whenever possible. Let them structure their own work and be there to support them. Active involvement is important from all parties, and this includes individuals from the sponsoring company.
4. *Document.* Translation quality results from proven quality control processes (Kelly, Beninatto and DePalma 2008). Support the sharing of best practices in the community. Document translation processes and methods. Help members spread their tool experience around the community. Rather than dictating tools or methods, engage members in a frank discussion of the pros and cons of the technologies you would like to use.
5. *Motivate.* Understand why members of the community participate in the project (see Table 2). Whether it is a commitment to learning, a need for professional recognition, or a desire to advance their careers, discover their motivations, and keep nurturing them with rewards and incentives. Something as simple as a certificate can be a powerful form of recognition.

Table 2. What motivates translation volunteers. Source: Common Sense Advisory, Inc.

Motivation	Driver
Loyalty	Commitment to company and products
	Commitment to a cause
	Sense of ownership in product
Altruism	Desire to give back to community
	Desire to share expertise
	Not for money
Growth	Desire for professional recognition
	Desire to network professionally

Best practices for creating a robust, sustainable community
However strong the member community is, it cannot excel on its own. Every crowdsourcing group needs to be defined, nourished, and managed.

- *Formalize the community's structure.* Whether the project enlists developers, partners, users, linguists, or university students, it is important to identify the project managers, liaisons with internal staff, and language service providers. Outline any hierarchies, process maps, and procedures so that everyone knows what is expected, when, and from whom. Maintain constant communication with the community. Over time, volunteers will rise to the top and volunteer to lead the community.
- *Devise a recruitment strategy.* To capture the interest of volunteer translators, go where they go and develop programs that encourage them to participate. Some techniques include involving user groups, posting announcements widely and frequently, advertising on the websites where potential volunteers congregate (including your own), identifying organizations and venues to which they flock, getting involved in related communities, participating actively in communities around Launchpad and other open-source projects, and bringing your local subsidiaries into the recruitment effort.
- *Develop a recognition program.* Highlight and showcase member contributions. The crowdsourced translation pioneers discussed in this chapter have found the "leader board" to be an effective tool for recognizing their most productive members. But remember that not everyone has the time or the ability to contribute at such high levels, so be sure to recognize community members at every level of participation. How? Try showcasing individual contributors, involving them in local company events, or sponsoring user groups. Don't forget simple expedients such as t-shirts, coupons for pizza parties, and sponsorship of local activities and charities in the name of the volunteers.
- *Involve professionals where needed.* Commercial LSPs perform the heavy lifting for translation quality reviews, terminology and style guide consistency, and

integration with the source content. We have heard of one project where the organizers found initial translation quality to be unacceptable; a language service provider cleaned up the site, virtually re-translating what the community had done. Timely checks assured that the errors were caught in time, that fixes were implemented, and that quality came in at the desired level.

Step 3: Build a platform for collaboration

The technology foundation for community translation projects depends on the complexity of the undertaking. Simple, low-volume initiatives can proceed with minimal software support, e.g., wikis for the platform, email and chat for communication, spreadsheets for job control, and Google Docs for real-time collaboration. Adding more content, code, and languages to the mix, however, requires more complex software to manage the projects. While nurturing the community, it is also necessary to design a project-friendly infrastructure that allows sponsor and members to:

- *Congregate.* Every project requires its own landing page to inform the community about projects, member registration and account management, the terms and conditions, the tasks and roles that are provided for, recognition of members, and other application-specific details. Initially, this page may simply be a dissemination point to let prospective and current members know what is planned. Over time, it will become a true "town meeting" for two-way communication between sponsor and members, and among members working on the same projects.
- *Participate.* Fundamental to any crowdsourcing environment is the ability to opt in or sign up. Once in, the landing page includes a portal for basic project management and the ability to assign roles such as translator, administrator, project manager, moderator, reviewer, and language service provider. The project management piece includes task descriptions, assignments, and monitoring. It will also define access control for members, the type and amount of content they will translate or localize, and potentially even remedies in the event of non-performance. However, even defining what non-performance means in a crowdsourced translation project will be a challenging task for most organizers.
- *Collaborate.* Crowdsourcing organizers must provide support for the basic collaboration tools. Many Web 2.0 (and "wannabe" Web 2.0) firms probably already have some elements of the necessary infrastructure in place to support community translation, e.g., direct communication tools such as email, instant messaging and chat, shared workspaces, webcasts, and Google Docs. Add glossaries for terminology and style guides for the right expression of brand.
- *Translate.* Most community translation projects launch with rudimentary translation tools, but soon see the need for a translation framework nested in the target application. Otherwise, volunteers cannot see their work in its final context. As in

any translation project, crowdsourcing organizers will march through a succession of core tools for terminology development and search, translation memory, and in-country and specialist review. The choice of tools will range from open-source products to run-time variants of commercial solutions to the emerging category of open Gmail-like translation environments from companies like Elanex, Lingotek, and Lionbridge (DePalma 2007).

- *Localize.* The more deeply volunteers are involved in global content and code life cycles, the more likely it is that they will be exposed to engineering tools such as file format converters and more advanced tools that touch the software development stack – databases, version control system, bug tracking system, and the resulting product or website user documentation. Most companies will reserve the right to perform integration internally, restricting the type and level of content or code that may be adapted by the community to documentation, user interface text, externalized strings, and messages.
- *Manage.* For more complex projects, the landing page looks more like a translation management system (TMS) than a simple platform for collaboration (DePalma and Sargent 2008), offering a linguistic tools component, systematic project management, a business and vendor management module, connections to corporate systems of record and website data sources, and business process monitoring tools for more detailed job analysis. While it is unlikely that many crowdsourced translation projects will bring volunteers into their TMS systems, most will draw on these resources for use in populating their terminology databases and translation memories.

Crowdsourcing inside the firewall: The corporate model

What if you don't want to involve an outside community in your projects or you work for a language service provider that feels threatened by this approach? The same techniques that pertain to external volunteers could very easily be adapted to work inside a corporation. For example, IBM involved many of its worldwide employees in a crowdsourced approach to correcting and otherwise validating machine translation output (Cohen 2009). On the LSP side, some agencies have already begun experimenting with the asynchronous model for translating large volumes of information.

For behind-the-firewall community initiatives, the moral of the story is that it is not necessary to be a high-tech company to make crowdsourced translation a success. However, the experience of Facebook, Microsoft, Plaxo and Sun Microsystems proves that you do need to be able to adeptly manage online communities and the information that both results from and sustains them.

References

Beninatto, Renato S. and DePalma, Donald A. 2007a. "The end of localization Taylorism." *The Global Watchtower* [Common Sense Advisory blog], Oct. 16. http://www.globalwatchtower.com/2007/10/16/end-of-tep/

———. 2007b. *Collaborative Translation*. Lowell, MA: Common Sense Advisory.

Cohen, Noam. 2009. "A translator tool with a human touch." *New York Times*, Nov. 22: B5.

DePalma, Donald A. 2007. "A Gmail model for translation memory." *The Global Watchtower* [Common Sense Advisory blog], Dec. 12. http://www.globalwatchtower.com/2007/12/12/gmail-tm/

DePalma, Donald A., Beninatto, Renato S. and Sargent, Benjamin B. 2006. *Localization Maturity Model*. Lowell, MA: Common Sense Advisory.

DePalma, Donald A. and Sargent, Benjamin B. 2008. *Evolution and Revolution in Translation Management*. Lowell, MA: Common Sense Advisory.

Howe, Jeff. 2006. "The Rise of Crowdsourcing." *Wired* 14 (6): 176–183. http://www.wired.com/wired/archive/14.06/crowds.html

Kelly, Nataly, Beninatto, Renato S. and DePalma, Donald A. 2008. *Buyer-Defined Translation Quality*. Lowell, MA: Common Sense Advisory.

Sargent, Benjamin B. and DePalma, Donald A. 2007. *Unleashing the Global Customer Experience*. Lowell, MA: Common Sense Advisory.

———. 2008. *Website Globalization: The Availability Quotient*. Lowell, MA: Common Sense Advisory.

Additional resources

Associations

Association Francophone de Management de Projet (AFITEP), http://www.afitep.org
Global Alliance for Project Performance Standards (GAPPS), http://www.globalpmstandards.org
International Association of Project and Program Management, http://www.iappm.org
International Centre for Complex Project Management (ICCPM), http://www.iccpm.com
International Project Management Association (IPMA), http://www.ipma.ch

> IPMA member associations are found in more than 50 countries. For more information, see http://www.ipma.ch/membership/memberassociations/Pages/default.aspx

Product Development and Management Association (PDMA), http://www.pdma.org
Project Management Institute (PMI), http://www.pmi.org

> There are currently 250-plus active PMI chapters in more than 65 countries. For more information, see http://www.pmi.org/Get-Involved/Chapters-PMI-Chapters.aspx

Online resources

All Project Management, International Institute for Learning portal, http://www.allpm.com
"Project management module," online translation project management course created as part of the EU-funded eCoLoTrain project (Developing Innovative eContent Localisation Training Opportunities for Trainers and Teachers in Professional Translation), http://ecolotrain.uni-saarland.de/index.php?id=1924&L=1
Gantthead.com, community for IT project managers, http://www.gantthead.com
NASA Earned Value Management website, offering a tutorial, glossary, as well as schedule and work breakdown structure (WBS) handbooks, http://evm.nasa.gov
NASA Headquarters Library, bibliography of introductory project management texts, http://www.hq.nasa.gov/office/hqlibrary/ppm/ppm1.htm[1]
PM Boulevard, program, portfolio and project management portal, http://www.pmblvd.com
PM World Today, a global project management e-journal, http://www.pmworldtoday.net
PMForum, a resource for information on international project management, http://www.pmforum.org

---

1. See also the links on the NASA page to bibliographies on earned value management, management communication, managerial core competence, project budgeting and cost control, as well as project risk management.

Project Smart, project management articles, templates and discussion forum, http://www.projectsmart.fsnet.co.uk

ProjectsAtWork, project management resources and agile approaches for the management of portfolios, programs and teams, http://www.projectsatwork.com

"The risk doctor," website of risk management expert David Hillson, http://www.risk-doctor.com

"Top 100 project management blogs," a good overview of online project management resources, http://constructionmanagementdegree.org/blog/2010/top-100-project-management-blogs

"Max's project management wisdom," website of project management expert Max Wideman, http://www.maxwideman.com

Suggestions for further reading

Binder, Jean Carlo. 2007. *Global Project Management: Communication, Collaboration and Management across Borders*. Aldershot, UK/Burlington, VT: Gower.

Cleland, David I. 2004. *Field Guide to Project Management*. 2nd ed. Hoboken, NJ: John Wiley & Sons.

Cleland, David I. and Gareis, Roland (eds). 2006. *Global Project Management Handbook: Planning, Organizing, and Controlling International Projects*. New York: McGraw-Hill.

Cleland, David I. and Ireland, Lewis L. 2008. *Project Manager's Handbook: Applying Best Practices across Global Industries*. New York: McGraw-Hill.

Cockburn, Alistair. 2006. *Agile Software Development: The Cooperative Game*. Upper Saddle River, NJ: Addison-Wesley.

DeMarco, Tom and Lister, Timothy. 2003. *Waltzing with Bears: Managing Risk on Software Projects*. New York: Dorset House.

Edwards, Peter J. and Bowen, Paul A. 2005. *Risk Management in Project Organisations*. Amsterdam/Boston: Elsevier/Butterworth-Heinemann.

Fähndrich, Ursula. 2005. "Terminology project management." *Terminology* 11 (2): 225–260.

Frame, J. Davidson. 2002. *The New Project Management: Tools for an Age of Rapid Change, Complexity, and Other Business Realities*. 2nd ed. San Francisco: Jossey-Bass.

Highsmith, James. 2010. *Agile Project Management: Creating Innovative Products*. Upper Saddle River, NJ: Addison-Wesley.

Hillson, David. 2004. *Effective Opportunity Management for Projects: Exploiting Positive Risk*. New York: Marcel Dekker.

International Project Management Association (IPMA). 2006. *IPMA Competence Baseline (ICB) Version 3*. http://www.ipma.ch/Documents/ICB_V._3.0.pdf

Jonasson, Hans. 2008. *Determining Project Requirements*. Boca Raton, FL: Auerbach.

Kendrick, Tom. 2003. *Identifying and Managing Project Risk: Essential Tools for Failure-Proofing Your Project*. New York: AMACOM.

———. 2006. *Results without Authority: Controlling a Project When the Team Doesn't Report to You*. New York: AMACOM.

Kerzner, Harold. 2009. *Project Management: A Systems Approach to Planning, Scheduling, and Controlling*. 10th ed. Hoboken, NJ: John Wiley & Sons.

———. 2010. *Project Management Best Practices: Achieving Global Excellence*. 2nd ed. New York: John Wiley & Sons.

———. 2011. *Project Management Metrics, KPIs, and Dashboards: A Guide to Measuring and Monitoring Project Performance*. Hoboken, NJ: John Wiley & Sons.

Lewis, James P. 2007. *Fundamentals of Project Management*. 3rd ed. New York: AMACOM.

———. 2010. *Project Planning, Scheduling & Control: The Ultimate Hands-On Guide to Bringing Projects in on Time and on Budget*. 5th ed. [New York]: McGraw-Hill.

McKethan, Kenneth Jr. 2003. "Controlling project churn: A case for reality-based project management." *The ATA Chronicle* 23:9 (September): 19–22. ftp://ftp.software.ibm.com/software/globalization/documents/controlling_project_churn.pdf

———. 2004. "Project churn: Counting the cost." *The Guide to Project Management*. Supplement to *MultiLingual Computing & Technology* 15 (4): 15–16. http://www.multilingual.com/downloads/printSupp63.pdf

Morris, Peter and Pinto, Jeffrey K. (eds). 2007. *The Wiley Guide to Project, Program, and Portfolio Management*. Hoboken, NJ: John Wiley & Sons.

Office of Government Commerce [of the United Kingdom] (OGC). 2009. *Managing Successful Projects with PRINCE2*. N.p.: TSO (The Stationery Office).

———. "P3M3 [Portfolio, Programme, and Project Management Maturity] Model." http://www.p3m3-officialsite.com/P3M3Model/P3M3Model.aspx

Richardson, Gary L. 2010. *Project Management Theory and Practice*. Boca Raton, FL: CRC.

Shenhar, Aaron J., Milosevic, Dragan, Dvir, Dov and Thamhain, Hans. 2007. *Linking Project Management to Business Strategy*. Newtown Square, PA: Project Management Institute.

Turner, J. Rodney. 2009. *The Handbook of Project-Based Management: Leading Strategic Change in Organizations*. 3rd ed. New York: McGraw-Hill.

United States Government Accountability Office (GAO). 2009. *GAO Cost Estimating and Assessment Guide*. http://www.gao.gov/new.items/d093sp.pdf

———. 2010. "Draft revised scheduling best practices." [Draft addendum to *Cost Estimating and Assessment Guide* to be published as a separate appendix to the *Guide*.] http://www.houstonscea.org/GAOHQ-4115068-v2-COST_GUIDE_SCHEDULE_APPENDIX_BEST_PRACTICES_REVISED_DRAFT.pdf

Wideman, R. Max. 2004. *A Management Framework for Project, Program and Portfolio Integration*. Victoria, BC: Trafford.

Wysocki, Robert K. 2006. *Effective Software Project Management*. Indianapolis, IN: Wiley.

———. 2009. *Effective Project Management: Traditional, Agile, Extreme*. 5th ed. Indianapolis, IN: Wiley.

———. 2010. *The Business Analyst/Project Manager: A New Partnership for Managing Complexity and Uncertainty*. Hoboken, NJ: John Wiley & Sons.

———. 2011. *Executive's Guide to Project Management: Organizational Processes and Practices for Supporting Complex Projects*. Hoboken, NJ: John Wiley & Sons.

Contributors

Alain Chamsi is CEO of JiveFusion Technologies Inc., a company that specializes in the development of computer-aided translation software. Alain holds a Bachelor's degree in Computer Engineering and worked in the telecommunications industry for 21 years. He entered the language industry as regional manager of Canada's largest LSP. He then took the reins at JiveFusion Technologies, combining his language industry and software development experience. Alain became a member of the Board of Directors of AILIA (Canada's language industry association) in 2005, and Chairman of the Board in 2006. He was previously a director of Languages Canada and the Language Technologies Research of Canada.

Karen R. Combe is Vice President of Localization at PTC, where she is responsible for product localization as well as localization support for Global Services, Technical Support, and Marketing. Previously, Karen was the president of the internationalization and localization consultancy firm Combe Consulting, and Senior Vice President at International Language Engineering, where she managed Client Services, Sales and Marketing. Karen holds a B.A in Linguistics from the University of California at Berkeley and a post-graduate degree in Social Anthropology from the University of Cambridge. She has served in the Peace Corps in Senegal and in International Voluntary Services in Algeria.

Don DePalma is the founder and Chief Strategy Officer of Common Sense Advisory, Inc, a research and consulting firm specializing in the on- and offline operations driving business globalization, internationalization, translation, localization and interpreting. Previously Don was co-founder of Interbase Software, vice president of corporate strategy at translation technology supplier Idiom Technologies and one of the first analysts at Forrester Research. While at Forrester, Don launched the firm's coverage of various sectors, including content management, application development for strategic internet systems, digital marketing technologies and customer relationship management, ethnic marketing, knowledge management, and business globalization. Don holds a Ph.D. in Linguistics from Brown University with specializations in generative grammar, computational linguistics, and the historical phonology of Slavic languages. He is the author of *Business Without Borders: A Strategic Guide to Global Marketing* (2002).

Elena S. Dunne is an Account Executive at Advanced Language Translation Inc. Since joining the company in 2003, she has managed hundreds of projects and played a key role in the development of Advanced Language's proprietary terminology management and ISO 9001 quality management systems. She has also volunteered and consulted on the Project Management Institute's Unified Lexicon Project. Elena holds undergraduate degrees in Linguistics and Cross-Cultural Communication and in Psychology, as well as a Master's degree in Translation. She is currently a doctoral candidate in Translation Studies at Kent State University. Her primary research interests are project management, risk management and terminology management.

Keiran J. Dunne is an Associate Professor of French and a member of the faculty in the Institute for Applied Linguistics at Kent State University, where he teaches graduate courses on computer-assisted translation, localization, project management and the language industry. Drawing upon more than a decade's experience as a French localization and technical translation subcontractor for Fortune 500 companies and other corporate clients, his research interests include localization, project management, terminology management and quality management. He is the editor of the collective volume *Perspectives on Localization* (2006).

Salvatore Giammarresi is Localization Director at Yahoo! Previously he was Vice President of Products at HomeGain.com; Director of International Product Management at Homestore.com; Senior Localization Manager at Kana Software; Engineering Program Manager at Electronics for Imaging; and an independent localization consultant. Salvatore holds a Ph.D. in Applied Linguistics from the University of Palermo, where he has been a Visiting Professor teaching localization, computer assisted translation (CAT) tools and global product marketing. He is the author of a textbook on CAT Tools and has published several papers on localization and applied linguistics.

Nataly Kelly is Chief Research Officer at Common Sense Advisory, where her primary focus is remote language mediation services such as telephone interpreting, video interpreting, and other forms of on-demand speech-to-speech language conversion. She has worked in the language services industry since 1996 as a certified court interpreter, freelance translator, and in upper management of some of the world's largest translation and interpreting suppliers. Nataly is a former Fulbright Scholar in Spanish sociolinguistics and has studied at the university level in Ecuador, Ireland, and the United States. She is the author of *Telephone Interpreting* (2008).

Mark Lammers has worked at Microsoft since 1999 in project management roles in software and content localization as well as Website development. He holds a Project Management Professional (PMP) certification from the Project Management Institute (PMI) as well as a certificate in Software Localization Project Management from the

University of Washington. He also holds a B.A. in Anthropology and International Studies from Macalester College as well as an M.S. in Library and Information Science from the University of Illinois at Urbana-Champaign. He lives in Seattle.

Natalia Levitina, PMP is a Localization Program Manager at PTC, where she manages the Marketing and Technical Support Localization programs as well as the translation management system implementation. Natalia has 15 years of experience in the localization industry on both the vendor side and the client side, in areas ranging from operations to business development and from product management to program management. Her previous positions involved managing a desktop publishing team, performing user training for localization tools and processes, as well as testing and technical writing responsibilities. Natalia holds an M.A. in Journalism from Moscow State University.

Richard Sikes has been immersed in technical translation and localization for over 25 years. He has managed localization teams at several industry-leading software companies, and he is well-known as a frequent speaker at industry conferences as well as for his articles in *MultiLingual* magazine. In his current position as Solution Specialist at MultiCorpora, Richard focuses on translation technologies, industry best practices, and project management solutions. Richard holds a B.A. in Fine Arts from the University of California, Diplom Betriebswirt (FH) from the Fachhochschule Heidelberg, and an M.B.A. from the University of Toronto's Rotman School of Management.

Willem Stoeller, PMP, a Director at Lingotek, Inc., has worked for two decades in the translation industry. Willem is a Certified Project Management Professional and an active volunteer for the Project Management Institute. He is an active participant in the Translation Automation User Society (TAUS) as well as a co-founder of the TAUS Data Association. He can be reached at willem@intlconsultingllc.com.

Natalia Tsvetkov, PMP, is an international project manager for the Windows Localization group at Microsoft. She has more than 20 years of experience in the IT and localization industry and has successfully delivered over 100 complex projects in 35 languages for HP and Microsoft. She has presented at numerous international conferences on the subject of project management and cross-cultural communication. Natalia holds a B.A. and an M.A., and is currently pursuing an M.B.A. She speaks English, French, Russian and Italian.

Veronica Tsvetkov is a project manager and website marketing manager for localization company Translated. She is also a freelance management and online marketing consultant focusing on helping start-ups and small businesses define, improve, and strengthen their corporate and online marketing strategies. She completed her studies in Business Management at Concordia University's John Molson School of Business,

Montreal, and is currently living and working in Rome. She has worked internationally for companies in the United States, Canada, and Europe. She can be reached at veronica@veronicatsvetkov.com.

Ping Zhou, PMP, began her career managing the localization of games into Chinese. Early projects that she managed were among the first electronic games from Western countries made available to Chinese players. Thereafter, she was responsible for technical localization projects for Asian markets (Japan, Korea, and Great China), before moving into game development as an associate producer managing day-to-day game production. Her credits include *Heroes of Might and Magic II* (PC, Chinese), *King Kong* (PS2, Japanese), *Splinter Cell: Pandora Tomorrow* and *Chaos Theory* (Xbox/PS2, Japanese/Korean) and *Ghost Recon Advanced Warfighter* (Xbox/PS2). She currently works in the aerospace industry and lives in Toronto.

Alexandra Zouncourides-Lull is a founding partner at Double Masters LLC, a developer of project management simulations and workshops. Drawing on nearly two decades of project management experience in the software globalization industry, where she managed multi-million dollar international projects in internationalization and localization, Alexandra also teaches project management at Boston University and is an instructor for the Project Management Institute (PMI). Alexandra holds a B.A. in International Relations, a B.S. and an M.A. in French Translation, an M.B.A., and has a Project Management Professional (PMP)® certification.

Author index

A
Aberdeen Group 183
Akamai 314
Allen, J. 272
Allied Business Intelligence 272
Altay, N. 325
Alvarez, A. S. 129
Anderman, G. 6n4
Angelelli, C. V. 7
Angelone, E. 7, 269
Apgar, D. 227
Applebee, A. N. 283
Ashworth, D. 6
Asnes, A. 19, 26
Association for Project Management (APM) 120n2, 120n3
Association of Freelance Editors, Proofreaders & Indexers 137
ASTM International 137

B
Bacon, G. C. 26
Baer, B. J. 6n4
Bailey, B. P. 130
Baldauf, R. B. 177
Barabbam, V. P. 262
Bar-Hillel, Y. 177
Barnes, M. 119–120
Bass, S. 131, 172, 172n12
Bawane, N. 174n2
Bean, J. 244
Beath, C. M. 120
Beck, K. 167
Beninatto, R. S. 2, 5, 19, 24n7, 26, 108n8, 120, 154n2, 160n4, 169, 170, 215, 236, 272, 325, 379, 401, 403
Berry, D. M. 158, 166
Bhattacharya, S. 26
Bickhard, M. H. 278
Bilsky, W. 300

Bodily, S. J. 149
Boehm, B. W. 28, 165, 166
Bohmer, R. 274
Bowker, L. 6
Brentani, C. 23n5, 44
Briggs Myers, I. 192, 193
Brigham, E. F. 60
Brisset, A. 268
Brooks, F. P. 144–145, 149, 166
Bruner, J. S. 275, 276
Byrne, J. 159–160, 183–184

C
Cantlon, D. J. 276
Carnegie Mellon University 68n4
Cascio, W. F. 290
Chenu, A. 129
Chin, W. W. 325
Chriss, R. 131
Chryssochoidis, G. M. 44
Cismas, S. C. 163
Clark, D. 277, 278
Cohen, N. 406
Colina, S. 7
Cooper, R. G. 26, 29, 42–45
Crenshaw, D. 208
Czarnecki, D. 18n2, 20, 241n2

D
Daly, E. B. 28
Dancette, J. 269
Danks, J. H. 269
Darwish, A. 177
Davis, A. M. 28, 30
Davis, T. 335
Day, D. 100n4
de Bono, E. 303
de Geus, A. 54n2
de Mooij, M. K. 244n3
de Ridder, H. 240n1
De Young, C. 18n2

Deitsch, A. 18n2, 20, 241n2
DeMarco, T. 148, 253
DePalma, D. A. 19, 22, 23, 24n7, 26, 47, 108n8, 154n2, 160n4, 169, 170, 236, 244, 272, 281, 379, 382, 401, 403, 406
DeSanctis, G. 274
Dietz, F. 351
Dobson, M. S. 324
Dr. International 214n2
Driscoll, K. 18n2, 241n2
Drucker, P. F. 2, 121, 153–154, 274–275
Dunne, E. 6n5
Dunne, K. J. 6n5, 7, 23, 26, 28, 46, 133, 160, 172n12, 174n14, 176, 178n16

E
Ebert, C. 30
Edgell, S. J. 26, 29, 42–45
Edmondson, A. 274
Edward, K. A. 120
Einstein, A. 194
Ellis, K. 158
Ericsson 310n5
Esselink, B. 2, 6, 18n2, 137, 214, 249
Eurostat (Statistical Office of the European Communities) 2n1
Eveleens, J. L. 266n2
Even-Zohar, I. 268

F
Fagan, M. E. 28
Farn, C.-K. 325
FCC (Federal Communications Commission of the United States) 313n6
Ferris, S. R. 304–305
Field, J. C. 368

Fitzgerald, G. 325
Ford, H. 173n13
ForeignExchange Translations 169
Forsyth, D. 133
Fraser, J. 6n4, 176, 281
Friedman, T. L. 289

G
Gerzymisch-Arbogast, H. 6n4
Giammarresi, S. 23, 26
Goetschalckx, J. 271
Goldratt, E. M. 147n17
Goldsberry, L. 172
Goles, T. 325
Gollner, J. 124n5
Gonzales, L. 265–266, 267
Goodman, M. B. 198, 200
Gouadec, D. 6n4
Grant, T. 169n9
Greaver, M. F. 334
Griffin, J. 269
Grinold, R. C. 45

H
Hall, E. T. 176, 199, 201
Hamel, G. 4
Harkins, S. 307
Heerkens, G. 23n5, 149
Heiman, G. W. 174
Highsmith, J. 25n8, 167n8, 168, 373, 374
Hodock, C. L. 18
Hoffman, C. 262
Hoffman, E. 166
Hofstede, G. 203, 204, 300–302, 304
Hofstede, G. J. 203, 300–302
Holmes, J. S. 1–3
Holton, D. 277, 278
Holz-Mänttäri, J. 268
House, J. 7, 269
Houston, J. F. 60
Howard, R. 18n2, 241n2
Howe, J. 379
Huang, L.-T. 325
Hull, R. 207
Humphrey, W. 166n7

I
Iansiti, M. 26
Illegems, V. 129n6

ISO (International Organization for Standardization) 7, 154, 155, 157, 160–161, 178, 180, 181, 183

J
Jääskeläinen, R. 269
Janis, I. L. 307
Jiang, L. 274
Jonckers 169
Jordan, P. W. 244n3

K
Kahn, R. N. 45
Kano, N. 18, 241n2
Kaplan, R. 101n5
Kaplan, R. B. 177
Kasdorf, W. E. 169
Keller, H. 276n6
Kelly, D. 7
Kelly, N. 2n1, 154n2, 160n4, 272, 403
Kern, T. 325, 334
Kerzner, H. 51, 163n5, 324
Keyson, D. V. 240n1
Kezsbom, D. S. 120
Kinds, H. 160
Kiraly, D. C. 6n4, 6n5, 7
Kleinschmidt, E. J. 26, 29, 42–45
Kliem, R. L. 120, 131n9
Koby, G. S. 6n4
Koh, A. 169, 170
Kolko, B. E. 362, 363
Koller, W. 268
Konstan, J. A. 130
Konsynski, B. R. 325
Koo, S. L. 160
Kostur, P. 262
Kotonya, G. 28
Krishnan, V. 26
Kroeger, O. 194

L
Lai, M. 276
Langer, J. A. 283
Lapalme, G. 177
Latané, B. 307
Laufer, A. 166
Laverty, K. J. 257n4
Law, N. 276
Leary, L. 169, 170
Lefevere, A. 6, 268

Leffingwell, D. 28
Lencioni, P. 206
Levý, J. 177
Lionbridge 169, 178n16
Lipnack, J. 290, 307
Localization Institute 131n7, 261n5
Lok, J. S.H. 18n2, 241n2
Lommel, A. 18, 105
Lörscher, W. 268
Ludin, I. S. 131n9
Luong, T. V. 18n2, 241n2

M
MacDonald, H. 324
Mackiewicz, W. 6
Macklovitch, E. 177
Mahajan, V. 26
Maia, B. 6n4
Malmkjær, K. 6n4
Manning, S. 262
Marasco, J. 4
McCarthy, B. F. 257n4
McFarlan, F. W. 325
McGhee, S. 207, 208
McGrath, M. E. 43
McIlvor, R. 334
McKay, C. 131
McKenzie, J. 279, 282, 283
Medina, J. 208
Mehnert, T. 262
Mehrabian, A. 304–305
Meier, J. 334
Mersino, A. C. 336
Microsoft 107n7
Miller, W. C. 120
Mironov, R. 23n5, 33
Mirsky, S. 194
Müller, E. 137
Myers and Briggs Foundation 192

N
Newbold, R. C. 147n17
Nguyen, N. T. 177
Niranjana, T. 6, 268
Nock, H. 169, 170
Nolan, R. L. 325
Nord, C. 6, 173, 175, 176, 177, 180, 268, 270n5, 280
Norman, D. A. 244n3

O

O'Connell, F. 266
OECD (Organisation for Economic Co-Operation and Development) 313n6
O'Hagan, M. 6
Olohan, M. 6n4

P

Perinotti, T. 18n2, 241n2
Peter, L. J. 207
Pharro, R. 335
Pisano, G. 274
Platt, L. 307
PMI (Project Management Institute) 3, 5, 7, 52, 73, 75, 82, 83, 84, 85, 87, 91, 92, 96, 99, 113, 121, 122, 125, 126, 129, 130, 139, 140n13, 144, 154, 157, 182, 212, 213, 219, 223, 230, 266, 320, 323, 361
Prahalad, C. K. 4
Praxiom Research Group Limited 157n3
Priestly, M. 100n4
Project Management for Development Organizations (PM4DEV) 189
Pym, A. 6, 268

Q

Quine, W. 177
Quinn, J. B. 325

R

Ramírez Safar, Y. 271
Rätzmann, M. 18n2
Ray, J. J. 239
Rayner, K. 133
Reiss, K. 6, 175, 268
Rico Pérez, C. 6n5
Robinson, D. 6n4
Robinson, J. P. 129
Rockley, A. 262
Roehler, L. R. 276
Rogers, M. 6n4
Ross, G. 276
Royce, W. W. 163
Rozendaal, M. 240n1

S

Saladis, F. P. 163n5
Samuelsson-Brown, G. 6n4
Sandrini, P. 6n4
Santana, J. 334
Sargent, B. B. 24n7, 26, 108n8, 236, 382, 401, 406
Savory, T. H. 177
Savourel, Y. 18n2
Schell, D. 100n4
Schilling, D. L. 120
Schwaber, K. 373
Schwartz, S. H. 300
Séguinot, C. 269
Sense, A. J. 275
Sereno, S. C. 133
Shaefer, A. 169, 170
Shreve, G. M. 2, 6n4, 7, 160, 269
Shurygailo, S. 290
Sikes, R. 149, 236
Simon, H. A. 303
Smith-Ferrier, G. 18n2, 241n2
Society for Editors and Proofreaders 137
Sommerville, I. 28
Speier, C. 130
Spitzer, D. R. 59
Spivak, G. 6, 268
Srikrishna, C. V. 174n14
Stading, G. 325
Stamps, J. 290, 307
Standish Group 266
Stephenson, W. E. 28
Stewart, R. 2n1
Stoeller, W. 5, 6n5, 173, 364
Sun Developer Network 326n2
Swisher, V. 262
Symmonds, N. 18n2
Szalay, L. B. 190

T

Taylor, D. J. 18n2, 241n2
Taylor, K. 276n6
Texin, T. 170
Thayer, A. 362, 363
Thuesen, J. M. 194
Treasury Board of Canada Secretariat 189
Twomey, D. F. 262
Txabarriaga, R. 171, 172n12, 281

U

United Nations Office of the High Commissioner for Human Rights (UN OHCHR) 303
Urien, E. 18n2, 241n2
US OMB (U.S. Office of Management and Budget) 2n1
Uyttewaal, E. 122

V

Valacich, J. S. 130
Venuti, L. 6, 268
Verbeke, A. 129n6
Verhoef, C. 266n2
Vermeer, H. J. 6, 175, 268
Verzuh, E. 52
Vesey, J. T. 108n9
Vessey, I. 130
Victor, D. A. 201–202
Vygotsky, L. S. 275, 276

W

Wang, F. 172, 173
Washbourne, K. 6n5
Wegner, P. 166n7
Werchan, A. 276n6
West, D. 169n9
Westland, J. C. 28
Wideman, R. M. 364
Widrig, D. 28
Wiegers, K. E. 29, 34, 37, 38
Willcocks, L. 325, 334
Williams, K. 307
Williams, M. 7
Wilss, W. 130, 177, 271
Wood, D. 276
Woolf, M. 122
Woyde, R. 271
Wright, S. E. 3n2, 154n2, 178n16
Wysocki, R. K. 3, 129–130, 133, 144, 148, 158, 162, 163n5, 164, 166, 168, 173, 284

Z

Zaltman, G. 262
Zielinski, D. 271
Zydron, A. 131n7

Subject index

A

acceptance 116
  criteria 111, 112, 361–362
  of project 116
  testing 66–67
  See also risk response strategies: accept
activity
  definition 122–125
  duration estimation 86–87, 129–139, 141, 144. *See also* work effort
  resource estimation 128–129, 142
  sequencing 125–127. *See also* decomposition; dependency; logical relationships; WBS (work breakdown structure)
adaptive learning 267
agile methodologies 133n10, 164–168, 181–184, 372–376. *See also* Scrum methodology; waterfall methodology
analogous estimating 130–131. *See also* expert judgment; parametric estimating; three-point estimating

B

baseline. *See also* change management; reporting
  cost 81–83, 340, 342–343
  schedule 76, 91–92, 146
  scope 76–80, 111–113, 117
business case 34–35, 97, 149, 244–246. *See also* return on investment
business requirements 27, 29, 33–37

C

CAT (computer-assisted translation) 23, 64, 135, 138. *See also* translation memory (TM)
change control. *See* change management
change control board 91–92
change management 73, 91–92, 117, 147–148, 341–342, 370–372
change request 91–92, 117, 147–148, 371
client review 112–113, 171–173, 177, 183, 271, 279–280
communications management 84–85, 205–208, 299, 309–313, 359–361
configuration management 92, 258
contingency planning 224, 225–226, 227, 368
cost performance index (CPI) 90–91. *See also* cost variance (CV); earned value management (EVM); schedule performance index (SPI); schedule variance (SV)
cost variance (CV) 90–91, 342–343. *See also* cost performance index (CPI); earned value management (EVM); schedule performance index (SPI); schedule variance (SV)
crashing 88–89, 99, 144–145
critical path 87–89, 93, 144, 147, 230–232
crowdsourcing 293, 378–382, 406
customer satisfaction 160–161, 168

D

decomposition 24, 76, 113, 123–124. *See also* risk breakdown structure (RBS); WBS (work breakdown structure)
dependency
  discretionary 125
  external 126
  mandatory 125
  See also activity: sequencing; logical relationships
development methodologies 25, 325–326, 373–376
dimensions of culture 203–205, 301–303
  individualism index (IDV) 203, 204, 301
  long-term orientation (LTO) 204, 301
  masculinity index (MAS) 204, 301
  power distance index (PDI) 203, 204, 301
  uncertainty avoidance index (UAI) 203, 301
DITA (Darwin Information Typing Architecture) 100
DTP (desktop publishing) 100n4, 137

E

expert judgment 130–131, 133. *See also* analogous estimating; parametric estimating; three-point estimating
earned value management (EVM) 89–91. *See also* cost performance index (CPI); cost variance (CV); schedule performance index (SPI); schedule variance (SV)

F
fast-tracking 88, 145–146
float 144. *See also* slack

H
high-context culture 176, 199–201, 306, 309–312. *See also* low-context culture
human resource management 7, 83–84, 299. *See also* resource assignment

I
internationalization 18–20, 26–27, 31, 36–37, 43, 46, 83, 91, 92, 98, 105, 176, 216, 235–239, 240–243, 247, 250, 254–259, 294, 320–321, 323, 326, 327, 328, 332, 343, 363
  hard-coded strings 91, 255, 363
  string concatenation 241, 277, 321, 332
  testing 250, 255–258, 321, 327. *See also* pseudo-localization
  text expansion 104, 214, 241, 242
iteration
  in product development 373–376
  in SDLC 58
  in project management 166–168
  in quality management 181, 183
  in requirements specification 181–182, 274, 281. *See also* progressive elaboration

K
knowledge asymmetry 276, 284

L
lag 126, 142, 143, 145
lessons learned 92, 93, 163, 206, 219, 267, 297, 333, 366. *See also* post-mortem; post-project review

life cycle
  product 25–26, 47, 246
  project 73
  systems development (SDLC) 57–58
  translation company (LSP) 52–54
linguistic style 107, 178–179, 180, 182, 183
locale 101, 239–240
locale neutrality 240, 244, 250, 254–255
locale-specific requirements 32, 35–36, 38–40
localization kit 39, 340, 357, 371–372
localization-readiness testing 250, 255–257
localization testing 249–250, 321–322
logical relationships 126, 140
  finish-to-finish 126, 145
  finish-to-start 88, 99, 140, 145
  start-to-finish 126
  start-to-start 88
low-context culture 176, 199–201, 306, 309–310. *See also* high-context culture

M
machine translation (MT) 101, 109–111
  rule-based 109–110
  statistical 109–110
  hybrid 109–110
market requirements 27, 29, 33, 37–38
maturity 67–68, 108n8, 171, 236, 238, 262, 281, 331
  Capability Maturity Model (CMM) 68n4
  Localization Maturity Model 24n7, 236–237
metrics
  cost, for budgeting purposes 139n12
  cost, for reporting purposes 342–343
  earned value management (EVM) 89–91

performance of system 59
productivity, for reporting purposes 342
productivity, for scheduling purposes 130–134, 136, 139, 253
quality 83, 180,
volume of linguistic tasks 102–104
volume of non-linguistic tasks 104
monochronic culture 201–202. *See also* polychronic culture
Myers-Briggs Type Indicator (MBTI) 192–197

N
non-verbal communication 304–305, 316

P
parametric estimating 82, 130. *See also* analogous estimating; expert judgment; three-point estimating
personality type 192–197
phase-end review 29–30, 34, 37, 41, 45
polychronic culture 201–202. *See also* monochronic culture
post-mortem 111, 219, 333. *See also* lessons learned; post-project review
post-project review 206, 219, 267, 333, 342. *See also* lessons learned; post-mortem
post-release localization 355–357, 364, 366, 368, 371–372. *See also* simship (simultaneous shipment)
product development process 25–41, 373–376
product requirements 26–29, 33, 38–41, 97–98
progressive elaboration 181–183, 267, 274, 278
project budget 81–83, 88, 89–91, 103, 110, 116, 296, 340, 341–342
  contingency reserve 81–83

Subject index   423

project charter 73, 74
project management
    knowledge areas 7–8, 72–73, 297–298
    plan 74–87
    triangle 120–121, 336
Project Management Professional (PMP)® certification 72, 294n2
project model
    linear 162–163, 164, 168–171
    incremental 164–166, 168, 171
    iterative 166–167, 168
    See also agile methodologies; Scrum methodology, waterfall methodology
project network diagram 126–127
project procurement management 87, 298, 299–300
project schedule 76, 121–122, 139–143
    compression 88–89, 99, 144–146
    contingency reserve 82, 139, 147
    control 146–148, 296
    development 134, 139–143
project scope 76, 95, 96, 111, 113, 280, 335n3, 361
project scope statement 75, 111–113. See also statement of work (SOW)
pseudo-localization 44, 91, 255–256, 327. See also internationalization; testing

Q

quality assurance (QA) 27, 32, 83, 155, 174n14, 179–180, 181, 257–259, 299, 321–322
quality measurement 155–156, 174, 179–181, 401
quality control (QC) 83, 155–156, 174n14, 179–180, 181, 257–259, 299, 385
quality requirements 83, 106–108, 173–180

R

reporting 59, 63, 89–91, 148, 207, 342–343, 360–361, 400–401. See also status updates
request for quote (RFQ) 339–340
requirements engineering 29–30
requirements specification 38, 161, 181
resource allocation 42, 43, 44
resource assignment 143. See also human resource management
return on investment (ROI) 26, 42, 97, 101, 217, 320. See also business case
risk analysis 82, 366–367. See also risk prioritization
risk breakdown structure (RBS) 213–218. See also decomposition; WBS (work breakdown structure
risk categories 85, 213
risk event 82–83, 212, 221–222, 228. See also trigger
risk factors
    external 367
    internal 367
risk identification 218–220, 224–227, 228, 366, 369–370
risk management plan 85–87
risk matrix 221, 367
risk monitoring 227–229, 369–370
risk prioritization 220–222
    probability and impact matrix 221, 367
risk register 82–83, 91, 146, 219–220, 228
risk response planning 223–224, 227, 230, 367–368
risk response strategies 85, 218, 225–227, 367–368
    accept 85, 224
    avoid 85, 223, 368
    contingency 224, 368
    enhance 85
    exploit 85
    mitigate 85, 223–224, 368

share 85
transfer 85, 224, 367–368

S

Sarbanes-Oxley Act of 2002 309, 341
scaffolding
    created by project manager 279–282
    expert 277–278
    peer 276
    reciprocal 278
    self- 278
schedule compression 88–89, 99, 144–146
schedule performance index (SPI) 90–91. See also cost performance index (CPI); cost variance (CV); earned value management (EVM); schedule varance (SV)
schedule variance (SV) 90–91, 146–147, 342. See also cost performance index (CPI); cost variance (CV); earned value management (EVM); schedule performance index (SPI)
scope creep 76, 361
scope definition 96, 100, 111–113, 123, 361–364
Scrum methodology 372–376. See also agile methodologies; waterfall methodology
SDLC (software/systems development life cycle) 25, 57–58. See also life cycle
simship (simultaneous shipment) 31–32, 98–99, 323, 327, 330, 355–359, 364, 365, 372, 376, 377. See also post-release localization
slack 88, 144. See also float
stakeholder 30–33, 75, 84–85, 97, 270–271, 299, 323–324
statement of work (SOW) 74, 81, 82
status updates 207, 341, 358, 361. See also reporting

T

terminology
  development 23, 108, 261, 351, 383, 390, 397
  management 261, 391
  requirements related to 83, 108, 178
  risks related to 215, 226, 251–252, 273, 387
  review 108
  specification of 83, 279–280, 281, 385, 386
  user contributions to 386, 387, 389–393
test plan 67, 83, 258
three-point estimating 130. *See also* analogous estimating, expert judgment; parametric estimating

total cost of ownership (TCO) 59–60
translation expertise 4, 7, 271–272
translation management system (TMS) 109, 313, 406
translation memory (TM) 102–104, 107, 109. *See also* CAT (computer-assisted translation)
trigger 219, 220. *See also* risk event

U

use case 58
use case scenario 28

W

waterfall methodology 25, 162–163, 373. *See also* agile methodologies; Scrum methodology
WBS (work breakdown structure) 76–79, 82, 92–93, 96, 97, 113–115, 117, 123, 350. *See also* decomposition; risk breakdown structure (RBS)
WBS dictionary 79, 115, 117
work effort 129–139, 141. *See also* activity duration
work package 76, 79, 82, 113–115